SKIPJACK

The Story of America's Last
Sailing Oystermen

Christopher White

St. Martin's Press

New York

www.stmartins.com

Grateful acknowledgment is made for permission to reprint the following:
"Mrs. MacDonald's Lament" © 1969 Gordon Bok/Timberhead Music and
"Drudgin' Is My Drudgery" © 1979 Tom Wisner on Folkways/Smithsonian's album
Chesapeake Born (32410)
Oyster drawing © 1989 by Karen Teramura

Library of Congress Cataloging-in-Publication Data
White, Christopher P., 1956–
  Skipjack : the story of America's last sailing oystermen / Christopher White. —
1st ed.
        p. cm.
  ISBN 978-0-312-54532-1
  1. Oyster fisheries—Maryland—Tilghman Island.   2. Tilghman Island, (Md.)—
Social life and customs   3. Fishers—Maryland—Tilghman Island.   4. Skipjacks—
Maryland—Tilghman Island.   I. Title.
  SH365.M3W45 2009
  639'.410975232—dc22   2009024031

First Edition: November 2009

10 9 8 7 6 5 4 3 2 1

SKIPJACK

For Donna, who knew from the beginning

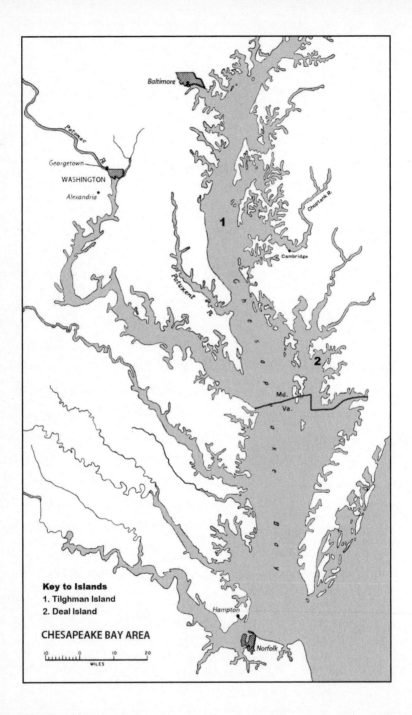

Key to Islands
1. Tilghman Island
2. Deal Island

CHESAPEAKE BAY AREA

10   0   10   20
|⊢⊢⊢⊢⊢⊢|⊢⊢⊢⊢⊢⊢|
        MILES

Contents

When the wind's away and the wave away,
That crazy old fool will go down on the bay,
Dodging the ledges and setting his gear,
And come back when the wind drives him in.

He knows full well the fishing is done;
His credit's all gone and the winter is come,
But as sure as the tide will rise and run
He'll go back on the bay again.

When the snow is down on the western bay,
That fool will go running the fiddler's ground,
Hauling his gear in the trough of the sea
As if he'd no mind of his own.

His father's gone and his brothers are gone,
And still he goes down on the dark of the moon,
Rowing the dory and setting the twine,
And it won't even pay for his time.

When the wind's away and the wave away,
His children go down on the morning sun;
They go rowing their little boats out on the tide,
And they'll follow their foolish old man.

Well, you blind old fool, your children are gone,
And you never would tell them the fishing was done.
Their days were numbered the day they were born,
The same as their foolish old man.

Gordon Bok, "Mrs. MacDonald's Lament."

SKIPJACK

Prologue

Come late March along the Chesapeake, winter often lingers, reluctant to let go. The pattern is familiar: A nor'wester shuttles in a cold front from the Canadian plains and thoughts of spring are pirated off to sea. The night air drops to freezing, rebounding just a fraction—perhaps into the low forties—by noon the next day. The sun climbs high and the wind lessens. But the Bay itself remains frigid. Its waters are slow to revive; they stay wintry till May. Only then will hibernating crabs emerge from their muddy repose. Yes, four or five weeks till any market, the locals say. Oyster dredging is over, and the crabs haven't started to crawl. In the idiom of the Chesapeake, it's "slack time." Slack season, especially when the weather is raw.

On one of those cold, slack nights—neither winter nor spring—I drove a little too fast down Route 33 on Maryland's Eastern Shore, the left bank of the Chesapeake, toward Tilghman Island, to board the skipjack *Rebecca T. Ruark* before she left port. Built in 1886, she was among the last sailboats still employed in commercial fishing in North America. Only nineteen of her sister skipjacks remained. The wind-powered fleet had just completed another season dredging oysters from the bottom of the Bay—by sail, the only legal way to dredge for these shellfish in Maryland, most of the week. To some an anachronism, to others a symbol of sustainability, skipjacks had been dredging on the Bay since the 1880s, and I had always wanted to see one up close—before they disappeared.

But my mind was elsewhere. The LED numbers on the car's digital clock warned: 3:10. *Rebecca* would depart the dock in twenty minutes. I was running late.

The evening before, on the phone, Captain Wade Murphy had said I should arrive at the wharf by three thirty. "We'll eat breakfast on the way to the orster beds," he had said, startling me. I had actually blinked. The first time you hear "three thirty" from a "waterman"—the Chesapeake name for a fisherman—you figure he must be talking about the afternoon. But he isn't. Murphy had said to get a good night's sleep; tomorrow would be a long day.

I had known Wade Murphy since the early 1980s, when I worked as a biologist for the Chesapeake Bay Foundation, a local conservation group. More recently, as a science writer, I had interviewed him at public hearings on the Bay's troubled fisheries, to get the waterman's point of view. Captain Murphy, fifty-five, was outspoken—proud of *Rebecca* and his place as one of the few sailing captains left on the Bay. And since skipjacks were the last commercial sailing fleet in North America, he had a sense of his place in history as well. When I saw Murphy at the March shellfish hearing, where watermen and state officials debated the reality of the oyster crisis, he invited me to observe seed oystering—what they call "spatting"—aboard *Rebecca* during the annual restocking season.

"Ain't drudging again 'til November," he had said at the meeting. "But right now we're planting seed for harvest in two or three years. If ya'd like to go spatting one day, ye're welcome to it. Just don't be late." Watermen are known for being punctual—it is an obsession, though nothing else in their lives is kept up to date. As keepers of an ancient art, they abide by a different calendar.

At this, their most crucial moment in history—the likely crash of the oyster—the majority of watermen stuck to their old ways: independent, stubborn, distrustful of others. Thus, for two weeks I had been talking to scientists and resource managers, getting only half the story. Oysters, like other Chesapeake fisheries, had peaked years ago (15 million bushels in 1884), and more recently—after years in the 2-million-bushel range—had plummeted, dipping below 200,000 bushels in 1996. Formerly the nation's largest producer of shellfish, the Chesapeake was no longer king of the American oyster. But what was causing the drop in landings? Overharvesting or mismanagement? Pollution or shellfish disease? The usual suspects. Some environmentalists claimed the fishery would vanish in a couple of years unless a ban on harvesting was imposed. Others said a moratorium wouldn't work. The camps were divided. But I had not yet heard the waterman's view, on his own ground—in the middle of the Bay. His opinion would likely be telling. More than the fishery was at stake for the waterman. At stake was his way of life, a lineage for Wade Murphy going back three generations.

So I was quick to accept Murphy's unexpected invitation—to observe oystermen at work. An equal attraction was the chance simply to ride aboard a skipjack, the last in a long line of oyster "dredge boats" that have plied the waters of the Bay. One thousand boats had fallen to twenty; my voyage was likely to be one of the last. Like a passage to some far horizon, today's sail held many promises, any one of which was enough justification for me to get up in the middle of a frigid night.

Tilghman Island—home port to more than half the remaining skipjack fleet—lay twenty miles down the road. From the landscape, each mile traveled could have been another ten years regressed into the past. After bypassing the town of Easton and the Black & Decker power tool plant, the road to Tilghman had become more rural and serpentine. Streetlights vanished. Shoulders disappeared. Years peeled away. Under the moonlight, empty fields stretched away from the road like black cloaks. A river appeared to the right—the Miles—and a hump of an old bridge took me over Oak Creek. The car shimmied with a gust of wind.

Up ahead the Victorian architecture of St. Michaels, a former watermen's haunt, loomed into view. Gingerbread houses. Antique stores. Real estate offices. A maritime museum. The residents of St. Michaels no longer lived exclusively off the water. Here Chesapeake workboats were artifacts of history, not the living skipjacks I expected down the road.

I recalculated the distance: twelve miles to go. The clock said: "3:15." Fifteen minutes left. Three small bedroom communities were perched along the hooked peninsula between St. Michaels and Tilghman, a limblike appendage known as Bay Hundred. Gabled homes from the days of schooner captains loomed in the moonlight.

The last five miles to Tilghman Island lasted forever. The clock gave me nine minutes. Watermen houses now lined the highway; crab pots overflowed from pickup trucks onto front lawns. Then, up ahead, I spied the tall masts of the skipjacks across Knapps Narrows, the slim channel dividing Tilghman from the peninsula. The half-dozen, fifty-foot sailboats rose out of the dark water like white ghosts. The drawbridge was down. On it a sign offered FRESH BAIT: EEL AND BULL LIPS and a phone number. Tilghman Island, one of the last authentic watermen villages around.

As I sped across the drawbridge, the iron grates clanked under my tires. Looking left toward the Choptank River, I saw the running lights of a dozen low-lying workboats getting under way. Beyond them, two tall skipjacks were silhouetted in the moonlight near the eastern entrance to the narrows. To my right—west toward the Bay—the treelike masts of four more dredge boats lined the channel, their white sails aloft. My heart raced a little. I had stepped back into the Age of Sail. Like a time traveler, I had entered another world.

Each of the six skipjacks was over seventy-five years old; under the spotlights of the wharf, they looked their age. After a long winter of dredging in storms and ice, the two-sail wooden boats needed dry dock and a coat of paint. Their former bright-white sides were a dull gray. The gold leaf on their trail boards and nameplates had peeled, and the vintage dredges were rust-red. But despite being rundown, they had assembled in Knapps Narrows for one more task before retiring for the summer—carrying seed oysters (spat) thirty miles up the Bay, to plant them for eventual harvest. The state would pay for their trouble. For the past two years dredge boats had moved young oysters from saltier southern waters, where a shellfish disease was rampant, to northern, where they were more likely to grow and survive.

The wharves resembled a nineteenth-century painting and were brimming with activity. Men, in pairs, lifted baskets onto the boats. Captains called on their crews to hurry. Hand over hand, men raised sails to dry them out from yesterday's rain. Others ran down the rickety pier, the boards warped and buckled like broken piano keys. The whole entourage moved in concert, with the purpose of a racing crew. The air smelled of brine, and I inhaled it deeply, leaving the window down as I scanned the docks for *Rebecca*. I spotted her southwest of the bridge.

Thanks to strong currents, the narrows was ice free throughout the winter. For this reason, during much of the past thirty-two years, Wade Murphy has tied up his first skipjack, *Sigsbee* (1901), and (more recently) *Rebecca*, to Buck Garvin's dock on the narrows. It was shallow there, and the captain had to raise each boat's centerboard to gain clearance. I pulled into Buck's yard, grabbed my thermos, and ran toward the dock. Sails were flapping in the breeze, the rigging rattling against the mast. These gentle sounds were suddenly interrupted by a loud backfire as an engine gasped, sputtered, and then conked out.

My wristwatch glowed "3:25 A.M." as I crossed the deck of *Sigsbee* and jumped aboard *Rebecca*, spanning three feet of open water, just as the crew cast off the bow line. "Well, it's about time," the captain barked through the dark. He was tall and lanky, like a teenager, and clean-shaven. The rest of his features were obscured by the night. I said good morning to Captain Murphy, noting that I was five minutes early.

"Heading out a bit arlier than expected," he called out above the slapping of the sails. "Put that gear below. We're having a few problems and ya might learn something." Surrounding me were the tackle and trim of a sailing ship—three-pulley wooden blocks, oak deadeyes, varnished spars, brass fittings, mast hoops—enough nineteenth-century hardware to make an antique dealer swoon. Setting my hand on the cabin top, I discovered it was slick, coated with ice. I regretted leaving cap and gloves in the car. With the wind chill it was well below zero.

In the cabin below I poured the last of the hot coffee from my thermos, forgoing the Nescafé instant that was crusted in a jar next to the propane stove. Four blue flames from the burners gave off some welcome heat. Over one sat a kettle, which was letting off steam without a whistle. Ripe with the odor of decay, the cabin was strewn with oilskins and rubber boots and gloves, as if the crew had shed their skins in a hurry. But no one sat on the benches. Then someone twitched in a quarter berth. I looked left, then right. Two of the crew were fast asleep, nearly hidden between wool blankets and the unpainted hull. Carved on the bulkhead was the year "1886." Another man came below as I headed up through the hatch. He was wearing a Baltimore Orioles' cap, bringing me back to the twentieth century. On the Chesapeake Bay, centuries don't follow each other; they coexist.

"I'm David," he said in answer to my question. "So ya come along for the ride. A piece of advice for ya: keep out of the captain's way." David gathered several quarts of oil out of a box and reascended. I followed. The captain was shaking his head, studying the engine in the yawl boat off the stern. (A yawl, or "push," boat about the size of a rowboat is used to propel a skipjack in and out of the harbor. By law, this auxiliary must be hauled out of the water when sail dredging begins.) Murphy had been fiddling with his new Oldsmobile 350 engine since three o'clock, and it still was not making quite the right noises. It was also guzzling oil. With a rusted knife, the captain cut the corroded lead off the posts of a recharged twelve-volt battery and reattached the wires. Out in the narrows another dredge boat motored by, its sails flapping and flashing white and black between moonlight and the shadows.

Murphy squinted into the dark. "*Nellie Byrd*," he said, meaning Daryl Larrimore, the boy captain, had headed out even earlier than we had. "Make it quick, David. I'll be damned if anybody gets to the seed area before me."

David Fluharty, today's first mate, leaned over the stern railing and poured oil into the crankcase of the yawl-boat engine. The yawl boat hung off two steel arms, called "davits," extending beyond the stern like the lifeboats on *Titanic*. Murphy leaned over and jiggled the battery-cable leads again. They sparked against the night, as if they were shooting stars. Encouraged by that, he reached for the key on the instrument panel. *Pop. Pop. Brrrrr.* The engine blasted thick smoke into the air and came to life. Captain and first mate unhitched the bow and stern lines that held the yawl boat on the davits and lowered the tender into the water. The yawl boat was now ready to push the skipjack, like a tug.

At the captain's order, I tossed *Rebecca*'s stern line onto *Sigsbee*. Wade Murphy had put *Sigsbee* up for sale, but so far there were no takers. Not many watermen had the skill to captain a skipjack—an art passed down from father to son. And with oysters on the decline, it was not the wisest investment. *Sigsbee*'s substitute skipper hired by Wade Murphy that day, Patrick Murphy, a cousin, had not yet arrived.

Captain Wade threw the transmission into gear and revved the throttle. The nose of the yawl boat lurched forward against our stern. *Rebecca*'s bow inched away from the dock, westward toward open water, but there were more obstacles to overcome. Buoys dotted the narrow channel. Slapping the hatch cover, the captain hollered sharply into the cabin. A second man emerged, wiping the sleep from his eyes. He walked around the cabintop, across the middle deck, toward the mast. Murphy shoved a six-volt flashlight into my hands and pointed me forward. I took it up to the man on the foredeck, Bunky Deale.

In front of the mast, at the base of the bowsprit, was the Samson post, which held the bow lines (and anchor chains, if need be). A horseshoe was nailed to it—a large one, probably from a draught horse. Striking up a conversation with Bunky wasn't easy with buckets of ice-cold spray assaulting us each time the bow dropped over a wave. They were salty to the taste. I handed over the light. Bunky shined the spotlight on the buoys that marked the western mouth of the narrows, identifying their position for the captain. I pointed to the horseshoe.

"We'll need more than luck to get through this day," Bunky said. "Look at that full moon—you can bet Wadey'll have his fangs out." The skipper's reputation preceded him all over the Bay: the irascible captain, a common affliction among professional (and even amateur) sailors. "In town, he's Mr. Wadey, a real nice guy, man of his word," said Bunky, "but out on the water he's Mr. Hyde. Just stay out of his way. You bet. Every day he singles out one guy to pick on. Last week it was me." Spray from a rogue wave slapped his face.

Bunky, all of six feet with short-cropped hair and a Norman Rockwell face, pointed the light at a green beacon, just ahead of us. Seeing this, Murphy spun the wheel to avoid it, and we fell off (downwind) a little, then made for the open Bay. Perched on the deck that night was like standing at the edge of a vast wilderness. The territory ahead was unknown to me. *Rebecca* sliced through the water as had the countless boats and ships that had charted this coast, from John Smith's day on down. Now she was nearly alone. I was mesmerized by the expanse of black water, by the moon and the lights on the far shore. Inexplicably, there was a feeling of safety. *Rebecca* seemed to know her way across the water.

The captain broke the silence by ordering all crew on deck. "Okay, boys, let's heist the main." As three men hurried forward, I followed, taking off the sail stops as we went. The stops held the furled mainsail to the fifty-two-foot-long boom, which, longer than a telephone pole, reached well aft of the stern. Two men hauled in the main halyard, hand over hand, while a third held the down-haul line taut to keep the three-pulley block from hanging up at the shrouds. Quickly, the halyard climbed the sixty-nine-foot mast, pulling the huge sail upward. The men puffed through the last few feet, and two of us hung by our hands, feet off the ground, to make her tight. A figure-eight wrap around a wooden cleat made the halyard fast. Then, quietly, the men sauntered below for another hour's sleep before we reached the oyster beds.

Still cold, I offered to pour a cup of coffee for the captain as an excuse to warm up in the cabin. Murphy declined, telling me a story about his reticence over hot drinks from the boat's galley. When he was a teenager crewing on his father's skipjack, they kept an enamel pot of hot chocolate on the stove. One day, the pour spout became clogged and, to clean it, Murphy lifted the lid, only to find a dead rat floating in the hot brew. He dropped the pot. The crew, he quickly realized, had been drinking from the pot for days with the fanged "beast" inside. Since that day, Murphy told me, he had never drunk a cup of hot chocolate.

I passed on the coffee.

The captain announced we were heading to Stone Rock, an oyster bed just this side of Sharps Island Light. Oyster beds are regularly called "bars" or "reefs" by scientists. Rarely called reefs by watermen, however, hard-bottom oyster beds are more often referred to as "hard bars" or "rocks." There are hundreds of oyster rocks throughout the Bay and its major rivers. This one, he said, was named for the baseball- to boulder-size stones embedded in the reef. They made dredging difficult, but the state had planted old oyster shells here last summer, around spawning time, in order to host larval oysters, which can swim, as they settled on the reef. The settlers, called seed or spat, attach to the oyster rock. Adult oysters are sedentary, glued to each other or anything that's handy—especially old shells and stones. Both the plantings and spawning had been a success, and the "spat set," the gathering of seed oysters, had yielded a record count. The Stone Rock nursery was the watermen's best hope for a future harvest.

I had to wonder why the oyster was in jeopardy. From the beginning its survival seemed assured, for as early as 1865 the Maryland legislature passed a law limiting dredging of oysters to sail power. With the potential arrival of steamships, it was one of the earliest conservation statutes in the country. Its continuance has been the equivalent of favoring the horse-drawn plow over the tractor, in what has been termed "enforced obsolescence," to preserve the reefs. Skipjacks are inefficient—that is their saving grace. The measure had its early hurdles, however, with almost every sailboat in the Chesapeake rerigging for dredging through the 1880s. After the inevitable boom and bust, the harvest settled into a sustainable 2 million bushels for almost forty years. A few hundred dredge boats worked within the limits of the fishery—in startling contrast to overworked fisheries elsewhere around the world. Then, in the 1960s, along the Bay, the fabric began to unravel. What upset the balance? Perhaps my voyage that day would tell.

In the last minutes of moonlight, two dredge boats passed us by. I asked the captain the name of the skipjack to our right. He cupped his hands around his eyes to shield the moon. Only a dark silhouette glided along the water, mast and sails reaching toward the stars. "*Lady Katie*," he said. "That's Daryl Larrimore's uncle, Stanley. Thar're only a few drudging families left." Six skipjacks had set sail, nearly a third of the fleet. The remaining captains sat out the spatting season for fear it would cripple their boats, which were already in ill repair. The fleet was in critical condition. After years of braving winter waters, timbers were weak—bone tired. Many skipjacks were unsafe to sail.

"We lose a couple of drudge boats either year," Murphy said, using the vernacular "either" to stand for "every" or "any." "We're down to a dozen or so Tilghman captains and half that at Deal Island farther south. That's only a few boats still living. Even if thar were more captains coming along, the rest of the boats are now dead."

The captain was steering from the mahogany wheel aft of the cabin. He leaned forward into the northwest breeze and, as the boat heeled over, braced against the gusts that filled the sails. As we gathered speed, he leaned farther forward, his coat ballooning like a spinnaker. The captain then fell off the wind, adjusting *Rebecca*'s course to south by southwest. The oversize rudder was sluggish; the boat responded slowly to the turn of the wheel. Captain Murphy steered broadly for Sharps Island Light, a red steel cylinder, fifty-four feet high, which tilted to one side like the Tower of Pisa. Ice had crippled the light three decades ago, and it had never been fixed. The lighthouse marks the footprint of an old island that has since washed away. We could see the red beacon flashing every eight seconds across four miles of water.

On the voyage south, Murphy turned his attention to the past year's oyster season. "I've been drudging for thirty-nine years," he said, "and last season was the worst year of my life. We've got the little ones; that's not the problem. It's the dying. The dying's been something awful."

The dying off of the oyster population had been underway since the 1960s, after a disease named MSX invaded the Bay's southern, saltier half. Like a blight, it invades a reef, turning live oysters into empty shells. The same disease had wiped out oysters in Delaware

Bay and Chincoteague Bay, which are more saline than the Chesa-peake and thus more vulnerable. Since then, MSX had crept north-ward, killing off most of Tangier Sound in the Lower Bay and now threatening the middle Bay and its rivers. Oyster harvests had plummeted at least in part due to the disease. And recent high oyster spawns had not made up the difference. The terrible paradox is that oysters spawn best in saltier water—exactly where MSX thrives. Murphy summed up the dilemma: "South of Stone Rock, half the big orsters are dead but the seed looks good. It'll take two or three years for that seed to grow, if it lives or if we move it. Anyway you look at it, it's just gonna take a long time getting the Bay straight." Everywhere predictions for the coming season seemed dire. The watermen would have to fight for every shell.

"I've seen good harvests come and go," the captain continued, "days when we caught 354 booshels in three hours—clear orsters—and days with only twenty booshels working all day, sunrise to sun-set. It's gonna get better again—always does. But this past season was unreal. Drudge after drudge coming up with 'boxes'—that is empty shells, dead orsters." Murphy looked over the cabin at the middle deck. "You ever seen a deckload of dead orsters?" he asked.

I said that I had not seen a deck full of live oysters. This was my first dredge boat.

"It's a sorry sight. And, you, ye're green then." He shook his head. "I don't have time to watch out for ya. So don't be a Jonas." He winked, then narrowed his eyes again. "And stay out of my god-damn way."

As we headed south, the gusty wind continued to blow from the northwest at about twenty miles per hour. We were on a "broad reach," the wind off our starboard hindquarter. *Rebecca* moved beautifully, slicing up, over, and through the waves. I had never be-fore sailed at night. With the moon nearly setting, the stars became clearer but offered no warmth. Black sky, black water: only the white skipjack lit up by the moon. In the dark, with the boat prancing and sails billowing, it could have been a night voyage in any one of the past five centuries. Clipper ships. Schooners. Bugeyes—the local two-masted dredge boat. They had all passed the torch to the skipjack. The moon as witness shone like a spotlight on our sails.

The captain spun the wheel of *Rebecca* to the right, to starboard, to the southwest. Each time Murphy turned his head, the hidden half of his face emerged from the shadows. He pulled in the main sheet a little and sent me forward to do the same to the jib. We were getting close to Stone Rock. In the growing light before dawn, we could see the white workboats gathered in a circle about a mile away. At that distance they looked like whitecaps breaking across the jet-black water.

Finished with the jib sheet, I came back aft. I had been gone only a minute, but, inexplicably, Murphy was furious, red in the face, mad as hell. What had I done?

"Tha're all thar," he spit, pointing into the twilight. "One, two, three, four. Four skipjacks on the rock before sunrise and here I am a mile behind. My crew has been late every day this week. Tommy didn't show up again this morning, so I left him at the dock. I may have to farr his ass."

I was surprised to hear one of the crew was not on hand. I had thought all four of them were asleep below. The captain's apparent frustration over the state of the fishery—and being late for its revival—was spilling over onto the crew. His temper flared and flickered in rapid succession. Even if the odds weren't against him, it was clear Murphy would be a relentless boss, expecting each man to carry his weight and then some.

"That's all I ask—they show up on time," the captain explained. "Once I got them aboard they can't go anywheres. They have to work. All I have to do is encourage them a bit: give them some ambition." Murphy, still flushed, turned back to the wheel. The captain's sudden outbursts were landing too close to my proximity; I vowed to stay clear of his wrath.

But as I turned away, he cuffed me—grabbed my sleeve—and leaned forward, his mouth close to my ear. "Things were diff'rent crewing for the Old Man. Nobody dared be late. And everybody worked harder than the next guy. We competed—culling, reefing, shoveling, whatever. It was a matter of pride—being the first aboard, first boat out, last boat in. And the Old Man worked me the hardest. Whenever he needed something, he shouted at me. 'Wade, reef that sail,' 'Wade, lower the yawl boat.' 'Wade, shovel them orsters back.' I believe he only knew one name on that boat—mine. He was either teaching me or trying to get me to quit. I think he wanted me to give up and go back to school." Murphy stopped talking for a moment to turn the wheel, then leaned toward me again, looked at the cabin, and lowered his voice. "See, I hated school and quit when I turned sixteen to crew on my father's skipjack, the *George W. Collier*. November 1957: first week of the season and the weather was bad. The wind was nor'east. Freezing rain. It rained the first day—ice-cold, drenching rain. Rained the second day. And the work was hard—two men lifting a four-hundred-pound drudge. By the third day it was still raining and I was ready to quit. School was looking good. But I stuck with it, the weather got better, and I grew to love sailing. Nothing like handling a skipjack. Crewed for the Old Man for seven years 'til I got my own boat. And here I am almost forty years later. Once you get it in your blood, it's hard to stop."

Dropping the air of co-conspiracy, he let go of my sleeve and returned to the helm. An orange-yellow sun lifted above a bank of clouds to the east, beyond the mouth of the Choptank River. At the same instant the full moon dropped below the western shore. One light out, another turning on. The captain's face at last came into full view. He looked like a young Karl Malden. His complexion was ruddy, an artifact of his Irish heritage. Below his white cap, his brown eyes were perched above a fleshy nose. His mouth was broad and grinning. The wrinkles spoke of hard time on the water—older than his years. Here was a man who wouldn't give up easily.

Rebecca approached the other boats; twenty-four in all fanned out over Stone Rock bar. Beyond some twenty low-slung workboats, typically employed for tonging oysters (with scissorlike rakes) or crabbing, the four skipjacks stood out with their tall masts. Universally white, the two fleets swayed in the steep waves. One by one the dredge boats came about and glided in front of the other pack. Then *Lady Katie, Kathyrn, Martha Lewis,* and *Nellie Byrd* tightened the noose, circling the smaller workboats, like sharks patrolling a school of fish. Dredgers and tongers were always the worst of friends; however, today they would not be competing: The workboats would fill more quickly, but the state would pay each captain the same for a bushel of seed.

Captain Wade opened the doors of the cabin and dropped to one knee. "Okay, boys," he called to the men below. "Let's go. We've missed half the morning." This was answered by creaks and groans and epithets not unique to the Eastern Shore.

In the sunlight, I could see the deck was stacked with painted plywood boards cut into various shapes. Two-by-fours were nailed onto the deck and cabin in strategic places. Donning boots and sweaters and caps, the crew began to assemble the plywood forms, which fit into grooves made by the two-by-four studs. Quickly, a huge plywood box, about five feet high, took shape around the edge of the deck. The middle of the deck was left open so that the box resembled a storage bin with two open doors on the sides. In this way all the area between the mast and the helm was semi-enclosed.

By the time this assembly was completed, *Rebecca* had arrived on site and joined the promenade. We were the fifth skipjack to join the fleet; only *Sigsbee* was still behind us. Wade Murphy glanced back at her and shook his head. Any straggling, any mishap, he knew, could tarnish his reputation with the fleet. The captain would need to find a way to recoup his losses—both *Sigsbee* and his crew being late.

Stone Rock was situated about half a mile northwest of Sharps Island Light in about fifteen feet of water. The Bay, though 195 miles long running north to south, was only about ten miles wide here; the rock was on the eastern edge of it. Stone Rock is a huge oyster bar: only a quarter of it was planted with shell and staked out for catching seed; the rest of it—a square mile or so—was "natural," unplanted and available for harvest during the season. I measured the salinity with a kit I had brought along. It was about half the strength of seawater. An estuary like the Chesapeake Bay is a mixture of freshwater and saltwater, fresher at its headwaters and saltier at its mouth. Oysters grow from mid-Bay to the ocean entrance. Stone Rock, at half the salinity of seawater, was perfectly placed for growing oysters and for spawning seed.

The crew took up their positions. Two men—David and Bunky—stood ahead of the starboard dredge, toward the mast. Each of them had a shovel in hand. On the port side, aft of the dredge and just in front of the cabin, was Johnny Murphy, another of the captain's cousins. It had taken two men to lift each 160-pound dredge out of the hold, so it seemed improbable they could get along short one man.

Wadey eyed me with mischief and relaxed the lines of his face (all but the crow's-feet) and said, "Well, here's yer chance to catch some orsters. I'm a man short. Ya got any boots?" He grinned.

I shook my head no. My pulse had quickened.

"Thar's some down below," he pointed to the cabin.

"Ya got any oilskins?"

No, again.

"Ya can use mine."

Down below, I quickly put on the gear. What had I gotten myself into? I had sailed on pleasure yachts, but this was a whole new world. I climbed up to the deck, partially dressed, and checked over Bunky's gear. I was missing something. I looked back at the captain, half hoping the deficit would disqualify me. He handed me his gloves. "Take mine," he said.

I crossed the thirty feet to the starboard station and listened to Bunky as he gave me an instruction or two. I was in the dark, leaning forward to catch his words.

"This is a flat-plate drudge," he said with his hand on the dredge cable. "Since we're working Stone Rock, you don't want any teeth snagging on stone. So we use this drudge that doesn't have teeth on it. We call 'em 'gummers.' Tha're heavy and sink right to the bottom." The dredge resembled a triangular cage with a chain-mail bag at the broad end, where oysters were scooped and caught.

"Now, we'll try unloading the drudge together when it comes up," Bunky continued. "If ya catch onto the rhythm, then we'll keep going. Otherwise, I'll do it alone and ya can just help out with the shoveling."

At exactly 6:00 A.M. by my watch, the captain called out: "Heave!" Immediately, David and Bunky threw their dredges overboard, one each off the port and starboard sides. Long steel cables followed the dredges into the water. They ran off two large windlasses, like lines playing out from two huge fishing reels—runaway spools of frayed cable.

I kept clear.

Like the other skipjacks, *Rebecca* had her sails furled—the crew had hauled them down and wrapped them into a bundle—and she was now propelled solely by the push boat. This auxiliary power, banned during sail dredging, was allowed during spatting. The skipjacks traversed the bar in a wide arc, skirting the smaller workboats and trailing their dredge lines at a safe distance. Workboats, operated by tongers, can dredge over an oyster bar only during the spatting season. During the actual oyster season, hand tongers anchor their boats while they work their long-shaft tongs;

patent tongers employ a similar anchor weight and lift their oyster catch vertically when engaging their patented hydraulic scoops. That past winter, only skipjacks could dredge. But now the two classes—workboats and skipjacks—created an inner and outer circle, all dragging their dredge cables like so many spiders in a complex web.

On the bottom of the Bay, the dredges scoured the bed for a new growth of young oysters. Quite quickly, the gummers, with leading edges made of truck springs, sliced and scooped up the spat and deposited it in the chain-mail bags, not unlike the leaf bag on a mower.

After less than three minutes, the captain signaled David and Bunky to wind in the dredges. He caught their attention by pulling a long cord attached to the throttle of the winder engine. (The gasoline engine used to lift the dredges was the only motor permanently allowed on a skipjack.) Wadey pulled the string harder. The *ptt . . . pttt . . . ptt* of the engine climbed an octave. The men knew the signal; they engaged the winders. Wet dredge cable rolled onto the spools as the windlasses groaned under the strain of four hundred pounds of iron, oyster shells, and stones. At nearly the same instant, both dredges emerged from the water and jumped across the rollers, easing the cages onto the deck.

Smiling gleefully at being back at work, Bunky lifted his side of the dredge with his right hand and, with his left, clasped the "dump ring" and pulled. I imitated him, move by move, so that together we dumped the entire load. The catch, spread out on deck, looked like a load of oyster shell for a driveway, only wet and swarming with life. Clumps of live oysters were mixed with shell and rock and writhing creatures. Small fish flapped on deck. Seven female blue crabs snapped their red-tipped pincers. Anemones whipped their tentacles back and forth. And attached to the shell itself, I could now see, were hundreds of dime-size spat—still round, not yet elongated into the typical shape of an adult oyster.

All these sights were nearly overwhelmed by the stench of oyster mud—like swamp gas—wafting across the deck.

Pulling some slack on the dredge cable, Bunky swung the empty dredge over the roller and tossed it back into the Bay. Then we bent to shoveling. From each of the crew came a spray of airborne oyster shell as they tossed each load overhead to the four corners of the plywood box. I hefted my first shovelful and threw it behind me. It was like shoveling brick. Slowly, by imitating the others, I got the technique down. The trick was to pry under the shell at a low angle in order to raise the oysters off the deck. And to be quick about it. We four had about three minutes to shovel five hundred pounds of spat and shell before the next load came aboard.

"Hurry up," grumbled the captain. "Can't you shovel faster than that?" I quickened my pace. So did the others.

"Shovel some over here," Murphy snapped at his cousin. Johnny lifted his shovel to drop some shell on top of the cabin, just within reach of the captain. The skipper inspected the seed and shell. "Better than last year," he said. "Back then, we hardly caught spat in either load." But this spring already showed promise. The spawn and spat count were high, thanks to a drought that had elevated the salinity at Stone Rock. Very impressive, we all agreed. And yet, I was most impressed by the skill and hard work of the men. The dredges were extremely dangerous to handle—they could break an arm or drown a man—but the crew managed them with a light combination of caution and ease. Rather than complain about the heavy work, the watermen talked about their hopes for the catch.

Bunky fixed me in his gaze. "Stone bottom catches real perty orsters," he said, holding up a specimen. "Here's a top-quality orster. This crop of seed will yield thousands of booshels. That'll pay my mortgage." All prayers, he said, would be answered next year.

The sounds of wave and wind had given way to the scraping of shovels and the crashing of shell as it bounced off the plywood baffles and hit the deck. After a few dredgefuls we fell into a rhythm:

wind, dump, shovel, toss. The oyster spat piled up on top of the cabin and on the foredeck against the mast. The piles drifted so high it was hard to see the crew.

After an hour of shoveling, the captain ordered David and Bunky to hold the dredges, not to toss them back in. A break. We were halfway done. It had only been an hour, yet it seemed like three. I welcomed the breather. "Ten minutes," said the captain, but it turned out to be a bigger respite for me. One of the Tilghman tongers brought his workboat abreast of *Rebecca*, and a young man leapt from one boat to the other. He was shy of six feet, but barrel-chested and too big for the jumpsuit he wore. He was unshaven and looked as if he had just rolled out of bed. It was Tommy Briggs, our missing crew member. Without a word exchanged with me or the captain, Tommy grabbed the shovel out of my hand and bent his back to work. He was a hefty man and made better progress than me. As I backed away, Bunky whispered, "Tommy can shovel for a big guy. Most big guys are no good, but he's a bull. Once he stepped on an eighteen-penny nail—pierced through his foot—and all he could say was: 'That'd give you one helluva flat tire.'" Relieved for the backup, I climbed aft over the seed oysters and plywood baffles to stand next to the captain. He glanced at me without a smile. I wiped my brow of mud and sweat. To him, I must have seemed exhausted, even though my shift had been a mere hour. And these guys worked sixteen-hour days, as their grandfathers had before them.

The crew of *Rebecca* joined in with Tommy, giving up their break to catch up with the rest of the fleet. Now that the dredges were rolling again, shells were flying. Once in a while, a random adult oyster came up with the spat. "You like orsters?" the captain said. I smiled back and he began shucking a large oyster with a knife from the cabintop. While it may have been a bold man that first ate an oyster, I required no pluck or prompting. Fresh out of cold water, that oyster was the best I ever tasted—meaty like a sea scallop, succulent and salty. "Fat as butter," said the captain. "Course, orsters taste best off a drudge boat." Another wink.

AFTER HALF AN HOUR of the second shift working flat out, *Rebecca* was nearly full. With the boat now sitting two or three feet lower in the water, waves spilled over the gunwales. Meanwhile, the crew was shouting, encouraging one another. Above the din, Murphy yelled forward to cousin Johnny. "How're we doing?"

"Looks good," said Johnny. "Maybe one more lick—throw that load up aft—we'd be done. That's one and a half hours, not bad. The best we could do."

The captain shook his head doubtfully. "Nearly eight hundred booshels on board," he said, "but we're overloaded on one side—that could sink her. Bunky, shovel some over thar—to starboard. Too damn much over here." A wave smacked into Bunky and he lost his balance. One of his shovelfuls went overboard, and the captain jumped to his feet. But he thought better of rebuking the crewman. "Watch this," he whispered to me and held out his open hands in silent exasperation. The deckhand owned the error by nodding back at the helm. Johnny and David stepped forward to help Bunky even out the load. In ten minutes they corrected the lopsided freight. With two fingers to his cap, the captain saluted the men. "They've got some ambition now," he said. "All I had to do was farr 'em up a bit."

At about this time the government boat, *El Sher Don*, came alongside *Rebecca*. Standing in the stern, the supervisor for today's spatting, Bradley Bradford, passed a ticket to us on a gaffer hook. The slip confirmed our cargo. "You run up the Bay now, Wadey," he said. "It's slack water so you'll not be bucking the tide." Everybody but the crew apparently called him "Wadey," his childhood nickname—the moniker of choice around the Bay.

Rebecca set a course for Six Foot Knoll, a shoal area, essentially an underwater plateau, in the Upper Bay opposite Baltimore

Harbor. Together with two other reefs in the northern Bay—Seven Foot Knoll and Snake Rip—this was one of the most important bars to the skipjack fleet. Dredgers always planted half their seed quota there. The other half was planted in the Choptank River near Tilghman. Some bars were left unplanted—completely wild. We had a headwind, still blowing from the northwest, so no sails were raised. Tacking back and forth would have taken too much time, so the yawl boat did all the pushing. The knoll was four hours away.

During the voyage, the crew took it easy. As soon as we were under way, they came aft, climbing over the shell piles to reach the cabin. Under their heavy boots the shells crunched but did not break. Oysters are the only seafood you can step on with impunity. David Fluharty stopped at the helm before going below.

"Are you a hunchback now?" he asked.

I straightened up. Breaks your back, I told him, if you haven't done it before.

"Breaks your back even if you do it all the time."

The men were wired after shoveling two hundred bushels of shell apiece. "After getting all pumped up," said Bunky, "you bet it's hard to relax. I'd like to go below and sleep but I can't."

"I can't sleep, either," said Johnny. "Let's make dinner." It was ten o'clock, the usual time for a waterman's midday meal.

The men tramped into the cabin behind Johnny, who was designated cook. The faces of the crew looked prematurely old. The creases in their faces had deepened with the exertions of the morning. None was over thirty years old, but each looked ten years older. Oyster mud coated their necks and caps. Down below, Johnny began the meal by cooking some blue crabs, ones brought accidentally aboard by the dredges. He added vinegar and Old Bay Seasoning to the water, and the cabin quickly became pungent with the sharp odor of crabs steaming. That took up one of the stove's propane burners. The other three burners were taken up by coffee, french fries, and fried oysters. Tommy had shucked a few for dinner.

He spoke to me through the hatch to the galley. "We rarely go to the grocery store," he said with a deep drawl. "Take this dinner. We've got all we want right here in the Bay. If they put up that drawbridge tomorrow, Tilghman Island would get along just fine."

The odors wafted up from the cabin and became too much to resist. I climbed through the hatch and down the ladder to claim a quarter berth among the crew. They were now talking about the captain, who remained at the helm just out of earshot, since he was hard of hearing.

"He's a good waterman," said one. "He knows the Bay like nobody's business."

"He'll make you money," said another.

"If only he didn't fly off the handle like he does, yelling and cursing at everyone, I'd come back next year," said a third. "The other day he was screaming cause the forms wouldn't come off. And then someone got the line caught in the wheel and his face was bloodred and his ears were hot, and we told him he better stop or else he'd have a heart attack right thar on deck."

Just then, Wadey popped his head through the companionway and asked for a sandwich. Everyone looked around, a bit guiltily. He smiled and returned to the helm. "Don't worry," said Bunky, "he's deaf as a bat. He can't hear thunder."

"Same thing on Thursday," said David. "He was out of control— yelling and screaming. We either loaded too slow or too fast. He got boiling mad. Told that little guy, Charlie, the bricklayer who worked for just two days, that he was worthless, a disgrace. 'Shovel, boy,' he says, 'or swim home.'"

Surprising the crew again—their eyes opening wide—the captain stepped below and said, "That boy claimed he was going to faint, and I said, 'Now, listen, remember and tell your grandchildren some day that you came to Tilghman's and you couldn't shovel.'" Wadey looked around at his crew. "He couldn't shovel with the Tilghman boys, so I farred the son of a bitch." Wadey took the sandwich out of Johnny's hand and returned to the wheel. Apparently, he wasn't as hard of hearing as they thought. Truth be known, he cultivated every rumor to his own liking.

Wadey stayed at the wheel for the rest of dinner and ate his meal there. He did not ask anyone to relieve him. And nobody offered. They knew he was tied to the helm. It was his birthright, his domain: He held the wheel as if he had sprouted whole at birth from the wood. Even as I climbed out of the cabin, I kept my distance, out of respect. We passed Annapolis and rode a nascent flood tide under the Chesapeake Bay Bridge. On the horizon the smokestacks of Bethlehem Steel marked the port of Baltimore. In the shipping channel a monstrous Maersk Sealand container ship, looming ten stories high, bore down on us, and *Rebecca* lithely moved out of the way. She was one hundred years out of place in the shadow of such high technology and yet here she was, pine mast, boom, sails and all.

Tommy emerged from the cabin and looked at the skipper. "Cap'n, how many weeks' work we got spatting?" he asked.

"Four weeks, Tommy, if you want the work." The last was a reference to his being late today. Wadey had half-forgiven him.

"I need the money," Tommy said.

"It's something more than money we get for hauling seed," said Wadey. "That seed's our future. If it doesn't live, we'll lose our boats. Then again, the competition may ruin us, too."

"I knowed it," said Tommy. "I crewed for Stanley all winter on the *Lady Katie*. Neither orster was living down the Bay. Something killed 'em. We had to give up and come—"

"Now," Wadey said as if he hadn't heard, "if we can keep them patent tongers off this seed, we'll have a better chance, too. Them hydraulic boats catch the new orsters every autumn before we can reach the rocks. That's yer overharvesting. The disease kills fewer orsters than those greedy sons of bitches. They catch illegal small orsters all winter long." Tommy walked away. The captain turned to me in confidence. "Just hired this crew," he said. "Won't be long before they think they know more than me. Then I'll have to farr them all. Happens either year."

Wadey tapped his cap farther back on his head and said, "I wish my two boys were old enough to crew. They'd earn their keep." The captain's sons—Li'l Wade, sixteen, and Billy, ten—would, he hoped, become the fourth generation of dredge-boat captains in the family. If the oysters held out. The skills to be handed down by their father would take a lifetime to master. And the apprentice-ship would be tough. "The Old Man was rough on me when I crewed for him and I'll probably do the same to them," he said. "You can't show favoritism on a dredge boat. The rest of the crew may mutiny."

The Murphy men have gone to the other extreme and ridden their sons hard. It all began with James Murphy, Wadey's grand-father, who arrived from Ireland in the 1880s, settled on Tilghman, and became an oyster schooner captain. Rumor has it, he beat at least one crew member. His hard ways, some say, cost him dearly.

"In 1913," Wadey explained, "my grandfather fell or was pushed off his schooner. He drownded. One version of the story has it that a young black boy, who lived on his property, was suspected of breaking into his house. My grandfather nearly beat the boy to death, and the boy ran away. A few years passed and my grand-father hired a young man for dredging of similar looks who may have been the same boy. But he wasn't sure. He told his wife about his suspicion and promised to fire the boy when the season ended. But next time they went drudging, it was too late. Old James went overboard. The young boy disappeared, and the rumor spread that he had murdered my grandfather for revenge." Wadey looked around. "Now don't repeat this—I don't want my crew to get any ideas." That wink again.

The skipjacks gathered around Six Foot Knoll, frightening a flock of sea ducks, which ran along the water into flight. The smaller workboats had already unloaded their seed and gone home, leaving the dredge boats to finish the job. The crew pulled the plywood baffles out of their positions and shoveled the seed overboard. It took only twenty minutes to scatter the catch, which had taken two hours to load. The crew moved quickly, still trying to catch up with the other skipjacks. Absorbed in his own task, the captain concentrated on moving *Rebecca* slowly over the area to cover the bar uniformly.

Like a priest presiding over a baptism, Wadey took his hat off and watched the seed scatter into the waves. He seemed to discount the virulence of the disease. "I have a good feeling about planting this seed," he said, his eyes drifting out over the water. "Up here the death is not our worry. It's too many boats. Patent tongers—hundreds of 'em. We can't cull what we used to—the big orsters just aren't thar. But I believe I'll be back at the top of the season in two years to harvest this seed. Not with power, but sail drudging. Better be. It's all I know how to do."

At that moment the oyster crisis started to come into focus for me: Overharvesting, if it was in play, had a whole new relevance with the oyster population already depressed by the disease. The diminished stocks could no longer accommodate the same number of oystermen as before. Pollution would compound the effect. Each threat was intertwined with the others. Little wonder the captain was frustrated. The oyster fishery was tangled into a knot.

Yet it had been a good day. Prime seed had been carried to a safer place for growth and survival. Even though the competition would have a leg up, the bet on Six Foot Knoll was the best gamble the dredgers could make. The day also provided captain and crew with some cash. The boat received $1.05 per bushel, or $840. The boat got a third, and the remainder was split five ways among the captain and crew, mimicking the old "shares" on a whaling ship.

Each man made $110. This wage was as good as an average day oystering and was a fair amount easier. Winter oystering, beset with fierce winds, ice, and freezing water, was brutal and dangerous work. On top of the backbreaking culling and dumping of dredges was the handling of sails and rigging—all this with nearly frozen hands. The crew and captain couldn't be out here for just the money, I thought. There were safer, less strenuous jobs on shore. Yes, it was what their fathers had taught them, but something more immediate kept bringing them back to the water, year after year. What was it? I kept remembering Bunky's smile, beaming as he worked.

The crew seemed to know their place in the world, happy to preserve it, not improve upon it. This attitude was the antithesis of our acquisitive society. Here was no burden of upward mobility. The men's desire was simply to follow the water and pass on a livelihood to their children.

The captain ordered the crew to lift the yawl boat out of the water, and he turned the wheel hard to starboard, aiming *Rebecca* southeast toward home. When we came about, the wind was at our backs—a fair breeze—and now Wadey was smiling. "Put yer jib up and be quick about it," he barked, and the men rushed into action. Then, at the captain's nod, all four hoisted the mainsail as if it were a circus tent. He cursed out more orders, and I let out the main sheet so that the boom could swing over the water, offering full canvas to the wind. *Lady Katie* took our sails as a challenge and, though she was ahead of us, raised her sails as well. So did *Kathryn* and *Nellie Byrd*. *Martha Lewis* followed suit. It took little provocation, I could see, to solicit a race home to port. The five skipjacks were now in tight formation: four abreast with *Rebecca* trailing. With a fair wind blowing over their sterns, their mainsails and jibs were stretched wide, opposite each other like an open book—what is called "wing and wing." From our vantage, the others looked like white birds skittering across the water.

Wadey grew impatient. "Let's get more out of her," he growled. He loosened the hitches that held the centerboard lines to their cleat. Hand over hand, he raised the centerboard as far as it would come and cinched it tight. Next, he grabbed the main sheet out of my hands and let the boom out—farther and farther until the spar was nearly perpendicular to the boat. We heeled over—baskets and buckets and brooms rolling across the deck to starboard— and the boom tip touched the crest of a wave. Just then, I lost my footing but luckily recovered. Within the boat, timbers creaked and groaned. *Rebecca* was gaining on the other boats thanks to our full canvas; we had full sail while the others were reefed. And we had the tallest mast. The crew climbed to the high (port) side of the deck and hugged the railing. Water rolled over the bow, and, at the stern, Wadey was splashed by a wave. He stood braced, legs apart, right hand on the wheel, as if he were just another part of the rigging. In contrast, I clutched the railing as if it were gold. I looked over at the crew huddled together but confident. They had bet on their skipper. And it was quite a ride.

I had stepped back in time to the days of wooden sailing ships, of whalers and schooners. And skipjacks. It was a voyage into an all-but-forgotten world of reading the sky and the water, of harnessing the wind to catch your supper. A lost art, too, of trimming sails for dredging and for racing—the ancient pastime of matching sailboats bound for home. The Chesapeake was a singular place, where men still scratched a living from the bottom of the Bay, a place where lives and livelihoods still depended on the generosity of the wind.

As we raced back to Tilghman Island, that fair wind in our sails, I realized that I had crossed over some invisible line, some great divide. Not that I wasn't still green. I was still a novice, but I had peered through the window, if but for a day, into the water-man's world. Here life was spare and more clear-cut. I had always admired the dredge-boat fleet from a distance, their majestic sails aloft at the annual skipjack races. From onshore those boats and their crews had seemed romantic, a pleasant anachronism. But today I had seen them up close: Far from quaint, they were kept afloat by grit and tenacity, by sweat and muscle. Each waterman, I could now see, was a piece of the water, a strand in the web. There was my threshold: For the first time I saw the waterman as part of the ecology of the Bay.

Up ahead Tilghman Island was already in sight. It was anyone's guess who would win the race, but I put my money on *Rebecca* and *Lady Katie*, hedging my bets. The Larrimores and Murphys had been winning these races for years. And their rivalry was legendary. Like many captains, Stanley Larrimore was over sixty-five and threatening retirement, but he was racing like a young man today. The tailwind had been steady for twenty minutes, and no one had the advantage. Then a slight puff of wind blew across the water from the west and *Rebecca* surged ahead. Overtaking the fleet, Wadey had recouped his reputation for the day.

I caught myself writing down *Rebecca*'s win in my notebook, amid the hollers of the crew. I knew then, that very moment, I had to tell their story, if only to discover what had pulled me in. At the time, I was simply in awe of the beauty of the boat, of the dangerous and demanding work, of the remarkable legacy of a rare breed of men. Captain and crew seemed to take it all in stride. Bunky looked behind at the four skipjacks trailing us and asked who would come in second. Wadey shrugged it off.

But I already had my mind on the future. How long could the skipjacks survive? They had sailed through two centuries; could they coast into a third? Perhaps it depended on the oyster. Or the boats. Or the men. They seemed inseparable: wooden boats and shellfish. Improbably, here was a fleet of men that still followed the water, like their grandfathers before, when the rest of the world embraced the modern. After a single day aboard *Rebecca*, I could not help but wonder how they had preserved their traditions. More basic than that, I was curious why they were so drawn to the water, so captivated by the wind. And that curiosity brought me back, time and again, to work the middle deck, to handle the sails, to read the water.

And even that did not quench my thirst. I longed all the more for the rhythms of a world where nature and man were joined.

So, after two more years of occasional crewing on skipjacks, I settled into a small cottage on Tilghman Island to live and work among the watermen. Perhaps there was still time before their way of life disappeared. Spring was just turning into summer: The slack season had closed with another run at spatting. By then, the crabs were crawling—bushels of steamed jimmies were flooding the market. Crab feasts were under way. The previous oyster season, worse than ever, could briefly be forgotten. All thoughts turned to the promise of a new season. Before long, it would be time to sail north again. The seed from Stone Rock was reaching harvestable size.

1

A Waterman's Summer

Tilghman Island in summer, like John Steinbeck's Cannery Row, is a "stink." Walking along the wharves of Knapps Narrows or the other moorage, Dogwood Harbor, one is overwhelmed by the oily odor of rotting fish. Which is not to say sweet-sounding, eponymous names don't hold their meaning. They do. Dogwood Cove still has flowering trees along the shore. In late spring the aroma of magnolia and dogwood is simply overpowered by the smell of ripe bait. Come June, more than a dozen charter fishermen and fifty crabbers work out of Dogwood Cove, harvesting seafood from the "protein factory" of the Bay. Even more tie up in the narrows. The crab potters scent their traps with "alewives" (menhaden), a noisome odor next to the rank bull lips and pig tongues employed by the trotliners, the old-fashioned watermen who crab with a baited line. Not just fishermen are to blame. Rancid crabs and fish, discarded by the tide, bake along the wrack line of the shore. All this carrion, gamy as it is, is a mild stench compared to the thick musk of salted eel, when it is available—my favorite, and the preferred bait of trotliners, one and all.

I had not yet grown to love these smells when I moved to the island in May. It was no longer spring on Tilghman Island; the month had merged into summer. In fact, for most Chesapeake watermen, there are only two seasons. Oystering is restricted, more or less, to the cooler months—an extended winter. Summer begins when the crabs crawl or, for charter-boat captains, when game fish start to bite. The biting and crawling had just begun when I arrived on the island, U-Haul in tow, looking for Gibsontown Road, my new address.

Directions were easy enough. I simply followed my nose to Dogwood Harbor, then turned left. My road was in sight of three-quarters of the island's skipjack fleet. As I drove along, masts appeared intermittently between houses and over vacant lots, flashing like cards shuffled in a Player's deck. One waterman stood at the edge of his lawn as if penned in, the balance of the turf taken up by stack upon stack, row upon row, of crab pots being prepped for the summer. Farther along, an old captain fixed his pots with galvanized repair wire. His grandchildren were painting Styrofoam buoys with stripes and colors (yellows and blues) emblematic of the family. In another yard, a woman and her daughter painted a small workboat with bright white paint while a man looked on. All told, the street had half a dozen families pitching in, as if it were a barn raising. No one is more industrious in pursuit of the edible than the waterman and his clan.

I was relieved to see the rumored development of the island hadn't yet begun. Tilghman was still a workingman's community: Detroit pickups, baseball caps, and Budweiser beer. Oxford and St. Michaels up the road had already become havens for tourists; they were enchanting, quaint, sedate. Hardly anyone made the extra pilgrimage to Tilghman, unless one was a serious sport fisherman. It was too remote, too coarse, too alien. A blue-collar town.

And yet it had a certain serenity, a quiet charm of its own. More than thirty genial houses, mostly dressed in white, bordered my new street. Magnificent trees—silver maples, hickories, walnuts, holly, tulip poplar, and magnolia—had survived the recent harsh winters and flourished. Still, two features stood in contrast: one supporting my preconceptions of the island, the other shattering them. First, the entire street lacked fences or hedges. Everyone was free to wander into his neighbor's yard. Doors were unlocked. The community was open and safe. On the other hand, while most houses were shipshape, every fifth dwelling or so was dilapidated. Down the street, seafood plants were boarded up. The disrepair reflected a community frayed at the edges. And aging. On Gibsontown Road, houses built in the 1940s still dominated the street, mostly one-story saltboxes and cottages. But one or two barns spoke of a time before the automobile—the first on the island being a 1910 Studebaker. On Tilghman, history was visible. The old was woven in with the new, like a mended net.

Finding a house had not been easy. On Tilghman, resident watermen owned and occupied most of the homes. In those days only a few houses were part-time residences or rentals—typically weekend retreats for "chicken-neckers." That is the local name for Washingtonians or others from the western shore of the Bay, derided for their amateur crabbing technique of tying raw chicken parts to the end of a string. Even these weekend homes were infrequently rented, and if so, only for a short term. So I was pleased to hear about a rare rental—the tip passed on to me by one of the dredge-boat captains—with a year's lease on Gibsontown Road.

I drove to the end of the street. Here, along a wide hook of land between the harbor and the Choptank River, the master shipwright, John B. Harrison (1865–1940) built his boats, his name, and by necessity houses for his five children and his sister. Mister John B., as he was known far and wide, was "the best damn boat builder on the Chesapeake Bay." He built at least three skipjacks, including *Emily* (1901), but was best known for his log canoes and bugeyes. His six houses—mine being the second—hugged the outside corner of the big turn on Gibsontown Road.

Realizing I was about to move into one of the Harrison houses, I felt as if I was trespassing. Nonetheless, I parked my rig and began unloading furniture and boxes onto the front lawn. After an hour or two, I had placed everything inside the front porch, a screened portal with a roof abutting the second floor—that is, everything except the bedroom furniture. Inside the house, I discovered a narrow winding staircase to the second floor, tight and awkward as a lighthouse. Neither bed nor bureau nor chair would fit up that stairway; everything had to come through the window. I borrowed a ladder from my landlord.

Perched on the roof, I was negotiating the mattress through the second-story window when a sweet, if wavering, voice called me from below.

"Hello, neighbor!" she shouted, as if hard of hearing. "I'm Pauline Jenkins. This is Max." She pointed to her dog, a shepherd mix. "And this is Cat." She was walking Cat, a white tabby, on a long white leash.

I descended the ladder to greet her properly. She had cloud-white hair and an angelic face, wrinkled from smile lines. She giggled at my handshake and offered to brew me a glass of iced tea, then turned and walked Cat back to her house. Max stayed with me.

Halfway to her cottage, she turned and hollered, "Don't hurt yourself on top of that porch roof, young man. I dare think my father built it good and strong, but it's a long drop to the deck." Miss Pauline, recently widowed and without children, still went by the name she held as a schoolteacher on the island for fifty years. In fact, older island women were always called "Miss," regardless of marital status, as a token of respect, in the same manner that men were called "Mister." My landlord had already informed me that Miss Pauline, eighty-four, was the middle daughter of Mister John B. and unofficial historian of the island. Her husband, Wesley, had been a dredge-boat captain. Scratch any family on Tilghman and you come up with a skipjack.

Miss Pauline returned with the tea, and after I cleared two porch chairs of pots and pans, we sat to enjoy our cold drinks. I thanked her (and Max and Cat) for the welcome party to Tilghman.

"*Tilghman's*," she corrected me. "This is Tilghman's Island. Maps say 'Tilghman,' but they're wrong. Mathew Tilghman inherited the island in 1741; his predecessors stole it from the Indians. All my children get it right now, but I'm still correcting their 'tookens' and 'ain'ts.'" By her "children," Miss Pauline meant all the pupils she had trained over fifty years, essentially the entire island population over thirty—some six hundred people.

I drained my glass, ready to get back to work; however, Miss Pauline was not letting go.

"You're moving into my Aunt Vesta's house," she said. "I'm happy for it; the house has been empty too long. Of course, everyone now calls it 'Lawrence Tyler's house,' but he only lived in it for thirty years." So it will be known long after my landlord and I and a dozen more chicken-neckers have come and gone.

With a sweep of her hand, Miss Pauline pointed out my neighbors: "Over there is my sister Emily's house—she kept boarders for years; she's ninety-four. Your landlord has it now, but I don't like the cut of his jib. Across from me is Miss Ethel—she was born on Poplar Island. She's ninety-four, too. Born two days before my sister. Across from you is Miss Mary. She's just a kid"—meaning, I think, that she was under eighty. "Behind her is Pete Sweitzer—he's the skipjack *Hilda Willing*, I guess you know." Beyond the houses lay Dogwood Harbor. From my bedroom window, I would be able to watch the skipjacks come and go.

"Pete was one of my boys," said Miss Pauline. "I taught just about all the boys on this island." By "boys" she meant her favorites: the captains of the skipjack fleet—for the most part, sons of other captains, the island elite. "I had my hands full, keeping them from climbing trees, pretending they were up the mast of some drudge boat," she scoffed. "And now you are up on the roof!" Miss

Pauline asked me if I had been sailing with Pete, but I told her my crewing had been limited to the Murphys and Larrimores.

"Wadey," she jumped in, "was a shy child. We couldn't keep him in school. He ran away so that he wouldn't have to attend first grade. By noon, the darling returned home. His mother took him in, but he cried and cried. Next day I took him to the head of the class and held him in my lap while he wept in front of all the other children. He just about stopped bawling, when I said, 'Now, Wadey, don't you want to cry some more for the other children?' And that made him cry all over again, until all his tears were gone. He came into school each day after that."

Miss Pauline completed her circle and her commentary on the neighborhood. "And my little house," she said, turning around, "was built in Aunt Vesta's vegetable garden in 1928 by my father." The white bungalow cost $500, she told me—$100 to Aunt Vesta for the lot and $400 for the lumber, which her father had left over from a bugeye to build his daughter and her husband, Wes, a home.

"Now remember all that," she said. "There will be a quiz. And stay off that roof." Suddenly, she stood up and announced she would go home and bake me an apple cobbler, the first of many. I'd be working up an appetite with all this heavy lifting, she said, so I'd better not balk. In forty minutes I had been chastised, informed, and adopted as a surrogate grandson, and been told, in gestures universal and maternal, it was pointless to resist.

LATE THAT EVENING, while I was unpacking a box of books, there was a sharp rap on the windowpane of the back door. Wadey Murphy stepped into the kitchen, then straddled the open door of the living room where I sat. He filled the space, his white hat tilted far back on his head, nearly touching the top of the doorframe. His broad shoulders were clad in a white T-shirt, which was tucked neatly around his thin waist. He leaned forward on the balls of his feet, as if permanently braced against the wind. Wadey looked awkward without a deck under his feet.

"Honey, welcome to Tilghman's," he said. This traditional salutation between men on the island was a little disconcerting the first time I heard it. Murphy surveyed the room, stepping over a box on his way to the northwest window. He looked out. "Honey, you know Miss Pauline?" he asked, turning around. "She loved me so much that she kept me back in first grade twice." He smiled. "She didn't want to see me graduate to the next teacher."

I told him Miss Pauline had already promised me an apple cobbler. "Did you bring her some apples?" he laughed. I didn't yet get the joke.

"What're ya doing tomorrow?" Wadey said next. He took off his hat briefly and wiped his brow. I felt a proposition coming on. The hat went back on, even farther back on his head than before. "Got any plans?"

I offered that I was pretty free.

"You want to come dragging with me? I need a man. It pays seventy-five dollars for the day."

I said that would be fine, but I didn't know what dragging was.

"Bagless drudging," Wadey explained. "It's like orstering, except we carry no chain bag in the drudge. We drag over the orster bars to clean 'em up—scrape the silt off—so the new orster spat can attach to the bar after spawning. If you don't use it, you lose it. We have to work these bars to keep 'em living. With all those farms upstream washing their topsoil into the Bay, we have plenty of sediment to scour from the rock."

That silt and other pollutants, such as an overdose of nutrients, bring on stress for the oyster and other Bay species. Nitrates and phosphates from fertilizers, agricultural waste, and sewage treatment plants stimulate algal blooms that prevent sunlight from reaching submerged aquatic vegetation, a valuable habitat for blue crabs. While phytoplankton is the main food source for oysters, not all is consumed. A surfeit of dead algae chokes deep-channel oyster beds, turning the surrounding waters anoxic—devoid of oxygen. These deepwater reefs, in turn, die off. The onslaught of pollution is staggering. Nearly 5 million tons of sediment wash into the basin each year, an assault three times precolonial levels, thanks to the clear-cutting of forests. Over 303 million pounds of nitrogen and 20 million pounds of phosphorus are also introduced, mostly from human activity. When the wastewater streams from the Bay's three hundred sewage treatment plants and power plants are summed, their combined flow makes up the fourth largest tributary to the Chesapeake, just short of the Susquehanna, Potomac, and James. The result is a cloudy, oxygen-deprived estuary—abused and neglected and begging for rescue.

Thanks to a startling statistic, oysters may offer one of the best remedies to nutrient and sediment overload: Each oyster pumps up to two gallons of water through its gills every hour. Before the 1870s, the enormous colonies of oysters recycled the entire 18 trillion gallons of the Bay in just a few days, filtering out sediments, consuming algae, and depositing nutrient-rich waste on the bottom. The clean water of those years sponsored prodigious growth of submerged grasses and deepwater reefs. Today, however, with diminished oyster stocks, it takes more than a year to filter and recycle the water of the Bay. The expected benefits of a renewed oyster population—as filters and habitat—gave Wadey and the other watermen an added incentive for replenishing the reefs.

To this end, oyster renewal requires a three-pronged effort. Besides spatting and dragging, the third prong in the forty-plus-year replenishment initiative has been the planting of old oyster shells— 2 to 5 million bushels a year—on seed areas and commercial beds, to give oyster larvae even more hard substrate, or "cultch," on which to better bond and grow. Oysters spawn at least three times over the summer; each time the resulting free-floating larvae wander for up to sixteen days until they encounter suitable oyster grounds, at which point they adhere in a matter of hours to either the natural bed or to cultch placed by resource managers. In years past, freshly shucked shell from oyster packers had been used as cultch, but with Maryland shucking houses closing down and canning shifting to Virginia, the state now planted mostly fossil oyster shell dug from deposits in the northern Bay. Now, here in May, a month before the first spawning, shell plantings should already be under way to lay the groundwork for spat, but the barges were empty. The state was consistently late, usually spreading shell around July Fourth and sometimes burying seed. The watermen looked to bagless dredging as the only guarantee that a few bars would offer a clean surface for larvae in June.

"Meet me at Gary's at six A.M.," Wadey said. "We'll go from thar. And pack some sandwiches. We're not cooking anymore aboard *Rebecca*." He started for the front door, then caught himself and turned around to exit through the kitchen. It's an island superstition, I would learn later, that you must exit a house through the same door you enter. And there was nobody more superstitious than Wade Murphy. I wondered how many other doors he had passed through twice in search of crew that evening—before settling on mine, the greenest door on the island.

GARY'S STORE WAS brightly lit well before dawn the next morning. Known as Fairbank Tackle to outsiders, the store sat next to Tongers Basin, a cove off of Knapps Narrows, providing gas and merchandise to watermen. When I arrived, over two dozen pickup trucks were parked in double rows in front. Gary's was the local gathering place. It opened at 5:00 A.M. all year long, when men crowded into the store for coffee and conversation, to hire crews, and to argue over politics, perceived slights, and the price of seafood.

I entered the store and the conversation died. Twenty grizzled men stared at me, my foreign hat, and my foreign shoes. Wade

Murphy turned around from the coffee machine and said, "Thar's my crew—he's paying me to take him." Another said, "How much?" Half the men laughed. They were mostly Murphys. And the conversations resumed—today mostly about how the governor wanted to put the Maryland watermen out of business. They claimed he would prefer a handful of seafood corporations, engaged in oyster farming, to two thousand renegade fishermen plying the waters of the open Bay. Even though the independent watermen were a Maryland tradition, they feared all that could change overnight.

The Chesapeake Bay has traditionally been a public fishery. Unlike the extensive private shellfish operations of New England and the Pacific Northwest, aquaculture is a relatively minor concern here. Anyone with a license can drop a hook—or its equivalent—anywhere in the Bay, a commons open to all. The Chesapeake is the largest and most productive of the nation's 850 estuaries—semienclosed coastal basins where fresh- and saltwater mix. More than 200 million pounds of seafood are pulled from its waters annually, with a dockside value exceeding $1 billion. But this open fishery, though world-renowned, has lost its stature of late. The fabled harvests of blue crabs and striped bass have been cut in half. Other commercial species have fared even worse: The American shad, for example, has dropped to a fraction of historic landings, prompting a moratorium on fishing. A similar ban on striped bass, now lifted, helped restore stocks somewhat—a success that has prompted proposals for moratoria on shellfish.

The well-loved American oyster (*Crassostrea virginica*), which—in the middle of its geographic and salinity range (Nova Scotia to the Gulf of Mexico; brackish to marine)—finds its perfect home in these waters, has suffered the greatest setbacks, especially over the past decade. The Maryland oyster catch had dropped from 400,000 bushels to 199,000 bushels, only 10 percent of early-1980 levels. Scientists now agreed that most Bay fisheries had declined from a combination of habitat loss, pollution, and over-harvesting. The American oyster has the additional vulnerability of being prone to disease. After collapsing, oyster stocks have stayed depressed. The Chesapeake is not as resilient as it once was. Not surprisingly, the spring that I prepared for bagless dredging, the skipjack fleet had lost two more boats: The captains of *Dee of St. Marys* and *Connie Francis*, faced with slim prospects, decided to retire early. No young captains were coming along with the skill and know-how to command a dredge boat, so the two boats became idle, too. One now offered educational tours to schoolchildren. The fleet slipped to eighteen—twelve on Tilghman's, six on Deal. After a bitter season of captains competing against one another for an ever-shrinking resource, the summer chore of bagless dredging afforded the men at Gary's a chance to work together for a common goal.

Aboard *Rebecca*, we made ready for travel. The yawl boat was lowered—not an easy job with only two men—and I (as first mate) climbed into it to guide *Rebecca* through the narrows. The yawl boat's diesel engine was deafening, and the auxiliary made a poor tugboat. Skipjacks were designed to be sailed, not to be pushed. Knapps Narrows connected the Choptank River to the Bay, and thus separated trotlining from crab potting, the provenance of open water. From the air, Tilghman's Island hangs like a huge crab claw reaching southward into the mouth of the river. Today we would venture east from the pincers into the Choptank, the biggest river on the Eastern Shore and most important oyster grounds to Tilghman's fleet.

During the hour voyage upriver to Lighthouse Middles, the oyster bar that was our destination, Murphy spent most of the time on the marine radio talking to other skipjack captains. Their topic that morning was the recent meeting of the county oyster committee, a group of watermen who advised the state on the annual seed program and planting of oyster shell. Wade Murphy was chairman of the Talbot County Dredgers' Committee. Every year Wadey threatened to quit, resigning as chairman, and "either year" the other captains talked him back into it. He had just cause for rebellion. This past season not all of the dredgers' quota of seed had been planted on Six Foot Knoll and Howell Point, as the dredgers had requested and as the state managers had promised. "They lied to me," Wadey said, "and it's the last time. If we—us sail drudgers— have seed coming, we ought to be able to harvest it 'stead of the state giving it to them tongers. But the bureaucrats don't care for us. Hardly anybody likes a waterman and nobody loves a drudger."

Dredging the Chesapeake has had a spectacular history, full of exploits by outlaw sailors, rivals with tongers for the reefs. Still, the two shared a common fate in the future viability of the oyster. Since our spatting trip two years before, the young oysters on Six Foot Knoll and elsewhere had fared well. A series of unusually wet springs and summers had decreased the salinity. While this fresh-water infusion had limited spawning success and spatfall, it had also kept MSX, the oyster disease, in check. (MSX stands for "Multinucleated Sphere Unknown," its original designation before the single-celled protozoan was renamed *Haplosporidium nelsoni*; the original acronym stuck.) On many bars, spat and young oysters from previous spawnings were surviving. On other beds, the dying continued: the victims mostly older oysters. But, in the watermen's estimation, things were looking up: They had youngsters in the pipeline. Now they hoped spawning would pick up on the Choptank, too.

The Oxford Lighthouse was up ahead, and the tongers' white workboats were already circling the oyster bar just west of it— Lighthouse Middles. They commenced dragging. All twelve Tilghman skipjacks were out scraping today as well. From a distance the vessels looked as tightly packed as a raft of canvasbacks. When we approached the bar—marked with flags—Murphy and I ran forward and tossed the two dredges over the rollers and into the water. The dredge teeth began to comb the bottom, and we joined the circle of skipjacks on the perimeter of the bar. The oyster rock was fifteen feet beneath us, worn down from its previous heights. In colonial days, reefs jutted toward the surface like mountain ranges and were a hazard to navigation; now they are flat, leveled in the early days of the oyster boom and rendered susceptible to siltation. In twenty minutes we completed a circuit; then we began again. There was nothing else to do. We had eight hours of circling back and forth, of cleaning the bar, to look forward to. Wadey Murphy and I traded stories most of the day, but there's only one I remember in any detail. Or at least the only one that was totally true.

"Dragging is easy," he said, "but some drudging is a challenge—a challenge to not get caught." He winked. "Now on Wednesdays through Saturdays, only drudging with sail power is legal, but some captains break the rules when the marine police aren't looking. Push drudging in the fog with a yawl boat, when no one can see you, is one way. Or drudging at night. In the winter, my father would tie up his skipjack in the evening and go poaching in his powerboat. One dark night, the Old Man and his brother-in-law crossed the Bay to the western shore to sneak-dredge for orsters. The other boat caught fire—a gasoline engine—and my father helped put the fire out. But in the meantime that burning workboat lit up the water like a house fire. Some of the local watermen saw it and gave chase, shooting across his bow. Thar was the Old Man, towing a burnt boat and the posse after him. Crime doesn't pay."

Murphy leaned over to read my watch. Like most watermen, he didn't wear one. It was 2:00 P.M. "Well, say," he said, "that bottom must've cleaned up an hour arlier today than yesterday." We headed in with the other boats. Only they motored in. For the pure joy of it, we raised the main and sailed for home. Back at the dock in Dogwood Harbor, we secured *Rebecca*, placing extra spring lines off her bow and stern. She would claim this berth each evening until she was hauled for repairs in August. She needed a new foredeck and a coat of paint. The captain offered me a beer, and we rode in his red truck over to his house.

The Murphy house was situated on a quiet side street populated by watermen. Planks were laid across the wet yard, which was soaked with groundwater. That day, I noticed clothes flapping on the clothesline. Jackie Murphy, Wadey's wife and mother of three, stood at the back door with her hands on her hips.

Wadey said, "I'm picking up some marine white for the boat."

"How about paint for the house?" she answered.

"Boat needs it more," he said.

"I'm telling you," she said, nodding at me, "if I nailed a bowsprit to this house, is the only way it'd get painted." She glanced over at Wadey, who threw up his hands in supplication.

After another beer, Wadey offered me a job dragging for the week. I headed home, happy to have an island vocation.

ON MOST SATURDAYS that summer I observed and wrote about wildlife, mostly birds and invertebrates traipsing along the shore, in the wetlands and shallows near my house. Besides journaling, I busily prepared a study guide and poster to accompany a Chesapeake field guide I had written a few years before. The fringe marsh at the end of Gibsontown Road, along the Choptank River, was bristling with aquatic life. Periwinkles climbed the stems of cordgrass, and mussels clustered at the base, clinging to the clumps of earth and shell that were covered by the tide twice each day. When exposed, the peat began to crawl with fiddler crabs, a favorite food of the great blue herons that stalked the shallows. White egrets often joined in, dining on minnows. Red-winged blackbirds nested in the cattails, flashing their scarlet epaulets. At low tide, I could reach out a few feet and gather all the oysters I desired. Fringe wetlands, bordering the entire island like a beard, would become my weekend sanctuary.

Other times, I explored Tilghman's streets and wharves, something I did the following Wednesday after another morning of dragging, when I wandered up Main Street in search of groceries. It was a sweltering day, and everyone was stripped down to his T-shirt, invariably white with no lettering. Mine was splattered with mud from *Rebecca*. I strolled along the wet shoulder, saturated with water like the Murphys' lawn, as if the Bay was intent on reclaiming the island. Pickups cruised up and down Main Street, some loaded with crab pots and bushel baskets. Others were empty and stopped to offer rides to the young boys sauntering up the road to Gary's Store. Whenever two trucks passed each other, I noticed a few fingers rose from each steering wheel—two or three, never a full hand—in friendly acknowledgment.

Halfway to the narrows I passed the Volunteer Fire Department. The twin garage doors stood open, and I saw two fire trucks, shiny with new wax. Two watermen were coiling a hose. Another was polishing brass. Jimmy Murphy, Wade's younger brother, was sweeping up the garage floor. Clenching a pipe between his teeth, he stopped briefly to wave. "He's over to Gary's," Jimmy said between puffs, meaning Wadey was at the store, which he also assured me had some groceries.

Just as I approached, Captain Wade pulled away from the gas pumps in his red truck and, crossing the drawbridge, headed into the mainland. As it happened, his departure opened up a new island nook to me, a world of yarns and inspired deceit. In front of Gary's was a long split-rail seat, good enough for three people, informally known as a liar's bench. Three older watermen sat there now, watching me as I stepped closer. I knew the bench by reputation. Here old-timers would talk all day long about how they were going to caulk their leaky boats, good as new, and get back on the water. They would say it every day with conviction. It's hard to let go of the water. The same elderly trio held court most days, watching who crossed the drawbridge, who came in too early from crabbing or tonging or, a boon to reputations, who stayed out late. The trio knew what everybody else was doing, news they would trade for a better story. This kept them in the know. On Tilghman's, gossip was hard currency.

Today, Mister Dan, Mister Jack, and Mister Clifford were in fine form. You could learn all of the Eastern Shore dialects from their chatter. They were "tarred" and ready to "retarr." (It looked like they already had.) A "farr" on the "alland" would be a "gawdawful" conflagration—simply "turrable." It was "flat ca'm" today, a poor wind to "drudge an orster." "Neither breath of wind." Just too "slick ca'm." In a phrase, it was "slickity slatey." The language smacked of Cornwall and Devon, ancestral homes to most watermen originally from southwestern England.

On my approach, the threesome caught me in their crosshairs.

"Working for Wadey, are ya?" said one as I ambled by.

I nodded my head and cap.

"He best paid at least fifty—what the state give him for drudging crew."

"Dragging that is," said another old-timer.

I confirmed fifty was at least what he paid. They winced at my accent.

"Ya from Bawlmer?" said the one.

I allowed as I was born in Baltimore.

"Thought so," said the other.

They scanned me top to bottom—sunburned face, muddy pants, wet boots—then stared at my eyes, sizing me up.

"Looks like river mud. You can always tell," the first one finally said.

This brought the third waterman—Mister Jack—out of his apparent slumber. He flashed a broad smile, glanced left and right at his brethren, and began his story in a slow cadence, swallowing his consonants and turning each *i* into an *e* or a long *a*.

"Ben Harrison—that's Miss Pauline's brother—could smell mud and he know'd where'd it come from. One season he had a new drudge boat and a green crew. First day out, his Aunt Vesta put some flowers in the boat for good luck. They drudged all morning and caught a mess 'f orsters, then fog set in like pea soup. The crew wanted to anchor—wait her out. But ol' Ben wanted to be the first to sell them orsters. He told them he could navigate directly back to Tilghman's, if they'd drop a lead line every twenty minutes and bring the mud it collected to him. Cap'n Ben then put his first mate at the wheel and went below to rest."

Mister Dan picked up the story. "After a piece, the crew brought him the lead line. Ben felt the mud, sniffed it, and said, 'We're right off Sharps Island Light. Keep heading to the north'ard.' After a while, the crew took another sounding and brought him the sampling. He said, 'We're right off Knapps Narrows, a little southwest of the channel. Bring her to the east'ard—to leeward.'"

Mister Clifford held up his hand and continued: "The fog was so thick you couldn't see your breath, and the crew became suspicious of Ben's talent, so they played a trick on him. The first mate, Joshua, scraped the flowers on the foredeck and got enough mud to fill the lead line. The crew took the tampered lead down into the cabin. Ben smelled it, tasted a piece, and threw it aside. Then his eyes opened wide. He rushed up the cabin steps and yelled at Josh, 'Keep her off, hard to port. We're right in the middle of Aunt Vesta's flower garden.'"

"Yes, sir," said Mister Jack. "Ben Harrison could solve a mystery with that nose. And, honey, that's just about the smart of it."

All three men laughed, delighted with some deeper amusement. I bowed my head and stepped into the store. At 10:00 A.M., it was nearly empty. I spotted a couple of teenagers in the back room—beyond the fishing tackle display—playing pool. Watermen had finished their coffee hours ago and were about their business. There was no produce in the store, as I had been led to believe, so I bought a soft drink and headed back down Main Street, toward home, to buy some tomatoes and corn at McCarty's Grocery.

Miss Mary McCarty, ninety, had run a roadside grocery on the island since 1933. She supplied dredge boats with food for their galleys and saved Tilghman's residents from weekly visits to the supermarket in St. Michaels. Everyone was on credit during slack time, till the crabs came in. As I approached her store, several brown chickens clucked from wire-mesh coops, from where they kept the town supplied with eggs. Miss Mary was sweeping the front step. I hid my soda. "Don't worry," she said. "All us merchants look after each other." I told her I needed some garden vegetables. "Everybody here just about grows their own," she responded. "I don't have any today, but you can check with Hardy—he's down at the old drugstore." I thanked her. My search was taking on Odyssean proportions.

Just beyond the stone memorial to watermen who had died on the water—over thirty familiar names: Larrimore, Murphy, Harrison, Cummings, Haddaway—stood the red-brick Tilghman Elementary School, where Jackie Murphy worked. It was still in session. Children were playing on the swings. If history proved true, many would not graduate from high school and take to the water instead. Tilghman's Island Hardware was next, an abandoned blacksmith shop with rusty dredge winders and a banged-up yawl boat in the front yard. The brick bank building and post office, the only new commercial buildings on the island, were nestled against the old blacksmith shop. I'd found the center of town.

In an abandoned lot, next to the bank and the post office, a blue truck was parked under a walnut tree. Behind the pickup, an old man napped in a green plastic lawn chair, a bottle of rum protruding from his pocket. The bed of the truck was piled high with tomatoes, onions, green and yellow beans, and, trucked in from out of state, blackberries and strawberries.

"What can I get ya, today?" said Hardy Jackson, rising with difficulty from his chair. He wore a straw hat and seemed overtaken by the sun.

I pointed to some tomatoes and a box of blackberries, and then he caught me searching around. "It's too arly for corn," he said. He told me that most of his produce came from Caroline County, just southeast of here. "Corn will be ready in a month. We used to grow Silver Queen here. On the island, it's all horse corn now." He noticed my skipjack cap.

"So yer the one working for Wadey," he said. "I had a few drudge boats in the old days," he continued. "*Cecrops* was the last one—all skipjacks, all gone now. Never did figure out where that last one got her name. She was cranky. Pete Sweitzer and I owned the *H. A. Parks* together for about a month, in 1947, until I farred him. In them days we had an all-white crew, and they threatened to quit if I didn't git rid a him. He thought he knew more than anyone else.

"I drudged on, good Lord, the old *Mollie Leonard*—she was a sloop like Wadey. I drudged on a schooner, too—the *Clara Garrett*—and a couple of two-masted bugeyes—the *Thomas M. Freeman* and the *Coronet*, a square-rigged bugeye, she was. Tha're all dead now.

"On their papers you'll find George F. Jackson or Franklin Jackson. That's me. Nobody knows it. I never went by George. Never went by Franklin, neither. Always Hardy. Truthfully, my brothers and I—well, in those days, everybody on Tilghman's—went by nicknames. When all of us kids was coming up, I had a taller brother, two years older—we was kids, you know, fighting all the time—and when Walter and I tangled, I'd get my arms around him. I was a li'l more chunkier than he was. He'd always slip out of my hold somehow, tall and slim as he was, even though I was harder or bigger, I guess. 'Look,' they'd say, 'Hard Knot and Slip Knot are at it, again.' Hard Knot dwindled down to Hardy, and here I am today." The old man staggered with an uncertain gait toward the truck, which he called "Topper." Nicknames are de rigueur on the island, where the likes of Ebb Tide, Hooch, Toadie, Big Daddy, and Biscuits can be found.

Hardy Jackson put my tomatoes and berries in a sack, then handed me an extra box of blackberries. "For Miss Pauline," he said. "My favorite teacher. I recall every scolding. Two pints is just right for a pie, you'll see." Suddenly, Mister Hardy waved his hand over the vacant lot. "Jackson's Drug Store is gone, too," he said. "Nothing's left. Father was a druggist, pulled teeth and made milkshakes. Stanley Larrimore used to eat a lot of milkshakes right here. So did the rest of the fleet. In better times."

I thanked Mister Hardy for the produce and headed on my way.

But Hardy grabbed my arm, and I spun around. He had just taken a bite out of a large tomato as if it were an apple, and wiping his mouth, pointed down the street just north of Rose Garvin's Nothing New Shoppe. "See that two-story house, all boarded up? That was Old Man Murphy's. He was the *George W. Collier*, a good skipjack. Bart and Wadey grew up thar—best brothers. Now they don't speak at all." Hardy offered no other words on the subject, but I suspected my curiosity would be quenched in good time. The house was empty, a derelict with two bookend chimneys. Across Main Street, just short of the Methodist Church, was Bart's house, white with bright green shutters. Down a lane, behind Rose's, was Wadey's house. The brothers lived only a hundred yards apart. And their father's house stood between them.

I CROSSED MAIN Street and passed Harrison's Chesapeake House, the popular local hotel and restaurant, and with my groceries in hand, made my way toward Dogwood Harbor. The combination of a land breeze and the scent of the flowering trees had nearly erased the odor of bait. Like Tongers Basin off the narrows, Dogwood Harbor was square with a tight entrance: seventy yards across with a bottleneck egress into the Choptank River. An asphalt landing, with room for parking, swept around three sides of the basin. The harbor was full today, overflowing with boats and trucks. On the north side, twenty white workboats claimed all the slips: *Donna Gail, Gracie E., Miss Kim, Miss Marly II, Annabell II, Island Girl, Albatross, Gray Hare, Big Daddy,* and others, each a personification of its owner or his sweetheart. On the south side, the skipjacks floated in three sets: three abreast making nine. (Another three were sequestered in Knapps Narrows.) After dragging, all would be tied up for the summer; the skipjack captains employed their regular, motorized workboats for crabbing, until oystering came back in the fall. Nonetheless, each spare minute, the skippers were aboard their dredge boats, painting the decks and spars, sprucing up anything dry and above water. Towering over the men, the nine masts, each over sixty feet tall, presided over the harbor like sentinels.

I rounded the harbor with the thought of getting home to another cool drink. By noon, the humidity had descended on the island like a plastic sheet. But then I spied the captain of the first skipjack waving me over. It was Pete Sweitzer, seventy-four, my neighbor, aboard *Hilda M. Willing.* He was talking with Bart Murphy, whose *Esther F.* was tied alongside. Black Bart, as he was known, was shorter, slighter than his younger brother, Wade. Here were two of the island elite, men of the first water. Out of three hundred watermen on the island, only twelve were dredge-boat captains, and they usually kept their own company. Within this tight circle, they traded news and gossip, even among rivals, though "rivals" was a generous characterization of these two. They barely tolerated each other.

"Getting ready for drudging?" Pete said to Bart.

"No, I'm getting her stripped down for the races—taking the winders off and all that cable. Stowing the drudges. Painting the bottom. If I had some goose grease, I'd slick down the hull." The first of the autumn skipjack races, an annual tradition at Deal Island on Labor Day, was only nine weeks away. The purse was one thousand dollars for first place, a free-for-all. No size divisions. No handicaps. The best captain, crew, and craft would win.

"You better pray for light air—for a small boat to win," Captain Pete said.

"Light or heavy, I just want to beat him." Bart tilted his head toward *Rebecca*. "Well, I've got some errands to run." Suddenly, he drove off.

"Probably gone to drink a beer," Sweitzer said. Captain Pete was an unforgiving waterman with the work ethic of a farmer and the constitution of an ox. "Whenever thar's painting to be done, some captains run scarce. Or just talk about it. That one's got more mouth on him than a catfish." He removed his hat, revealing a crop of white hair. "A piece of advice for you: Stay away from them Murphys—bastards every one of 'em." Word around Gary's was that Pete had a similar affliction. The dredge-boat fleet was made up of hard men, what they called "hard rollers." I didn't take Pete's caution to heart.

My street had its own warning system. As I hurried home, Max barked proudly, the screen door opened, and Miss Pauline stepped outside to hand me a warm plate wrapped in foil. Suspecting some injustice, I quickly reached into my sack and handed her Hardy's and my berries. "Too late," she said, peeling back the foil. "Blackberry pie," she whispered with a devilish grin.

"That was fast," I cried.

"You got me good, but now I've gotten you one better," she gloated, tickled with herself. It was becoming clear I had a challenge on my hands to get ahead of Miss Pauline.

I juggled my tomatoes and pie on the short path to my back door, blessedly unlocked, as was the island custom. It had been an eventful day, but I was ready to wash the mud off my clothes and get back to chronicling the island's natural history, though I had run into some of its most colorful species on my walk.

THAT SUMMER, I RECALL one continuous banquet from the hands of watermen and the kitchen of Miss Pauline. Like errant school children, the crabbers brought their favorite teacher apples, garden produce, and tributes from the sea. Bushel after bushel of crabs landed on her doorstep, which she turned into crab cakes or crab imperial to stuff the flounder and rockfish she also received. And, invariably, Miss Pauline would invite me for dinner to help divest her of this plentitude. With a seat at her table, my own kitchen fell into disuse.

By the end of June, I had paid part of my rent by bringing my landlord half a bushel of crabs. That was, in turn, my earnings for helping Wadey trotline one morning in Harris Creek. That sunny and sultry day, begun at 4:00 A.M., was one of the highlights of my summer. Wadey already had a helper—Billy, then twelve—so I mostly came along for the ride. We were aboard *Miss Kim*, a thirty-eight-foot wooden workboat named for Wadey's daughter. Our goal was simple: to fill five bushel baskets or more with savory blue crabs. Father manned the dip net and steered the boat; son sorted the crabs: large males ("number one jimmies" with blue claws), "fat" medium-size males ("number twos"), "light" males ("number threes" or "whities"), females ("sooks" with red-tipped claws), and peelers (crabs about to molt). The challenge was to keep them all alive, while out of the water, until unloaded at the dock. The solution was to return to the harbor before the sun was too high in the sky. Wadey would exceed his goal, selling eight bushels for $240. A crabber earned from $15,000 to $20,000 during the summer season. Double that by oystering. That's an impressive pile of shellfish. Maybe too impressive. Crab potters were now allowed nine hundred pots per boat, which seemed excessive to the old-time trotliners like Wadey.

Billy showed me how to spot a peeler. He grabbed a she-crab (an immature sook) from his father's net and turned her over. He pointed to a red smudge in the second-to-last segment of the swimming leg. "She'll molt in the next two days," said Billy. Softshell crabs are, next to oysters, perhaps the greatest Chesapeake delicacy—at least to Billy and me. Returning to the wharf at Knapps Narrows, we sold our peelers (at fifty cents each) to Lula Mae Aerne, one of the island's many "peeler dealers." She kept them in water trays until they "shed," and resold them for $1.50 a piece.

By noon, we had tied *Miss Kim* back in her slip in Dogwood Harbor. Then Billy and I indulged in our other passion: baseball. Fast friends, we played the island's sandlot diamond all summer long.

The Fourth of July brought the watermen off the water early in the day. By midafternoon, red-checkered tablecloths were spread on picnic tables in just about every backyard. But there were no barbecues. No chicken or burgers or dogs. On the tables instead were wooden mallets and mounds of brick-red steamed crabs. I soon realized what separated Chesapeake watermen from other commercial fishermen across the country: their choice of cuisine. Maine lobstermen prefer steak over lobster. Monterey seiners do not favor sardines and squid. And Alaskan fishermen opt for caribou over halibut. But Chesapeake watermen have dozens of recipes for their oysters and crabs, as I learned at Hunky Lednum's.

Hunky, sixty-two, a hand tonger and trotliner, was Wadey's best friend. (They had a running argument over whom Miss Pauline loved best.) On Independence Day, he put on a crab feast for forty people. All his guests brought food: crab cakes, crab imperial, crab creole, deviled crab, scalloped oysters. And, of course, jumbo blue crabs for steaming. The kitchen looked and smelled like a boiler room peppered with Old Bay. Six picnic tables were smothered with crabs. I sat next to Wadey and Billy, and we made a dent in the bushel before us—a couple of dozen a piece. Luckily, I had skipped breakfast—only because Miss Pauline hadn't been baking that morning. But I was still beholden to her for the latest apple cobbler. My dinner mates had a solution.

Wadey, Billy, and I presented her with some of the most beautiful and plump crustaceans in recent memory. Tip to tip, the claws spanned the length of a ruler. The picnic hardly missed them. For the moment, Miss Pauline and I were even, but I knew that wouldn't last.

JULY PASSED BY without incident—men crabbed and caulked and painted; women picked crabmeat—until the twenty-fifth, when "all hell broke loose," as Captain Pete put it. And the island rallied, neighbor helping neighbor. Most of the island was asleep early that morning after a sweltering night. I awakened to a loud blast, more like a thunderous "pop," followed by a long "whoosh." A minute later the piercing sirens of the Volunteer Fire Department rose above the island, climbing the scales like a tenor. A workboat, *Levronson*, had exploded in the harbor. While fueling, a spark from a bilge pump ignited the gasoline. The captain, Sonny Murphy, a cousin of Wadey's, was blown overboard. When I got there, the firemen were pulling Sonny out of the water. He had minor burns on his arms; otherwise, he was uninjured. Most remarkable was the response from the community. Dozens of trucks rushed to the narrows; everyone offered help, extinguishing the boat and the wharf, which had been set aflame. The firemen swiftly got the fire under control. On Tilghman's Island the fire brigade was as vital for putting out conflagrations as for saving men from sinking boats. Today, it had done both.

THE COOL MORNINGS of August prompted the captains to lift their noses to the wind. Autumn would not be long in coming. Meanwhile, excuses were running lean. Throughout the summer, skippers had tinkered with their skipjacks. They had painted the decks, overhauled the winder engines, and varnished the masts and booms and spars. But there were limits to what they could fix while the boats were in the water. As much as they'd like to put it off indefinitely, it was time to haul the skipjacks onto dry land. This was an annual affair, but the captains rarely got used to it.

The lifting of the hulls put enormous strain on the timbers. Nobody liked it less than Stanley Larrimore, sixty-eight, the captain of *Lady Katie.*

But Captain Stanley, a huge man and top competitor, had racing on his mind. Even though dredging was three months away, the upcoming races—two in September, one in October—made his appointment with the boatyard more pressing. The skipjack fleet always turned out in perfect repair and adornment for these contests. Not just prize money was on the line. Reputations hung in the balance. Suddenly, at every boatyard, preparations were under way with the urgency of the paddock at Churchill Downs.

Knapps Narrows Marina was nearly full the day *Lady Katie* was lifted from the water. And Stanley was a wreck. *Lady Katie* creaked and groaned as the steel "travel lift" carried her across the yard. It wasn't unusual for the procedure to open up a leak in a skipjack. A look of anxiety on his face, Stanley leaned his immense frame forward with anticipation. I hovered at a safe distance. The thought of fifteen tons dropping onto the oyster shell (or my foot) gave me pause. But Peter Mathews, the operator of the travel lift, was skilled at his job; he gently lowered the skipjack toward the ground, resting her securely on wooden blocks and steel braces. Once she was safely settled, Stanley relaxed his massive shoulders and noticed me for the first time. His huge hand enveloped mine like a baseball glove.

"Where've ya been?" he asked. His generous profile filled my view: a mountain of a man so formidable he made his own weather.

I told him I'd been working for Wadey.

"He pays better'n I do, I imagine," he said, chuckling to himself. It was well known that Stanley Larrimore had trouble parting with a dollar. Always self-effacing, he was the first to make a joke about himself, either his weight or his wallet.

Over the previous two years I had sailed and dredged aboard *Lady Katie* many times, including a memorable trip on a Thanksgiving Saturday when *Lady Katie* cut through the ice in Trappe Creek like an icebreaker to get to the oyster grounds. It was an unspoken rule that racing crews for the autumn skipjack races helped the captains with caulking and painting over the summer. I was scheduled to crew for Stanley at the Sandy Point Races, the third leg of this year's Triple Crown. So I showed up at *Lady Katie* for work.

Lady Katie had been placed on blocks next to *Kathryn* (1901). Out of the water, their different hull designs were obvious, revealing a vagueness in how a skipjack is defined. *Lady Katie* was clearly the more classic skipjack, her hull like that of a huge rowboat. She was built recently, in 1956, one of three sisters constructed by Bronza Parks, legendary builder of skipjacks. Viewed from her sharp clipperlike bow, she had vertical sides that ended abruptly, just below the waterline. From there, the bottom planks were nailed crosswise to the keel. This sharp turn in the shape of the hull on a classic skipjack is called a "hard chine," as opposed to a "soft chine," which *Kathryn* had. *Kathryn* was planked lengthwise from stem to stern over a frame, completely perpendicular to *Lady Katie's* design. Head on, *Lady Katie's* hull had the profile of a V, what's known as a "deadrise," with vertical topsides rising above it; *Kathryn* was U-shaped, with no abrupt change in shape at the waterline. Round-bottom, soft-chined, frame-built—all these terms distinguished *Kathryn* from *Lady Katie*.

Rebecca T. Ruark (1886) also had a U-shape, much like *Kathryn*. However, *Kathryn* had always been rigged as a skipjack, with a simple mainsail and jib, whereas *Rebecca* may have originally been a gaff-rigged sloop. Thus, the dispute: Does the hull or the rig define a skipjack? Must a skipjack have a V-bottom hull or simply the right sail plan? This is an important debate because only "skipjacks" are allowed to compete at the autumn races. Each year, a protest against *Rebecca* was launched, but each year Wadey convinced the race committee that his boat qualified as a skipjack because of her sail plan and rig. A skipjack's rig is defined as the mast height being equal to the length on deck plus the beam (or width). *Rebecca* now fit this to the inch. Wadey made sure of it. In any case, the rounded hulls of *Rebecca* and *Kathryn* made them faster than ordinary skipjacks. They were the two boats to beat at the autumn races.

We were unloading tools and nails and paint from Stanley's truck when Gene Tyler, sixty-four, stopped by. Gene was a Smith Islander and captained *Martha Lewis*, always the last procrastinator to make it to the boatyard. They fell into a conversation about Bronza Parks, as they often did. Each had a fierce affection for Bronza's boats.

Most of the youngest dredge boats in the fleet were Bronza's design. He had lived and worked just across the Choptank River, in Dorchester County, and had the reputation of being a fine craftsman, a perfectionist, and an obstinate son of a bitch. That's what probably cost him his life. As the story goes, a man had commissioned Bronza to build a replica skipjack to be used as a pleasure yacht. Bronza kept adding features to the boat without the man's permission, and the price kept going up. The client showed up once to protest, then again. The man was livid. After the third fight over costs, the man's temper flared beyond control. He shot Bronza dead, right in the boatyard.

That was the end of an era. The last three skipjacks that Bronza designed and built were sister ships and are still afloat—*Rosie Parks* (1955), *Martha Lewis* (1955), and *Lady Katie* (1956). He laid out their keels side by side and built them according to the same plan, which was in his head. He couldn't read blueprints. They were classic skipjacks with sharp bows and transom sterns, hard chines, and cross planking, what he called "herringbone" construction. He built *Rosie Parks* for his brother Orville; she was named for their mother. Orville, the winningest racing captain of recent years, died in the 1970s, and the boat is now owned by the Chesa-

peake Bay Maritime Museum in St. Michaels. Gene Tyler and
Stanley Larrimore now owned the other two, and they often compared notes on how well they matched—in dredging, racing, and
longevity.

"Look at this, Gene," Stanley said, climbing up a ladder to the
port railing of *Lady Katie*. His bushy eyebrows twitched in frustration atop an eaglelike nose. Gene grabbed another ladder and
stepped up to Stanley's height. "How could anyone sink two bolts
that close together," Stanley continued, "and this close to the edge
of the board? It split. Should've split years ago. Now I have to replace all the rotten wood around it."

"Suppose you'd have to ask Bronza," said Gene.

"I don't want to go where he is, just to ask him."

Gene laughed. "You wouldn't want to get thar the way he did,
either," he said.

"No, and I'm not so certain which place to look for him."

"He had his way, you know," Gene said. "I can imagine how he
could get someone mad enough to shoot him. He always did it his
way."

"I suppose I'm the same," said Stanley. "I gotta do it my way.
But if someone has something to say, I'll at least listen before I go
do it my way."

They climbed down the ladders and looked up at the side of
Lady Katie and then stepped back to see her lines. Stanley was the
first to speak.

"Captain Orville told me he could take this boat and beat *Rosie
Parks*, you know. He just thought this boat was faster than his."

"I suppose he could, Stanley," said Gene. "His brother improved
as he went along. Got meaner, too." They both shook their heads.
Stanley then lifted a saw, which must have made Gene nervous.
He quickly protested that he had a lot of work to do, then opened a
beer and motored off. We finished unloading the truck.

Stanley assigned me to sanding the bottom of the boat—removing the old red copper paint—and renailing any loose planks. To find where nails were missing, he handed me a nail punch and a hammer. It was like dentistry, he assured me. Simply find the cavities and then hammer in new boat nails with a sledgehammer. Swinging a sledgehammer uphill, against gravity, was the trick, he warned. It would be a good workout. "The bottom is the most work," he said. "You might as well get it out of the way first."

Meanwhile, Stanley turned his attention to the port log rail, next to the errant bolts. The oak log runs around the boat on top of the outside edge of the deck, what is known as the "waterways." Holes are cut in the log to allow water to run off the deck, over the waterways, and over the side of the boat. Below the waterways is the "bends," the planking that wraps around the side of the boat. Stanley feared that the rot in the log and waterways had extended into the bends.

Grabbing the power saw again, Stanley climbed the ladder and surveyed the damage. The oak log was rotten both fore and aft of the cylindrical roller over which the dredge cable ran. "I'll have to go back and forward to hit timbers under the deck to tie the new log in," he said. "Yes, sir. No easy job." Slowly chunks of oak came free. But the more he cut out, the more he could see the rot was widespread. It extended farther toward the bow and the stern, and ran deeper, as he had feared. By late morning he had removed fifteen feet of log and a five-foot section of the bends. "It's easy to tear out," he said. "What's difficult is putting it back in."

While Stanley had been cutting and tearing, I checked for missing nails with a blunt hand awl. This worked better than the nail punch, which was too short. I found twenty-three nail holes in the planks that were missing nails. The brackish water of the Bay had corroded the nail heads, or they had simply popped out. I retrieved a handful of galvanized, four-inch boat nails from the truck and renailed the bottom. Stanley was right: hoisting a sledgehammer upward against gravity was a terror. It was arm-numbing work. Luckily, Stanley was ready for lunch.

"Hold that, please," he said, nodding toward the bottom of the ladder. "As big as I am, if I fell it would spell trouble. I gotta be careful with only one kidney. Hold that ladder now, I'm coming down."

He eased down off the last step, and gravel crunched under his feet. "Everyone kids me about how big I am," he said. "Well, this heat is harder on a fat man." I noticed an eagle on his left forearm. The tattoo—a relic from his days in the navy, was large and covered his huge forearm, which was the size of a normal man's calf. "This is too much work for one man," he continued. "That's what happens when you get old—the timbers start to go. *Lady Katie* and I are in the same shape. We need a makeover."

It was noon. Stanley invited me to his house in Fairbank, at the south end of the island, for lunch. I inspected my shirt and pants, took off my hat. I was covered with red and white dust, head to foot. The hair on my arms appeared to be speckled with powdered sugar. What about this? I gestured. "She don't mind," he said. "Remind me to pick up another hammer while we're down home."

We parked the truck at his house but walked across the lane to his father Glendi's house, which Stanley and Loretta now owned and were restoring. Glendi had captained two skipjacks, *Laura M. Evans* (1911) and *Laura J. Barkley* (date unknown); Stanley learned his trade on both. The house was at the same stage as *Lady Katie*— they were still tearing walls and ceilings off it. Stanley shouted into the door and his wife appeared in a cloud of black dust. Her blond hair was coated with soot. She could have made the casting call for an episode of *I Love Lucy*. We all laughed. While pulling plaster slats off the attic ceiling, the insulation had fallen on her. Like her husband, Miss Loretta, when she got her mind set on something, went right ahead, one gear only—full speed. "I guess I pulled out them slats too quickly," she said, smiling. "Lunch is almost ready."

Glendi's house bordered on Bar Neck Cove, and we wandered down to the water outside a marsh where Stanley was building a dock for *Lady Katie*. "I want to get her out of Dogwood Harbor," he said. "It's a fire hazard—lightning. I've already been hit twice. Of course, the lightning will probably follow me here." He shuffled down to the shore with a rolling gait and pointed to a derelict, half-sunken skipjack at the head of the cove. "That's the *Geneva May*. My nephew Daryl bought her but let her die. My brother's bugeye, the *R. H. Daugherty*, died right alongside her. When I was a boy, this cove was full of skipjacks. Every one of these houses was a captain: Wood Somers, Funny Parks, Ernest Jenkins, my grandfather Addison—he was the bugeye *Frank B. Legg*. I'm the only one left. Three generations of Larrimores drudged out of this cove, from bugeyes to skipjacks." The varnish doesn't fall far from the mast.

Stanley pointed out a cannonball nestled amid some cattails. He explained it was from the War of 1812; he had dredged up history while sailing under Calvert Cliffs across the Bay. "Yes, sir, plenty of relics around here," he said, slapping his chest. "Ya're looking at one."

We sat down to lunch. Even after washing our hands, the three of us looked like we had been tarred and feathered. Loretta served fried soft-shell crabs and homemade lima bean soup, made with fresh limas, corn off the cob, and dumplings. As an afterthought she had baked fresh zucchini bread with summer squash out of her garden, raisins, walnuts, and ground flour. We washed all this down with sun tea. The soft-shells were crispy, the fins like french fries filled with crab. It's called Eastern Shore cooking, and after the first bite, I couldn't get enough of it.

I learned that their daughter, Rhonda, lived in Easton, and son, Steve, lived in Tilghman's. Both have sons. Steve had tried being a waterman, dredging with his father in winter and crabbing—trotlining—on his own in the summer. But he discovered nature wasn't consistent. Poor harvests came in waves. Steve now works as a rigger in an Oxford boatyard.

As we stood up to leave, Stanley complained about a blister on his hand from this morning's work. "Well, you have those baby hands!" Loretta said. "You get blisters 'cause you haven't been working much lately."

"Not much on the house," Stanley agreed, smiling at his wife. "You wouldn't want to switch jobs, would you?"

Back at the boatyard, we were greeted by Daryl Larrimore, Stanley's nephew, who was standing next to *Lady Katie* smoking a cigarette. Daryl, thirty-eight, was the youngest captain in the skipjack fleet, and his boat—*Nellie L. Byrd* (1911), was one of the largest. He was as tall as Stanley but rail thin. As the watermen say, he had to drink muddy water to cast a shadow. Daryl never wore a hat; his Dutch-bob haircut was crowned with a blond cowlick.

"What do y'know?" Stanley said.

"I've got the afternoon free," Daryl answered. His speech was clipped, the cigarette dangling from his mouth. The nephew was a good boat carpenter and had agreed to hire out to Stanley for fifteen dollars an hour to help replace the port side. Daryl scrutinized his uncle's handiwork. "You about done cutting?" Daryl asked.

"She's all torn out," Stanley said. "Seven feet on either side of them bolts."

They talked about where to find the lumber they would need. Old-growth pine was the best. Salt-treated was a second choice. Aged untreated wood was a distant third but cheapest. "I think'll go see that man with the *Claud Somers*, see if he'll sell some of that aged pine he's got for the deck. I'll never find any salt-treated. No, sir. Not enough of these old boats left to make it worthwhile for the lumberyards to produce it." A Baltimore skipjack aficionado, Gary Lambert, had bought the old *Somers* at salvage and was now restoring her at Severn Marine, the second boatyard on the island.

"All right then, I'll try to buy some lumber off Mr. Lambert," said Stanley. "First I'll slip down home and pick up that hammer I forgot at lunch." He ambled toward his truck, while I lifted two cans of white paint off his tailgate and slammed it shut. "I'll get some more thinner, too," he said as he drove off.

"Better paint quickly before he waters it down," said Daryl. "He hates to buy another can. I'm closer to him than my own father, but I'll tell you what—he's the tightest man with a dollar other than me."

I started painting the starboard side of the boat down to the waterline, which was a black stripe at the border between the red bottom paint and the white upper sides. I noticed some of the side was covered with copper sheathing to protect the boat from ice in the winter. Glass ice—the sharp, thin layer that first freezes on the water surface—can cut the hull planks of a skipjack, so the metal sheathing is nailed along the waterline from stem to stern for protection. Daryl had a trick for painting the copper siding.

"Wash it down with vinegar," he said. "I have some in the truck. It etches the copper, making it hold the paint better. Only problem is it makes you hungry—smells like steamed crabs."

Daryl fetched a bottle of vinegar. "Don't worry," he said on his return. "I'll charge Stanley for it." He grinned. Then he took a tape measure from his pocket and began planning his carpentry work. The vinegar brushed right on and dried quickly in the heat, so I was able to paint most of the side with white—in an hour or so—by the time Stanley got back.

The truck arrived in the yard with two long boards of seasoned pine. He intended to cut these into two-by-twos for the deck adjacent to the waterways. Four twelve-foot boards of green wood were also tied to the roof. These would be reserved for the bends. Stanley had forgotten the hammer again. "I've slipped down the road twice today and I haven't picked up that hammer yet," he said, shaking his head.

While we unloaded the lumber, another truck rolled over the

gravel and stopped at *Lady Katie*'s stern. It was Leland "Puss" Larrimore, Daryl's father and Stanley's brother. He spoke to his brother without getting out of his truck.

"The whole side's bad, I see," Puss said.

"Coupla weeks' work. Daryl's helping."

"I see that."

"You staying?"

"Gotta go," Puss said, after he nodded in Daryl's direction. Whenever there was work to be done on *Lady Katie*, family and friends became scarce.

"Dad was the *Esther W.*," Daryl said to me, after his father had left. "A big skipjack. One-thousand-bushel boat. Not fast but a good drudge boat. He was that bugeye, the *R. H. Daugherty*, too."

Far and wide, Puss Larrimore had a reputation. One summer about thirty-five years ago, he was crabbing—trotlining—on Black Walnut Sands, a large oyster bar off the southeast side of the island. Nearby, a few boat lengths away, was Old Man Wade Murphy trotlining another "lay," or spot for crabbing. There was disagreement over whose lay was whose, and they yelled back and forth. All of a sudden, Puss turned his boat toward Old Man Wade and gunned the motor. Puss hit him broadside and sank the boat, leaving Murphy to drown, leaving him for dead. Old Man Wade was rescued, and he pressed charges. Puss pleaded guilty to assault, Daryl confirmed, and spent a little time in jail. During this time, Stanley and Loretta took in the young Daryl and his brother, Dennis, raising them with Steve and Rhonda in their Fairbank home. Ever since Puss's arrest, there had been bad blood between the Larrimores and the Murphys, like a backcountry feud.

Daryl and Stanley now went about measuring the hole in the bends to begin the repairs, working from the bottom up. Once they measured the boards to cut, they would set them in place, glue them, and bend the green wood with clamps. Lastly, they would bolt them through, tying them into the boat's timbers.

First, Stanley showed me what he wanted painted. While he did, he poured thinner into my paint can. He told me to paint the port side after I finished the starboard and then he'd show me how to design the waterline and the red bead, a thin red stripe on a groove that marked the bends. But first the marine latex. Painting the broad sides with white was easy, and after Stanley had watered the paint down with mineral spirits, it brushed more easily, too. "It's thinner now," said Stanley. "You'll get farther with it. But it's just as white. They say they put blue in it to make it that white." Daryl cracked a smile from the bow of the boat.

Next, I attacked the waterline. There was no groove to follow, and I had already covered most of the old black line with white paint, over the copper, so I had to start from scratch. The waterline, I was told, always had to be repainted, so don't sweat it. But with Larrimore eyes upon me, I painted like a perfectionist. The black stripe went on smoothly: From a distance it almost looked straight. Then, when I was three-quarters of the way down the boat, I heard a whistle. Then two. I turned around. The two Larrimores were sitting on trestles watching me paint. "A regular van Gogh," Daryl said, with a little applause.

"Yes, sir," said Stanley. "Putty and paint. Putty and paint makes her what she ain't." He smiled. "That's why we name these drudge boats after women."

At 6:00 P.M. we began cleaning up around the boat. We loaded the tools and materials—everything except the lumber—into Stanley's truck. "People love these old wooden boats," he said, "but they have no idea about all the hard work and foolishness it takes to keep 'em afloat." He turned on the ignition. "Yes, sir. After a day like this, you'll appreciate orsters all the more next time you eat 'em. See ya tomorrow." Stanley drove home to another fine meal.

Over the next three weeks I would help Stanley prepare *Lady Katie* for another season of oystering and racing. Stanley and Daryl would concentrate on the repairs to the port side, and I would caulk and paint the hull, a huge job, and the topside, including the bowsprit—with the thinnest paint on the island. For now, however, I was content to walk home under the cool light of an August evening. Tilghman's Island, its walnut-lined streets and busy harbors, had become home for me. I felt at ease knocking on any door, hailing any captain. The watermen had shed their myth but not their stature: They were flawed, yes, but still a breed apart. Independent, self-sufficient, unconventional. In a word, original. I had stumbled upon one of the last true fishing communities, a people and a place with an enduring mission and compass.

Up ahead, I could see the men loitering outside Gary's. Now for a cold drink.

The glass door of Gary's Store was wide open, unusual for August. I noticed the air-conditioning was busted, as I shuffled through, pausing briefly to wave at the pair on the liar's bench. Both tipped their hats—a rare courtesy. It had taken me all summer, but I had finally arrived.

Inside, a couple of captains were milling about: Gene Tyler, on another break, and Bart Murphy, buying a six-pack of beer.

"When ya hauling yer drudge boat?" Gene asked Bart.

"Soon as you do."

"Only three weeks till the races."

"I'll be thar. All I've got to do is copper my bottom."

"Ya'll need that centerboard fixed if it's heavy weather."

"I'm counting on light air."

"We've gotta gang up on them Deal Islanders," said Gene. "We better win and take that trophy away."

"I don't care about beating them Deal boats. Let 'em win."

"Where's your pride, Bart!"

"Hell, I just want to beat my brother Wade."

2

At the Races

For Chesapeake watermen, all news begins with the wind. Good or bad, all forecasts, all tidings, float in with the breeze. Whether a skipjack captain can work on a given day, whether he can lie low, is determined by the speed of the air. Upon waking, a waterman listens to the night. If it's too quiet or too fierce, he might catch a few more winks. But if the morning sounds promising, he rushes to catch the first breath. By dawn, each gust brings the expectation of a good harvest. His prospects, his day, will be shaped by the wind. A seasoned skipper plays this breeze to his advantage, reading every nuance, harnessing every whim. Above all, his fellow fishermen measure him by his prowess with the wind.

At no time was this truer, I thought, standing on the bow of *Rebecca*, than on this day, the first Monday of September. The Labor Day Race at Deal Island was getting under way. We had sailed ten hours south to Deal, home of one-third of the skipjack fleet, the day before, affording us a chance to check the rigging. That fifty-mile voyage was about the range of a skipjack. Now, after a poor night's sleep on the deck of *Rebecca*, we were making for the start of the race. All entries were required to rendezvous at the race committee boat northwest of the island at 10:00 A.M. sharp. The gun and flag that would mark the start of the race were still more than forty minutes away, yet the sun was already high in a flawless blue sky.

The wind had swung clockwise during the night. The southerly breeze of the afternoon before had turned west and was blowing northwest by morning. And it kept turning. Even now, the wind was breezing up nearly due north, right down the length of the race-course. Ninety percent of all skipjack races are won "on the wind"; that is, facing the wind. So, with the wind parallel to the course, it was shaping up to be a good race day. Blowing nicely, too—about twenty miles per hour—and that was good news for *Rebecca*: She sailed best in heavy air. Poor news for smaller boats like *Esther F.*, with Bart Murphy at the helm.

It was thirty-two minutes before the start when we passed the channel buoys that marked the entrance to Deal Harbor. Wadey began barking orders. He was on edge. Racing brought out the worst in him, and he took it out on the crew. "Heist the sails, boys," he shouted, "and be quick." Wadey then turned the bow north into the wind. Four of us hauled the main, which rattled up the mast with the aid of classic wooden hoops, and secured it with a fast-releasing slip knot; two others handled the jib. The jib halyard twisted and the whole thing had to be downhauled, set right, and raised again. "Jesus Christ," snapped Wadey. "Get it right, god-damn it." The wind was to blame, not the crew.

Wadey's racing team comprised serious amateur sailors who crewed for him every Labor Day. The only watermen were cousin Lawrence Murphy and Hunky Lednum. The others were Jack Dunham and Fred Whittaker, both of Wilmington, and Ray Saunders and me from the western shore. Li'l Wade, eighteen years old, the captain's son, made seven. Wadey's advice to the crew was simple and brief: "Everybody keep their heads down after the start. Unless something needs fixing, I don't want to see anybody. For heaven's sake, keep out of my goddamn way."

Racing was a blood sport to Wade Murphy. For years aboard *Sigsbee*, a "dumb" boat, he had lost race after race. Now, with arguably the smartest racing boat in the skipjack fleet, he had something to prove. With the sloop's only real competition, *Kathryn*, not appearing at the Deal Races this year, it was Wadey's race to lose. There were no other fore-and-aft-planked skipjacks at the race. The cross-planked boats were decidedly slower, unless a lucky captain caught a puff of wind while *Rebecca* was in dead water. Bart was hoping for just that, but it hadn't happened on a Labor Day yet. Wadey had caught good breezes and won the trophy the last two years.

Dredge-boat captains had been racing one another since the dawn of oystering on the Chesapeake Bay. In the early days of schooners and bugeyes, the dockside price for the day's catch fluctuated hourly. Consequently, captains would race one another to port to get the better price. Later, when skipjacks were born and joined their larger and faster cousins on the oyster rocks, buy boats anchored near each fleet to buy oysters at midday. Captains raced to these buy boats every time their decks were filled. It became important not only to have a good dredging boat but a good racing boat as well. Soon, skipjack captains began matching their boats for the sheer joy of it. And their reputations as skippers depended as much on their successes in racing as by the number of bushels they caught.

In 1960, Ben Evans and Clifton Webster of Deal Island approached the local Lions Club and persuaded them to create a homecoming event on Labor Day, complete with a skipjack race. Thirty captains showed up, and the races have run annually ever since. They now come with a combined purse of $1,750 for the first three finishers, provided by sponsors, mostly local newspapers and banks. During the first thirty years, the winningest captain was Stanford White Jr., whose *F. C. Lewis* won ten times. The next most successful captain was Orville Parks, considered the finest tactician, with four wins. At least a few Tilghman boats traveled to Deal each September to try to take the trophy away from the local captains. The rivalry between the two islands became intense. So far, most years the Deal Islanders have kept their trophy at home.

But last year was a different story. The Labor Day Races got off to a poor start, or rather a contested one. That Monday, at ten o'clock, the only boat at the starting line was *Rebecca*. It was the official time for the start of the race and Wadey was ready to go. The seven other captains, comprising Bart Murphy and six Deal Islanders, were late getting to the committee boat. Wadey started without them. He rounded the course and crossed the finish line, an eight-mile run (an extended course), before many had set their sails. *Rebecca* was given first place, but the Deal Islanders disputed the win and have been complaining about it ever since. The central argument revolved around whether a race starts when the official time passed or when the gun was fired.

Just this morning before we got under way for today's race, one of the Deal captains, Ted Webster of *H. M. Krentz*, had berated Wadey for last year's debacle.

"If it had been me at the starting line, I would have waited for you," Ted had said. "Don't you have any principles?"

"Yes," Wadey answered.

"So why don't you use them. Nobody farred the gun."

"When I race I'm serious, Ted, and ten o'clock is ten o'clock."

"You should have waited. If it had been a fair race, I would have beat your ass."

"How much air do you think I need to win?" Wadey asked, referring to *Rebecca*'s proficiency in heavier weather.

"Twelve or fifteen mile," said Ted, abbreviating miles per hour, "and it was blowing light and I would have beat you. And you knew it. That's why you jumped the start."

Wadey pushed his cap back on his head and said, "Well, it's blowing today, so try to get to the start by ten o'clock, and I'll beat you again."

AS OUR SHAKEDOWN cruise continued, I checked my watch: 9:40 A.M. Plenty of time to test the sails and to show up at the starting gate. The captain was pacing like a cat, however, back and forth in front of the helm. Something caught his eye. He bent over near the gunwale and picked up a shiny new penny. "Good luck," he said. Removing his left shoe, he placed the copper penny inside carefully, face up. It "tinked" as it nestled beside the other pennies already there. He laced up his shoe. Wade Murphy was taking no chances this race day. He carried three two-dollar bills in his wallet. A polished horseshoe was nailed to *Rebecca*'s Samson post. Spars were varnished; everything else aboard was painted bright white; not a single color interrupted the motif. All this was designed for good luck as well. Blue paint was considered bad luck (it had been the color of the Spanish armada, enemy of the watermen's ancestors), as were walnuts, fried chicken, and upside-down hatch covers.

Perhaps the most obvious manifestation of the captain's superstitions was the lack of women aboard *Rebecca*. The other skipjacks left the docks loaded with spectators, including women and teenage girls. But Wadey carried only a minimal racing crew—all of us had assigned jobs—and no spectators, no women aboard. The captain felt they were unlucky. And like all superstitions, there was a story behind it. At the races in 1968, Wadey's cousin's daughter fell overboard. He dived in to save her, and both of them nearly drowned. He hasn't allowed a woman aboard at the races ever since.

Wadey performed a few practice tacks to satisfy himself that the rigging was secure and everything was running smoothly. To tack, or come about, is the act of turning the bow through the wind so that the breeze crosses to the other side of the boat. The wind then hits the opposite side of the sails and the boat can change course. During each tack this morning, the crew ducked to give Wadey a clear view, to sidestep his temper.

I made the first mistake. I walked over to the cabin and lifted a pair of binoculars from the cabintop. I might have obscured the captain's vision for a split second but that was enough. "Give me those damn glasses," he roared, taking them from me. "Now keep out of sight." After a few seconds he did smile at me, however. After all, they were my binoculars.

Wadey raised the field glasses to his eyes and scanned the boats. Eight wooden masts punctuated the horizon. With *Rebecca* that made nine—nine captains here to sail for the prize. A thousand or more spectators lined the docks and beaches and motorboats at the edge of the racecourse—all the anticipation of the Kentucky Derby. Time was ticking toward the start.

At eight o'clock that morning, before Wadey and the others got under way, the race committee had held the obligatory skippers' meeting to lay out the rules of the race. Also called the "reading of the clock," the gathering permitted the captains to synchronize their watches with that of the official timekeeper. This year's meeting was especially tense, with the Deal contingent protesting Wadey's "false start" all over again. After the ranting, I stepped up with two watches and synchronized them with Deke Sheller's, the race director's. While Jack Dunham was first mate, I had been Wadey's timekeeper for the past couple of years. It was a nerve-racking job. I hated to think the wrath I'd earn if I made a mistake.

Just then, Wadey approached me. "Get it?" he said, eyeing my stopwatches.

I nodded. Wadey stared me down for a second or two and then

strode off to *Rebecca*. The other captains scattered as well. I checked both watches. It was time to get under way.

On the walk to the boat, Jack and I had overheard Bart talking to Gene Tyler, the captain of *Martha Lewis*. "I'm only here to beat one boat, and damn it, thar's too much wind. If I push it, I'll break something." Just about everyone was gunning for *Rebecca*. You could hear the chorus—from family, rivals, and friends. The only one missing was Stanley Larrimore, who was stranded in Tilghman's with a bad yawl-boat engine; he would save *Lady Katie* for the next two races, the wrap-up of the Triple Crown.

BY THE TIME we reached the committee boat, *Becky Ann*, Wadey was still steaming from his encounter with Ted Webster over last year's contested start. Others had chided him at the skipper's meeting; the locals had gotten under his skin. He gathered us, his crew, together near the cabin and tipped his cap back on his head.

"These Deal Islanders have made me mad this morning, carrying on like that, how I should wait for them," he said. "I don't wait for anyone. Well, today we're gonna show them what a sailboat can do. I've been holding back last couple of years. But today we've got something to prove. I don't care what it's blowing; just as long as thar's a breeze we'll do fine. We're going all out, boys. I'm putting all the sail up—no reefs—if it's blowing less than thirty mile. If we break something, you'll just have to fix it."

Jack and Lawrence and I looked at one another with wide eyes. The last thing we wanted to witness was a mast or boom crashing to the deck. That could kill somebody. But we all thought better of voicing caution to the captain. "Whatever you do," Jack said, "don't ask him any questions or, for Gawd's sake, offer any advice. This is a dictatorship and there's room for only one tyrant aboard."

Wadey paced the deck but never more than a few seconds away from the wheel. The starting line stretched east-west, perpendicular to the wind and to the length of the race. Eight skipjacks gathered just south of the mark, jockeying for position. They made short tacks east and west just leeward (downwind) of the line in order to be close to the start at the sound of the gun. *Rebecca* had a different strategy. We sailed right up to the line and, setting the stopwatch, turned and headed south for five minutes away from the wind, then came about and returned to the starting line. We did this twice, testing the north wind and the tide and *Rebecca*'s speed. In this way, Wadey knew exactly how far away to begin his charge toward the start at the five-minute gun. It also gave the crew practice jibing, which would be required at the northern buoy on the course. Jibing was the act of changing course by swinging the stern through the wind, rather than the bow. It was a dangerous move. The boom typically swings violently across the deck as the position of the wind changes, and this whipping of the boom can snap it in half. For this reason, Lawrence Murphy, the biggest and strongest man aboard, was positioned to haul in the main sheet (the line to the boom) when it swung across the deck—to cushion its force.

At the wheel now, the captain stepped onto his soapbox. He was selling bravado to the crew. "I'm not saying we're gonna win. That would be bad luck. I'll brag after the race. But I'll tell you boys one thing: We're not gonna lose."

Each time we approached the line, the other skipjacks flew past our bow, each captain measuring time and distance instinctively so as not to collide. Two auxiliary committee workboats sped around, guarding the raceway, fending off the hundred or more spectator boats—Chris Craft, bay-built workboats, and fiberglass sloops—that crowded the course.

At the ten-minute cannon (and raising of the white flag), we had just jibed and were heading southwest away from the starting line—to get a running start. *Rebecca* was in fine form; she sliced through the water like a knife. I resynchronized the watches. We were five seconds ahead of the cannon's time, but I figured there was a delay in its firing. Close enough. I would compensate.

"Tell me when it's five minutes," the captain shouted at me. We were on a starboard tack, still sailing away from the start.

"Now," I told him. "Five minutes to go. I can't hear the cannon, but the blue flag is going up right now."

The captain, figuring he had plenty of time, spun the wheel hard to starboard. *Rebecca* came about, salt spraying over the bow. The mainsail filled, obscuring my vision like an enormous flag. Lawrence pulled the main sheet tight, and the boom was trimmed close to the boat. With the bow now just to the right of the wind, the boat was said to be "close-hauled." The wind came over the left side of the bow so we were on a "port tack." She was also heeled over, her deck tilted to starboard from the force of the wind on the sails and mast. To compensate, the crew climbed across the deck to the port rail, on the windward side, but their weight did little. With the water swishing over the starboard rail, their escape was more for safety. *Rebecca* was in beautiful trim cutting through the water, heading northeast toward the start.

We were more than halfway there.

"Give me some time now. Give me some time."

"Two minutes."

Rebecca closed in on the start but was on a collision course with *City of Crisfield*, the lead boat of the Deal fleet. The *City*, captained by Art Daniels, the senior man, was on a starboard tack so she had right-of-way over *Rebecca*. But Wadey held his course. It was going to be close.

"One minute."

As if threading a needle, *Rebecca* glided toward the narrow passage between the committee boat and *City of Crisfield*. With this objective, Wadey could call for buoy room, thus canceling out the standard right-of-way. These sailing regulations were a mere formality, however—rarely observed in a dredge-boat race. More often than not a skipjack simply gave way to the older man. Other than that, it was hang the rules and race to win.

"Thirty seconds."

Rebecca was nearly there.

But Wadey blinked. He turned the wheel to port, slowing the boat on tacking. *Rebecca* nosed up into the wind, coming parallel with the *City*. His motivations were unclear. Maybe he was coming on the starting line too swiftly. Or maybe he bowed to the older captain. In any case, the game of chicken was over. *Rebecca* regained her speed. We both ran northwest now, neck and neck, bowsprit to bowsprit, toward the start.

"Fifteen seconds."

The distance closed, almost too quickly. I looked at the captain. He swiveled his head, awaiting my call.

"Ten seconds."

My responsibility for the countdown had soaked my shirt in sweat.

"Five seconds."

Please fire the gun, I thought. Or else we'd be jumping the start.

"Three . . . two . . . one."

Crack-boom, the cannon reported, the smoke blowing south as we squeezed by the line, only twenty yards ahead of the *City of Crisfield*. A red flag and a perfect start.

The wind now breezed up to twenty-three miles an hour and rushed down the course. We were in the teeth of the wind. Since the first turn, a bell buoy, was a mile ahead, due north, the skipjacks had to tack back-and-forth in a zigzag course, first northwest, then northeast—to make headway, like climbing a ladder. On *Rebecca*, the captain was on his feet, his head bobbing and weaving each time the boom swung across the deck. Despite the head wind, we made good time. The tide was with us. It was flooding from the south.

Eleven minutes into the race, we were on our second tack (wind to port) and one hundred yards ahead of the competition. The *City* trailed, followed by *Caleb W. Jones*, *Helen Virginia*, and *Esther F.* On each tack *Rebecca* pointed closer to the wind—nearly north-northeast and north by northwest. Her sails were trimmed closer to the boat. This gave her greater speed. Some dredge boats naturally sail closer to the wind and hold up better against the tide. *Rebecca*'s U-shaped hull gave her an advantage over the V-bottom designs of the other skipjacks in the field that day. She had more draft, which acted like a deeper keel and gave her stability. Also, Wadey had his centerboard down for the beat to the first mark, which added steadiness. His raked mast gave him another edge. All this helped Wadey keep a point of sail as close to the wind as possible.

At 10:19 A.M., we made our third tack, now starboard, and took aim at the bell buoy. Wadey started screaming again. He roared at Lawrence, telling him to pay out the main sheet as we rounded the buoy so the wind would catch the mainsail and bring us around, circling the buoy to the north. "Tend the sail. Slack the sheet."

It looked as if we would smash the buoy, but Wadey had expertly gauged the wind and the tide. We passed within a few feet of it. The outstretched boom nearly touched it. Wadey now turned the wheel hard to the left and the bow edged west and then southwest. The stern swung through the wind in a classic jibe. *Rebecca* had completed the first leg, and we set sights on the southern mark. The eight other skipjacks were still sailing north.

Wadey pointed at Li'l Wade and me and said, "Let's go! Get that centerboard up!" Without facing a head wind, there was less need for a centerboard, and, with a fair wind, the boat was faster without it. Heading south now, with the wind dead behind us, the sails were "bellied out," filling like spinnakers. After a couple of boat lengths past the mark, *Rebecca* was back up to speed—about seven or eight knots.

The captain yelled to Jack up near the bow, "Where's our next mark?" Jack lifted his binoculars and strained his eyes over the three-mile distance. After a couple of minutes, he called, "I got it," glancing back over his shoulder at the captain. "Just off the port bow. Five degrees." Wadey gently turned the wheel slightly to the left. "Okay, Captain," Jack shouted. "That looks good!"

I had walked forward to assist Jack, but his eyes were better than mine. I dropped my binoculars around my neck. "We're ahead and gaining," I said to him.

"We have the better boat," Jack said.

Hunky had joined us and was listening to Jack. "We have the best captain," he added, "but that doesn't mean ya're gonna win. Now, Orville Parks, he was the winningest captain, but he was overbearing. He said he could jump into any boat and beat anybody. It isn't true. Most of it's the boat." Hunky asked to use my binoculars, but I barely got them off my neck.

"You three up thar on the bow," came the captain's booming voice. "Get down. I can't see a goddamn thing." We dispersed. Jack dropped to his knees next to the jib traveler in case it hung up. Hunky and I crouched aft and sat in front of the cabin, out of the wind, which had picked up to twenty-five miles per hour. We still had full sail up. The canvas was stretched tight as a drum while we ran down the course at close to hull speed, our maximum velocity for our type of hull and the length of the boat at the waterline.

"We're walking the dog today," Hunky said. "The wind's got us on a leash."

The captain held us on a close port tack—the white sails bulging to starboard and the deck heeling over in the same direction. His strategy was to guide us on long tacks toward the southern mark, changing direction as little as possible. Each unnecessary jibe lost time. The other skipjacks employed a different maneuver. *City of Crisfield* and *Caleb W. Jones* rounded the northern mark and then spread their sails—mainsail to starboard and jib to port—with the wind directly behind them in that sail formation known as "wing and wing." They looked like a pair of clouds skimming along the water. This tactic potentially netted more speed as long as the wind did not shift. *Helen Virginia,* the fourth boat, now came around the mark and adopted a wing-and-wing flight, too. The Deal Islanders were going all out to catch *Rebecca.*

Meanwhile, the Tilghman boats had fallen behind. In the wind's wake, casualties had mounted. *Martha Lewis* cracked her boom when jibing around the bell buoy, and Gene Tyler was now pushing her back to the harbor. *Esther F.* was taking on water from a chronic leak worsened yesterday when she was towed to Deal Island through rough seas. Like Gene, Bart Murphy was forced to return to port, missing the chance to better his brother. His boat was simply in too poor shape. In any case, there was too much wind for the smaller skipjack to win.

The Deal detachment had sustained injuries, too, but only one was lethal. Stan Daniels's *Howard* broke her rudder, leaving Stan dead in the water. Most of the fleet was not in good enough repair to hold up to a steady blow.

In all, three boats had dropped out of the race, leaving a field of six. The next skipjack to round the mark was *Thomas Clyde,* followed by *Somerset,* both without mishap. Out of the money, they adopted a port tack, like *Rebecca,* for the three-mile run to the southern mark. Wadey was now an eighth of a mile ahead, and the wind was building, to his advantage. "It's gusting to twenty-eight mile," he said. "It's a strong breeze."

On the water, skipjack captains are able to measure the wind's speed with remarkable accuracy. They don't use wind gauges but rather a method of observation centuries old. It was quantified in 1806 by Admiral Francis Beaufort of the British Navy in a wind-ranking system from "1" to "12," from "calm air" to a "hurricane." The concept behind the method was that trees on land and waves on the water had distinct patterns of motion when subjected to wind along this gradation. For example, a Beaufort number of "2" (4–7 mph; 4–6 knots), called a "light breeze," caused leaves to rustle and "small wavelets with crests of a glassy appearance that do not break." A "moderate breeze" (13–18 mph; 11–16 knots), at "4" on the Beaufort Scale, moves small branches and lifts leaves and dust; small waves have numerous whitecaps. A "gale" (39–46 mph; 34–40 knots), at "8" on the scale, breaks twigs and small branches off trees and the crests of high waves break into spindrift and foam. By observing the trees and waves and clouds and even smoke from a chimney, Beaufort proposed that one could accurately predict wind speed. A waterman has a modified version of the Beaufort Scale in his mind and uses it daily. Just now the moderate waves, with a long fetch, and whitecaps steadily increasing, told Wadey we had surpassed a "fresh breeze" (19–24 mph; 17–21 knots) with gusts approaching a "strong breeze" (25–31 mph; 22–27 knots). If it kept strengthening, he'd be forced to reef the sails. He calculated this almost without thinking.

Watermen measure wind speed in miles per hour but the speed of a boat in knots. A knot is one nautical mile per hour or about 1.15 miles per hour. (To calculate number of knots, multiply number of miles per hour by 0.87.) This can be a little confusing until you get used to it: One knot is slightly faster than one mile per hour.

Rebecca was flying downwind at about eight knots (or about nine miles per hour). This was fast for a trailing wind of twenty-five to twenty-eight miles, the waterman's shorthand for speed, and was approaching the sloop's hull speed of nine knots. This was Wadey's goal—an elusive velocity. At hull speed, additional power (in the form of wind) does not result in extra velocity. *Rebecca* and *Kathryn* had the highest hull speeds in the skipjack fleet by virtue of their frame-built, lengthwise-planked, rounded bottoms (and their length at the waterline) and would always win in heavy air, all things being equal. Small skipjacks could win in light air because they were overrigged—having an enormous sail area for the length of the boats—and since nobody in such a race is approaching hull speed.

At 10:30 A.M., we were halfway down the second leg of the course, still the leader. *City of Crisfield* and *Caleb W. Jones* were close behind, within a couple of hundred yards. If the breeze shifted, they could run right by us, but so far the wind was steady and due north behind us. We were on our second run, now starboard, and it looked like it would only take two more turns to round the southern mark, a round orange buoy resembling a huge balloon. *Rebecca* cut through the water, the tops of each wave spraying over the bow each time she surfed over a crest and nosed down into the sea. The captain held steady at the wheel, steering for an imaginary point around which he would turn. The crew stayed out of his way, all except one.

Li'l Wade, tall as his father but even skinnier, looked over his shoulder and saw the two other skipjacks bearing down. He was brave enough to step back to the helm and ask his father about them.

"Those boats ain't getting any farther away, Dad."

"Tide's starting to ebb. We'll round the mark soon and then they won't be able to catch us. Then everyone'll be against a head tide. I can keep up against the tide and the wind better than any of them. They'll have to sail farther off the wind."

"They know the local waters. What if they have a secret plan?"

"It's open water. We'll be all right. I can beat all these skipjacks. The only way one of 'em can beat me is if I'm in dead water and tha're off to the side and catch a puff of wind."

Li'l Wade stared at his father and decided not to respond. But he turned his head and said, under his breath, "That's just what I mean."

Wadey looked at me and repeated his point. "The only skipjack rig that ever outsailed *Rebecca* was *Sallie E. Bramble*, a converted bugeye, and she's dead—sitting on blocks in a yacht yard in Cambridge. *Rebecca*'s the last sloop hull still living. If this wind holds, we'll be fine." It sounded like the captain was trying to reassure himself as much as the crew.

Back on the bow, Jack Dunham was more cautious in his outlook. "Three boats have already dropped out thanks to this wind. And look who's left: Dickie Webster has torn the sails on *Caleb Jones*, and Art Daniels broke his traveler. That's what I heard over the radio. Something could break here, too. We're sailing with full canvas; everyone else has reefed their sails. That's a lot of force on the rigging, especially when we tack or jibe. Sailing with Wadey, you can appreciate why they call it Murphy's Law. Anything that can go wrong will go wrong, at the worst possible time."

At 10:45 A.M., Wade Murphy called the crew to prepare for rounding the leeward mark, the downwind buoy. Lawrence grabbed the main sheet and got ready to pull it tight as we began our counterclockwise turn around the buoy, through the wind. Li'l Wade and I assisted him. Jack and Fred handled the jib traveler. Hunky looked for crab pots, a racing hazard. Rounding the leeward mark requires precision. Acting too soon can spell a collision with the buoy. Bringing the boat about too late can mean overshooting the mark altogether. The rule of thumb is to change course when the mark is seventy degrees off your bow, or when you are just shy of right angles to it. Wadey had such calculations ready-wired in his brain and executed a perfect turn. The crew scrambled to keep up, but everyone handled their job nicely.

It was another three minutes before we fully rounded that southern buoy, again close enough to touch it. As we swung around into the wind, we naturally adopted a port tack, and the captain kept it to maintain our speed. The slapping sails echoed like a rifle report. He dropped the centerboard, anticipating the new headwind, and pulled in the main sheet and jib. With the sails trimmed the captain set a course northeast, just right of the eye of the wind.

The five Deal boats were headed right for us. The lead boats were still in extended formation, their sails ballooned tight like kites flying low across the water. Wadey saw a gap and sailed *Rebecca* right between *Somerset* and *Thomas Clyde*, the last two boats. At 10:55 A.M., *City of Crisfield* and *Caleb W. Jones* rounded the mark only seven minutes behind us. The race was far from over. And a battle for second place was under way. Shortly after rounding the mark, the *City* crossed *Caleb Jones's* bow and tacked at exactly the right moment to block her wind, blanketing her— hardly an easy maneuver in a skipjack. The sails of *Caleb Jones* fluttered—"luffed"—and she lost headway. In a skipjack race, stealing someone's wind was just another way of saying hello. The *City* pulled away, safely holding on to second place.

The wind freshened and began to waiver, dodging east then west, as if trying to make up its mind. Wadey responded with a quarter turn of the wheel. He leaned into the breeze like an autumn tree. When a gust hit, he guided her up into the breeze a little bit more, and he eased her off when the wind softened, always holding the hint of a quiver in the main, keeping the jib full. The captain became one with the boat. And the skipjack became a part of him.

In this way he made incremental gains on the blustery, or "flawy," wind—still strong, pushing the thirty-mile-per-hour mark. (A "flaw" is a sudden burst of wind.) Hunky pointed up to the pine mast. It was bending far back under the pull of the full sails. It could break, but the captain pretended not to notice. Jack pointed to the committee boat two miles ahead, and Wadey affirmed that he saw it. *Rebecca* was already aimed right for it, or rather just east of it on this port tack. The finish line was the same line as the start. It would be like pushing a stone uphill—headwind and head tide off our bow. The tidal current was ebbing now and was strongest in the middle, at the edge of the channel.

This retreating tide and inconsistent breeze seemed to dictate the next moves of our competition. The Deal boats had a plan. Behind us, Art Daniels in *City of Crisfield* made a long port tack into shallow water, closer to Deal Island, and then made another long starboard tack to come along our right flank, just to the east of us. Similarly, Dickie Webster in *Caleb W. Jones*, after rounding the southern mark, came about sharp for a starboard run and, gaining ground, made a port tack, west of the channel, where the tide was also weaker. He came alongside our left flank. We were boxed in.

Caught in the middle, *Rebecca* depended for her lead on the wind remaining northerly. Wadey made short tacks to cover each aggressor: a port tack to cover the *City*, then a starboard tack to cover *Caleb*. A smart strategy. If one of them caught a puff, Wadey planned to race over to catch that breeze, too. On the Bay a flaw can hit one place while a hundred yards away it is dead calm. Therefore, Wadey couldn't afford to sail too far away from either of them. His frequent tacks meant he lost distance each time he came about. That was the price he paid for playing it safe, covering the other two boats. Captains Daniels and Webster, in concert, were betting on the breeze shifting one way or the other, when Wadey wasn't looking. Then one of them would break free.

Trolling for a flaw, the *City* and *Caleb* zigzagged widely in shallow water and the channel, respectively, like twin shadows flanking *Rebecca*. Then the inevitable happened. Certain, but just a little early for Wadey, the wind shifted to the northeast: a land breeze, favoring Art Daniels.

Rough green water rippled along the shore and danced across Tangier Sound toward the regatta. *City of Crisfield* caught the first puff and surged forward, heeled over, and plowed through the water. As it happened, *Rebecca* had been on a port tack heading above the *City* when the new wind hit. This was lucky. Wadey responded instantly. He fell off the wind and rushed over to the northeast to harness the new gust, barely staying ahead of Art Daniels.

There are three principal points of sail, orientations of a sailboat with respect to the wind: close-hauled or beating (next to the wind), reaching (wind to the side), and running (wind behind). This race had been, at times, either close-hauled or running, at least until the wind switched. While dredging during the winter oyster season, nearly all sailing is reaching, with the wind abeam, since this is the position from which the most power can be harnessed to pull the dredges. Reaching is further refined into three classes: close reaching (wind off the side of the bow), beam reaching (wind fully abeam), and broad reaching (wind off the side of the stern). Close-reaching and running bookended these three, so there are, practically speaking, a total of five points of sail.

Sailing upwind, whether beating or close-reaching, necessitates trimming the sails just right. Now, Wadey ordered Jack and Fred to raise the jib farther and trim it aft. Meanwhile, the captain himself hauled in the main sheet to flatten the sails more as we beat east, to cover *City of Crisfield*. For his part, Art Daniels was skirting away, far into shallow water. His son, Robert, was sounding the bottom with a long pole. When his reading dipped to six feet, Art was forced to tack. Immediately, Wadey came about, too, assuming a starboard tack with Art Daniels behind him—shadowing him essentially. Jack had noticed that *City of Crisfield*, with a crooked mast cut from a gnarled tree, sailed poorer on a starboard tack so, for the moment at least, we had the advantage. Still, our captain looked concerned.

"He's gaining on me at each port tack," Wadey complained. "I hope he's worried, because I sure am."

The green-hulled *City* had been boosted by puffs of wind. She had gained on us and was only 150 yards behind. By contrast the red-hulled *Caleb W. Jones* had lost her gamble and was now far back—a quarter mile or so. The new breeze had only benefited the *City*. And the finish line was less than half a mile away.

Despite his torment, Wadey kept an outward calm. Even with the *City* gaining, his strategy remained the same: cover the competition with a zigzag pattern of tacks, regardless of whether the greater number of tacks—two to their one—slowed him down. He was ahead, so he could afford some yardage. With the wind to the northeast now, he sailed close with a bearing north, right toward the finish line.

On a final gamble, the *City* tacked again and made for green water, which suggested wind turbulence, to the northeast. She was pointing higher than *Rebecca* now. With a weak tide in the shallows, she was closing fast. The green hue of the waves indicated that more gusts were coming. Art Daniels figured one good flaw might carry him across the finish line first.

Rebecca tacked to cover him. But Wadey was conservative about it. He kept within one tack of the finish. Again he was lucky: The wind was mercurial. By the time Art Daniels reached the green water, the breeze vanished like a dream. The wind skipped right past him and slapped the water half a mile away. Art, I heard later, shook his head in disbelief. Seeing that the *City* was now in dead water, Wadey came about and made a run for the finish. He was in the clear. *Rebecca* rushed forward, sails at their limit, the wind bearing down. No stopping her now.

At 11:35 A.M., *Rebecca* crossed the finish line. The gun fired, and a flag whipped down. The crew cheered. Wadey Murphy had won his third Deal Island race in a row.

In just over an hour and a half, Wadey had again beaten the competition. Art Daniels brought the *City* across the line next. Dickie Webster carried third, despite splitting his bowsprit on the beat upwind to the finish. (The tension from his jib had cracked it.) The other three boats—*Somerset, Helen Virginia,* and *Thomas Clyde*—far back in the field, limped across the line under reefed sails, some of them torn. But only slightly. No reason to push their rigs today with the prize money beyond their grasp.

Only *Rebecca* completed the course with all her sails up. Wadey had preferred damaging his rigging rather than losing. As it happened, nothing broke. And Wadey made his point: a fair start and still he won.

Once we tied up to the wharf, Wadey calmed down. While we scrubbed the deck, erasing all evidence of sweat and toil, he stepped onto dry land and strutted through the long aisles of booths of the Labor Day Festival, the land complement to the races, nestled among the low-lying salt marshes common to Deal. Wadey seemed out of place among the landlubbers, who collected bets from the races. Along the wharves, spectators viewed other competitions. The Lions Club was putting on a docking contest (for workboats), a fishing tournament, a canoe race, a swimming contest, and a swimsuit contest for teenage girls. The food featured Eastern Shore specialties, right down to roast oysters and deep-fried, soft-shell crabs.

But the biggest onshore event was the presentation of trophies, which commenced shortly after all the skipjacks arrived in port. Deke Sheller took the podium, tapped on the mic, and the crowd gathered round. Calling the three top winners in reverse order, each of them—Dickie, Art, Wadey—stepped up to receive a check and a trophy. Wadey, as the winner, was asked to say a few words. He was all modesty.

"Thank you," he said to the applause. "It was a tough race. Anyone could've won this morning. It's no secret Art Daniels is the best sailor on this island. I just got lucky today."

Wadey handed Hunky the trophy and asked him to stow it on the boat. He kept the check himself, slipping it among the two-dollar bills in his wallet. Fans gathered around to congratulate the captain, but they stepped aside when Captain Art Daniels walked over to speak to Wadey. Up close, Captain Daniels showed his seventy-six years but had a boy's glint in his eye, a spring to his gait. He wore a white T-shirt and a red cap tilted to one side, obscuring his left eye. Twists of white hair peeked from under his hat. A spot of skin cancer showed on his nose—the price of decades on the water under the harsh sun. He had worked outdoors as a dredge-boat captain for more than fifty years, as a waterman for more than sixty. Here was the man who had given Wadey a run for his money. Giving him room, the other Deal captains stepped aside.

Art Daniels said, "Wadey, that was a good strategy, covering us like you did. You sailed that race just like Orville would have done." By all accounts, Orville Parks was the best racing captain of all time. Art's compliment was high praise.

"Thank you, Captain Art," said Wadey. "If you had gotten that breeze a little arlier, I'd be the one congratulating you. I'm just fortunate the race was only six miles. You were gaining fast."

Art Daniels smiled and tipped his hat and walked away. He never stayed for the land festival because beer was always served. Captain Daniels was a Methodist preacher and a teetotaler. He lived on the southern end of the island in a village called Wenona where most of the Deal skipjacks lived. His son, Stan, lived next door.

Wadey watched Captain Art stroll down the wharf and he turned to me and said, "Art's a gentleman, a good waterman, and a good sailor. He knows more about sailing than I'll ever know. But he had me worried. If we switched boats, he would have beaten me by a lot more than I beat him." By then, the crowd had closed in and a local television cameraman was elbowing his way toward Wadey. Yet the captain kept his attention on his fans. Playing off the audience, Wadey raised his voice, and the crowd of twenty fell silent. He was a natural showman. He leaned forward slightly, his arms and shoulders drooped, hanging at his sides like a lanky teenager. As the camera rolled, Wadey began talking about what it takes to win.

"I have a good boat and a good crew," he announced. "That's how we did it. The boat is ninety percent of it. A good crew is the rest."

"What about the captain?" a young woman asked. Groupies are not unknown to sailing races.

"Well, the captain helps a little. But these skipjack captains sail every day of their lives in all kinds of weather. They race each other whenever they can. Tha're the best sailors on the Chesapeake, so any one of these captains can race any boat here to its best advantage. It's mostly the boat that wins. Her and the crew. Maybe a little luck."

At this point, Li'l Wade walked over to his father to tell him a couple of old dredgers were looking for him. Wadey took one more pass at the TV camera. "I'm a third-generation waterman, third-generation drudge-boat captain. Here's the fourth. My son is drudging with me now. He'll be a captain some day." Wadey waved at the dispersing crowd and walked with his son back to *Rebecca*, tied along the wharf next to *Esther F*. Wadey strolled past Bart, but the brothers didn't acknowledge each other. Two blank stares into the distance, though Wadey wore a grin. Bart had missed his chance; he'd have to wait another year.

Back on *Rebecca*, two elderly black men were leaning against the cabin. They stood up when Wadey jumped on the boat. "Howdy, Cap'n," they both said, shaking hands with Wadey.

"Melvin, Juney, what are you doing here?" Melvin White, near ninety, had been a dredge-boat crewman for many years. Juney Harris, seventies, had dredged on *Rebecca* for six years when the previous owner, Emerson Todd, was at the helm. Old deckhands never forget a skipjack.

"I was picking up a mess of crabs when I saw the race was on," Melvin said. "How do the arsters look for the coming season?"

"Tha're looking good," Wadey said. "Plenty of small ones. Now, it'll only be a light skim. Won't last for long. But then you don't want to catch too many." ("Skim" is the local term for the year's fresh crop of legal oysters.)

"No, sir," Melvin said. "Catch too many and the buyers drop the price on you."

"That's right. And I like to leave a few for next year." Wadey turned to face the other man. "What you been up to, Juney?"

"Watching the race. I knew you'd win. The only boat that can beat you is a boat like the *City*, if she snares a piece of wind you don't. I crewed for Art Daniels; his father, too. He's a fine sailor. Good man. Preacher, too."

"Best sailor on Deal Island," Wadey said. "Best drudger, too. Tell me, June, were you thar when those men drownded off *Rebecca*?"

"One of them men fell overboard when I was crewing. He just wasn't paying attention. Drudge come aboard and hit him in the leg. Lost his balance. Over he went. Captain Emerson couldn't bring the boat around in time to save him. Man couldn't swim. The other drowning was before my time. But that made two for Emerson Todd. Bad luck if it came to three. And I was careful after that. Damn if I was going to be the third man and bring *Rebecca* that bad luck." Juney smiled and a big gold tooth caught the glint of the sun.

Next on board the winning vessel were two young men, late teens, carrying a six-pack of beer. Aaron and Jerry Langford. High school dropouts. They crewed on *Rebecca* last oyster dredging season and were here today looking for a berth this coming winter. They lived in Crisfield, twenty miles south of Deal.

"We'd like to go this year, Cap'n Wade," Aaron said.

"Okay," Wadey answered. "See if ya can get three more head. We'll need six men, but my son will be crewing this year. We'll be sail drudging at first and need that many. Six. Later, when we're only power drudging—pushing on Mondays and Tuesdays—after Christmas, we can get rid of some of 'em. I'll only need four men then. I think we'll have enough of a skim in November to sail, at least for a while." The two Crisfield men would have a two-hour commute to Tilghman's, but jobs were scarce and they needed the work. They sauntered off, chugging their beers. Li'l Wade followed them, taking a Budweiser. Aaron let out a cat whistle in the direction of the swimming suit competition and crushed a beer can on top of his head.

Wadey was already talking to Jesse Thomas, a retired skipjack captain now in his eighties. Captain Jesse was a brother-in-law of Art Daniels and skippered *Seagull* for many years. Among the old-time dredgers, he was one of Wadey's favorites. Captain Jesse, though a Deal Islander, had ridden on *Rebecca* in past races to keep Wadey company. He was the one member of the racing crew that Wadey did not dare reprimand.

"I thought you'd sail with me this year," Wadey said to the old man.

"I'd worry I'd be a jinx," the old-timer laughed. "I haven't hit a piece of luck since I caught 550 booshel on Flat Rock thirty years ago—opening day. That was a sight."

"No, Cap'n Jesse, you're welcome anytime. I could use the advice."

"I'll tell you one thing, Wadey, you should move that mast forward some." Jesse Thomas pointed up the mast. "Yer sail is too loose. She needs tuning."

"I knowed it," Wadey said. "The sail wasn't curling right, but I didn't have time to fix it."

"One other thing, Wadey, you looked heeled over too much, even in that heavy wind."

"I never had any water on deck, Cap'n Jesse."

"Just the same, I'd put five tons of lead bars in the hold next to the keelson—give her some momentum. But don't change the line of a good sailer like her. Keep her on her feet."

"I knowed it. I just didn't have time to get to it." Wadey stole a glance to see if anyone else was listening. "If I had had that weight in her, I would have finished ten minutes arlier."

It was afternoon by now, and the festivities were winding down. Local Deal Islanders had won the docking contest and the canoe races. But a teenage girl from Ocean City had pirated the swimsuit competition away from the local girls. The beer truck was exhausted. Art Daniels returned to sail *City of Crisfield* back to Wenona Harbor. The other four Deal captains untied their skipjacks and did the same. Only *Thomas Clyde* was left behind in the northern harbor. She was up for sale and would not be dredging next season.

The three Tilghman boats—*Rebecca, Esther F.,* and *Martha Lewis*—also pulled stakes and began pushing out of the harbor. It would be a long sail home to Tilghman's, a headwind, and they would arrive well after dark. Wadey had won the first leg of the Triple Crown, but the toughest competition lay ahead. He was undaunted. Trophy in hand, a pocketful of cash, and several pennies in his shoe, he was looking forward to the next two races. "We'll be thar," he said, getting under way. "We'll be thar with the best of 'em."

But the talk on the sail home was all about oysters. Jesse Thomas and Juney Harris had set the mood. A strike of oysters, one hundred bushels or better on opening day, were the words on Wadey's tongue. Yes, a couple of races and then the big money: Sail dredging, the calling of generations, would commence in November.

3

November, Howell Point

The night had been clear, but fog now overwhelmed the Choptank, cloaking the river in white. Everything disappeared, as if we were floating in a cloud. The shoreline dissolved, and the water vanished. Even our sails melted into the mist. Yet the change had been incremental. In the hour before dawn, under a bright full moon, the fog had slowly enveloped our fifty-foot skipjack like a tiptoeing ghost. At last sight we had been running parallel to the shore. Now strange shapes materialized, left and right, then evaporated as if they were apparitions. A bell buoy clanged nearby, its direction uncertain. Hearing it, the crew grew more nervous. They were already on edge, and the fear on their faces was palpable: We could run into a boat or a buoy any second. If tragedy struck, the river water was too cold to survive for long. Only Captain Art Daniels seemed calm, unruffled at the helm.

Now, just before sunrise, there was another illusion: a slight diffused light—perhaps dawn approaching—but it seemed to come from all directions. North and south, east and west, were indistinguishable. How would we find our direction? A green "can" buoy took shape to our starboard, but in the haze, its number—painted black—was obscure. Little matter to the captain, it seemed, for in the midst of all this confusion, I saw him quietly examining the ripple of current against the can. Art Daniels, white-haired, well into his seventies, was reading the tide—to him as good as a compass. The tide was ebbing, flowing toward the open Bay. From his memory of the river—upstream was east—he knew the sun would rise behind us. He was on course: bearing west downriver toward Tilghman's Island.

We were sailing aboard *City of Crisfield* (1949), just out of Cambridge Harbor and heading for Howell Point, the most prolific oyster bar in the Choptank. It was a Wednesday—November first, opening day of the sail-dredging season. At the helm, Captain Daniels directed his crew to stand watch so they could join him in trying to outwit the fog. His son Robert and grandson Bobby took the bow, while brother Jimmy manned the port side with the cook, Howard Jones, and me. On starboard, Howard's two brothers, Larry and John-Boy, searched for boats and buoys at midchannel that might emerge from the mist. The three brothers were sons of Elmer Jones, for fifty years the black cook aboard Art's father's skipjack, *Robert L. Tawes* (1901)—a tenure spanning the years from the First World War past the Great Depression to the moonwalk. On the Chesapeake, little had changed. The captain sailed downriver through the mist, in the family tradition, a light touch on the wheel, guiding the wooden craft through the current.

Captain Art showed no fear in his eyes—a piercing bright blue. He simply steered *City of Crisfield* around Cambridge Light as if it were a sunny day—no radar, no depth sounder, no loran, just his memory of the lay of the river and the tide. He knew each bar and beacon, each ripple, by heart. Of the many drawbacks to fog for sailing was this: light air. "Hardly a breath," the captain said. "Till this lifts we won't get more than a puff. What we need is a little breeze—to blow this fog away." He was anxious to arrive at the oyster reef to begin the season, if there was enough wind downriver to pull a dredge.

Yesterday, Captain Art had invited me to sail *City of Crisfield* (affectionately known as "the *City*") north from Deal Island to Cambridge—a ten-hour trip—to begin the season. Having planned to sail with Wadey, I begged off, but was eventually talked aboard. The *City* was short a man, while Wadey's *Rebecca* had a full house. I was also curious to board a Deal skipjack; word had it that most were antiquated, even for a skipjack, sporting primitive navigation gear, crew quarters, and a cook in the galley. The southern fleet was also in notoriously poor shape. "Take your own life vest," was the advice of Hunky, Wadey's old friend.

Art Daniels and crew sailed north from Deal Island without mishap, out of Tangier Sound, north along the Bay, and into the Choptank River, three miles wide at its mouth. On the way Captain Art lamented the scarcity of "arsters" in Tangier Sound—Deal Islanders say "arster" instead of "orster," in a dialect uniquely their own. "The arsters have died back a little," he said. "It's winter kill, that's all. We've seen it before—nature runs in cycles." Others claimed the oyster disease, MSX, had crawled up that leg of the Bay like gangrene, killing Tangier Sound for good. They maintained the disease killed an oyster in three years, on average, just as it was reaching legal size. But the captain was insistent. "Thar's no such thing as MSX," he said. "The freeze last year just trimmed back the population some. In other words, I plan to drudge near home again, as soon as the little ones grow. God'll bring them back." In the meantime, Captain Art and his crew would dredge the Choptank beds, the closest living oysters to their home. Somewhere in the fog the other boats in the Deal fleet had the same idea. Maybe the Tilghman skipjacks, too.

When we had arrived past midnight in Cambridge Harbor, all eight of us decided to sleep aboard. The harbor was quiet. Like Oxford across the river, Cambridge was no longer the home port to any skipjacks but historically had been a busy hub for oyster dredging. When it was still strong, the Cambridge fleet had wielded considerable political power locally and, with Orville Parks taking the lead, was responsible for setting aside Howell Point as a sail-dredge-only bar. This happened about the same time the relaxing of the oyster laws allowed power dredging elsewhere on Mondays and Tuesdays; that is, dredging with the small push boat rather than sails. Captain Orville Parks and the Cambridge captains had wanted to preserve Howell Point against power dredging, and their call for the conservation measure was prescient: Subsequently, while other Choptank bars had been worn down by power dredging two days a week, Howell Point remained robust. The oyster bed has been a consistent producer and is the rock of choice at the beginning of each season for both Tilghman's and Deal. It always held the promise of the best catch. We would sail and dredge there today—alone or with a crowd. In the fog it was impossible to tell.

THE SMELL OF BACON grease and smoked sausage rose out of the cabin, forcing the crew (with the captain's permission) to abandon their posts. While the captain stood at the helm scanning the mist, everyone else piled into the galley for breakfast. Howard Jones, youngest of the three brothers, served up fried eggs and toast and scrapple in addition to the sausage and bacon. The crew of six was silent as each man ate the steaming hot food. The men requested prodigious quantities for a first helping. Larry, at 260 pounds the biggest of the Jones brothers, ordered a "setting of eggs"—an even dozen.

"This is mighty good—sausage hot and spicy," said brother John-Boy.

"Mighty good—sausage hot and spicy," said Howard, also known as Cookie, who was in the habit of repeating anything said to him. In addition to cooking, he doubled as a culler on the middle deck; he and I would alternate positions. "I'm frying chicken and arster cakes for dinner today, if we catch some," he said.

"We better catch some," said Larry, taking a break from his eggs. "We might catch a load if we had Howell Point to ourselves. That and some wind."

"Fog'll lift, come sunrise," said John-Boy, "then we'll catch a mess o' arsters. Until then, brother, neither Tilghman boat can make it here. Not in this fog."

"Not in this fog, that's right," said Cookie.

Stan Daniels, at fifty-seven Art's oldest son, captain of *Howard*, came even with us now and yelled over the bad news. "Daddy, tha're coming—the whole Tilghman fleet's coming upriver to Howell Point. Just heard Russell and Robbie talking on the radio. Gave it away. Tha're burning diesel fuel fast, with the sails up, to get here by sunup. Somebody saw us sailing by Tilghman's last night. They knowed we was here."

Up ahead, a low bank of fog still gripped the river, but above its ceiling—only forty or fifty feet above the surface—was blue sky. And there they were: above the fog, a dozen mast tips, some brightly varnished, some white-tipped, some with golden globes. Whatever their adornment, all reflected the rising sun behind us. They flashed brightly, beacons above the mist. "Damn," said Cookie. Now, one at a time, their bows broke out of the fog, as a slight breeze rippled our sails. One boat. Three boats. Five, eight, nine. Ten Tilghman boats sailed out of the curtain, all on a starboard tack, their sails stretched full and wide. The two fleets approached Howell Point from opposite directions, east and west, like two armadas ready for battle.

Dawn loomed behind us. At first there was a diffused yellow, but almost immediately the mist burned off, revealing the bright red aura of the sun, which still hung beneath the eastern horizon. The captain stared at it for a minute. "And then thar was light," he said in his Methodist preacher's voice. Robert, Art's second son and a minister in his own right, completed the passage: "Yes, sir, 'Thar was light in the dome of the sky to give light upon the earth.'"

I had been forewarned: If you are going to sail aboard the *City*, you are going to get some preaching. Art Daniels was prone to spontaneous recitations. Apparently, his son Robert was, too.

The scarlet sun now broke loose of the horizon in a spectacular sunrise. The color spectrum ran from saffron to magenta. "Legal to begin dredging now," said Jimmy, a smoker, in a voice like sandpaper. He was younger than the captain but, like him, weathered and spry, short but agile. He wasn't as handsome, however; Art resembled a graceful cowboy, fair and thin and saddle-worn. In the shadow of the leeward shore, Joe Jones, a marine policeman, had been hovering in his Boston Whaler, spying on the fleet, waiting for one of the vessels—considered outlaw oyster boats to him—to try dredging too early. The antagonism between lawmen and oystermen had a long history. But today nobody jumped the gun. Arriving at the bar, the Tilghman skipjacks spread wide. They hauled their small yawl boats off the water and started their dredge "winders," the only motor permanently allowed on a skipjack. We sailed straight ahead, a little to the right of the fleet. Bart Murphy (*Esther F.*) and Pete Sweitzer (*Hilda Willing*) were the first to reach the main part of the bar, and each cast in a single dredge. The Tilghman boats had full sail—main and jib fully aloft. The southeast breeze was light—around six miles, that measure watermen prefer to knots. In the light wind it would be difficult to pull two dredges. The rest of the fleet dropped just one.

Art Daniels held off, peeling away from the fleet as he searched for the part of the bar he liked to work: a small "spot" in shoal water just inside the long submerged arm of sand that protruded from Howell Point. The rest of the oyster bar was hard-packed reef and extended to midriver. The *City* arrived in position. Ahead of us a raft of oldsquaw ducks, or southerlies, which had been feeding underwater on reef fish, took wing. The captain called the men on deck.

"Heave yer wind'ard," he yelled. John-Boy tossed the windward dredge overboard—starboard on our current tack. The single dredge, a three-foot-wide, triangular cage, splashed loudly into the water, played out, and touched the bottom, then began to rake over the reef. The crew that handled the starboard side—Jimmy, Larry, and John-Boy—assembled at midship, awaiting the captain's next order. The winder engine sputtered and coughed: *pttt, pttt, pttt.* Four minutes elapsed. Then, on the captain's signal—he pulled a cord attached to the throttle of the engine, which raced on cue— John-Boy engaged the clutch on the windlass and the dredge cable reeled in. Shortly, the dredge jumped out of the water and onto the steel roller. John-Boy and Larry then grabbed the rings at either side of the dredge and—with a gasp of effort—dumped the heavy load. Stones, shells, and oysters clattered on deck—mostly stones. Larry and John-Boy were joined by Jimmy in culling the oysters. They tossed nineteen "keepers"—legal oysters over three inches long—behind them and shoveled the smaller oysters, stones, and lone shells overboard. It was a poor catch. Apparently, the dredge had not dug sufficiently into the reef.

Art Daniels came about and set a new course southwest, exactly opposite the first "lick," as each run across the bar was called. "We'll try it again," he said, "but let's give them drudges more line." The captain ordered Larry to let out more cable on each dredge by cutting the "becket," a loop of manila line that cinched the dredge cable at set intervals to the windlass. When a dredge ran out, the steel cable unwound from the windlass until it hit a becket. There were multiple beckets tied along the cable, forming stops within the spool. By cutting off a single stop, the cable ran out an extra six feet. The longer lines, the captain explained, would allow the dredges to dig deeper into the reef.

"See, it's always the same at the start of the season," Captain Daniels said. "The arsters grow tight as bedsprings all summer, and we have to break into them. It takes a few days each autumn to loosen 'em up. See, drudging's good for the bar. What we don't catch we leave behind as single arsters, broken free from the others, and these grow bigger and more plump, like thinning a row of

squash." Skipjack captains call this "cultivating the bottom."
Dredging is criticized by some for damaging the reefs (and inexperienced captains can be at fault), but, when worked properly, the
opposite is true. Sail dredging renews the reef, clears silt, and produces the single oysters most prized by the shucking houses.

"Ho, yer wind'ard."

Larry released the becket and threw the port dredge
overboard—now to windward. The dredge bag—a net made of
parachute cord—flung outward, wringing wet, drenching the crew
like cold beads of sweat. I took up my station next to Robert and
Bobby on the port side, to get ready for the next haul.

On the new tack, Captain Art adjusted the sails to optimize his
speed while still retracing his northeast-southwest course—
backtracking precisely over the same ground. He let out the main
sheet, allowing the boom to swing out to starboard. This pulled the
mainsail away from the boat, stretching it over the water, the best
way to harness the wind when it is abeam; that is, perpendicular to
the boat—a beam reach. Dredgers like to sail on a beam reach (or
slightly ahead of it) and prefer a ten-to-twelve-mile wind, which
allows them to pull two dredges without reefing the sail. They call
this a "drudger's breeze."

After about four minutes and a hundred yards, the captain
pulled the throttle cord again. The *pttt, pttt* turned to a *grrr*. Robert engaged the windlass. The single dredge came onto the roller,
and Bobby and I dumped the catch: Oysters and shells crashed into
a sprawling mound. Even with the dredge less than half full, I
broke into a sweat, and we slowly selected forty-six legal oysters
from the tangled pile of mud, sticks, and shells. Mixed in with the
live take, ten or more dead shellfish, with gaping valves, littered
the deck. Cookie and Bobby discarded these with disgust. Robert
held his finger to his lips and said, "Boys, don't even spell the letters MSX aboard this boat." Bobby stole a glance at his grandfather and kept on sorting. With the small catch, culling was fairly

easy—there was plenty of time to pick out the big oysters, legal ones that Jimmy called "markets." The shells were razor sharp and cut my gloves.

"Looking better, Daddy," Robert called back to the captain.

"Here, too, Daddy Art," Bobby shouted to his grandfather, a term of endearment shared by all eighteen grandchildren.

"Okay then," said the captain. He lifted a plastic gallon milk bottle off the cabintop and tied a twenty-foot line to it and a piece of scrap iron to the other end. As he came about, he threw the makeshift buoy off his stern. This would mark the northern end of his run. The jug bounced in the current like a toy.

"If it breezes up, we'll catch fifty or sixty booshel," the captain said. "A little wind, see, and with two drudges we'll break into them good." Captain Art tipped his bright red cap to the side so that it was cocked to the left, giving him a rakish appearance. Captain and crew wore oilskin overalls but no coats. Just hooded sweatshirts, jeans, tall rubber boots. And cotton hats. The autumn morning was shaping up to be warm and mild.

"Ho, yer wind'ard." The starboard dredge plunged into the water.

"These drudges're hard killers," said John-Boy. "Near to break your back." Hard dredges, made heavy for hard-bottom reefs, were used on Howell Point and they weighed 140 pounds each. With a bag full of oysters and stones, they topped 400 pounds. During the day, John-Boy and the others, in pairs, would lift them more than a hundred times. I'd tally half that.

"Larry, check yer cable," Captain Art called out after we had sailed for a couple of minutes on our third lick. On command, Larry grabbed ahold of the dredge cable where it ran over the roller into the water. It was taut as piano wire. And it quivered slightly in Larry's hand, like the first bite of a game fish, as the dredge raked over the uneven features of the oyster rock.

"Ye're on 'em, Cap'n," said Larry, his big paw feeling the cable and the bottom. Hearing this, Captain Art threw another buoy overboard, marking his southern run. He was now "buoyed off." He had claimed the lick; other dredgers beware. On the next two runs, the dredge broke the surface with a full load, and I was pressed to keep up with the culling. Between each lick, I had less than five minutes to sort hundreds of oysters into legal and smalls, and toss them with other winners into keeper piles or with other losers overboard. I felt like a croupier at a busy roulette table.

The good news was that most of the oysters were living. MSX disease may have obliterated the oyster in Tangier Sound, but here the oysters looked healthy. Less than ten percent of the catch presented with a gaping shell (a "gaper") or an empty one (a "box"), two visible manifestations of infection. Howell Point, located in the fresher reaches of the Choptank River, had a lower incidence of MSX than the oyster beds in the saltier, lower Bay. Salinity and (probably) pollution encouraged the attack. (In laboratories, adding pollutants to shellfish tanks stimulated the disease in oysters, so the correlation is likely in the wild.) In any case, the disease was unusual in two respects that had allowed the Choptank oyster fishery to survive so far despite some infection. First, the pathogens could infect one bar in the river but not another, even though they were adjacent. Nearby, Tred Avon was riddled with disease while Howell Point itself was relatively free of it. The other fortunate trait was that infected oysters were perfectly edible—harmless to humans. The diseases wasted away the tissues of the oyster, but anyone could eat them. It took three years, on average, for 90 percent of a heavily infected oyster reef to die and within that time many of its oysters were harvested and went to market with nobody the wiser.

Approaching his northern buoy, Art Daniels clutched the main sheet and prepared to tack. He shortened the line through a series of wooden pulleys to cushion the momentum of the boom as it pitched laterally above the cabin. Spinning the wheel hand over hand, he brought the *City* nose into the wind. She hesitated, like a wind vane, then bobbed past the eye.

As we swung around the milk bottle and came about, I noticed a greater design in the sail tending of the captain. To successfully sail-dredge this diagonal lick, he had to accommodate the waves and the wind and the tide—the latter two sometimes at odds with each other. The trick for the captain today was to stay precisely on the same northeast-southwest line between his buoys even though the wind and tide were pushing him downriver. This was akin to swimming parallel to a shore while a riptide was pushing you out to sea. On a sailboat, deft handling of the sails was necessary to maintain this challenging course—all the more so with the *City*'s crooked mast.

"Ho, yer wind'ard," Captain Art called. His grandson heaved the port dredge over, which landed with a belly flop. There were many other subtleties to sail dredging that were not readily apparent. The boat must be kept straight while winding in the dredges. Otherwise, the dredge line could be caught in the rudder, or worse, when hauling two dredges, they could become entwined under the boat. The only sure remedy for this was to send a skin diver down to release them. The dredge lines must be adjusted from lick to lick, depending on the depth, the wind speed, and the nature of the bottom. And five different dredges must be kept on deck for different types of reef—mud, stone, sand bottom, and others. Not to forget the sails. To regulate the speed of the vessel, sails must be reefed and sheets trimmed. No matter the force of the wind, skipjacks had to be held to a slow pace (about three knots), so the dredges did not skip off the bottom or dig in too deep. Sailing too fast, the mistake of some young skippers, quickly exhausts the reefs.

Requiring the greatest finesse was simply finding a patch of oysters and staying on it. Art Daniels knew the "marks" for hundreds of oyster bars in the Chesapeake Bay. He knew their depths and contours. He knew which dredges and dredge lines were best suited to each. He knew which bars were best worked with a certain wind: which could be productive in a light southerly breeze and which were sheltered enough to allow working in a northerly gale. When the tide shifted from ebb to flood, he could stay on a spot by taking advantage of the counterbalance of tide to wind. And he knew when to drop the centerboard, when to lift it. In all, sail dredging was more art than science, a feat of legerdemain. The improbable in search of the edible.

At 8:30 A.M. the southeastern breeze was still light, still too gentle to pull both dredges. The sky was bright blue, the fog long forgotten. To the west of us, in deeper water, the balance of the fleet was sailing about in seeming chaos, in all aspects to the wind. Close hauls. Broad reaches. Only some abeam. Howell Point bar was large—nearly a mile square—and the boats were scattered across it. Some sailed south toward the channel, some in the middle of the bar, and us alone in the shallows. They crisscrossed each other without regard to right-of-way. It seemed a miracle there had not been a collision. Watermen called this "broadcasting," dredging over a wide area in search of a rich lick. When broadcasting was not successful, captains often trespassed out of frustration. Captain Art had been the only one to buoy off so far that morning, and it was just a matter of time before the salty dogs came sniffing around.

Captain Art lifted his binoculars and scanned the fleet. Too far to read the gold-leaf nameplates or board numbers of the boats, so he had to rely on distinguishing marks. From the quantity of boats, he knew that almost everyone was here today, but he wanted to see just who had made it to the rock. He counted them off.

"One: That's Wadey Murphy—his mast and boom's the longest. Two: *Martha Lewis*—she's plumb like the old *Rosie Parks*. Three: *Kathryn*—Russell's a little bigger than Wadey and he's got a gold globe atop the mast; that means she's paid for. Four: *Wilma*

Lee—Robbie's always next to Russell. Five, six, seven: *Hilda Willing, Esther F.*, and *Virginia W.*—tha're all small; working together. Eight: *Maggie Lee*—raked mast; she was my father-in-law's boat. Nine: Daryl's *Nellie Byrd* has the widest beam. Ten: *Minnie V.* has a carved eagle below her bowsprit. That's ten Tilghman boats shopping around the bar. Make that eleven: here comes *Lady Katie*. She's the prettiest, but don't tell Stanley I said so." He swept over the fleet as if they were birds to be identified from a field guide and turned his attention to five boats dredging alone near the channel. "See, them's the Deal boats. *Caleb W. Jones* is the widest. *Helen Virginia* has a red jib. The Benton brothers have *Fannie Daugherty* and *Somerset*. Stan's on *Howard*. And we make six. Only Ed Farley is late. Almost the full fleet."

Daryl Larrimore's appearance had surprised the captain. In October, Daryl had said he was done with dredging and had put *Nellie Byrd* up for sale. He had one prospective buyer, a novice, who couldn't come up with all the money—$30,000 was the modest asking price—so he rigged the boat for another year. "Daryl's suited up," said the captain. "Those Larrimores say tha're gonna sell, but they can't get sail drudging out of the blood."

Then the predictable happened: Two boats broke off from the pack and headed our way. In single file, *Kathyrn* and *Wilma Lee* sailed nose to the wind to cross over to shoal water. Captain Art held his course and completed another turn around his buoys. On the southwestern run, Russell Dize, forty-eight, on *Kathyrn*, came close enough to speak over the calm water.

"Good morning, Cap'n Art," Russell said, cupping his hands over his mouth so the words would carry. Art's radio was disconnected. Russell and the rest of the fleet had been trying to raise him on the VHF all morning to see how his licks in shoal water were coming along. Art had been happy for the anonymity. Until now. "Like bees to honey," the captain said under his breath. Russell was heading right for our buoy.

"Go easy now," Captain Art called.

"I see yer buoy. I'm in the clear."

"Okay then."

"Are you breaking into some orsters?" Russell continued. "We're just sailing around—"

"Congratulations, you've been crowned," Art shouted, changing the conversation to Russell's victory at the Sandy Point races the weekend before. "Yer the king!" In fact, *Kathryn* had beaten *Rebecca* in the last *two* races—at Tilghman Island Days and at Chesapeake Appreciation Days ("Sandy Point")—spoiling Wadey's bid for the Triple Crown. The Tilghman race was lost when *Rebecca* ran aground, a disappointment, but the last race had really unsettled Murphy. Sandy Point was hotly contested, the finish called early by the race committee when a screaming gale brewed up in the middle of the last leg. The committee feared someone would get hurt and, looking for an easy fix, declared *Kathryn* the winner before the last mark, to end the race, even though *Rebecca* had been gaining. Both men were sailing flat out, with only a hundred yards between them, and neither could have cared less about casualties. But the committee didn't consult them, in waving the checkered flag. Back in port, Wadey chewed out the judges and refused the second-place money. Needless to say, Russell and Wadey were no longer speaking. But Art gave all the credit to Russell, as he shouted again, "Yes, sir, you've been crowned the king!"

"Temporary. Wadey'll probably win next year." Modesty triumphed over Russell's grin.

"Every dog has his day," said Captain Art as he turned the wheel hand over hand and came about. He had dodged the buoy and Russell's question about the oyster bed as well.

Next in line to break our defenses was Robbie Wilson, thirty-nine. He maneuvered *Wilma Lee* alongside of us, to windward, and stole our wind, as if slowing us down for a chat.

"How ya think ya'll do, Cap'n Art?" he said, in a thick drawl.

"Okay, I imagine, if we get a breeze."

"How much water ya got?" Robbie asked, wondering whether Art was atop a hill.

"About eight feet I figure," Art guessed without benefit of a depth sounder.

"Ya got a lump, Cap'n Art?" Robbie persisted.

"A little hill. Just enough room for one drudge boat."

Robbie chuckled at this. He peeled off our course, briefly giving way to the older man. Our wind returned and Captain Art revved the winders. We pulled up another load, a writhing mass of crabs, fish, and (mostly) oysters with a small complement of boxes, gapers, and stones. A pungent scent arose from the mud-soaked oyster pile, an odor not unlike that of a wrack of seaweed at low tide. Inexplicably, hidden now within the fetid muck, the prime oysters upon shucking would have a fresh aroma—each worth a dollar at the raw bar, gems amid the rubble.

The precious catch was getting better with every lick. "Throwing over a buoy brings in a crowd," the captain said. "You can't blame 'em really. This is the best lick, right here." The pair had gravitated toward success, a mixture of envy and respect. Competition is the lifeblood of the fleet: Captains, especially the young ones, vie each day for the biggest catch, the best price, and covet Art's standing as the dean of the fleet. Even with the jealousy, conversations today were friendly, however. All sins absolved. Opening day was like the reunion of a very exclusive club.

When Wadey came by, he tipped his hat at the senior man and gave me a scowl. I had wondered what his reaction would be to my sailing on a Deal boat. Watermen are possessive if they are anything, and loyalty is the measure of a man. Still, of all the boats for me to be shanghaied on, I figured Wadey and Stanley would object to the *City* the least. They honored the old man. "Art's a fine drudger," they had both said. The highest praise. Then Wadey had added, "Just don't sail with anyone else. Half these captains are common as hell."

A wedge of geese flew over us, and the lead gander raised a racket: *honk, honk, honk.* Art lifted his eyes, tilted his cap over even farther, and smiled. The crew looked up as well. "Perty today," Art said. "Perty as it gets. All these boats. If a man loves life, loves nature, it doesn't get better than this. Sailing for a living—thar's the gift. You've gotta love what you do."

Art Daniels was looking at the fleet half full. He had seen many more boats than this in his day, and he recalled the days when hundreds of dredge boats showed up on opening day.

"I was thar when they opened up Poplar Island bar in 1949," he began. "Thar must've been 150 drudge boats—schooners, bugeyes, sloops, skipjacks—the whole lineage of Chesapeake sailing craft. It was December first. We had been drudging for a month, but Poplar Island had been closed for three years, to let the seed arsters grow. The state used to do that in them days: set aside a big bar as a sanctuary for a few years then open it up for Christmas. I was sailing the *Mollie Leonard* then. We caught 260 booshel the first day and then 300 or so each day after that. This was before any maximum limit. The big boats—schooners like the *Anna and Helen*—caught more than 500 booshel. It took five days to clean that bar out. The packers cut the price to three dollars, but we made a week's work. It was a beautiful sight. All those rigs, all that sail. Schooner rigs. Gaff rigs. Three-sail bateaux. Drudge boats as far as you could see." He waved his hand over the remaining fleet. In his mind's eye he saw a grander day.

In addition to *Anna and Helen* (1911), which ended up being the last schooner to work the Bay, on the rock that day was the schooner *Mattie F. Dean* (1884), which Art Daniels had apprenticed on as a young boy in the 1930s. The last gaff-rigged sloop, *J. T. Leonard* (1882), and the last bugeye to dredge oysters, *Edna E. Lockwood*, built on Tilghman's Island in 1889, sailed that week as well.

Skipjacks dominated the fleet, however. More than a hundred of them dredged and culled a boatload. Glendi Larrimore, Stanley's father, dredged *Laura J. Barkley*; Wade Murphy Sr., was at the helm of *George W. Collier*; Jesse Thomas skippered *Mamie Mister.* Most of those hundred skipjacks are long since "dead"—sunk or abandoned or burned.

As a young culler in the 1930s, Art manned a rowboat to get to and from his father's skipjacks, moored off Deal Island. No yawl boat. They sailed in and out of port, totally dependent upon the wind. Instead of depth sounders, they used sounding poles. It was Art's job to endlessly sound the bottom with a long bamboo pole to check the depth of a bar and to see how thick the oysters were. When they were dense, he claimed they would "bite the pole." The tip of the pole would wedge in among the oyster clusters and seemed to get gripped, or "bitten." In lieu of winder engines, the crew employed hand winders to reel the dredges in, adding another arduous chore to landing the catch. These hand cranks required strength and endurance, and not a few crewmen dropped dead on deck, overcome from the effort. Today's deckhands (and I) were sweating and groaning, so one could only imagine the toil in Art's father's day.

Suddenly, on a northwest tack the sails fluttered. Snapping their heads, captain and crew looked up at the main. It was chaotically whipping like a flag. Little puffs of wind were hitting us now, ruffling the loose jib. By this time, the fleet had spread to the four corners of the bar. Wade and Stanley worked their own buoys along the shore, just to the north of us. On the top of the reef the younger dredgers—Russell, Robbie, Daryl, Bobby, Frank, Freddie, Johnnie, Ed—were still broadcasting, each covering a large area on every tack. Only two of the eight had fathers who were dredgers; the rest had missed out on apprenticing within a sailing family and thus were prone to bad habits. Sins such as grinding down a reef by keeping their dredge lines too long, or keeping and selling small oysters. Next to us, Stan Daniels had run aground in shoal water during the ebb, but a change in tide was coming; it was slack water just now but getting ready to flood.

Downriver, ripples appeared in the water a couple of miles away. The surface looked dark green with a calmer light green beyond. "Here comes yer wind, Art," said Jimmy in his gravelly voice. "Here comes yer flaw."

Abruptly, our world changed. The water around us turned a frothy green. And the blustery wind hit fast. The mainsail and jib, which had been luffing, filled with air and stretched full, ballooning. The breeze instantly doubled in force, originating now from the southwest. Quickly, the *City* picked up speed. With the windward dredge aboard, Art tacked and came about. He straightened up the boat, taking aim at a southern mark—the green beacon that marked the edge of the channel—and signaled the crew to release both dredges.

"Heave," he called, and pointed to each dredge, port and starboard, with an extended forefinger like a conductor instructing his choir. Or a preacher. Bobby and John-Boy at port and starboard tossed the two dredges. Their mesh bags flew out, releasing a fan of water, and hit the surface, sloshing, then sinking fast. Art said, "Now we'll catch a few."

With the benefit of the stiff breeze, the oysters were easier to break into. Inexplicably, the oysters were bigger, too, and with two dredges we were catching them twice as fast. Twice the catch. Twice the noise. Twice the work on deck. Most of the catch was living. All the skipjacks kept full sail and, with canvas bulging and boats heeled over, cutting through the water, it was a glorious sight. Art said this speed was his best wind—topping off that "drudger's breeze."

"That's Daddy Art's wind," said Jimmy.

Art smiled. "Only four disciples were fishermen—John, James, Peter, and Andrew—but you wouldn't know that today. Look at this fleet—over one hundred men, both captains and crew. See what I mean." He lifted his hands to the sky. " 'If you follow me, I'll make you a fisher of men.' " On a day like this, on a skipjack flying fast, he could probably convert a boatful of souls. He worked on me all day long.

On the second lick of the new course, Cookie culled a grand-daddy oyster and waved it at the captain. Art signaled him to come aft and Cookie arrived with the oyster—half a foot long—in his hand. Pulling a yellow tape measure out of the cabintop shelf, Art measured the oyster, which recorded a full six-and-a-half inches—twice the size we had been catching. It had a wide flange and a tight hinge and was gnarled, like a well-worn bedroom slipper.

"You can tell how old it is by the ridges on the shell, like the rings of a tree," the captain said. He counted them with a stubby finger: one, two, three, four, five, six. It was six or seven years old. "This Methuselah proves it," he said. "He lived past three years. Thar's no disease—it's a myth."

"I'll cook him for dinner," Cookie said. "Arster cakes. This monster will fill one all by hisself." I shared with the cook the like-lihood that an oyster this old was probably a female. Many male oysters switch sex to produce millions of eggs in their second or third year.

"That sexual razzle-dazzle could come in handy," Cookie said. "Devil knows what trouble I'd get into with that talent. I guess I'll cook her just the same."

"That's a good idea, Cookie. Why don't you get dinner ready?" It was 10:00 A.M.

Forty minutes later, after ten good licks, a cowbell clanged from the galley. The smell of galley-cooked food drifted onto the deck. Art signaled the dredges to be brought aboard—by now there were twelve bushels on deck—and the crew literally ran aft toward the cabin. I learned about fried chicken on a dredge boat that day. By the time I reached the galley, all that was left was a wing.

Seven of us crowded into the cabin; only the captain remained on deck. The space was claustrophobic, like a mountain tent. Except for the four-burner propane range that had replaced a wood-stove cooker, the cabin looked the same as the first skipjacks in the 1880s. With the crew covered in oyster mud and with no way to wash up, the dinner scene looked like a photograph of trench warfare—faces splattered with mud and the weary look of tired men.

A bowl of soup—hot navy beans and bacon—was passed up to the captain, who sat down on the wheelbox. Robert said a short prayer and the captain called out, "Amen." Then everyone was free to eat. The chicken was demolished quickly and the crew turned to the soup (served with two biscuits) while Cookie prepared the fritters—"oyster cakes," he called them. The conversation, at the beginning, was mostly about food.

"This is down-home cooking," said Robert.

"Down-home cooking, that's right," Cookie repeated. "Eat as much as you like. That's all the chicken, Reverend Robert, but I'll have these arster cakes ready in a minute."

"Oh, yes. He gave us dominion over the birds of the air and the fishes of the sea," said Robert. "Don't you know it."

"I'd like a few more birds of the air," John-Boy said.

"I could use some knucklebread, black molasses, and hog meat," said Larry, who worked summers on a poultry farm and had seen enough chickens. "Now that's eating."

"Down home, my wife makes a fine sweet potato pie," said Jimmy. "You need a good oven, though."

"A microwave will make you a lazy wife," said John-Boy. "Don't buy her one, Jimmy."

"She's a good cook, don't worry," Jimmy said.

"I can cook for myself," said Bobby. "I don't need a wife, not yet anyway."

"You want to cook for a skipjack crew sometime, Bobby?" Cookie said, looking at the twenty-year old. "Watch me make these cakes. Now pay attention. Mind your Cookie. You shuck your arsters— half a dozen for each cake, a dozen for each man. I shucked a hundred this morning in between culls, just for dinner today. You dice your onions up real small; place 'em in a bowl; add a quart of flour, a couple spoons of mustard, and three or four eggs. A little condensed milk. Stir it all together. Put the grease in the pan. Let it get real hot. Make your cakes—like a pancake—and add your arsters. Fry 'em good. No spices needed. You get that natural arster flavor. Yes, honey. Yes, indeedy."

Four fritters were just then sizzling in the pan. Art could smell them and leaned his head into the cabin. "Cookie, I like mine lightly fried—just brown, tanned a little and juicy inside. Don't overcook 'em."

Cookie was hurt—he began wiping the stove with a wet rag— but he was polite. "Aye, aye, Cap'n, these are ready for you. Piping hot and juicy inside. Pop right in your mouth." He handed a plate with two oyster cakes up to the captain. The other two went to Jimmy and Robert Daniels, the senior men, who were literally speechless while eating the delicacies. Maybe only on a family farm is a hot meal so appreciated at midday, or midmorning. After hauling dredges, nothing is more gratifying. As Jimmy Daniels said, "Everything tastes better drudging."

"These arsters shucked real good," Cookie said. "I can only fit four in each cake." He flipped the second batch of cakes with a spatula.

"I shucked some, too," said Larry. "Howell Point looks good— perty. With this wind we can make some money."

"We're gonna make all our big money, if any, by Christmas," John-Boy said. "Then the price will drop. Happens either year."

"I'm gonna fly to Seattle after Christmas," Cookie said. "Crew on a salmon boat. They've got steel boats out thar. Metal. Don't leak like these damn wooden boats."

"Steel sinks faster than wood," John-Boy said.

"Faster than wood," said Cookie. "I don't know—sometimes wood's faster when the wood's full of holes. And I'm always in the galley—that's closer to the bottom."

"I'll tell you what it's closer to," said John-Boy, "and it's not heaven."

"It's not heaven, that's right, and I'm getting off this drudge boat and onto a salmon boat. Tha're made of steel."

"I'm gonna buy me a skipjack," Bobby said. "Daddy Art's got one; Uncle Stan's got one. Dad had one. I'm gonna get one, too. Maybe the *Thomas Clyde*. She's in Deal Island harbor in good shape. Charlie Abbot's got her for sale, right, Daddy?"

"Ya can get her if ya can find the money," said his father, who once owned the skipjack *Stanley Norman*, now a "floating classroom" for schoolchildren. "Twenty-five thousand. She's worth a hundred. Maybe he'll take payments."

"Ya can only make money in the water business if ya have yer own boat," said Larry.

"Yer own boat, that's how it is," Cookie said.

"Brother, get one in good shape, not like this one," said John-Boy, looking up toward the captain to make sure he was out of earshot. "Ain't many left in good shape."

Jimmy and Robert kept their tongues quiet during the Jones brothers' rant. It would be bad luck and poor form to criticize Daddy Art's boat, especially while under way. But they didn't contradict the Jones boys, either. "It's only a few boats left," Larry said. "It takes all yer catch just to keep 'em afloat."

"I'm buying one anyway," Bobby said. "Maybe my brother will join me. He works in the prison, as a guard. Down home, that's just about all thar is to do. Not me. I'm gonna follow the water. That's the family business. That and preaching, and I'm no good at that."

Just then Larry stabbed an oyster cake off of John-Boy's plate with his fork. John-Boy jumped up and hit his head on a bulkhead. He reached for his brother. "I'll kill you," he shouted.

"I didn't think you wanted it," Larry said. "It was just sitting on yer plate. Cookie will make you another one." John-Boy scowled and handed his empty plate to the cook.

Jimmy Daniels now spoke up. "When we was little, during the Depression, we always fought over food, Art and me. Booshel prices were rock bottom. We were poor, but we never went hungry."

Larry said, "We was poor *and* we went hungry."

"We went hungry, that's right," Cookie said. "That's the difference between white folks and black folks—when ye're poor ya wear old clothes, when we're poor we don't eat."

"We share our bounty today," Robert said, pitching his voice like his father, the captain and preacher. "Bounty from the land and bounty from the sea."

"Are you trying to save us again, Reverend Robert?" John-Boy said.

" 'Brothers, whoever brings back a sinner from wandering will save the sinner's soul.' James, chapter 5."

"Hallelujah," said Cookie. "I know yer talking about me! Tell it like it is!"

"Amen, amen," Larry said with a grin. The Jones brothers were in the habit of serving as flock and supplicants to Reverend Robert when at sea.

Having received his admonishment, the crew funneled up through the companionway and regained their stations. All except Cookie, who stayed behind to wash the dishes; I would man his post on deck. As he waited for a pot of dishwater to boil, Cookie busied himself caulking a leak he had discovered on the cabin wall, high on the hull. The caulkage was best applied from the outside but the first aid gave him some peace of mind. "I don't like either leak in my kitchen," he said as he spread the mixture into the wet crack with a putty knife. "This galley's surrounded by water. We're just one rotten board away from it." He shook his head in disgust, then his eyes lit up.

"Did you ever hear about the old cook with the pots and pans?" he asked. "Well, this old cook worked aboard a leaky dredge boat, the *R. H. Daugherty*, Puss Larrimore's bugeye. Leaked all day and night. The crew kept her pumped while drudging but at night the cook had to get some sleep. So he turned those loud pumps off and took all his pots and pans and spread them out on the cabin floor. Then he lay down in his berth. Middle of the night the cabin would start to fill with water. The pots and pans would float up off the floor and start clanging together. Made a racket. Woke him up. That's when he knew it was time to bail the boat. Them pots and pans were his alarm clocks. Set 'em every night." Cookie laughed. "I don't need no pots and pans, though. I can see we're leaking right now."

Within minutes the crew and I fell back into our old routine: winding the dredges, dumping the oysters on deck, heaving the dredges back overboard, culling the catch, then hauling the dredges aboard again. We worked fast but rarely enjoyed a rest between hauls. Only Larry diverged to clear the jib traveler, which hung up each time the boat nosed into the wind. Of all these chores, the real talent was culling. This began with what the dredges scooped up.

As each triangular dredge hit bottom, it swiftly collected the catch by making a three-foot-wide swath across the top of the reef, like a garden rake. Unseen and unheard, the dredge teeth combed oysters, reef animals, and debris from the bed, all of which then rolled back into the chain bag. After less than five minutes, the dredges, now full, were reeled in. The crew had to keep clear of the dredge line. It was made of steel cable and, whipping across the deck, could decapitate a man quite cleanly. The cable ran over the culling area, so it was hard to avoid. As if it were packed with high voltage, the crew carefully ducked under it or gingerly stepped over it to get to the dredges.

Upon dumping the take, the art of culling came into view. Jimmy, at sixty-eight, was still the ultimate culler. He squatted like a jockey on his toes and haunches in front of the dredge pile. With a cull hammer (a thin hammer with a three-inch measure along the shaft, like calipers) in one hand, he grabbed a cluster of oysters and knocked them apart. Mussels were similarly removed. Legal three-inch oysters passed between his legs into his pile of keepers. Small oysters, fish, and empty shells were tossed overboard. Jimmy culled fast. He had less than five minutes to go through the entire pile— four or five bushels of markets and "trash," his name for the bycatch—before the next load came on deck. A good cull would net a bushel of keepers out of those four or five bushels gross, but today Jimmy and his team were averaging less than a quarter bushel each lick per dredge. Either the oysters were "tough breaking into," or they just weren't there—lost to Art's winterkill or the disease.

Culling styles varied. There were as many ways to cull an oyster as there were to pronounce it. While Jimmy squatted with his wiry frame, his nephews, Robert and Bobby, leaned over from the waist to cull from a standing position. Larry kneeled on his right knee and extended his left foot to the side. He was too big to throw market oysters through his legs so he tossed them over his shoulder. John-Boy knelt on both knees and culled them like a center hiking a ball to a quarterback. He was the fastest culler, flipping each oyster with the flick of a wrist. With six men culling, the markets kept coming, bouncing and clicking like marbles across the deck. I imitated John-Boy as best I could.

By 1:00 P.M., the captain estimated that we had twenty-five bushels, about six bushels in each of four piles scattered strategically around the boat. "We should have thirty-five by now," said Captain Art, turning the wheel, "if we had this nice breeze all day."

"Shellfish are hard to catch this arly in the season," said Jimmy, rasping his voice. "We'll break into 'em next couple of days."

"Yeah, we might catch a few, next month or so," Robert said, "but not all season long."

"That's right, it looks like it's just a light skim," Jimmy said. "Lucky I'm on Social Security."

In the early afternoon, four or five skipjacks returned and swarmed around our buoy like predators searching for a weakness. But they could not "get straight." They sailed wide—outside the bounds of the hill. With the new southwest wind, there was only extra room for Stan Daniels, who worked to the leeward of us. Certainly, the depth sounders on the other boats told the captains that the underwater hummock, the "lump," was too small, but that did not prevent the younger captains from seeking some purchase on the small hill.

When we bore southeast on a starboard tack, heading toward our southern buoy, a lone skipjack crossed our path on a port tack heading north. Art was forced to fall off the wind and passed behind her stern, missing his lick. Art had right-of-way—he was the starboard boat—but that did not seem to matter to Freddie Williams, next to Daryl the youngest captain. "All's farr in love and war," he called from the helm. "You might have more orsters than me!" Art shook his head, resigned to the contest, but didn't react further. He was a tolerant man. Pulling in the main and tacking to port, Art got back on course, but by then ten minutes and half a bushel were lost. Freddie had cost him money. And perhaps his winning edge.

Though little gusts now and then struck the sails, the dredger's breeze held firm. *City of Crisfield* lurched forward each time the wind freshened. "I need the wind more westerly—to work the rest of this hill—and that's just what it's gonna do," Captain Art said. I looked downriver but could not yet see any sign that the wind would continue its clockwise swing and move farther west. "That's what it always does on the Bay," the captain said. "See, if the wind's sou'west, it wants to come nor'west. It may take a a couple of hours or a few days, but that's what it does. We depend on it."

Art stood in front of the helm as if it was his pulpit. "Here it comes," he said. And then I saw the ripples of green water and whitecaps roll in our direction, darkening the water as they came. Bits of spray lashed our faces. Just as he had predicted, the new, stronger breeze was due west. He had seen the distant green water before I had. With the wind now west at eighteen miles, we were able to work due south off the northern buoy. But first Captain Art had to slow us down; the dredges were bouncing off the bottom. He ordered a single reef added to each sail. The Jones brothers took down the main, tied the reef points, and raised the sail again. The bottom three feet of the sail had thus been rolled up and se-cured, leaving the main with 15 percent less sail area. The Daniels clan also shortened the jib, a trickier job since Bobby had to crawl out on the bowsprit, what he called the "bowsplit," to tie those points, something akin to straddling the mane of a galloping horse. The two families competed, friendly but dead serious, in their quest to shorten the sails in record time. They tied the sail stops by rote, a talent mastered in their teenage years. Two more rows of reef points, which could be secured in even stronger winds, were left untied. The second set would be employed if the wind reached twenty-one miles, and the third would be battened down at twenty-six or even thirty miles, a strong breeze. At that point, the captain would take down the jib. (These general thresholds were often ad-justed, depending on the tide.) Right now, with one reef, we slowed down to our former speed, about three knots—the right velocity for dredging Howell Point.

Just after two o'clock on a new course across the hill, we struck it rich. "Hallelujah!" sang Larry as the dredge came up at the end of the lick. A full dredge of live oysters spilled onto the deck. The captain did not bother to drop a new buoy at this point. He had a mark on the other side of the river—a clump of trees on Horn Point—that would serve just fine. As he came about, he picked up his binoculars and viewed the horizon. "Ca'm down river," he said. "Breezing up over to Trappe Creek." He explained that these signs meant that the ever-shifting breeze was turning northwest. "A cold front," he said. "Winter's coming. Let's make another lick. It'll be slick ca'm here in a bit." He dropped the glasses on the cabintop. "The breeze is flawy today—we'll miss the next wind I'm afraid. Quitting time is three o'clock."

At 2:45 P.M., we made our last lick, another beauty—what the captain called "clear arsters." Too bad it was the witching hour— the marine policemen hovered nearby to guarantee it. The next batch of clear oysters would have to wait until another day. All bets were on Art Daniels finding them again. He didn't jot down any coordinates. Like other marks on the river, they were stored in his head. His son said the old man could toss a brick overboard one year and pick it up the next.

Meanwhile, this day had not quite met its promise. The *City* carried thirty-two bushels of oysters into port, the largest tally to-day. Yet that was only 20 percent of her legal limit of 150 and, even with the tightly packed reef, a poor showing for opening day— pollution-stimulated disease or not. The dredgers would earn thirty dollars per bushel for their harvest, or $960 for the day, net-ting the crew eighty dollars apiece, a modest take for a twelve-hour shift.

Thanks to a fair breeze, Captain Art sailed on a broad reach home to Cambridge; the wind was just behind us to port, the sails in perfect trim. The bow cut through the water like a straight ra-zor, and spray washed my face. When the *City* turned upriver, the balance of the Deal fleet followed him in single file, taking his lead like a skein of geese. They followed a path worn into the water. Oystermen had carried their catch from Howell Point to

Cambridge for generations. Art Daniel's father had sailed this channel in the late 1890s. No wonder Daddy Art could stay on course in this morning's fog or, now, in the darkening afternoon. Meanwhile, the Tilghman boats headed downriver, some under sail, some pushing against the wind. They were spread out, as if still broadcasting, no leader among them. Art Daniels's generation, an old man at the helm, was just about gone.

Halfway to Cambridge, we passed over Sandy Hill, a popular hand-tonging area that was off-limit to dredgers. Jimmy and Robert stood next to the captain and passed a pair of binoculars back and forth. A dozen workboats floated in their field of view. The tongers balanced their long shafts, the poles bending under the strain, like huge saplings dipping into the water. "Tha're not catching the limit, either," Robert said, scanning the scene.

"That's bad news for us," Jimmy replied. "Them hand tongers'll give up on the river and go patent tonging out in the Bay—on drudgers' ground. Thar's not enough arsters for us both. We can't afford more overfishing."

"Skipjacks'll be surrounded by hostiles, wagons circled, making a last stand—"

But Art wasn't listening. He was preoccupied with minor adjustments to the rigging. Just now he let out the main sheet a few feet to harvest a little more wind. Scanning the horizon, he adopted the thousand-yard stare of the veteran waterman, sailing by feel, by touch, the wind tickling the back of his neck. "Fair wind, fair tide," he said to me with a smile. "All the wind we need. See, nature provides. That's heaven's way." It became clear that sailing was his second religion. To him, God and water were pretty much the same thing.

I wandered up to the bow where Bobby kept watch with the Jones brothers. As I approached, Bobby stared past the mast and me, over the cabin, at his grandfather. I glanced over my shoulder, too, and saw the old man searching the sky for one last gust to carry us home.

Bobby lifted his voice like a preacher's son. "Down from the mountaintop," he said. "That's Daddy Art in all his glory."

"All his glory, that's right," Cookie chimed in. "Cap'n's the best damn sailor on the Chesapeake Bay."

4

The Water Trades

Early one Wednesday I awoke to the hollow, ringing sound of iron striking steel. The clanging noise echoed down Gibsontown Road, so I stepped out of my house, oriented toward the sound, and followed it. After a few paces, it became clear that the cacophony originated at Henry Reecer's property—called Riverview—at the far end of the road. He was the island blacksmith and by reputation the last great dredgesmith on Chesapeake Bay. The entire skipjack fleet depended on him for their "drudges."

It was a cool, sunny autumn day with the musty smell of fading oak leaves heavy in the air. From the road I could see hand tongers clawing the bottom for oysters in the Choptank River. A good dozen of these tongers toiled over Middle Ground bar, about a mile off the shore just east of my house. The river was flat as glass, and the bright white workboats stretched out in a line on the smooth skin of the river like pearls in a necklace. As I walked south along Gibsontown, a peninsula between river and cove, I could also see the dredge boats moored in Dogwood Harbor just to the west of me. Eight skipjacks sat idle, stranded by the lack of wind, but captains and crews were busy on deck. They tuned engines, replaced lines, and inspected dredges and rollers, tightening the ironwork that made dredging possible. In just three weeks—eighteen days of sailing—the skipjacks had run up a list of repairs. Many could be handled by the captains alone; others were the domain of mechanics, sailmakers, and blacksmiths. Some of the younger skippers employed welders for ironwork, but the old guard—Art and Stanley and Wadey among them—were purists. Only a dredge-smith would do.

When I reached Riverview, I saw Henry Reecer hammering away at his forge. With the warm weather still spelling an Indian summer, the blacksmith had moved his tools and anvil and forge out of his shop and onto the lawn. Riverview, the Reecer family home ever since his father had moved to Tilghman's from Tennessee in 1923 to be the island doctor, was perhaps the best property on the island. Water on three sides. The waterman traffic, at arm's length, flowing in and out of the harbor gave Riverview the stature of a lighthouse. And Reecer anointed himself keeper of the flame. The skipjack fleet was both the backdrop and foil of Mister Henry's wit. He mercilessly graded each captain by how they treated his equipment and by extension how they honored the reefs at the bottom of the Bay.

Henry Reecer said hello to me—we were practically neighbors— and invited me to watch him work. He was making a new dredge for Stanley Larrimore, who had lost one the first week of the season—a shackle had busted, stranding it at the bottom of the river. An iron rod balanced gingerly in the blazing, red-hot forge. It was the first piece of the frame that would become an oyster dredge; assembling it would take three days. Although he could fashion a dredge without a blueprint, from only a design in his head, this light "mud" dredge was to be a duplicate of another one that lay at his feet. Stanley had salvaged half the pair and had commissioned Reecer to build him a replica. (A pair of dredges, port and starboard, had to be twins and balanced just right to catch evenly on both sides of a skipjack.) The surviving dredge was typical of the oyster scoops on every boat. Shaped like a triangular cage, the dredge had a broad end with teeth for scraping oysters off the bottom and a pointed end, which attached to the dredge cable. A chain mesh bag hung behind the dredge to hold the oysters. By law, the dredge bar was limited to forty-four inches across. The design had not changed much in 150 years.

"Anybody can lose a drudge," Mister Henry said, standing next to some heavier dredges. "I don't fault Stanley for that. But look at all these banged up and tortured drudges over here. That's the work of the young bucks who've bought themselves a skipjack without knowing how to sail. Their fathers weren't captains and neither should they be. You have to be born to it. And taught the rules."

Reecer lifted a hammer and banged the hot metal on his anvil. *Brring-brring.* It rang like a church bell. He was making an "eye," a loop at the end of the rod to serve as a ring on the center post of the dredge. I stepped closer to look at his handiwork. After flattening the top of the rod a little, he shoved it back into the forge to keep it malleable. Then he banged on it some more. Slowly, he curled the tip of the rod back on itself, making a loop. This was the primordial eye.

The forge itself was not enclosed but was an open hearth, accessible on all sides, more like a campfire than an oven. This "flatbed forge" was over eighty years old. It had come from the shop of Mister Henry's mentor, Adam Kapisak, the last island blacksmith to work full-time. (Reecer, seventy-two, was semiretired and only kept his forge lit because the captains had nowhere else to turn.) When Kapisak died, Reecer bought the forge and the shop's tools from the Kapisak family. The collection littered the staging area like a hospital operating room. On the left side of the glowing coal, thirty iron implements were scattered around the cement slab— round punches, chisels, and cutters among them—each with a special function for piercing, bending, slicing, or bonding hot iron and steel. On the right side, twenty or so hammers and iron mallets and sledges of various shapes and sizes lay about, ready to deliver the blows that would shape metal into gear useful to watermen. The forge was so hot that Mister Henry had to place the hammers in a barrel of water from time to time in order to swell the wooden handles, which were constantly drying out and shaking loose. He had primed the forge that morning by lighting an old rag soaked in oil. Placing this in the center of the forge, he turned the bellows on it, which ignited the coal fast. The bellows was actually an electric blower, more efficient than the old hand-crank bellows that Kapisak had employed. The industrial age ended there. Aside from the electric blower, the forge and its tackle and trim were lifted from another century. Mister Henry used soft coal, which was brittle and crumbly and turned to coke upon burning. It burned hotter and cheaper than acetylene.

Better at joining, too. He could put two pieces of iron in the forge, add a little flux, and "forge-weld" a bond as strong as the parent metal. This method was preferred over modern welding, which can be too brittle and is more likely to fail. Cutting was a little harder though. He had to chisel a hot iron bar with a hammer and wedge to break it in two.

But just now he was strengthening the eye by laying it in the coal with the blower set on high. The end of the tempered rod was sunset orange. Reecer explained that this rod was only one piece of the puzzle, but the linchpin. "The center rod is the spine. I position four more rods around it to create the frame—like a triangular box with a center strut."

Mister Henry was a stout man, short but powerful across the shoulders. He stood in a short-sleeve shirt with coal dust on his arms as he swung the hammer for emphasis. The hair on his hands was singed. "This is no lazy man's job," he said. "It takes a lot of work to turn a bunch of iron bars into a drudge. Once you get started you can't stop, either. Take this drudge. Once I have the center rod, shaped and hot like now, I turn it into a center post—you'll see that in a minute. All five of the bars have to be gathered and forged into a neck. Thar's your pointed end for the cable. It's a juggling act. Everything has to be heated up at once."

The blacksmith pointed to a second steel bar, about six-feet-long, and then at me. "Easiest with a helper," he said, motioning me to pick it up. "That's how I got started—hammering and banging for Adam Kapisak, the best dredgesmith ever on the Bay."

Like the island blacksmiths before him, Reecer could shape any of the ironworks that adorned a skipjack from rigging to anchors to dredge rollers. He could also forge hand tongs and gear for the other water trades. But the pride of the Chesapeake blacksmith has always been making dredges for the skipjack fleet. A good dredge catches oysters right; a poor dredge doesn't catch at all. And a blacksmith's reputation was always made or broken by how well his dredges caught oysters. Adam Kapisak's prized, sixty-year-old dredges, with patches and repairs, are still in use today. None catch better, but Mister Henry's are considered just as good.

Reecer took the virgin round bar from me and sat one end in the hot coals next to the center rod. The warm middle rested on a tripod brace, which stood in front of the forge. He held the other end—cool to the touch—in his hand and turned it slowly as if he were blowing glass. He cranked up the blower. Immediately, a yellow flame roared out of the coals, straight up into the air. The air around the forge appeared to boil—from my vantage the boats swam in the distance like a mirage.

Mister Henry withdrew the iron rod. The last twelve inches of it were red hot, like a poker. The tip appeared liquid enough to drop off. "It's still solid," he said, "but it's soft, like rubber."

Placing the smoldering tip on the huge anvil nearby, he grabbed a maul and hammered the end. Surprisingly, the iron swiftly changed shape. Still firm; however, it bent with each blow of Mister

Henry's hammer. Five blows and the iron bar acquired a right angle, turned downward. Next he spun the rod so the L-turn faced upward. Then he banged the end backward toward the main shaft—but not quite closing it. *Bang-bring. Bang-bring. Bang-bring.* Now the bar sported a hook at the end like a coat hanger. This hook would thread through the eye bolt of the center rod— loosely, affording some give-and-take to the spine of the dredge.

"Together the eye and hook and their shafts will make up the center post, running from the neck to the teeth. I build it stronger these days with power drudging allowed on Mondays and Tuesdays. If they hit a stone or something, the center post 'give' will keep the drudge bar and teeth from pulling out. Otherwise, those stones can yank the teeth out like a denture. The younger captains push too hard and knock 'em out all the time."

About this time, Stanley Larrimore's beige truck rolled through the gates of Riverview and over the oyster shell that lined the driveway to the blacksmith shop.

"How's that drudge coming along," he said as he rocked his huge frame out of the driver's seat, stepped down, and shuffled toward Henry Reecer.

"I started it today, Stanley," the blacksmith said. "I'll add a few improvements. It won't be any stronger than the original but it will handle better. Bet ya it will catch more orsters."

"Do you have the floor chisels to make them teeth?"

"Yes, I got 'em from Frank Lowery. He found 'em in New Jersey. I'll cut the ends off those chisels with a torch and weld 'em onto the dredge bar. They'll work just fine."

"Okay then, let me get these other drudges out of the truck." I helped Stanley unload a pair of heavier dredges, each weighing about 150 pounds. These were old dredges used for catching seed during the spatting season. Half the teeth were knocked out, the chain bags were rusted, and the "cotton bags" were frayed. The cotton bag (nylon today) held the chain bag in place and lightened the dredge.

"Let's just replace the teeth on these, Henry. Those floor chisels will do. And leave the cotton bag alone—I'll knit it myself." Stanley stared at the pair of dredges. "Who built these, Henry?"

"Adam did. You can tell by the round steel rods used as braces— all forge-welded. Other blacksmiths used flat-plate steel for bracing. And the shape is all Adam's. He did it all in the forge. Stronger that way. He didn't know how to operate a blowtorch. Too modern for him."

"It was something to see him work," Stanley said. "I'd watch him as a boy. Two big anvils, he had. Two men banging on the iron at each anvil with huge sledgehammers, trading blows. Metal ringing. Sparks flying. Yes, sir."

Henry nodded. "He could make anything. But all the boat builders were blacksmiths in those days. Miss Pauline's father, John B. Harrison, was the best shipwright but he also did his own blacksmithing. He used to set up a forge and shop in a stand of trees where he picked his lumber and built the boat right thar in the middle of the woods. No plans."

"Ever seen them pick out a mast, Henry? They'd walk through the woods and pick out a tree that looked good. Then they'd take a stick of a certain measure and stand it up a few paces from the tree. Then one man would take a couple more paces, lie down, and look up, taking sight on that stick and the treetop, and they could tell whether the tree was tall enough. Of course, they had big trees, seventy feet high, back then."

"Give me a couple of days, Stanley, and I'll have this new drudge ready for you."

"Okay. No hurry on these other ones."

Without saying goodbye, Stanley drove off, and the blacksmith returned to his forge. By now it was midday, and we watched the tongers come into the harbor. Most had their limit of fifteen bushels, typical success for the first month of the season. Rumor was, especially for tongers' ground, that this year's skim wouldn't last.

"These watermen are done for," Mister Henry said, rotating another iron rod over the flame. "They've caught most of the orsters. Crabs is where they make all their money now and that's just a few months each year. If the crabs disappear, I don't know what tha're gonna do. When I was a boy, the watermen would net fish during the slack months, between orstering and crabbing, but the fish are mostly gone. That leaves 'em with three months sitting idle. Nothing'll burn a hole in yer pocket quicker." The blacksmith withdrew the red-hot rod and dropped it in a bucket of water, which hissed and boiled over like the spout atop a kettle.

"The waterman is his own worst enemy," he continued. "He's always competing with the next man, trying to beat the next captain at his own game. Well, he's competing himself right out of his livelihood. Take the Murphys and the Larrimores—you crewed for them the past couple of weeks, you know—they've been feuding for years, ever since Puss Larrimore tried to drown Old Man Murphy. My father was from Tennessee; he said those two families were no better than the Hatfields and the McCoys. I wouldn't go that far, but I'll tell you: Bad blood is trouble for the water business. Hand tongers hate drudgers. Drudgers hate patent tongers. Tha're all rivals for the bottom. And they overfish. Too much competition is poison."

Mister Henry and I watched the tonging boats round his property as they left the river and headed for the shelter of Dogwood Harbor. He shook his head and summed up the decline of the oyster business. "Anybody with a pair of tongs can go out and try to catch some orsters," he said, scratching his head, "but you have to be foolish to think thar's a future in it."

For over three hundred years the forecast for the oyster trades was more optimistic. Before watermen claimed the Bay, Native Americans harvested seemingly boundless oysters from the shores of the Chesapeake. All they had to do was step down to the water's edge at low tide and pry a few bivalves loose for a meal. Then, in

1661, the Virginia colonial government decreed that all natives must buy a license to harvest oysters. Colonists were exempt. The license was a ploy to starve the natives, part of a wider campaign to force them inland. The strategy worked, and the colonists gained dominion over the Bay's bounty. Shellfish became a staple for the settlers. Soon, the shoreline beds between the tides were depleted, leaving oysters only farther out, beneath the waves. When opportunistic settlers took aim on these abundant deepwater reserves, another method of harvest was needed.

In 1702 the first shaft tongs were introduced on the Bay. These allowed fishermen to stand waist-deep in water or in a boat to pinch oysters from the bottom. The tongs looked much like they do today—a pair of raked heads atop two wooden shafts that were pinned together much like a pair of scissors or ice tongs. The heads were originally made of wood but later were forged from iron. The layout has hardly changed in three hundred years. Then and now, muscle power is employed to close and lift the tongs.

The history of harvesting oysters has largely been one of pushing the limits of gear in order to catch the bivalves in deeper and deeper waters. Shaft, or hand, tongs are no exception. As the colonists worked farther from the shore, the shafts were lengthened. Today, long tongs range between twelve feet and thirty-two feet in length. Plucking a bushel of oysters from the bottom with long shafts is backbreaking work.

The oyster dredge, designed for even deeper ground, first appeared in Chesapeake waters in the 1790s, arriving on opportunistic schooners from New England, where shellfish beds had already been depleted. The northern fleets journeyed south first to buy seed stock from tongers and later to dredge adult oysters from the bottom of the Bay. Local hand tongers protested, and in 1820 the Maryland legislature prohibited the dredge and the shipment of oysters out of state. (Virginia, which claims the lower Chesapeake, had done the same nine years earlier.) The northerners returned to

Long Island Sound. It wasn't until after the Civil War, in 1865, that Maryland changed its law, allowing the oyster dredge in the Bay proper but only under sail power. Steam power, a relatively new technology, was explicitly prohibited. Within five years, hundreds of freight-carrying schooners had been converted for sail dredging. The heyday of the Maryland oyster harvest was under way.

The 1865 sail law, the first conservation law of its kind, and its continuance to this day, has two major consequences: It has assured the longevity of the skipjacks and, until recently, has preserved the oyster beds. Keeping the law on the books is an anachronism to some and enlightened wisdom to others. It is difficult to think of another successful instance of enforced obsolescence that has survived over 140 years. Sailing is both less modern and less efficient than power dredging. In order to sail dredge, the wind's strength and direction have to be just right to work a given bar; on calm or stormy days the fleet stays in port, giving the oyster reefs a rest. This inefficiency, once the dredge-boat fleet was pared down to fewer than two hundred boats following the First World War, helped preserve oyster stocks for decades.

But enforced obsolescence would soon fray at the edges. Through the late 1800s, hand tonging and dredging were the only two legal means of catching oysters. With shoal-water oysters becoming scarcer, tongers wanted a means of harvesting oysters in deeper waters, like the sail dredgers. The answer came from two blacksmiths who each invented a new brand of deepwater pincers known as patent tongs.

The two inventions were apparently independent. In 1887 a patent was awarded to Charles Marsh of Solomons, Maryland, for his round-headed, deepwater tongs. A second patent was issued to William Dixon (and his partner, Joseph Bristow) in 1890 in Virginia for a head with a sharp right angle. The all-metal tongs were dropped into the water with jaws agape. When they hit bottom, a wooden latch floated upward, releasing the tongs and allowing the men to close them tight on the oyster reef. They worked well enough. In his first three years of manufacture, Marsh sold 1,200 pairs of tongs for sixteen dollars apiece. The Dixon & Bristow tong won a blue ribbon at the 1893 World's Fair in Chicago. Today, both the round-head and sharp-head tongs survive in the Bay oyster industry with two major modifications— how the tongs open and close and how they're lifted from the water.

The original patent tongs closed from the weight of the tongs (once the latch was sprung) and were pulled to the surface by hand winders. In the 1920s the hand winders were replaced by small donkey engines, an innovation that met with no resistance from the government. The daily "jag," the feasible catch, jumped from 30 to over 100 bushels. Finally, in 1958, two Maryland inventors created a hydraulically operated patent tong. (The idea for a hydraulic tong came from log loaders, the mechanical claws that pick up timber— whole tree trunks—and load it into flatbed trucks.) The tong heads are closed and opened with hydraulic power, with crushing strength sufficient to punch holes in oyster shells—just one of the hazards of the technology.

By the late 1950s most oystermen were hand tongers or patent tongers; dredgers were a minority. So there was little protest against the new machinery. And, as they have done so many times before and since, the Maryland Tidewater Administration gave in to the request of the patent tongers for more efficient gear. The hydraulics were allowed. The old Maryland code of enforced obsolescence lost some ground.

And the oystermen lost ground, too. Oyster ground. It didn't take long for the hydraulic patent tongs to destroy oyster reef after oyster reef. For this and other reasons, harvests dipped below 2 million bushels for the first time in twenty-seven years. Henry Reecer summed up their destructive power this way: "The oyster drudge is the equivalent of a horse and plow, but a patent tong—now that's a steam shovel. It could dig up this driveway."

However, not only patent tongers have abandoned the code of inefficiency. Periodically, sail dredgers also demanded leniency from the state, a watering down of the law that had brought these oystermen into existence. After a hundred years of sail dredging, six days a week, the skipjack fleet had a couple of bad seasons in the mid-1960s—ice and poor harvests—that led to complaints from a vocal minority of captains. State delegate Randolph Harrison, a Tilghman Islander, championed their cause and asked the legislature in Annapolis to relax the sail-only ban to allow dredging with a push boat two days a week, making for a more efficient harvest. Skipjacks would be able to work in calm or heavy weather, formerly impossible on a sailboat. During bad times, captains would have a guaranteed catch, or so the argument went. Despite protests from the old guard—Glendi Larrimore, Old Man Murphy, and their sons, among them—in 1967 the old sail law was modified, as requested by the few, to permit power dredging on Mondays and Tuesdays. It was a contradictory statute—sail only, except when power—and a precedent that would haunt the fleet. The senior men feared the measure would spell the end of sail dredging. The Larrimores worried about the precious few oyster hills, or "lumps," being ground down. Others were concerned the two-day limit would be violated. And, in the ensuing years, these abuses came to pass. The waterman is an enigma: part thief, part conservationist. Until his death, Junior Benton, the old-time captain of *Geneva May*, would drop his yawl boat illegally on a Wednesday, if there was no wind, and power-dredge. He'd get a ticket from the marine police, smile, pay the fine, and do it again the next day. Junior was one of the most blatant in a long line of outlaw dredgers—some active today. Their reputation goes back more than 130 years.

In 1879 an official report on the oyster industry warned:

Dredging in Maryland is a general scramble, carried on in 700 boats, manned by 5,600 daring and unscrupulous men, who regard neither the laws of God or man. . . . An honest captain who complies with the law by not working on Sunday, at night, or on forbidden ground, will take at least a week longer to catch a load of oysters than one who, disregarding the law, gets his oysters whenever and wherever he can. . . . The unscrupulousness of the captain is well assisted by the character of his men. These men, taken as a class, form perhaps one of the most depraved bodies of workmen to be found in the country. They are gathered from jails, penitentiaries, workhouses, and the lowest and vilest dens of the city. . . . As may be supposed, the life led by these men on board of the vessels is of the roughest kind . . . hour after hour winding away at the windlass, pulling a heavy dredge, or else stooping with backs nearly broken culling oysters. Returning from a trip, the men take their little pay and soon spend it in debauchery amid the lowest groggeries and dens of infamy to be found.

By the mid-1880s, nearly a thousand dredge boats worked the waters of the Bay. Over 7,000 captains and crewmen, ranging in honesty from pirate to parson, manned the fleet. To meet the demand for vessels, Chesapeake boatbuilding expanded and entered its most innovative period of the century. Specifically, it responded to the call for a boat that could navigate a wider expanse of the Bay. Just as the progression of tonging has been from shallow water to deep, the progress of dredging has been from deepwater to the shallows. The first dredge boats were deep-draft schooners that could only work in the Bay proper. The 1865 statute excluded them from bars shallower than fifteen feet, which remained the domain of tongers. Quickly, the deeper bars were cleaned out, the law was

amended, and there was a need for a smaller, shallow-draft dredge
boat. The bugeye, with two masts and three sails, for pulling the
heavy dredges, and with a centerboard for the shallows, was developed in the 1860s in time for the oyster boom, which reached a
pinnacle in the 1880s with regular hauls of 10 million bushels a
year, nearly fifty times what it is today. The first bugeyes were constructed from logs and were expensive to build and maintain. A
frame-built bugeye followed, perfected by John B. Harrison, but
not every waterman could afford one. Finally, in the 1880s, a
cheaper and shallow-draft boat was created—the skipjack. (The
origins of the name are lost.) Adapted from the flat-bottom skiff,
the skipjack was cross-planked but had a dead-rise, or V-bottom,
hull. *Eva*, at thirty-nine feet, was likely the first one built in
Dorchester County, prior to 1888; she was frame-built like *Kathryn*. She had a centerboard and, like the bugeye, could work in less
than six feet of water, if need be. The skipjack took hold, and by
1910 was the dominant dredge boat, its numbers well over five
hundred—enough pressure to assure overfishing. The oyster harvest dropped 50 percent between 1900 and 1925. At that point,
with fewer boats, the harvest—around 2 million bushels annually—
became sustainable for thirty-five years. Only a few skipjacks were
built between the great wars, with the last four launched in 1955–
56. By the late 1960s, with oysters on the decline again, all schooners and bugeyes had been retired, and fewer than fifty skipjacks
sailed the Bay—outnumbered and outcompeted by patent tongers.
And threatened by disease. On average, one boat per season has
dropped out each year since.

Today, there are five types of oystermen, each with distinct vessel and gear. The most recent technique is diving for oysters. The
air supply is stored on board and fed to the diver via a hose. It is
very dangerous. And expedient. Divers have denuded many beds.
Again, it is a mystery why the government permitted another

method of harvesting oysters that is more efficient than hand tonging and sail dredging. Under political pressure, Maryland regulators have often placed fishermen ahead of the resource. The trend has been, when faced with tough times or new technology, to open up the fisheries more with better gear. In their defense, the bureaucrats claim the greater efficiencies were offset by stricter bushel and cull limits. However, like many watermen, Art Daniels believes the motivation was to pit waterman against waterman. The five camps work with different seasons, hours, and harvest limits; they have access to different bars. All the contrary regulations cause bitterness among them. Divided, Daniels argues, they have little political voice.

Harvests have plummeted, experts agree, in part because too many competing watermen have been struggling over too small a resource. From an average 2,020 licensed oystermen over the past ten years, over 50 percent of the catch was landed by hand tongers, 27 percent by patent tongers, 19 percent by divers, and less than 4 percent by sail dredgers. Ratios have changed from year to year, especially recently, with the disease favoring patent tonging over hand tongers in many places. In the 1960s, Maryland first imposed daily catch limits on oystermen—15 bushels per man on a tonging boat (either rig) and 150 bushels for a skipjack, another sore spot in the craw of tongers. With the disease depressing the oyster population, dredgers rarely catch their limit now. Curiously, the annual harvest began a descent before MSX struck hard, when hydraulic patent tonging and power dredging became popular—in the 1960s. Many factors are afoot, so correlation is speculative; however, one can only wonder about the likely health of the Chesapeake oyster fishery if sail dredging and hand tonging had been left alone. In any case, Maryland's sail-only law was repeatedly abandoned.

A sixth harvest method, gaining popularity, is oyster farming, the transfer of barren bottom to private leaseholders for planting shell and seed. Many see private leases as the answer to the tragedy of the commons, where competing "free rangers" selfishly over-tax the public resource. But, among watermen, this has been the most controversial technique of all. For centuries the Chesapeake Bay has been a public fishery, a commons open to everyone. The constitution of the state of Maryland declares it so. Nonetheless, over 7,200 acres of bay bottom has been leased so far—a fair chunk of real estate compared to the estimated 36,000 acres of oyster habi-tat in Maryland. The watermen fear all of the Chesapeake, includ-ing natural bars, will someday be controlled by private interests, most likely seafood companies. They fear they will be forced to work for these enterprises rather than roam the waters freely, as they do now. Henry Reecer expressed the apprehension as well as anybody.

"What the politicians don't understand," he said, setting down his hammer for a moment, "is that just about everyone here on the Eastern Shore is self-employed. If you close down the public fisheries—open up leasing everywhere—thar're no jobs for these men to take. Some of the younger men have gone to the city—Baltimore, Washington, Wilmington—looking for work. But they have no skills other than the water business. Nobody will hire them. Wouldn't know how to follow orders anyway. They've never had a boss." He clanged an iron tooth against a dredge; it rang out like a brass bowl. "Even if the seafood packers don't take over, the watermen will still be looking for another job. Crabs and orsters will be gone. Give it ten years and they will have caught all the shellfish." He put down the chisel for a minute. "Of course, the gov-ernment let 'em do it—allowed the new gear, gave out too many licenses, let them catch too many—but the waterman knew better. Still, knowing that, he caught more than his share. He forgot the tradition. The old-timers did it differently. They always left enough orsters and crabs behind for next year."

BY LATE AFTERNOON, Mister Henry had assembled a rudimen-tary triangular cage—the five rods were forged at the neck, a feat of uncanny timing and balance. "Come back on Saturday," he said, "and I'll show you a beautiful drudge. That is, if you call me Henry." As he closed up shop, two young dredgers, Frank Lowery and Freddie Williams, stopped by to unload two pairs of heavy gummers with teeth, or rather a spattering of teeth. Each dredge was mangled, the frames bent and the center posts nearly pulled apart. Henry said, "You boys sure are hard on your drudges— power drudging with long lines in the river, pushing too fast, grinding down the bars to dust. No respect for God or man."

"Grind 'em and wind 'em," Freddie said, in a defiant grin. "If thar's one last orster on the bar when I finish the day, I haven't done my job."

"Your job is to hand down a living to our children."

"I see your lips flapping but I only feel the breeze."

Henry Reecer threw up his hands. "I guess I'm getting old. You boys have a different take on life than we did." With a wave in my direction, he walked back to his house. For me, it was time to shuck some oysters for my neighbors and turn in early. Tomorrow was Thanksgiving, and I had been invited to more than one meal.

EARLY THE NEXT DAY, I cleaned a quart of oysters, beauties from dredging aboard *Lady Katie*, and poured them into a Tupperware bowl—ready for Chesapeake haute cuisine. During the night, a nor'wester had blown across the Bay, bringing the first light snow of the season. Out my window, the northwest perimeters of the tall skipjack masts were coated with frost. More than ever, they resembled an isolated stand of woods.

At midmorning I tucked the oysters under my arm and negotiated the fallen branches on the shared lawn that spanned the distance to Miss Pauline's bungalow, already trimmed with Christmas lights. I heard her first: She played "Tennessee Waltz" on her upright piano, which she kept tuned to display her nimbleness with southern classics. My neighbor had never traveled outside Maryland but she was a patron of mail-order sheet music. At her door, I hid the container of oysters behind my back as if they were flowers. At my knock, the music stopped, and she answered the door. "I've put the turkey in," she smiled. "Now, if I only had some orsters." This was a tease; she was expecting my gift. "Oh, my," she said, inspecting the catch. "They're a nice size for scalloping. Let's save the oyster liquor—it'll come in handy." She weighed the bowl in her hands. "Well, I guess we don't need *all* these." Miss Pauline popped an oyster in her mouth and fed one to the cat.

Scalloped oysters were—like crab imperial—an island specialty, and reputations hung on the success of each family recipe. Miss Pauline inherited her scalloped oysters from her mother, Miss Lottie, second wife of John B. Harrison, and planned to bequeath the secret to her great-niece, Vicky McQuay.

"Wash your hands," Miss Pauline admonished. "You can chop. Start with the onions. Then we'll see how good you are with celery."

Miss Pauline arranged a layer of bread crumbs and oysters in a rectangular baking dish. Meanwhile, I finished up with the onions. "Three layers is what makes a good scalloped oyster," she said. "I'll put the casserole in the oven as soon as the turkey comes out."

An hour later, the neighbors arrived: Mister Boats, the island repairman, and Miss Mary, who was legally blind. The three of us made up Miss Pauline's immediate neighborhood. The other guests were family. Miss Pauline's nephew, David McQuay, showed with his daughter Vicky, at about noon. David, like his father and grandfather before him, was a shipwright. His specialty was restoring vintage log canoes, which sailed in the August canoe regatta on the Miles River off St. Michaels. David carved the turkey, which boasted a succulent oyster dressing. I longed for the ingredients. Prying a recipe out of Miss Pauline, however, was like trying to shuck a stubborn oyster: Even if you found a likely entrance, the valves were sealed shut. But the prize was always worth the trouble. I tested the waters by asking who had supplied the oysters for the giblet dressing, but she was bashful about it—the shellfish undoubtedly a gift from a former student earlier in the day. The Harrison recipe book was as big as a bible, but she would not budge, so I turned to other offerings: sweet potatoes, green beans with almonds, and sauerkraut. The scalloped oysters were impeccable. The shellfish melted like sweet butter in my mouth. Miss Pauline honored the island philosophy of preserving the natural flavor of the oysters—that's why she conserved the liquor. Suddenly, she pulled two pieces of paper out of her apron and placed them before Vicky and me. Without pushing, the latch had sprung open. One of the family recipes was at last within our grasp.

HARRISON FAMILY SCALLOPED OYSTERS

1 cup chopped onion (sautéed)
1 cup chopped celery (sautéed)
2 cups bread (or cracker) crumbs
1 quart shucked oysters (counts or selects); drain and
    reserve liquor
12 pats (or one stick) butter
Salt and pepper
⅔ cup heavy cream
2 eggs

Sauté onion and celery. In a buttered shallow casserole, place a thin layer of bread crumbs, then a layer of oysters and butter, next a thin layer of celery and onion. Repeat layers until dish is full. Season with salt and pepper to taste. Pour reserved oyster liquor and cream uniformly over all. Cover with bread crumbs. Bake at 350° for 30–35 minutes.

Balls. To the south are Chinese Muds, Sharkfin Shoal, Old Woman's Leg, Hurdle Braw, and my favorite, Tippity Wichity. Some are reserved for tongers; some for dredgers. Each of the latter is best worked with a certain slant of wind and, from the forge of Henry Reecer, one of the five dredges proven for its bottom.

Henry welded the last tooth onto the dredge and raised his eyes. Stanley Larrimore's tan truck was rolling down the driveway, crunching more oyster shells in its wake. Stanley stepped out of the truck.

"How's it look?" he said.

"Looks right, weight's okay," Henry Reecer said.

"How's the set? Will it catch the same?"

"Should catch better."

"If that's true, I'll come back here and ask you to build another one just like it."

"That's the idea." Henry smiled.

"So you're gonna get the price of a pair out of me anyhow."

"Now ye're thinking, Stanley."

"Thought I was. Yes, sir." They both laughed. Stanley walked around the new dredge, eyeing it. He nodded his head in approval.

The talk between the two men turned to island gossip, the ways of the waterman, and the trials of the water trades. Listening, I could only smile at the ease of the island life, at the familiarity of each neighbor, at the calm of knowing one's place in the world. On the island there was always time for shooting the breeze. Soon enough the water would call, and hard work would again be at hand.

"It used to be like this, during the Depression," Henry was saying. "When orsters were scarce the captains would fix up only one pair of drudges at a time."

"Looks like you got plenty of work now," Stanley said, waving his hand at the stack of dredges on the lawn. "Some of these drudges are fifty years old, I guess."

"Adam and I built them strong, built them to last. The only time

Beat two eggs, spread over top, and broil until golden brown.

Serves 6.

Over dessert—pecan pie—David said to me, "I hope you have a big second appetite. The Murphys serve again at four." I had been found out. As always, there were no secrets on Tilghman's Island. "Tell Wadey I have some large stainless-steel clamps in the truck that should fix his boom," he continued. "*Rebecca*'s got some splits in that pine. The clamps should help."

"I'll tell him," I answered. David had a soft spot for skipjacks, too.

"He needs a sail cover. It would drape the boom, sails and spar both. Nothing tears up a wooden boat more than the sun. His boom was exposed all summer. I tell all the captains, but they don't listen. Well, Wadey listens, but he takes his time getting around to it."

Miss Pauline saw me to the back door, and thanked me for the oysters. I said I was jealous that she had another admirer—the provider of the oyster stuffing. With a giggle she waved me off, then grabbed a box off the washing machine and shoved it into my arms. Inside was a tangle of green wire with tiny multicolored bulbs. "You are going to put up Christmas lights," she said. It was not a question. "I'll lend you a ladder. Just don't get caught in the rigging."

My second turkey was better than the first, but, alas, no oysters. True to form, Wadey had given his catch away. Every Thanksgiving, every weekend, he delivered free crabs or oysters to friends all over the island—to retired watermen and widows. This year, some of his fare may have found its way into somebody's stuffing. Just another attempt to win a teacher's heart.

TWO DAYS LATER, after a morning crewing aboard *Rebecca*, I heard clanging again upwind and returned to Henry Reecer's forge to see how Stanley's new dredge was coming along.

"Almost got her finished," Henry said, wiping the sweat from his forehead.

The triangular box frame—all steel—was complete and an iron bar ran across the leading edge of the front of the dredge. It was half full of teeth. Reecer was adding the others, aligning the old chisels in a straight line, matching them up like an orthodontist. He picked up his acetylene torch and cut the beveled head off another chisel and welded it to the dredge bar. It would take eighteen chisels to provide the teeth—each three inches long—for Stanley's new mud dredge.

"We always made five sets of dredges for each boat," Henry said. "Each was different and customized for the captain. We'd tailor a dredge depending on where you wanted to work. If you wanted a mud dredge for the river, we'd build it light. If you wanted a dredge for stone piles or packed-down cinder bottom, we'd make it heavy. Oysters live in a lot of places, so we'd make a dredge for each particular type of bottom.

"These days some drudgers—the younger ones—go into the river with heavy drudges, flat plates mostly, and they sink in the mud, dig up the bottom. On push days they can use power to overcome the mistake, but they can't fix it when sail drudging. Sail drudging's all finesse. That's why the best drudgers—Stanley and Wadey, Bart and Pete—still carry five sets. Tha're ready for whatever bottom they run across. It is not unusual for a good captain to install three different drudges during the course of a day."

Mud dredges are the lightest, about 100 pounds, and have long, three-inch teeth for raking oysters out of mud bottoms (e.g., Six Foot Knoll). Edge dredges, for the vertical side of a reef (a slightly harder place than a mud hill or channel), weigh 120 pounds and have slightly shorter (2¾-inch) teeth. Round-bar dredges (also called "hard dredges") are made with heavier gauge steel, weigh 140 pounds, and have moderate teeth (2½ inches). The harder the bottom the heavier the dredge and the shorter the teeth. Round-

bar dredges are used on bottoms with shell and small stones (e. Howell Point) or hard-packed sand (e.g., Black Walnut). Too gummers have short teeth (two-inches long) and a heavy flat bla made from an automobile spring. They are used where stones of moderate size. Lastly, gummers (or "flat plates") are the heavi (160 pounds) and lack teeth altogether so as not to snag on la stones or "hangs" at places like Stone Rock. The difference tween muds and gummers is also measured in sweat. After hours of culling oysters, each pair of crewmen has hauled s two tons more weight with a flat-plate dredge than with a dredge. And that's not including the stones brought on board, s weighing thirty pounds or more.

Those stones often provide the foundation for a fledgling Some reefs begin with a single spat adhering to a pebble sunken log, the bar growing eventually to a square mile in Free-floating oyster larvae (or "veligers") will attach to any surface, but the preferred real estate is old oyster shell, with rugosities, so the reefs are self-perpetuating (unless dug up patent tonger or overzealous dredger). The oyster cemen binds the reef together is the envy of chemists—strong, fast-a and durable, and it works underwater. Nearly every san every hill, and every stone pile in the Bay has been coloniz glued together by oysters at one time or another. Over five hu oyster reefs form a patchwork beneath the Chesapeake, son a hundred feet thick. Most once formed escarpments, stee rises" like coral reefs, that provided fifty times the habita given acre, than do the flat beds found today. The boom dredging and, more recently, patent tonging and clammi lopped off the summits of the old reefs. Over the years w have given the remaining bars colorful names, most of the exotic than Howell Point. In the Choptank, dredgers work Hill, Choptank Lumps, and Dawson's Discovery. To the r Hollicuts Noose, Turtleback, Tea Table, Man O' War, anc

Beat two eggs, spread over top, and broil until golden brown.

Serves 6.

Over dessert—pecan pie—David said to me, "I hope you have a big second appetite. The Murphys serve again at four." I had been found out. As always, there were no secrets on Tilghman's Island. "Tell Wadey I have some large stainless-steel clamps in the truck that should fix his boom," he continued. "*Rebecca*'s got some splits in that pine. The clamps should help."

"I'll tell him," I answered. David had a soft spot for skipjacks, too.

"He needs a sail cover. It would drape the boom, sails and spar both. Nothing tears up a wooden boat more than the sun. His boom was exposed all summer. I tell all the captains, but they don't listen. Well, Wadey listens, but he takes his time getting around to it."

Miss Pauline saw me to the back door, and thanked me for the oysters. I said I was jealous that she had another admirer—the provider of the oyster stuffing. With a giggle she waved me off, then grabbed a box off the washing machine and shoved it into my arms. Inside was a tangle of green wire with tiny multicolored bulbs. "You are going to put up Christmas lights," she said. It was not a question. "I'll lend you a ladder. Just don't get caught in the rigging."

My second turkey was better than the first, but, alas, no oysters. True to form, Wadey had given his catch away. Every Thanksgiving, every weekend, he delivered free crabs or oysters to friends all over the island—to retired watermen and widows. This year, some of his fare may have found its way into somebody's stuffing. Just another attempt to win a teacher's heart.

TWO DAYS LATER, after a morning crewing aboard *Rebecca*, I heard clanging again upwind and returned to Henry Reecer's forge to see how Stanley's new dredge was coming along.

'Almost got her finished," Henry said, wiping the sweat from his forehead.

The triangular box frame—all steel—was complete and an iron bar ran across the leading edge of the front of the dredge. It was half full of teeth. Reecer was adding the others, aligning the old chisels in a straight line, matching them up like an orthodontist. He picked up his acetylene torch and cut the beveled head off another chisel and welded it to the dredge bar. It would take eighteen chisels to provide the teeth—each three inches long—for Stanley's new mud dredge.

"We always made five sets of dredges for each boat," Henry said. "Each was different and customized for the captain. We'd tailor a dredge depending on where you wanted to work. If you wanted a mud dredge for the river, we'd build it light. If you wanted a dredge for stone piles or packed-down cinder bottom, we'd make it heavy. Oysters live in a lot of places, so we'd make a dredge for each particular type of bottom.

"These days some drudgers—the younger ones—go into the river with heavy drudges, flat plates mostly, and they sink in the mud, dig up the bottom. On push days they can use power to overcome the mistake, but they can't fix it when sail drudging. Sail drudging's all finesse. That's why the best drudgers—Stanley and Wadey, Bart and Pete—still carry five sets. Tha're ready for whatever bottom they run across. It is not unusual for a good captain to install three different drudges during the course of a day."

Mud dredges are the lightest, about 100 pounds, and have long, three-inch teeth for raking oysters out of mud bottoms (e.g., Six Foot Knoll). Edge dredges, for the vertical side of a reef (a slightly harder place than a mud hill or channel), weigh 120 pounds and have slightly shorter (2¾-inch) teeth. Round-bar dredges (also called "hard dredges") are made with heavier gauge steel, weigh 140 pounds, and have moderate teeth (2½ inches). The harder the bottom the heavier the dredge and the shorter the teeth. Round-bar dredges are used on bottoms with shell and small stones (e.g., Howell Point) or hard-packed sand (e.g., Black Walnut). Tooth gummers have short teeth (two-inches long) and a heavy flat blade made from an automobile spring. They are used where stones are of moderate size. Lastly, gummers (or "flat plates") are the heaviest (160 pounds) and lack teeth altogether so as not to snag on large stones or "hangs" at places like Stone Rock. The difference between muds and gummers is also measured in sweat. After ten hours of culling oysters, each pair of crewmen has hauled some two tons more weight with a flat-plate dredge than with a mud dredge. And that's not including the stones brought on board, some weighing thirty pounds or more.

Those stones often provide the foundation for a fledgling bar. Some reefs begin with a single spat adhering to a pebble or a sunken log, the bar growing eventually to a square mile in size. Free-floating oyster larvae (or "veligers") will attach to any hard surface, but the preferred real estate is old oyster shell, with all its rugosities, so the reefs are self-perpetuating (unless dug up by a patent tonger or overzealous dredger). The oyster cement that binds the reef together is the envy of chemists—strong, fast-acting, and durable, and it works underwater. Nearly every sand bar, every hill, and every stone pile in the Bay has been colonized and glued together by oysters at one time or another. Over five hundred oyster reefs form a patchwork beneath the Chesapeake, some over a hundred feet thick. Most once formed escarpments, steep "high rises" like coral reefs, that provided fifty times the habitat, for a given acre, than do the flat beds found today. The boom years of dredging and, more recently, patent tonging and clamming had lopped off the summits of the old reefs. Over the years watermen have given the remaining bars colorful names, most of them more exotic than Howell Point. In the Choptank, dredgers work Bunker Hill, Choptank Lumps, and Dawson's Discovery. To the north are Hollicuts Noose, Turtleback, Tea Table, Man O' War, and Minnie lls. To the south are Chinese Muds, Sharkfin Shoal, Old Woman's g, Hurdle Braw, and my favorite, Tippity Wichity. Some are reserved for tongers; some for dredgers. Each of the latter is best forked with a certain slant of wind and, from the forge of Henry Reecer, one of the five dredges proven for its bottom.

Henry welded the last tooth onto the dredge and raised his eyes. Stanley Larrimore's tan truck was rolling down the driveway, crunching more oyster shells in its wake. Stanley stepped out of the truck.

"How's it look?" he said.

"Looks right, weight's okay," Henry Reecer said.

"How's the set? Will it catch the same?"

"Should catch better."

"If that's true, I'll come back here and ask you to build another one just like it."

"That's the idea." Henry smiled.

"So you're gonna get the price of a pair out of me anyhow."

"Now ye're thinking, Stanley."

"Thought I was. Yes, sir." They both laughed. Stanley walked around the new dredge, eyeing it. He nodded his head in approval.

The talk between the two men turned to island gossip, the ways of the waterman, and the trials of the water trades. Listening, I could only smile at the ease of the island life, at the familiarity of each neighbor, at the calm of knowing one's place in the world. On the island there was always time for shooting the breeze. Soon enough the water would call, and hard work would again be at hand.

"It used to be like this, during the Depression," Henry was saying. "When orsters were scarce the captains would fix up only one pair of drudges at a time."

"Looks like you got plenty of work now," Stanley said, waving his hand at the stack of dredges on the lawn. "Some of these drudges are fifty years old, I guess."

"Adam and I built them strong, built them to last. The only time

I have to replace anyone's drudge is when they lose one—like you. Of course, you don't want to lose one the way Bart did. When he had the *Ruby Ford*, I built him a pair. He took them out first day of the season and, when he got to the rock, he shouted at the crew to toss over them drudges. Well, they hadn't attached the drudges to the cable shackle and they tossed them all right. Both cages went right overboard never to be found again. Made him another pair on the condition he fire his crew."

Stanley smiled. He had heard the story before and would hear it many times again. He scanned over the water's edge and asked Henry if he'd heard the news about the fall oyster survey. Conducted by the Tidewater Administration, this field analysis measured the health of the oyster fishery. "Somebody mailed me the report anonymously," Stanley said.

"What did the state boys find this time?" Henry asked. "Orsters are growing like weeds?"

"No, sir." Stanley Larrimore wore a frown. "Sure, seed from Tangier Sound used to ripen in three years, but now they say it's dying before it reaches legal size."

"All over Tangier Sound, Stanley?"

"Some bars have the death; some don't. Chain Shoal has only a few big orsters, and nobody's been working thar. Something's killing them. Sharkfin Shoal is a graveyard. Luckily, Kedges Strait is pretty free of the die-off; they found nearly fifteen hundred spat per booshel. Must be a record."

"Somebody better catch those orsters before they die," Henry said.

At about this time, a red truck appeared at the entrance to Riverview. It was Wadey. As he pulled up next to the two men, Stanley and the blacksmith kept talking, offering no greeting, since the close quarters of the island afforded no room for formalities. Especially the Murphys and Larrimores. An island tradition: Their fathers had hardly spoken to each other, before them. Just now Stanley and Wadey chatted through Henry Reecer, as if he were an interpreter.

"You done with Stanley's drudges?" Wadey asked, as he joined them—on Henry's right, the opposite side from Larrimore.

"Almost finished. What've you got?"

"I have two edge drudges in the truck, Henry. They need new teeth, a new set to the bars, and chain bags. I'll give you four booshels of orsters to fix 'em."

"Take me better part of a day when I get the chance."

Stanley shuffled his feet. "Where's Wadey gonna get teeth for his drudges?" he asked, avoiding Murphy's eyes.

Henry spoke for Wadey. "We'll use Frank Lowery's chisels. Same as the teeth on your drudge."

Wadey stared silently at the blacksmith regardless of where the questions had come from or who they were about.

"What price will Wadey be paying for 'em?" Stanley said, addressing the blacksmith again.

"Two dollars apiece. Frank's tight. He probably paid fifty cents a piece for them chisels in New Jersey."

Stanley smiled at the sly commerce, with the comfort of a compatriot.

Wadey risked a grin, too. "I don't know why I sail a skipjack. It costs a bundle. Tongers got it easy—no drudges, no chisel teeth to break, no bags to knit."

"Those tongers ain't getting much of a price for orsters," Henry said, changing the subject.

"Henry, thar'll only be a certain amount of orsters to catch this year," Wadey said. "Whether they get caught at twenty-five dollars or thirty, they'll get caught just the same. Might as well refuse to work for two days and drive the price up, but them tongers won't do it. If we sell off the skim at a low price, we have nothing to blame but our own dumbness."

Stanley chuckled to himself. "Even if we strike, Henry, afterward them buyers will probably pay me less than anyone," he said. "Usually do." Larrimore now took a step toward the driveway. "Well, I guess we've killed the morning. Better head up to Gary's and avoid doing some work over thar as well." As Stanley climbed into his truck, Wadey lowered his own tailgate to remove his set of edge dredges. I helped him lower them to the ground.

"Put 'em over thar," Henry said, pointing to the stack of dredges from other captains.

"I wanted to get 'em to you arlier but I didn't have time," Wadey said. "The first few weeks of drudging is all about working the kinks out—sails, cables, crew, drudges, too. It's unreal—you wouldn't believe what's held me up."

"Well, I wouldn't trade places with you. And I know where this conversation is going. Wadey, I know you're behind, but I'm still not fixing your drudges ahead of these others."

Wadey flashed a smile and laughed. "I knowed it. I knowed it. Just thought I'd try."

Henry shook his head and returned to Stanley's dredge, which was hanging from the rafters. He only had a couple of rows left to finish the chain bag, the chain mesh that holds the oysters kicked backward by the teeth.

"Is Stanley gonna knit his own cotton bag?" Wadey said.

"I think so."

"I'll do mine. It's a habit from the Old Man. Time to show L'il Wade how to knit one."

"I remember your father. He was an edge drudger, working those sides of an oyster bar where they run down into the channel. Made an art of it. When I was a little boy, him and the other old-time drudgers used to sail right to the dock, no push boat. On a northwest breeze they'd come up to Avalon Island, old Tilghman Packing Company's dock, over thar, reef down, luff their sails, pull into the wharf, and drop their mains. Stop right on a dime. Park their boats like a buggy. That was sailing."

"I would have liked to have seen that."

"In those days thar was thirty or forty skipjacks, schooners and bugeyes, too, that tied up in this cove. You could walk across the harbor on their decks. Lot of drudge boats sunk right here, too. The old schooner *Clara Garrett* ran aground over thar"—he pointed across the harbor—"in the hurricane of 1933. That was before they started naming hurricanes after women. One, two, three, four drudge boats died alongside of her. A few years later that old log bugeye *Coronet* sank thar, too. Right next to her, *Cecrops* collapsed—old age. Those are just the boats I know by name. Others are dead *and* forgotten." At the surface of the harbor, hovering above these shipwrecks the Tilghman fleet now floated peacefully, with the help of their pumps.

Wadey seemed curious but also a little embarrassed by this talk of abandoned boats. Straddling the past and present, old traditions and modern realities, was a daily burden. Like other captains, he focused on the living. He changed the subject abruptly by asking if I'd help him ferry his torn sails to the Easton sail loft for repairs. "The sun ate up my sails last summer. And the boom's split. Just haven't gotten to 'em, but now's no better time to keep a skipjack in trim." Or to fight back time. Just a short errand, he said. I waved farewell to Henry and jumped into Wadey's truck. One errand would likely turn into half a dozen and—with shooting the breeze— likely take the whole day. As Henry would say, murder the morning and hang the afternoon.

5

December, Gum Thickets

Yellow light poured out of the windows of Gary's Store and shone down the path like a searchlight. No other lights interrupted the night, save a few stars and the red-and-green flashers on the drawbridge up ahead. Clouds scudded across the sky, and the wind whispered in the trees. Two paper bags rolled down Main Street. Other than that, it was a peaceful night. But not for long. At 4:45 A.M., the island was stirring awake. Pickups were idling all over town, ready to make the pilgrimage.

Watermen are drawn to Gary's light just as sailors through the ages have been drawn by other beacons—from Pharos to Liberty—as they wandered away from home. If skipjacks are a second home to the captains, then Gary's is a third. It is boathouse, community hall, and rallying point. The first words of the day and the last ones, too, are traded here. For on the horizon is a lonely voyage on the water. Conversation and coffee at Gary's: for some, the only human connection of the day.

Into this oasis the men marched heavily, stomping out the cold, leaving their pickups running in the snowbound parking lot. It was the second week of December, and the price of oysters was up again. Christmas orders were spiking; time to catch as many bushels as you could before the price dropped. Around the corner lurked January, always a lean month on the water, so if real money was to be made, it was likely to be now. A dozen or so tongers stirred about the store, drinking coffee and talking about prospects for the day. They wore plaid wool shirts, two or three layers' worth, with red long underwear peeking out of the top. All of the tongers wore knee-high rubber boots and baseball caps announcing favorite teams or hardware or fishing tackle. Meanwhile, the skipjack captains, in the middle of the crowd, without exception were distinguished by hats declaring the names of their boats: *Esther F., Virginia W., Hilda Willing, Nellie Byrd, H. M. Krentz, Minnie V., Lady Katie,* and *Rebecca T. Ruark.* The eight of them—Bart, Bobby, Pete, Daryl, Ed, Johnnie, Stanley, and Wadey—clustered near the coffee machine and the cash register, which Gary Fairbank held on to as if it were going to fly away. Bart and Wadey stood apart, but the others moved freely between them.

Johnnie circled around the store, asking the hand tongers what price they were getting now that the holidays were just around the corner.

"Twenty-two dollars a booshel at the Oyster Peddler," said one. "That's for tongers—working in the river."

"Same price at Kool Ice Seafood," said another.

"It's twenty-three for river and twenty-seven for bay orsters at Harrison's," Johnnie said.

"The buyers've got their heads together," said another tonger. "It's nearly the same price everywheres."

"Drudge orsters are supposed to go up another dollar today," said Johnnie. "Those bay orsters will be twenty-eight dollars again." The larger, fatter bay oysters always sold at a premium, and sail dredgers worked the open water for them whenever the weather was right.

"That's what I'm catching today—*bay* orsters," said Ed Farley, stealing a glance at Stanley. In unison, the captains turned to stare at the big man while he filled his coffeecup.

"Everybody's gonna catch bay orsters today, if Stanley shows the way," Daryl said. "Only my uncle's got a secret." The word had spread about *Lady Katie* filling her decks with 120 bushels at the end of last week, and the fleet would retrace her steps if they could. She had hit the jackpot alone, somewhere off Kent Island, just north of here.

"Looks like tha're going to hound ya today, Stanley," Johnnie said.

"I know," Stanley replied, shaking his head. "Don't I know it."

It was common knowledge Stanley would be returning to Kent Shores today—he had blurted out as much—though where along that eight-mile stretch was unclear. Now that the fleet knew generally where his treasure was buried, Stanley had no choice but to sail there to catch whatever he could before the pack cleaned him out.

Bart Murphy was the next to speak. "So where'd ya catch all them orsters, Stanley?"

"I hit a spot."

"Where?"

"Hard to say."

"Hard to say? I bet it's hard to say. You giving us the slip, Stanley?"

"Trying to," he said, grinning. "Yes, sir, been trying to keep a secret around here all my life. Hasn't worked yet. No, sir."

Wadey Murphy set his coffeecup on the glass case next to the door. The merchandise in the store had changed over the past couple of months; the summer fishing tackle had been put away. In its place the owner had stocked his shelves with wool hats, oyster gloves, rubber boots, oilskins, and knee pads for culling oysters on deck—last-minute supplies gathered at five each morning. Two men on *Rebecca*'s crew were already on hand—Kenny and Hot

Rod, the two Welch brothers. Arriving next, Li'l Wade avoided his father as he walked around the store. He said "Hey" to Kenny and grabbed a Coke for breakfast. That made half of Wadey's crew. By contrast, all of the other crews had assembled. Wadey selected three pairs of rubber oyster gloves and laid them on the counter. He paid for them—fifteen dollars—and, avoiding his brother, Bart, walked briskly out the door. He wasn't waiting for anybody.

Outside the store, Wadey overheard Stanley and Johnnie talking about an oyster bar, though giving no name. "Thar's more orsters on them stones," Stanley said, "and thar's small orsters for next year." Stanley had nearly spoiled his secret in the store. Now he gave away a tantalizing clue. Wadey wouldn't be telling any other dredgers this hint about the stones.

It was a clear, cold predawn, just below freezing after the second snowfall of the year. Just a dusting, the snow had mostly blown away. The half moon had set around midnight, turning the sky ebony. At that moment the stars seemed to pop out of the sky, each one sharp and brilliant. Wadey stole a look at Arcturus, the brightest star on the eastern horizon, but it would be Polaris that guided him this morning. Since the moon's passing, the wharves had lost all shadow. Along the narrows the row of skipjacks was quiet, like a string of thoroughbreds sleeping, only the rigging rustling in the breeze. But this was false security. Heavy winds and snow were predicted for the afternoon. Among captain and crew there was a new caution. Make no mistake: Winter had arrived, the most dangerous time of the year.

We stepped aboard *Rebecca* and made preparations for setting sail. L'il Wade and I lowered the yawl boat, while the Welch brothers unfurled the sails. By the time the three Langfords arrived in down coats, the captain had lost his patience. Looking at them, Wadey set his jaw and ranted: "The first rule is to get here on time. I said we were leaving at five thirty this morning. Can't you get at least one thing right?" The brothers looked timidly away; there was no talking back. Under the cover of darkness they settled into the cabin for another hour of sleep.

We followed Stanley out of the narrows, bearing north into the Bay. To conserve fuel, *Rebecca* kept her sails flying and her push boat running, as if caught between two worlds. No crewman was needed in the yawl boat since its controls were on the cabin of the skipjack. A fresh breeze cut across our port bow from the northwest. The running lights on *Lady Katie* were visible on that dark morning, so Wadey was able to keep a respectful distance while not losing sight of the lead boat. In any case, the North Star beckoned straight ahead. Close behind, five skipjacks took up the slack, a string of scavengers fast on the scent. Kent Island was seven miles away.

Night and predawn sailing are always a voyage of discovery, especially in winter. Ahead, to the northeast, the sky erupted in a fireworks display: Hundreds of shooting stars raced across a patch of sky like tracer rounds. Each ball of white fell earthward, followed by a bright tail, and disappeared on the horizon—burning out like a bottle rocket. This was the Geminid meteor shower, so called because a large concentration of meteors appears for five days each December in the constellation Gemini. I had never seen so many meteors at once. "Beautiful out here," Wadey said, rubbing his hands together for warmth. "I wouldn't want to be anywheres else. I'd like a little more money, that's all."

Bloody Point Light, marking the southern tip of Kent Island, lay up ahead, flashing its beacon every eight seconds. It also marked the deepest point in the Bay, a hole reaching 174 feet down. Bloody Point itself was named for the spot where colonists massacred a group of Native Americans in the seventeenth century, though this history had long been forgotten on the Eastern Shore. We passed by to leeward, giving the lighthouse plenty of room. *Lady Katie* sailed on a northerly course, heading for any of several oyster bars off the western shore of Kent Island: Brick House,

Halfway, Kent Point. The sky was getting light, and Wadey lifted his binoculars to search the waters ahead. Half a mile off, *Lady Katie* turned broadside—she was bearing down on her prize. Wadey dropped his binoculars. "It's Gum Thickets," he said. "That's Stanley's bar." He opened the hatch to the cabin and yelled below, "Get up, boys. Take off the hard drudges and put on the gummers. We're gonna work a stone pile and catch some orsters today!"

Gum Thickets is a vast oyster reef measuring more than a mile long and a quarter mile wide, running parallel to the shoreline of Kent Island, the eastern abutment of the Chesapeake Bay Bridge. Like 20 percent of commercial landings, its catch was off a "natural bar," not planted with seed—a wild harvest. Earning its name from a clump of black gums growing along the creeks at the edge of the island, Gum Thickets is a hard bar riddled with stones. Thus, Wadey's call for gummers (flat-plate, toothless dredges), which tend to hold up best on a rocky bottom.

Wadey explained how different bars rank in priority. "Arly in the season we work hard bottom, like Howell Point, and after the year's crop is caught up thar, we move to cinder—beds of broken shell—and deep spots, mud mostly, which is difficult to cull. Stone piles usually come later—we wouldn't be here today if it weren't for Stanley hitting a gold mine."

Wadey broke off from our conversation to stir the crew again. "Come on, it's getting late," he called. "I'm feeling great for a Monday. Let's get going." With the captain in a good mood, I was disappointed not to be culling today; I came along for the sport of it.

Stanley quickly located the neighborhood of his previous strike, a spot no bigger than a football field in ten feet of water—one of the shallowest sections of the reef. Taking his bearings from trees and buoys nearby, he would, at first light, be able to position himself close to where he had scooped up his record catch. Now all he had to do was circle his claim and wait for dawn.

Wadey ordered the crew to lower the sails. We pushed toward *Lady Katie*, only to stop short of her circle, honoring the first man to prospect this spot. The sails were quickly furled; it was the first of the week, a power day: We would be pushing all day. Until 2002, all skipjack captains power-dredged on Mondays and Tuesdays, even ones originally against it, because they couldn't afford to be at a competitive disadvantage with the rest of the fleet. Looking back, Wadey talked about the heyday of Gum Thickets: "I used to catch my limit here, sailing, by ten o'clock, but we'll be working here all day long, I expect." He scratched his chin. "I think I may have sailed here on November 2, 1968, the day my daughter was born. Caught over 150 booshel. On her wedding day, I told my son-in-law that if he ever made her cry, I'd kill him. He must've heard of me." He winked. "I think it made his day."

With the sky brightening in the moments before dawn, we could see the skipjacks behind us more clearly. Four boats—*Minnie V.*, *H. M. Krentz*, *Virginia W.*, and *Nellie Byrd*—spread out across the bar. These were all young captains, mostly in their thirties. With the exception of Bobby Marshall (*Virginia W.*), they made a bee-line for Stanley's piece of the reef. Bobby sailed farther north to join Bart on Brick House; these two captains declined the assault on Stanley.

"If them young bucks stay clear of me," Wadey said, "we may catch seventy-five booshel today. With orsters scarce, I'd settle for that—half my limit. The young captains, pushing hard, might catch more, but on a sail day they can't compete."

Just after seven o'clock the sun rose over Kent Island, spreading a bright pink banner across the cloudy gray sky. Opposite the dawn, to the northwest, the sky appeared ominous; it pressed down against the water. The damp air smelled like snow. Autumn had given way to a winter sunrise. And Wadey didn't miss a beat. "Hey," he yelled at the crew, and two dredges ran over the sides in concert and descended to the bottom, sixteen feet below. *Rebecca* was not quite atop Stanley's small hill but maybe she'd find a strike of her own.

The dredges came up fast. On each side, port and starboard, two men muscled the dredge. The "third man"—Jerry Langford on port and Li'l Wade on starboard—manipulated the clutch lever on the winder engine to make sure each dredge rose up and over the side of the boat smoothly, without hanging up on the roller. The four outside men—two Langford brothers (Aaron and Matt) and two Welch brothers (Kenny and Hot Rod)—dumped the catch on deck and bent to culling, separating the chaff from the harvest. Wadey figured that stationing one set of brothers to port and the other to starboard would make them compete, to the benefit of the catch. About sixty market-size oysters were gleaned from each dredge, a good take on a first lick. The oysters were large, many nearly four inches long, but some were dead: two valves without the meat inside. These hollow boxes, called "coffins" by the crew, were more corpses left behind by the disease MSX. Perhaps ten of the sixty were dead. A couple of others were in their death throes, distinguished by their gaping shells. MSX invades each oyster through the gills, rapidly infecting the internal organs, leaving entire reefs dead or dying. The pathogen could kill half a reef in a season; some bars were more susceptible than others, depending on freshwater influx and drought. This morning the coffins and gapers were more prevalent than had been sighted in November on Howell Point, underneath a tributary and thus a fresher area than the open Bay. Gum Thickets was saltier and thus more vulnerable. "Good Gawd Almighty," Wadey declared at the sight of the fatalities. "I never thought I'd see orsters dying like this." Nonetheless, the captain was pleased with the fifty live ones. He threw a blue buoy overboard to mark the cache.

"Hey," he signaled, and the crew released the dredges again. They dived into the water with a resounding splash. "We may not be on Stanley's spot," Wadey said, turning the wheel hard, hand over hand, "but I'll take this part of the rock for now."

Nearby, the three other skipjacks were less patient. The young dredgers huddled around Stanley's run, two to the north, one to the south, boxing him in. Try as they might, the three could not dig into Stanley's spoils without tripping up on his buoys. They had to be content with the periphery of the hill. But Wadey's attention, his gaze, was diverted farther north, to Brick House bar. There Bart and Bobby leisurely combed virgin bottom, just past a raft of canvasbacks. He stared for a long time at the pair with his binoculars, then turned to me with a resigned air. "Bart and I used to be close," he said. "We helped out on each other's boats; I crewed for him at the races; we both looked after each other. But that's ancient history." I thought back about what I had heard about the impasse. Both brothers had crewed aboard *George W. Collier*, their father's skipjack, as teenagers. The brothers got along well enough as long as their father was alive. The Old Man may have played favorites, however, doting on the youngest, and perhaps the seed of the rivalry grew from there. The rumor around the island was that an argument erupted over the ownership of a set of skipjack winders from *Collier*. The Old Man left them to Wadey, who stored them at his house. Then, so the story goes, Bart asked to borrow them, and Wadey obliged. But when Wadey asked for them back, Bart claimed his father had bequeathed them to *him*. Wadey left, angry and empty-handed. According to gossip, the brothers had never broken their silence. And neither had ventured to comment.

Setting the glasses down, Wadey said, "Bobby may have some luck up thar, even if he's in mixed company." That was as far as Wadey would go. He ruffled his forehead and gave me a wink.

Wadey made a long lick before turning the boat again, to double back. He kept the inside (starboard) dredge overboard during this turn, like a pivot—something he'd never do while sailing. With more time in the water, the dredges caught more oysters on each leg of the circuit. This could add up considerably by the end of the day, producing a larger harvest, sometimes 50 percent heftier than when sail dredging. There were other efficiencies to power dredging, to be certain. The captain was able to steer the boat in any direction he chose. With sailing, he'd have to be abreast of the wind to pull the dredges efficiently, limiting the ground he could cover. With push dredging, he could direct the boat to wherever the oysters were most dense. He could turn quicker and keep a steady speed. He was not tied to the wind. But power had its detractions: Caught between the yawl boat and winder engines, the helm was a stereophonic hell. I longed for the relative quiet of sailing.

For the balance of that second run, I noticed the captain was smiling. He had hit some oysters and he had a compliant crew. He kept his lines short, to catch just the top skim, and his boat slow— just barely moving. This would preserve the reef. The gummers were scraping over stones, the impact reverberating along the cable onto the deck, but fortunately only small stones were coming aboard. Murphy's Law was in remission. But, as the law proscribes, all bad things come to those who wait.

For the next hour, we worked the same two buoys with fair success. On deck were four small piles—three bushels each up front and two bushels in each pile aft, making ten overall—loaded with mussels, but it was a good start: We were on our way to a hundred-bushel day. The only trouble had been the repeated jolts and shudders that resonated through *Rebecca* each time a dredge hit a big stone, hanging up for a minute before tearing loose. These "hangs" were a constant danger on a stone pile like Gum Thickets.

Elevator cable runs off each windlass to the steel dredge, but not all of the spool plays out on each lick. The captain can adjust the length of the line by ordering the crew to tie an additional becket to the spool at the appropriate spot. Imagine a fishing reel playing out till it hits a snag; the snag is similar to the rope becket,

only it's a separate loop of line, which limits the cable coming off
the spool. The two-foot becket cinches the steel cable like a noose.
In this way, any specific measure of cable, up to the two-hundred-
foot maximum, can be released (or withheld) from the windlass.
The becket, being manila, is the weak chain in the system and, in
fact, the captain counts on it breaking from time to time. If a dredge
hits an unforgiving hang, the becket breaks and the line plays out
another six feet to the next becket. The slack afforded by the
break usually allows the dredge to snap free of the obstruction.
The breach also limits damage to the boat. Today, on treacherous
ground like Gum Thickets, Wadey ordered the crew to cut halfway
through each becket with a knife so that, if the dredge hit a hang,
the becket would likely break, thereby freeing the dredge. The momentum of a fifteen-ton skipjack under power (or sail)—even at
the preferred slow speed of three knots—is enormous. While pushing with the yawl boat, the dredge is basically propelled by a truck
engine, and the force in snagging a hang can break a dredge, cut a
gash in the side of the boat, or tear the winders from the deck. Between the diesel engine and the steel cable is a boatful of wood,
and timber is the first to buckle under the strain. Worse still, a
frayed, lashing cable can cut a man in two. "I'm not taking any
chances," said Kenny Welch, as he cut a shallow groove in a becket.
A little too shallow, I thought.

At 9:00 A.M. the dredges surfaced with more stone—about the
size of bowling balls. The crewmen hurled each sphere into the
water like a shot put, all except Li'l Wade, who stood distant, out of
the fray. "Now they begin playing again," Wadey said. "I'll tell you,
it gets on my nerves. I get anxious about the boat or an accident. I
yelled at 'em all day last week."

Wadey turned the boat to starboard, releasing one dredge, then
the other. "It was diff'rent in the Old Man's day," he continued.
"On my father's skipjack, we competed with each other: who could
cull the fastest, build the biggest pile. In a gale, I'd be the first one

out on the bowsplit to reef the jib. We had pride and loyalty to the skipper. Now it's diff'rent. These boys don't help me none. Tha're supposed to call out the number of legal orsters on each lick. But they don't do it, unless I ask. Thank God, I have Li'l Wade aboard— besides Jerry, he's the only one I can count on, the only one with some ambition. I told him to set an example."

In between licks the crew gathered at the winder engines, except for Li'l Wade, who still remained aloof. They warmed their gloves by placing them over each exhaust pipe, which puffed up the fingers like a cow's udder. The trick worked until the next dredge poured cold water down their hands again. This congregation at the engine was the equivalent of chatting at a watercooler, and the conversation never strayed far from girls and sports.

From a distance, at the mast, Li'l Wade listened and watched. He was almost sullen. Yesterday, Wadey had chewed out the boy for not breaking the descent of a dredge in time, the reproof perhaps louder than warranted in an effort by the captain not to play favorites. The crew, he asserted, would ostracize his son if he was too lenient. The danger was going too far in the opposite direction. In any case, the boy was still smarting from the reprimand. As his father revved the engines, Li'l Wade took a last drag of his cigarette and, with thumb and finger poised, flicked it over the deck into the water. Even this gesture was in silence. He looked anguished, like a boy who had been gut-hooked.

Bad luck hit early. Underwater, a small boulder snagged our starboard dredge. No small calamity: The gummer bit hard against the granite, the dredge spilling its oysters. The whole boat shook, as if a small quake had washed over the bar. *Rebecca* lurched forward. She spun to the right like a carnival ride, and then abruptly stopped. Cinching tight, the cable bit into the roller and squealed. Surprisingly, the becket held—it had not been cleanly cut in half by Kenny. Nobody reacted until Li'l Wade cautiously reached over and cut the becket with one sweep of his knife. Immediately, the cable jumped off the windlass and into the deep. Underneath the waves, the dredge bounced free.

The crew simultaneously looked back at the captain. He was furious.

"Good Gawd, ya'll are tearing up my boat," he screamed. "Pay attention, goddamn it. When we have to stop to fix things, nobody's making any money. Ya're only making money when things are running right." He walked forward to the starboard roller. "Now wind 'em in, but first put a becket on every six feet and—for Christ's sake—cut it in half!"

I took over the helm while Wadey inspected the dredge and the winders, to see if any damage had been done. The equipment had survived the incident, but Wadey's irritation had not abated. He took one look at each oyster pile on his march aft, and each time shook his head in disgust. The mishap had set him behind. He lifted his eyes across the water and scrutinized *Lady Katie*, with no little envy.

Wadey reeled in the dredges, and the men dumped two wriggling mounds of sea life on the wooden deck. A few clumps of oysters (coated with inedible bent mussels) punctuated the gathering of reef creatures: anemones, barnacles, mud crabs, tubeworms, blennies and gobies (two small reef fishes), and bright orange Atlantic starfish, a voracious predator of oysters. Among the richest communities in the estuary, oyster reefs with their many nooks and crannies provide habitat for hundreds of species. Saltwater anglers know fishing is best above an oyster bar. The largest catch today was a foot-long oyster toadfish. A third of its body consisted of a grotesque head bearing sharp teeth and powerful jaws; two hollow spines on its dorsal fin were supplied by venom glands. Ugliness is in the eye of the beholder, and Kenny dispatched this singular specimen with a knife between the eyes, claiming the "big-headed monster chews up orsters like crackers." However, contrary to local folklore, toadfish do not prey on oysters and spat.

Rather they eat other reef denizens, particularly mud crabs that *do* prey on spat. In this regard, toadfish are guardians of the reef.

By far the most ignorant myth concerns the starfish. Watermen are familiar with their carnivorous nature: An infestation of sea stars can devastate an oyster bar. They can be prolific; their regenerative powers are prodigious. Each of the five arms, even if severed, is capable of growing a brand new starfish. Yet crewmen think they are easy to kill. Unwittingly, the crew just now hacked six starfish into pieces and threw the amputees overboard. Thirty new starfish would rise, each like a phoenix. I tried to stop them, but prejudices run deep on the Eastern Shore.

"I CAN'T STAY ON this damn junk too long," Wadey said, his voice shaking in anger. "Too many hangs and trash and distractions." He paced back and forth at the helm now, scrutinizing each dredge as it surfaced. The count climbed high—fifty markets per dredge—but both stones and oysters were now coated with inedible mussels. Buyers will reject a load of oysters covered with mussels because the mussels both exaggerate the volume purchased and make shucking more difficult. The crew would have to clean each oyster, freeing it of the mussels. The captain resigned himself to the inconvenience, in a surprising about-face. "Just shovel 'em into the piles now, boys," he said pleasantly. "We'll trim 'em up later." Maybe his more civil tone would bring the crew to attention. Inexplicably, Wadey seemed to relax.

During the lull, Wadey told a story about one of the old black crewmen on *J. T. Leonard*, built like *Rebecca* and the last gaff-rigged oyster sloop on the Bay. "Old Shad, he was quite a character—in the drunk tank either week and sleeping it off in the forepeak of that drudge boat the rest of the time. One week he had a little appointment at the Cambridge courthouse—for creating a public nuisance. The judge says, 'You've been here one time too many.' Shad says, 'Yes, sir, one time too many.' The judge tells him, 'Fifty dollars and costs, or jail time.' Shad says, 'Oh, I can't afford that, Judge. And I'm going drudging in the morning.' The judge then says, 'All right then, twenty-five dollars and costs.' Shad says, 'Oh, Judge, I can't pay that. Please, Judge, I feel turrable but I can't do it.' The judge tells him, 'Well, then, ten dollars and never let me see you here again.' Old Shad pulls out a roll of bills and says to the clerk, 'Can you change a fifty?' "

Lady Katie was pushing in a tighter circle, over shallow water about a quarter mile to the east of us, where there were fewer stones and mussels. Wadey suspected that Stanley and the other boats were catching more oysters than him, and he'd had enough heartache for one morning. He set his sights on a new lay, just northwest, to windward, of *Lady Katie*. Better ground, he hoped. On the way, I noticed the clouds had lowered, socking us in and obscuring the sun; it looked like more snow was coming. The temperature hovered in the midthirties, and the nor'wester barreled along at about twenty. The seas were short and steep.

Once he arrived on site, Wadey settled down to a north-south circuit just to the east of Stanley's east-west run. *Rebecca* and *Lady Katie* now sketched a (backward) letter L in the water, with the legs of the letter not quite touching. Still honoring the unspoken rule of letting the first man on location work his buoys, Wadey set up a perpendicular course in shallow water, giving Stanley sufficient room. The younger captains backed out of the way.

"Maybe we'll have better luck here," Kenny said to the captain.

"Luck's in the Lord and Devil's in the people," Wadey said. "That's what my mother said." He looked over the water, left and right, and pointed a finger at each dredge on deck.

"Hey," Wadey shouted and waved both arms like an air-traffic controller. The crew heaved the dredges overboard for our first lick of the new run. The oysters came aboard clean, with little trash. Culling was easier, which I figured was a benefit. But the captain quickly corrected me, as he spun the wheel. "Without those mussels to clean and those stones to hurl, them boys won't be as busy. That's why I didn't shorten the lines in shallower water. Last thing they need is a rest. Just watch 'em play."

As if on cue, the crew began their antics. It took them only a couple of minutes to cull the oysters, and then they started tossing bits of shell and mud at each other. This wasn't simply a paintball exercise; they were aiming at the face. A mud ball just now clipped Kenny on the chin.

"Children, that's what they are," Wadey said, his face reddening. "I can't farr 'em—and they know it. Crews are too hard to find. But you watch, somebody's gonna get hurt."

His anger barely in check, he stepped forward, halfway around the cabin and raised his voice only slightly: "Kenny fell overboard last week. Who's gonna be next?"

Last Wednesday, on Old Rock, Kenny had nearly drowned. His attention strayed while using a five-foot "turn stick" to right a dredge that had twisted in the water. Used correctly, the stick functions as a lever; used incorrectly, it becomes a catapult. The stick flipped Kenny over the side. Two things were in his favor: The water wasn't yet freezing and he was able to grab a life ring thrown by Li'l Wade. With the help of a boat hook, the crew pulled Kenny onto the gunwale and hauled him aboard. A close call but no injuries other than pride.

Stepping back to the helm, Wadey was visibly shaken. "After drudging with these children all day, it takes me three of four beers in the evening just to calm down."

This morning, Wadey had a devious way to quell the kids. "Two," he yelled forward, holding up as many fingers to his son. The signal called for the dredge lines, on both sides, to be let out two turns on the windlass, or approximately six feet—the typical interval for a becket. While the other crewmen returned to culling, Li'l Wade untied the beckets and reset them after the cable played out. He was careful—the cable winding on the drum was a hazard for fingers and hands. Beneath the waves the gummers bit deeper into the bar, dipping underneath the skim. When the next dredges surfaced, more shell and stones came aboard. The longer lines had done their trick: The crew would be kept busier, culling. Immediately, the games of the boys ceased. "They don't even know what happened," Wadey said. From the mast, Li'l Wade caught his father's attention and rolled his eyes. For the first time today, Wadey risked a laugh.

It was eleven o'clock, time for dinner. We had thirty or so bushels on deck, a slower rate now than for our first hour, so Wadey wanted to keep the dredges running, the crew busy culling. He announced there would be no break for the midday meal: The crew would eat in rotation, two men at a time. There would be no cooking, either, for good reason, as the captain explained it. Sandwiches only. Recently, Wadey had an old cook aboard, named Tom, who was in the galley slicing potatoes into a boiling pot one day. Hot steam flooded the cabin and streamed out of the hatch toward the captain at the helm. When Wadey peered below, beads of sweat from the cook's brow plopped into the soup. That soup went the way of hot chocolate on a dredge boat. Wadey refused dinner that day and he hasn't allowed cooking aboard *Rebecca* ever since.

Aaron and Kenny were the first to step back aft to retrieve their brown bags. "I hate sail days, too much wind or not enough," Aaron said to the captain. "If the wind ain't just right, ye're out of luck. I'd like to power drudge like this every day—guaranteed money."

Wadey took a long look over the Bay, deciding not to explain the facts of life. "Breaks my heart not to be sailing today," he said softly into the wind. "Good breeze for it." The boys hardly noticed, jockeying past the captain and scurrying forward to dine next to their brothers.

I witnessed again a curious phenomenon: The captain, given the choice, never turned his back on the crew—apparently not from fear but simply another superstition. "I was working right here on Gum Thickets," Wadey explained, "when one of the crew, this guy named Leroy, culled a nice flounder from the drudge. He tried to put it aside, for himself, but I told him it was mine—that's the captain's right. Leroy got mad and grabbed a shovel and came after me. I had a choice between a crowbar and a hatchet sitting on top of the cabin. I picked the hatchet. That was enough for him. He backed off." Wadey tapped his hat farther back on his head. "That was the day my crew robbed the bank in Tilghman's. Leroy was the getaway driver. Somebody should have put up the drawbridge, but the tellers forgot to call the bridge tender and lost a bundle. Better the bank than me. I had a bunch of outlaws aboard that year. Not anymore. Stanley's got all the outlaws now. I'll bet ya Leroy is working the log on *Lady Katie* right this minute."

I asked Wadey how the flounder tasted—grilled or baked.

"Just to make Leroy *really* mad, I threw it back overboard."

The crew—Matt and Hot Rod now on break—discussed the water trades over bologna and cheese. Hot Rod picked up on Aaron's sentiment: "Power drudging's the boss—only reason I show up. Sailing's not dependable. Last Friday was slick ca'm and we made neither dollar. And it was payday. I haven't been paid yet. Wind is the least dependable thing in the water business."

Matt said, "Blessed are the power days for they shall inherit the earth."

"My father did better by the water than any of us," Hot Rod said. "His whole generation. Look at Wadey—he owns two boats and a house. They had good catches back then."

"I pray for a strike of orsters," Jerry said. "My crabbing skiff needs a new engine. I just replaced the cabin and the deck. It's been dollaring me to death."

"Ya can't get ahead on the water anymore," his brother Matt said. "That's why I'm quitting, end of this season. Course, I said that last year."

"Take the good with the bad," Li'l Wade said. "Anyway, I promised him the season."

"My old lady's harassing me to get a job on dry land," Kenny said, with a goofy smile, "but I've got saltwater in my veins. All the hassling in the world ain't gonna change that."

Aaron seemed to wake up on that one, throwing his last keeper into the pile, overhead like a baseball pitcher. "I'm gonna drink beer, chase women, and work the water. Don't make any sense, but I always wanted to be a waterman."

Abruptly, *Rebecca* lunged to port, shimmied, and groaned, waking all of us from our reverie. The port cable stretched tight like a guy wire, and the becket split slightly, then completely snapped. As it shattered, six feet of cable rushed overboard, just missing Aaron's head. Avoiding it, he tripped over the oyster pile and landed on his back. It took less than a second for the cable to run to the next becket, which cinched tight with a thud. It held, then frayed. But the dredge pried loose from whatever obstruction had clasped it for the few seconds that had threatened the boat.

The captain scouted around for someone to blame but could find no one remotely at fault. This time the crew had cut the becket, which split right on cue. Like a few other minor hangs that day, this boulder was just another hazard of working a stone pile. Still, Wadey had had enough of this run. "Damn it," he whispered. "One hang too many and dead orsters. Let's get away from these coffins." We gathered our northern red buoy. The captain motored south, bypassing his white buoy and swiftly turning west. It soon became apparent where he was headed: the mother lode. We were going to invade Stanley's domain. Well, not exactly. Wadey left his southern white buoy where it was and began working a loop between it and Stanley's yellow mark. Technically, *Rebecca* was to the east of *Lady Katie*'s lay, but they now shared a common buoy. That yellow buoy marked a no-man's zone, and when turning, Wadey was at pains to avoid it.

"Hey, yer wind'ard," the captain called, as we turned in front of his own buoy, counting on Li'l Wade to know he meant the starboard dredge. Like clockwork, it bounced up and over the roller and into the drink, joining the inside dredge on the bottom. We lay a track toward no-man's land and Stanley, who was heading our way.

Notwithstanding the elaborate tricks of the power trade, mechanized dredging was easier than sailing. We had switched from a north-south course to an east-west one without having to reef a sail, trim a sheet, or adjust a centerboard. Retracing our path between the buoys was just a matter of keeping the wheel steady. No great talent required, and the crew had too little to do. (Wadey could have gotten by with four men today.) He was not above claiming an aesthetic. "It's more like plowing a mule than sailing. Thar's no magic to it."

As we pushed west, I estimated that we'd arrive at the yellow buoy exactly when Stanley would. But if both skipjacks turned ahead of the mark, as was the custom, a collision was unlikely. As it happened, *Rebecca* came around before *Lady Katie*, our captain giving the big man room. A hundred oysters spilled on deck, fifty from each dredge. Then, a curious thing happened. With Wadey's back to him, Stanley raised a pair of binoculars, scoping out our harvest. This was a common game of cat and mouse played out daily on oyster rocks across the Chesapeake Bay. Upon Stanley's rounding of the mark, with his stern now toward us, Wadey lifted his own field glasses and spied on *Lady Katie*. "Fifty, sixty bushels, if he's got one," Wadey said, in a pique of exasperation. "Twice our take. Well, we're back on 'em now."

The crew continued to cull, more busily with each pass, as the dredges cut into the reef. For every ten legal oysters, they threw another twenty undersized ones overboard. Dead shells, boxes, and mussels were also discarded. By the third run, the crew was harvesting seventy markets per dredge. "Eighty-two," Li'l Wade called back to the captain on a particularly good lick. Finally engaged, the men stopped hurling shell and stones at one another. They ceased chatting about women and baseball and began talking about the catch, as if the good luck had aged them. The adult was overtaking the child.

Rebecca and *Lady Katie* danced back and forth between the two far white buoys, turning again at Stanley's middle mark, their paths forming a figure eight. Their elegant curves were complementary, in step, a pas de deux. All they needed for beauty was a set of sails aloft. Both skipjacks gave ten or twenty yards' clearance to the yellow buoy. The Larrimores and Murphys seemed at ease. It was shaping up to be a beautiful day.

Then a bunch of things went wrong in short order.

First, human nature as it is, the crew slipped back into character. On the fifth run, *Rebecca* was slightly out of line and began catching large stones, the size of soccer balls (one hundred pounds apiece). The boys responded by rolling the mini-boulders onto each other's toes. Wadey, losing patience, raced forward to chastise the crew, and this delay placed *Rebecca* behind in her arc to skirt the yellow buoy. The captain was distracted for fifteen, twenty seconds, but that was enough. The starboard dredge was now on deck, and emptied, but Wadey could not release it again to create a pivot on the bottom because the port gummer wasn't yet aboard. A huge stone weighed down the bag. Try as they might, the Langford brothers could not lift the combined weight of the dredge and stone, some 450 pounds, over the roller. Jerry kept dropping the cage into the water, then winding it quickly, in an effort to use the momentum of the windlass to pull the full gummer aboard. *Swosh, kerplunk, splash*—the dredge entered the water like a belly flopper and sprayed the brothers each time it cut into a wave. On one of these dunks, *Rebecca* was turning a little too close to Stanley's mark. The dredge snagged the anchor line to Stanley's yellow buoy, which dipped underwater like the barrel on a shark. Wadey was on his feet instantly, boiling over at last, tearing a new exhaust pipe in each of the six crewmen.

"Jesus Christ," he said. "I'd rather have a bunch of women aboard than catch someone else's buoy."

If that was the worst of it, we could have unwound the buoy line and set it free, but when the men untangled the line and threw it overboard, the buoy didn't surface. The line had snared the rudder. Wadey cursed the crew, the buoy, and the moon. All hands on deck. I held Matt's legs as he dropped headfirst over the stern to extract it, but he couldn't get a purchase. Finally Hot Rod climbed into the yawl boat and clipped it with a boat hook; he pulled up hard, breaking the line. The weight dropped to the bottom, and Stanley's buoy popped up alongside the boat. Wadey tied thirty feet of new nylon cord to it and a piece of iron scrap at the other end and tossed it cleanly away from *Rebecca*. Without looking at Stanley, he returned to the helm, then blocked the crew's retreat.

He stared at them for a moment, then swiped his index finger across his forehead. "I'd rather be struck right here with a crowbar," he continued, "than steal from another captain. It's wrong and it's embarrassing. You boys were slow with that drudge." There was no protesting the weight of the dredge or the proximity of the boat to the buoy. One thing about sailing: It's never the captain's fault.

The mishap was an accident, but sometimes the theft of a buoy is premeditated and malicious. On the water, competition can give way to envy, and envy to caprice—a sudden turning on one's neighbor. Stealing another man's buoy, as an act of treachery, is second only to ramming another man's boat. One is the product of carelessness or capriciousness; the other is spawned by downright meanness.

Several years ago, on Todds Point, an oyster bar on the south side of the Choptank with stones much like Gum Thickets, the same two captains—Wade Murphy and Stanley Larrimore—were working off a single buoy. This time it was Wadey's. "Stanley was being greedy that day," said Wadey. "He tried to take over my spot. My boat, *Sigsbee*, couldn't keep up in the tide. *Lady Katie* had the advantage; she was the superior boat." Wadey got mad and ran broadside into *Lady Katie*, knocking the rollers loose. Stanley was hot, according to Wadey, and yelled at him, "I'll meet you at the dock!" Wadey, deferential to Stanley's size, wisely avoided him back at the harbor. He kept out of sight, and it never came to fists.

(Stanley had a slightly different version. He says there was only a light wind, and while *Lady Katie* was still able to drag two dredges, *Sigsbee* could drag only one. "I guess he got mad about it," Stanley has said, "and he rammed me. Hit me in light air, when he could get away with it. Didn't do any damage none.")

Back at the wheel, Wadey said, "I guess I've rammed everyone in this Bay at one time or another. Stanley, Pete. Even Emerson Todd, who owned the *Rebecca* before me. If anyone gets in my damn way today, I'll probably run over them, too."

On Gum Thickets, *Rebecca*'s catch was hard-won, and her blessings somewhat mixed. As Wadey would tell you, all bad things come in threes. The boys, the buoy, what next? But now he was prospecting the next best lay on Gum Thickets, second only to Stanley's claim. The plunder was getting better all the time.

"Nincty," yelled Li'l Wade.

"Ninety-four," echoed Jerry.

The other crewmen took their lead and bent to culling with greater care, counting as they went. Reckoning the totals, Wadey and I lapsed into a conversation about the tremendous reproductive prowess of the American oyster. *Crassostrea virginica* has a reputation for fecundity, aided by the ability to change sex, a strategy that has assisted colonization from the Gulf of St. Lawrence to the Gulf of Mexico. In a single spawning event, a male oyster may release over a billion sperm. Somewhat more modestly, a female over the course of a year (on average, three spawning events) may produce up to 300 million eggs. Not all are fertilized, and thanks to voracious predators (copepods to comb jellies), very few of the swimming larvae survive to adulthood, less than one in 10 million. In a perfect world, if all ova were fertilized and matured—settling as spat—and reproduced successfully for five generations, mathematicians predict the colony of resulting offspring would yield a volume one hundred times that of the earth.

"I've gotta wish," Wadey said. "I'd like to see, just for a day, the Bay drained, so we could count all the orster beds—thousands of 'em. I've been working all my life in the dark."

The captain clutched the winder cord to alert Jerry and L'il Wade to reel in the dredges, but they never got the chance. All of a sudden the skipjack shuddered, like an airplane hitting turbulence. With a jolt, *Rebecca* stopped dead in the water, then lumbered forward askew. The bow spun to the left, as if someone had dropped an anchor to port. Instantly we knew: The dredge had hooked a monstrous hang. Becket after becket snapped as more cable was yanked off the windlass. In the first twenty seconds, I counted three knots that broke, letting out eighteen feet of line, until the cable ran into a thick-roped becket tied sometime last week. Buried as it was, no one had thought to weaken it with a knife. It held tight while all of the other equipment on deck rattled like old squeaky bedsprings. The winders shook violently and threatened to be torn from the deck. The momentum of the boat kept us spinning to port. Within the first minute, as the boat came sideways, the steel cable wrapped itself around the vertical chock (which holds the roller). The chock, made of one-inch-thick steel, bent like rubber. The bolt holding the deck brace popped like a gun, sending the bolt head ricocheting toward the crew. The vertical roller jumped off its hinges and careened overboard, dropping to the bottom of the reef. The last becket broke with an audible *ping,* and the rest of the cable ran out like a fishing line that had hooked a marlin. It nearly cut Matt off at the kneecaps. The entire episode was over in a minute and a half. Remarkably, the dredge popped loose of its obstruction, and *Rebecca* floated free.

The captain ran forward to inspect the damage and took in the carnage with disbelief. All the steel forged to cushion the dredge cable had been mangled like a car wreck. The line now rested on wood and could not be reeled in. The port dredge dragged the bottom, with no clear way of getting it aboard.

Wadey ordered his son to take the helm, to slow the boat down. Li'l Wade marched aft, pleased with his new command, and straightened out *Rebecca* so the dredges were once again raking the bottom behind our stern. "Put her in idle," Wadey called back to him. Everything had happened so fast that the yawl boat, which had been pushing the skipjack, had been left running in low. Li'l Wade obliged. He depressed the throttle, which ran by a long cable to the yawl-boat engine. It was the first time he had been at the wheel all season. In a crisis the captain had turned toward one of the two crewmen he trusted most.

Then there were those he trusted least. As the crew gathered round the port chock, Wadey leaned forward in a threatening way and stared them down.

Matt spoke first. "It was a damn rock," he said.

"It wasn't Jerry," said Aaron, defending his brother, the winder man. "The drudge was already on the bottom."

"Must've been a boulder—a big mother one," said Matt.

Wadey was unmoved. "It wasn't the stone," he said, flushing red. "It was because you didn't cut the becket in half, damn it. Now you'll lose half a day's pay while we sail in early for repairs. It's yer money; it's my money. It's time you learned. Jerry is the only one getting it right." At that, Li'l Wade kicked a legal oyster back into the Bay.

Before departing, the captain had to jury-rig a substitute roller so he could wind in and store the port gummer. He remembered that the makeshift anchor for his white buoy was a metal sleeve, so he hauled this aboard and, inserting a steel rod, created a temporary roller. Once installed, the dredge came up quickly, bearing a few small stones—but no sign of the behemoth that had nearly torn *Rebecca* apart.

Heading south, we left Stanley, Daryl, Johnnie, and Ed behind. Bart and Bobby remained in the distance on Brick House. On the marine radio, Wadey called the attendant at Knapps Narrows Bridge, asking him to call Henry Reecer to get him working on two new vertical rollers. "I lost one and I have no spare," he said. "Tell Henry that." Maybe tomorrow, with two sets, Wadey could keep Murphy's Law at bay.

Li'l Wade sailed *Rebecca* the eight miles home.

SNOW WAS FALLING in big, wet flakes above Knapps Narrows. A freeze had been predicted for that evening, but at midafternoon the thermometer still hovered in the midthirties, so the oversize white crystals hit the piers, the pilings, and the water silently and anonymously, melting instantly. From a distance, the snowflakes landing on the wooden wharf at Harrison Oyster Company made wet paw prints, which then evaporated like a thousand little ghosts.

Harrison Oyster Company is the only shucking house on the island; during my time, it bought bushels from half the skipjack fleet, including Stanley and Wadey, who was now back at the helm. When relieved at the wheel, Li'l Wade had scowled, preferring the chance to steer *Rebecca* right to the dock. Just on the far side of the drawbridge, the landing at Harrison's required a deft maneuver, however: After passing under the span, Wadey had to jog right and back in, the equivalent of parallel parking. Li'l Wade wasn't up to it. Sonny Murphy stood on the wharf, catching our lines and guiding us in. He had recovered from his burns from the summer explosion of the *Levronson* and now orchestrated oyster buying for the company.

Once *Rebecca* was three or four feet away from the wharf, the crew jumped ashore and secured her with a series of bowlines, half hitches, and figure eights. Wadey and his son stayed aboard to fasten the boom. They swung the spar over the water on the port side to create clearance over the decks, above the four oyster piles. To hold it there, Li'l Wade propped a boat hook between the cabintop and the boom, like an airplane wing strut. We were now ready for the crane to off-load the oysters, a chore the captain ranked higher in priority than fixing the boat.

Each one of the crew, equipped with a shovel, stood at one of the four oyster mounds. Beginning with the starboard forward pile, the crane—actually a gaff-rigged boom, operated by Sonny—swung over the pile and dropped a bushel-size steel bucket. Li'l Wade then shoveled a bushel of oysters into the basket. From the countinghouse, a wooden shack charred by the *Levronson* fire, Sonny engaged the boom, and the steel bucket was lifted up and over the wharf to a conveyor belt, where a second man dumped the catch. The conveyor carried the first oysters noisily into a container truck, bound for another shucking house in Virginia. Meanwhile, on the port side, Aaron shoveled oysters into another steel tub. In this fashion, alternating between the starboard and port sides as the men shoveled, the boom slowly offloaded the oysters from the deck.

For every five buckets unloaded, Wadey called out, "One, two, three, four, tally." Each fifth tub was a tally, and the captain registered those sums in his head. In the countinghouse, Sonny also kept track of the tallies on his penciled pad, making four ticks and a slash mark for each series of five. The men would compare totals at the end. The system was efficient: With the crew keeping ahead of the boom, each seventy-five-pound tub was dumped in less than a minute. It appeared we had about forty minutes of "putting out" to be done. The operation looked like a road crew shoveling rock.

"One, two, three—," called Li'l Wade.

"—four, tally," joined Wadey, his voice overshadowing his son's. "That's twenty."

A little more than halfway through the process, with twenty-five loaded onto the truck, Sonny ordered a change. The next oysters were dumped into wheelbarrows, which were then rolled into the shucking house next door. To keep pace, two wheelbarrows ran back and forth. Island shuckers would assemble at tomorrow's dawn to pry open *Rebecca*'s harvest.

Li'l Wade lifted his eyes when a brown Buick rolled across the oystershell lot, next to the shucking house, and sounded its horn. He passed his shovel to Kenny and leapt ashore to greet his mother. Jackie had shown up to pay the crew for last week's landings on the Choptank River. This was typically a Friday affair, but since a waning breeze had left the crew at home, the Bay as "ca'm as a dish," the weekly disbursement had been bumped to Monday. Wadey now joined his wife and son, and grabbed a pad and pencil from the dashboard. "I'll pay off the crew by dividing the money up in front of them," he said. "Just like the Old Man did." Other captains who did their arithmetic in private held the risk of mistrust. "They won't question me," Wadey said, "because I have them check my math." Wadey sent his son to retrieve Jerry, the oldest deckhand, who would represent the crew in verifying the calculations. Li'l Wade appeared disappointed; he hurried off. The crew's split would be determined again by the formula of "shares" that dated back to the days of schooners and clipper ships.

"We sold 192 bushels over four days," Wadey said out loud for Jerry's benefit. "The price all last week was twenty-eight dollars. Friday was lower but we were in port. That's a total of $5,376 we grossed at the dock." He looked up at Jerry, then back at his scribbling. "Minus $100 for gas—diesel and gasoline—no food, gives us $5,276. The boat takes a third. That leaves $3,517 to divide seven ways, captain and crew." Wadey executed this by longhand. No calculator. Miss Pauline would've been proud.

"Jackie, the checks should be $502.47." Wadey turned to Jerry and said, "That okay with you?" Jerry said that it was, and Jackie made out the six checks, including one for her son. The unloading was just wrapping up; Kenny had started keeping count while Li'l Wade had fallen into silence.

"Tally. That makes forty-five even, Cap'n," Kenny called out.

"Okay, then," Wadey said, as he shut the car door and glanced at his wife. "I'm going to drink a beer. I need to calm down after a day with these children."

"They should work Saturdays," Jackie said to her husband. "They'd be too tired to fool around and their paychecks would be higher. Maybe orsters are scarce, but ya gotta at least try."

Just then, another skipjack, *Howard*, came through the narrows and rafted off *Rebecca*'s bow. Curiously, she had a blue cabin—the forbidden color. Captain Stan Daniels surveyed the last of our catch being carted away for shucking. He looked over our crew as they leaned against their shovels. "Boys," he said, "you all look tuckered out." Wadey stepped over to his friend—they were exactly the same age—and said, "We hit a hang and tore up the boat. And to think ye're the one with the blue paint! Lucky I had my boy along and he brought her home."

The snow was falling heavily now and muffled the captains' voices. Li'l Wade, out of earshot, stood on the bow by himself. He took a last drag on his cigarette and flicked it upward, over the narrows. A single, burning ember arched for a moment like one of those meteors that had beckoned the day, and then fell downward, extinguishing with a sizzle in the waters of the Chesapeake Bay.

6

To the Shucking House

A familiar melody filtered out of the oyster house into Main Street and took me by surprise. At 6:00 A.M. in mid-December, an hour before dawn, nobody expects to hear singing. Except perhaps on Tilghman's Island. Across the street at Gary's Store the old men listened and smiled. They remembered the glory days of Tilghman Packing Company, the huge canning operation now long gone, when spirituals danced across the island day and night. Today, the shuckers at the more modest Harrison Oyster Company were carrying on the spirit if not the exact words of that tradition. Christmas songs floated aloft this morning. The workers sang an accompaniment to holiday music trickling out of a radio inside:

I saw three ships come sailing in,
On Christmas Day, On Christmas Day.
I saw three ships come sailing in,
On Christmas Day in the morning.

But the radio provided only the background refrain. The shuckers' voices rose far above the orchestration. With lyrical sweetness

The Tilghman fleet sails out of the fog for a dredging day on the Choptank River. PHOTO BY CHRISTOPHER WHITE

top: Deckhands reel in the starboard dredge on the skipjack *City of Crisfield.*
PHOTO BY WILLIAM K. GEIGER

bottom: Crewmen on the skipjack *Rebecca T. Ruark* tend the jib.
PHOTO BY DAVE HARP

Captain Stanley Larrimore aboard the skipjack *Lady Katie*. PHOTO BY CHRISTOPHER WHITE

Captain Wade Murphy of the *Rebecca T. Ruark*. PHOTO BY CHRISTOPHER WHITE

top: Ruth Daniels, the only female deckhand in the fleet, emerges from the cabin of the skipjack *Howard*. PHOTO BY CHRISTOPHER WHITE

left: Captain Art Daniels spins the wheel on *City of Crisfield*. PHOTO BY CHRISTOPHER WHITE

above: Heading home. A skipjack is loaded with nearly seventy-five bushels of oysters, half her limit. PHOTO BY DAVE HARP

below: Breakfast time in the galley of the skipjack *Thomas Clyde*. PHOTO BY WILLIAM K. GEIGER

A classic skipjack on a starboard tack. Photo by Christopher White

above: Li'l Wade Murphy, first mate aboard the *Rebecca T. Ruark*, handling an oyster dredge. PHOTO BY CHRISTOPHER WHITE

below: Jimmy Daniels shucks an oyster aboard *City of Crisfield*. PHOTO BY CHRISTOPHER WHITE

The skipjacks *Kathryn* and *Howard*, in foreground, dredge early in the day.

their caroling poured out of the building into the falling snow. These were no amateurs. The group had clearly harmonized before—half in the white church, half in the black—and had practiced together in the oyster house for hours on end. The voices ranged from a deep baritone to a mezzo-soprano. I could only think that it was a requirement of the job—to be quick with an oyster knife and to sing on key.

On Christmas Day, on Christmas Day
On Christmas Day in the morning.

Stepping out of Gary's Store into the dark, I followed the music across the street to the shucking house, framed by tiny Christmas lights. I was curious to go inside but was stopped at the door, which creaked open, spilling a bright beam of light across my face. A man shouldered past me. Then I heard the gravelly voice of Pete Aerne, the oyster-house foreman, as he swept a flashlight across the yard. "Watch out, pussies!" he hollered. In the pitch black, while the singing continued, Pete began searching the grounds. He was shouting at the feral cats that patrolled the trucks and shell mounds on the south side of the property for mice. That summed up the oyster house: live oysters in one side, empty shells out the other, shuckers and shellfish and cats in between. Pete found three kittens, shooed them away to safety, and then tried to jump-start the motor to the old conveyor atop a flatbed truck. *Crunk-crunk-creee.* The gasoline motor kicked in. Shortly afterward, the conveyor belt carried pungent shells out of the shucking house, clinking onto the truck. The shuckers had taken the conveyor activity as a cue to begin.

Walking back to the side door, Pete focused his beam of light on a plywood sign hanging by hooks on the side of the building. In magic-marker scrawl it read: SHUCKING FRIDAY. This announcement had brought the workers out of their beds in the predawn hours. Of course, the dredgers had already left port an hour ago and were now halfway to the rock. It was a gusty day. Snow was falling at a sharp angle.

Pete invited me in, so I followed him through the side door, past a small office, down a hall lined with calendars of bikini-clad women, toward the shucking room. A chalkboard listed the retail prices for drop-in customers: thirty-five dollars a bushel, seven dollars a pint, and forty-two to forty-seven dollars a gallon, depending on the grade of oyster (standards, selects, or extra selects) sold that day. Opposite the sign, Pete informed me that today he would be filling holiday orders scheduled for shipping to the Midwest. To meet the demand, he had rounded up all the shuckers he could find.

We arrived at the shucking room, a long rectangle of cinder blocks dominated by an enormous shucking bench where a dozen workers now stood. It was a dark, gray room, lit by fluorescent lights. Windows were absent; only ventilation ports abutted the ceiling. The cement floor glistened from yesterday's mud and an aborted attempt to wash it down a drain. The place had the smell of wet gravel and seaweed and brine. In the middle of this gloom, a dozen people were singing about reindeer. Half the shuckers were male, half female. Half were white, half black. The men wore baseball caps, the women bandannas. The only common bond seemed to be their age: all but two older than fifty. A stack of oysters, impossibly high, stood in front of each shucker. Finishing the song, they laughed in concert. It could have been a Sunday picnic.

Next door, the oyster bin held about 150 bushels of oysters divided equally into two piles, like two heaps of poker chips. One comprised hand-tong oysters caught three days ago in the Chester River, and the other half were sail-dredge oysters caught yesterday in the open Bay by the *Rebecca*. Long and narrow, the hand-tong oysters seemed smaller, whereas the dredge oysters appeared oval and deeply cupped and huge. Wadey caught the latter on Old Rock, a hard-bottom bar on the western shore, opposite Tilghman's. Pete explained that the plan was to give the shuckers hand-tong oysters in the early morning and dredge oysters during the second half of their shift. "That'll make 'em happy right about when they start complaining," said Pete. "Drudge orsters yield more weight. And shuckers are paid by the pound." He added that the fastest shuckers can produce a gallon of fat oysters (about ten pounds) in an hour. At a dollar a pound, their wage can top ten dollars an hour, or eighty dollars a day.

Among the workers, I recognized a few by voice if not by sight. An infectious laugh erupted from Lula Mae Aerne, better known as Miss Luggi, a white-haired icon around the island. Pete Aerne married her twenty years ago and he was a forgiving boss. Her daughter, Donna, doubled the mirth and worked side by side her mother, both giggling incessantly. In summer, Luggi worked as a wholesale peeler dealer, the one who bought Wadey's peeler crabs when he was trotlining. In winter she shucked oysters. Luggi worked the center of the table and was considered a fine shucker, just shy of the three best.

As I made the rounds introducing myself, Luggi summed up the house atmosphere. "Shuckers are like a gaggle of geese," she said. "We quit each spring, but everyone comes back squawking in the fall. We can't help ourselves. It's one big family reunion." Far to the right of Luggi stood Woody King, the fastest shucker and at eighty-four the senior man. Woody was a short black gentleman, dapperly dressed. At the other end of the table, far to the left, Hobo Skinner, seventy, preened his mustache; he was nearly as fast and the "best" shucker because his skill was unsurpassed at quickly prying the mollusks whole and undamaged from their shells. Hobo towered above the others, a tall and regal-looking black man with salt-and-pepper short hair. To keep Hobo and Woody content, in the face of a dwindling quality and supply of oysters, these two shuckers received six dollars an hour over and above what they made per pound. Just to keep them around.

Scattered at the other stations, eight more shuckers tried to keep up with Hobo and Woody and Luggi. The largest family on hand today were the Lakes, a black family that had been shucking at Harrison's for twenty-five years. Jake and Mabel Lake had two grown children, Sheryl and Preston, working with them today. The four Lakes arranged themselves between Luggi and Woody. Donna stood on Luggi's left with a couple more Tilghman natives; next came Edith, one of Woody's girlfriends. Also on hand a familiar pair crouched next to the wall: Kenny and Hot Rod Welch, crew from the *Rebecca T. Ruark*. They had skipped out on dredging that day, leaving Wadey with only four crewmen in the driving snow. There would be hell to pay, but the Welch brothers figured it was worth it, that they'd make more money shucking than sail dredging in bad weather. Kenny was almost as fast as Hobo, and he stood next to the old man with his brother at his side.

Thus ranked the dirty dozen, their aprons already splattered with oyster mud, their wet rubber boots standing in gray water. Each shucker had an oyster knife or two, a whetstone, a black apron, a pair of gloves, and two one-gallon pails—one for standard oysters, the other for selects. Another three shuckers straggled in a little later and made it fifteen. This gave Pete Aerne hope that the oyster house could meet its quota for the day.

Each shucking day Pete wrote down a number on the chalk tally board, a target of what he thought could be shucked that day. Times were when Harrison's ran three shifts, shucking around the clock. Those days sported 2-million-bushel harvests on the Chesapeake. These days, with one-tenth that catch, they usually worked only one eight-hour shift in the early morning. Pete wrote down "130" on the blackboard. He expected to shuck 150 bushels, and since they were good quality, he anticipated getting a least seven pints of shucked oysters—seven-eighths of a gallon—out of every bushel, or a total of 130 gallons of shucked oysters by the end of the day, a high yield. This meant each shucker, on average, needed to shuck ten bushels, a little better than one an hour. That's over two hundred oysters, about four a minute. Woody, Hobo, Luggi, and Kenny would lead the way.

Pete's Christmas orders hung in the balance. This remained the last day to package and ship orders bound for both the Midwest and local markets—to arrive on grocery shelves a week before Christmas. To cover the territory, the oyster house sold oysters under two labels. Their B&L Brand went to the Ohio and Mississippi watersheds while Harrison Brand was distributed close to home, in the Mid-Atlantic.

A short hiatus had broken into laughter and song. "Jingle Bells" floated out of the radio and everyone joined in. It was contagious. I found myself humming, though not quite on key. The shucking also fell into a rhythm as each worker focused on the task at hand—breaking a fragile delicacy out of a rock. Shucking an oyster is the equivalent of opening a raw egg with a paring knife and scooping it out whole without breaking the yolk. I watched in fascination as Woody opened each oyster in one motion, tossing the shells one way and the naked oyster the other, into the pail. And he was fast, making it difficult to follow the sequence. Every few seconds he pried open another shell and a white succulent morsel emerged.

Luggi, a petite woman, stood on a wooden pallet to reach the height of the bench. She glanced sideways at me and broke the silence, or rather the singing. "Woody is the fastest shucker there is," she said, "but I'm prettier than he is." She laughed through a half-toothless grin. "Woody rushes hisself. He wants to stick his knife in too soon and pull it out too fast. So I hear." This brought roars of laughter up and down the shucking table. Luggi had scored a couple of points and the low shucking-house humor had begun. "Women always talking," said Woody, "usually about drudgers or us. Of course, we eat more orsters—makes you love longer—so ladies prefer a shucker." He smiled and his gold tooth caught the first dawn light coming through the high portholes.

Woody King has been shucking each winter at Harrison Oyster Company since it opened forty years ago. For all those years he has been the fastest shucker in the house. He had an advantage—he was left-handed, which, he claimed, shaved the time for shucking an oyster by a few milliseconds. The adductor muscle—or "heart" as it's called by shuckers—that holds the shell closed is easier to access for a southpaw, or so Woody insisted. Why this would be so was a mystery to me.

It took me several minutes of watching Woody's technique to break it down into a series of five lightning-quick moves that merged into one seamless motion. Woody wore two gloves: a black rubber glove on his right hand as protection against the knife held in his left hand, which was covered only by a cloth glove, now muddy and soaking wet. He held the oyster in this right glove with the cupped (bottom) side down and the flatter top shell upward. With the knife in his left hand he stabbed into the left side of the bill (just down from the hinge) until he caught the opening and popped it open. Then the blade was inserted fully and moved sideways, severing the heart. As soon as the heart was cut, he turned the oyster over so that the top shell was now in his right palm. The oyster liquor drained into the pail. He then sliced through the heart again, severing it from the top shell. The oyster was now loose inside. He pinched it between his left forefinger and the knife blade and tossed it into the gallon pail. This all happened in about four seconds. (I timed him.)

"They say I'm the fastest," said Woody, "but I know I'm not the best. Hobo shucks a pertier orster than I do. Never cuts 'em up. I bleed the orster sometimes. But I don't have time to shuck too perty an orster." He laughed. "I have to make a hundred dollars a day, *every day*. Oh Lord, the ladies cost me money. Oh yes, they do!"

Woody worked the middle deck of dredge boats as early as the 1930s, mostly out of Deal Island. He dredged on *Maggie Lee* with Clifton Webster, Art Daniel's father-in-law, and on *Mamie Mister* with Jesse Thomas. After moving from Guinea Neck on the southern Eastern Shore to Bellevue, a black town near Oxford, he crewed for Tilghman captains including Stanley Larrimore on *Lady Katie* and Ellis "Wild Bill" Berridge on the bugeye *Thomas L. Freeman.* "They were all hard rollers, hard-driving men," said Woody. "They had to be. Times were tough and they had children to feed. In them days we only got a couple of dollars for a booshel of orsters. There was no limit, though. Just fill up your boat. And thar was plenty of orsters to catch. It was nothing to catch 250 booshel in a day." Woody flipped another oyster into the pail.

"We worked in good weather and bad," he continued. "Captain Jesse would stay out in a gale no matter what. One day he had full sail in a nor'easter and wouldn't reef 'em. We were catching too many. Blew the sails right off the mast. Three hundred booshel aboard and the buy boat had to come to us and tow her in. Oh man, he was a hard roller. My, yes."

Woody quit dredging ten years ago. He had worked the middle deck of *Minnie V*, captained by Johnnie Motovidilak for Buddy Harrison Sr., up until the late 1980s. Until he was seventy-two. Now he spent his winters shucking but rarely had the water far from his mind.

"It's blowing thirty miles out thar today," said Woody. "I can hear it. Oh man, I can smell it." He chuckled. "Boiling through the narrows, too."

"We had gusts to forty yesterday," Kenny said to him. "We weren't catching anything, but Wadey wouldn't come in."

"He's a Murphy," said Woody. "The whole family's hard rollers. He'll lose a mast rather than be the first one in. Oh, man. Out there pushing the edge. Each day. *Every day.*"

Woody grabbed another hand-tong oyster and shucked it in record time. "These are perty but not fat. I'm ready for them drudge orsters. I'll take the catch off a drudge boat any day. Bring 'em on. Oh Lordy, yes."

Another Christmas carol—"Silent Night"—now piped out of the transistor radio, its raspy sound improved by the Tilghman chorus. As Luggi sang, she surreptitiously reached over to Preston Lake's pail and dropped three small stones in it. He didn't notice. Her daughter smiled, mischief in her eyes.

Once the song finished, someone turned the channel to the country-western station and Gene Autry filled the room: "Back in the Saddle Again." No one sang along. On Tilghman's, it would have been like interrupting the pope. The oyster-house repertoire weighed toward the South and West. It always had.

HARRISON OYSTER COMPANY was created in 1967 by Buddy Harrison Sr. to eliminate one level of middleman between waterman and the consumer. Buddy's father, Levin Harrison Jr., had operated a successful buy boat operation, purchasing oysters daily from dredgers and tongers out on the rock. His buy boats, *Nora W.* and *Levin F. Harrison*, moored in Black Walnut Cove to buy from dredgers; other buy boats serviced tongers. But Levin resold his oysters each day to Tilghman Packing Company, the largest of four packing houses then on the island, at a small markup. He often made less than fifty cents per bushel. Young Buddy had a better idea. By creating a fifth packing house and by sending "buy trucks" around the Bay to purchase oysters, Buddy cut the family into more profits. Today, Harrison Oyster Company is the third largest shucking house in Maryland and the only one left on the island.

The building of the oyster house was well-timed. For eight years—until MSX hit the mid-Bay—they had plenty of oysters. Recently, however, less than half of the bushels they buy from watermen are still shucked on site. The balance is trucked to Virginia for shucking, where labor is cheaper. Bevans Oyster Company and Daiger Brothers, both in Northern Neck, Virginia, essentially control the oyster business in the Chesapeake region now. Today, they shuck more than 60 percent of Maryland's oysters.

With Buddy's full attention now focused on the Chesapeake House's hotel and restaurant and on Harrison's Sportfishing Center, his son Bud (Levin Harrison IV) ran the day-to-day operations of the oyster house. Bud, forty, started with the company at age twelve, shoveling oysters after school. After college—Bud says "oyster" rather than "orster"—he began to share the responsibilities of running the shucking operations. Under his direction, he has seen the business move from only shucked oysters to a diverse line of products including retail pints and the "box trade"—oysters sold in the shell to restaurants for serving on the half shell. He bought over 15,000 bushels from watermen that previous year, shucking nearly 7,500 with the help of the oyster-house crew.

Even with that traffic, Woody can't get enough. He moonlights, shucking oysters for the raw bar at the Chesapeake House on Friday nights when an oyster buffet is served. Oysters cooked seven ways: oyster fritters, scalloped oysters, oysters Chesapeake (with crabmeat and bacon), oyster creole, sautéed oysters, oyster stew, and oysters on the half shell, courtesy of Woody. He has near-perfect technique and keeps his oyster knife sharp. The disconcerting thing is that he often closes his eyes while shucking—for practice. "You never know," he said. "The lights might just go out again. I was shucking orsters at the Tidewater Inn, in Easton, and the electricity went off for two hours. I kept shucking and the customers kept coming up to the raw bar with candlelight. 'Keep 'em coming,' is what they said. And that's just what I did." Woody's eyes were open now. He was shucking for speed not tips and he was shouting down the length of the table to Hobo—a running repartee.

"Faster now, Hobo, just a li'l faster."

"You bleeding those orsters again, Woody?"

"I ain't got time to shuck 'em too perty. If you were faster you'd know what I mean. Or more popular. Hobo, you need to get more popular."

"I shuck 'em so fast you can't even see it."

"And the ladies can't even feel it." This brings the house down again. Laughter and hoots and whistles. Something about oysters brings out the lewd innuendo. Talking is perhaps the greater aphrodisiac, but eating oysters has its advocates.

Hobo's shucking technique was altogether different from Woody's. For starters, Hobo was right-handed, a reputed disadvantage, but he made up for it with style. Hobo was smartly dressed today, wearing a wool racing cap and a red and blue checkered shirt. He looked more ready for dancing than shucking. From the oyster pile to his left, Hobo selected an oyster and, with his left hand, held it against a "shucking board"—a small wedge-shaped piece of oak—the cupped shell down and flat shell up. With the short thin blade in his right hand, he stabbed the front of the bill (directly opposite the hinge), found the crack between the shells, and jiggled the knife from side-to-side. The shell opened slightly. Next he pushed the knife down to the base of the heart and sliced it cleanly from the bottom shell. Then he slid the knife blade around to the left, prying the shell fully open to the hinge. Flipping the oyster over, upside down, in his left hand, he pushed the gills out of the way and cut the heart from the top shell, very cleanly, very close to the shell. The top and bottom of the muscle were now severed, leaving purple scars on the shells. The oyster was loose. With the knife and a forefinger he dropped the oyster into a pail.

The difference between Hobo and Woody was a murder of quality. With Hobo there was no meat left in the discarded shells and the oyster was shucked whole, unmarred and unbleeding. It kept its shape and its volume. His pails were filled by fewer, bigger oysters. Hobo opened an oyster from the front, Woody from the side—quicker but not as clean. Each shucker had perfected his technique over many years into a refined art.

"I've done it since I was nine or ten," Hobo said. "You get the hang of it. The secret is to have a short knife and go right for the heart. If the knife's too long, you'll cut the orster."

Hobo set three knives next to him along with a whetstone to keep them honed. They sat right next to his coffee thermos, his cigarettes and lighter, and his blue notebook and pencil, at the ready to keep track of his tallies. "Your knife has to stay sharp," he said again. "It has to break through shell and then cut through that heart cleanly. A dull knife will ruin an orster."

Every hour or so, the shuckers took their gallon pails to the weighing station, a window between the shucking and "skimming" rooms, the latter the place where oysters were cleaned. Pete weighed each pail of oysters on a scale and tallied the measures on a chalkboard next to each shucker's name. The pails ranged between eight and eleven pounds per gallon, a good weight. Some pails were not completely full. Also, the standard pails were slightly heavier than the selects because the smaller oysters packed tighter and there were more of them. There are four (sometimes five) grades of oysters: standards, selects, extra selects, and counts (sometimes "extra counts"). The grading is done by eye, and the larger oysters fetch a higher price. When Hobo weighed in, his two pails had a combined weight of almost twenty-two pounds—one just over eleven pounds, the other just under.

"Perty orsters," Pete said to Hobo, and Hobo smiled and walked back to his station. "When I have a special order, I set aside Hobo's selects. Tha're always perfect."

Next up at the scale came Preston. He dumped his standards into the skimmer and to his surprise several stones fell out of the bucket. "I thought they was too heavy," he said to Pete. Behind him in the shucking room, Donna and Luggi had a good laugh.

Nearly everyone had made three or four trips to the scales by the time a classic tune came over the radio:

Happy trails to you
Until we meet again.

The song was greeted by whooping and hollering. Like clockwork every day at 10:00 A.M. the country-western station played "Happy Trails," sung by Roy Rogers to the delight of the oyster-house crew. After four hours of shucking, the song marked the worker's midday break. Everyone joined in as they took off their gloves and untied their aprons to sing along. Between refrains nearly a dozen cigarettes were lit and inhaled deeply. The acrid smell of smoke mixed with the other scents of the oyster house—the sweet smell of fresh oysters, the pungent scent of bent mussels cracked open, and the rank odor of old mud at low tide. The shuckers had fifteen minutes to stretch their legs.

During the break, Pete tended the skimmer and evaluated the progress toward his daily quota. Over the first four hours, sixty pails had been turned over for cleaning. Another fifteen pails were still being filled on the shucking bench, pails that the workers had not yet topped off by break time. So, at midshift, he was pretty close to half of today's quota of 130 gallons. Pete was pleased. "We're shucking well today," he said in his sandpaper voice. "And we should pick up some speed later this morning—working on them drudge orsters."

The shuckers had now worked their way through seventy-five bushels of hand-tong oysters. Time to switch harvests. While the shuckers relaxed, Will, a house laborer, shoveled dredge oysters onto a steel dolly to load up the fifteen stations at the shucking bench. The oysters appeared bigger, and the shuckers smiled through the cigarettes dangling from their lips. "Bring 'em on, Will," said Woody. "Oh Lordy, yes."

Hobo used the break to sharpen his oyster knife. Woody saw this and looked at his own five knives stuck in the wood at his station and said, "I'll sell you a knife, Hobo. Sharper than any you got."

"I don't need no knife," Hobo answered. "Yours is too long anyway."

"That's right." Everyone laughed along with Woody. He was too quick for Hobo.

About this time Sonny Murphy entered the oyster house and saw Pete and me talking. "Why don't you put him to work?" he said. Pete agreed with a grin that would be a good idea. He handed me an apron, some gloves, a knife, and a wooden block, and pointed to a stall between Hobo and Kenny for me to begin. Like my first day dredging, I had no idea what I was getting into. It's one thing to watch, quite another to roll up your sleeves and meet a quota.

"Don't cut yourself," Pete said. "The only first aid I know is amputation." Like Woody, I put a white cotton glove on my left hand and a black rubber glove on my right.

"Good Gawd Almighty, ye're left-handed," Kenny said, returning to work, his eyes opening wide in envy. "Ye're gonna beat me. Either man is faster to the heart if he's a southpaw. The most right-handers can do is go in from the bill. I better not coach you any." He smiled his goofy smile. Kenny had no worries actually. He ranked third fastest in the room, just shy of Woody and Hobo and just ahead of Luggi. I was not in their league.

Slow was one word for my shucking style. The other would be "careless." No matter how hard I tried to cut the heart carefully without disturbing the oyster, I repeatedly sliced the body. My knife drove in too far, cutting the meat and the liver. Seeing this, Kenny agreed to give me some tips for clean shucking. "Go in from the side. Yeah, like that. Stab it. Then insert the knife, right, but only half an inch, and jiggle. Wiggle some more and she pops open. Then move the knife tip sharply down and to the left to cut the heart from the bottom shell. Never up. Then turn the orster over and cut it free. Simple really." Simple for him, I thought.

It took me a bushel of oysters to get the hang of it. There were so many steps to master. For me, the trickiest part was opening the shells just enough to slip the blade inside and cut the heart muscle but not too much to tear the oyster. (I broke an oyster knife just finding the opening of one oyster, and Pete scolded me.) Another challenge was simply identifying the top from the bottom shell. Though one is typically flatter and one more cupped, it isn't always so. Woody's trick was to feel it. The bottom side is usually more coarse, the shell rougher. These signs helped Woody in the dark and when he closed his eyes to practice. "Sometimes the orster'll fool you," he said. "I've been fooled plenty." The dredge oysters were indeed flat on top and easier to open. Still I stabbed my right hand several times until my black glove resembled a pincushion.

My select pail filled steadily; most of the dredge oysters were large and fat, a healthy white color. Pete announced that most of these were a grade higher, the size of extra selects, so he handed out a third pail to all the shuckers. The clinking of pails was greeted by cheers and cat whistles. Nobody loves a fat oyster like a shucker.

After an hour my pail was about half full. Other shuckers had weighed in their extra selects by then. I was going at half their pace, but I was falling into a rhythm and my accuracy had improved. Instead of tearing the oysters, I was shucking them more cleanly. I can't say my oysters were pretty but they were satisfactory. As an experiment I tried shucking a few like a right-hander and discovered it did indeed take longer to go in from the front of the bill. At least for me. I was happy to think I had at least one talent in common with Woody. Sinisterness. The other was the state of my clothes. Mud caked my sleeves to the elbow, and my pants and boots were covered with slime.

My own pail seemed to fill more slowly the closer it got to the top. Donna stepped past her mother and came to inspect my work. "Half the work is filling the pail," she said, "and the other half is topping it off. What you got is a hole in the bottom of your bucket. That happens to me sometimes." She smiled. Not only the oysters but the liquor and shell fragments went into the pail—to be cleaned later through the skimming process. In the meantime, I was thankful the debris helped to fill my pail. I had about twenty oysters left to go and two hours were nearly up. My left hand ached. I finished just as the noon siren sounded at the firehouse, the last to weigh-in: nine pounds in two hours. I had made four and a half dollars an hour, far behind the ranks.

NOON. PETE TURNED off the conveyor, signaling to the shuckers that it was lunchtime. The last shells of the morning were dumped onto the flatbed truck: *chink, chink, chink.* This "fresh shell" would be replanted on some oyster bars to serve as cultch, substrate for the attachment of spat. For six hours the conveyor had transported fresh shell to the truck where now over a hundred bushels' worth had accumulated in a six-foot-high pile. By day's end, rats would inhabit the pile, feasting on the shreds of oyster meat that still clung to the shells. And stray cats would patrol the oyster piles, taking care of the rats and mice. Such was the ecology of an oyster pile. Pete counted on his "pussies" to keep the balance.

The shuckers took off their muddy aprons and washed their hands in the sinks at the end of the shucking room. Miss Luggi offered me half a sandwich and a cupcake from her lunch box. I thanked her and devoured them. Nothing makes you hungrier than seeing several thousand oysters on the half shell flash before your eyes.

In the office Bud Harrison spoke on the telephone at a wooden desk. He was telling Daiger Brothers Seafood (Montross, Virginia) that he expected over 250 bushels of oysters today from his six dredge boats. They should send a truck to pick them up. Over Saturday and Sunday those bushels would be shucked in Virginia where shucking ran seven days a week. Bud wouldn't begin shucking again at his own oyster house until Tuesday, for Harrison Brand local orders. This weekend, Tilghman's only shucking house would be shut down. But today Bud was busy handing out money. The tongers had been stopping by all morning to get paid for the week's catch. Bud carried a roll of several thousand dollars in his pocket to pay off watermen. And now Captain Pete Sweitzer walked in. He had sailed the skipjack *Hilda Willing* back to Dogwood Cove early since the wind had persisted, the strong breeze turning into a raging gale. He was looking to settle up with Bud. Pete swept the snow off his hat and kicked his boots free of ice. Nodding to Bud, he flashed "fifty-two" with his right hand, and Bud began to count out the money.

"I'm done for the day," said Pete, the oldest dredge-boat captain on Tilghman's Island. "It's blowing smoke right off the water."

"The others coming in?" Bud asked.

"That young bunch's still out thar—you bet they are—drudging in a gale. Sailing too fast. The Gold Dust twins—Frank and Freddie—are grinding down another reef, looking for the big score. Greedy—that's all thar is to it. The boats can't take it and the or-sters sure as hell can't take it. Too much pressure on 'em drudging *every day* like that—regardless of the weather."

Bud nodded in agreement and handed him his money. Pete Sweitzer slapped the bills into the palm of his left hand. "That's all the money I need—one-third for the boat and some for me. But I'm from another generation. We're the last of the Mohicans. We're all dying out." Without another word he turned and walked out of the oyster house into the driving snow.

AFTER LUNCH, PETE Aerne had to finish cleaning and packing all of the day's shucked oysters in time for the shipping truck, due at four. So, while the shuckers put in their last two hours, Pete operated the skimmer and adjacent "blowers" at full capacity.

The skimming cycle commenced with each gallon pail that was brought to the weighing station. After weighing, Pete poured the oysters into the washbasin of the skimmer, essentially a huge colander welded and sunk into a stainless steel table. Here Pete washed the oysters with water from a jet-spray nozzle and drained them. He then scooped the oysters and dumped them into one of the two blower tanks—one for standards and one for selects. These vats, equipped with water jets like a jacuzzi, held two hundred gallons of water and thirty gallons of oysters. He mixed the oysters in this broth with a metal paddle and turned the blowers on. The vat swirled like a hot tub. Immediately, the lighter dirt, mud, and bacteria frothed to the surface. The heavier silt and shell fragments settled to the bottom. The oysters churned and turned over in the vat as if boiling, the salt from the oysters making suds. Cleaning the shellfish of grit and microbes took about five minutes. The trick, said Pete, was to blow them long enough to clean them but not too long or else the oysters would be purged of salt. (Salt gives Chesapeake oysters their distinctive taste.) Afterward, Pete scooped the oysters with a sieve into a second skimmer. From here, later, he would pack the B&L Brand plastic gallons.

"By the time we ship these orsters," Pete said, "tha're clean, clean as any other seafood you can buy. In a refrigerator they'll keep for two weeks."

The froth and water from the blowers overflowed onto the floor and traveled, by a series of aqueducts, toward the drains at the center of the building. Flecks and chips and grit from the shucked oysters were left behind on the floor, and these had the deep briny smell (and feel underfoot) of a wet beach. But above this residue was another scent—the tangy sweet odor of raw oysters. "I love the smell of orsters," Donna said, leaning against the skimming room door. "Makes me think of orster pie." She turned to face Pete and me. "Have you ever had a home-baked pie?" Pete said he hadn't, but would love some. Donna laughed. "Not for you, Pete. You've had plenty. I'm asking our newest shucker here." No, not yet, I said.

Donna said she'd give me her mother's recipe—basically a baked pot pie, steaming hot and bubbling over with oysters and vegetables. "Now, that's eating," she said.

Miss Luggi stepped up and said there was no reason to give me the recipe; she would bake it for me herself. "Stop by on Christmas and I'll give you one baked in a pan. All you have to do is reheat it." She asked Pete to set aside a couple of pints of Hobo's selects.

Discerning cooks always pick their grade of oysters according to what a recipe calls for. Not all oysters are equal. Baked recipes and oyster fritters call for extra selects or counts, the largest oysters that can stand up to a knife and fork. Oyster pie is best with selects—meaty but still possible to be eaten whole. Standards are reserved for oyster stew and oyster stuffing where oysters are not the dominant ingredients. Meanwhile, a four-to-five-inch dredge oyster—an extra count—produces a meal in itself.

Since shuckers are paid by the pound, they always prefer extra selects and counts over standards. It takes fewer of these oysters to fill up a pail or make a pound, while each and any oyster shell takes about the same time to open regardless of whether it holds a small oyster or a count. And you can't always tell from the shell. Approximately 250 standard oysters will fill a gallon, while it takes only 225 selects and 180 extra selects to do the same. Counts, which take 140 or 150 to fill a gallon, are nearly double the size of standards. When oysters from several boats are bought, Bud will do a sample shucking to see whose oysters are the best grade. The dredgers with the highest-quality catch may receive a tip: one or two dollars a bushel. When a good load comes in from a reef, word gets out. Like last week when Wadey caught 130 bushels of prime oysters on Old Rock, topping Stanley's strike, and half the fleet followed him there.

Pete concentrated on "canning" the oysters now. After cleaning the oysters in the blower, he sorted them in the skimmer and poured the strained oysters into gallon plastic buckets, which have replaced tin cans in the industry. He filled them about seven-eighths full, just below the top. From the skimmer he then added about a pint of the water-and-oyster-liquor mixture to the gallon bucket and closed it with a plastic lid. The gallon bucket read "B&L Brand Oysters: Standards," now worth forty-two dollars retail and ready for the Midwest.

During transport the live oysters will swell up with the water and fill fully the volume of the bucket. To take advantage of this, some packers are known to add two pints of water to a three-quarters filled bucket, but this usually backfires. "Orsters drink up the water going to market," said Pete, "but lose it when cooking. This disappoints the customer. We keep it to a pint or less."

The retail prices—forty-two dollars per gallon for standards, forty-four dollars for selects, and forty-seven dollars for extra selects—represent a 30 percent markup from wholesale. Margins are tight in the oyster trade. At wholesale—about thirty-three to thirty-six dollars per gallon—the oyster house only makes two or five dollars per gallon. Both produce and labor are expensive. To the dockside price paid to watermen (twenty-four dollars per bushel on average that day), add seven dollars for shucking. When overhead is also subtracted from the gallon price, little revenue accrues to the oyster house. Though squeezed, packers keep their prices as low as possible so as not to price their oysters out of the market. If they can make two dollars on a bushel or a gallon, they're doing well. And they must shuck a high-yield oyster to achieve this.

Profitability and market share have been shifting recently. Not surprisingly, retail sales, rather than wholesale, are more and more responsible for keeping the shucking houses afloat. And oysters are no longer cheap. They rank as a luxury item with steep prices that are susceptible to the whims of the economy. Carrying two brands helps the oyster house weather those economic tides, and their shift in relative dominance reflects the changing times. B&L Brand, which is a label actually controlled by another house, by Bivalve

Oyster Packing Company in Mt. Vernon, Maryland, used to dominate Buddy's gallon sales. Harrison packs the label for Bivalve. Originally, nearly 90 percent of Buddy's oysters were packed under that label and shipped to the Midwest like those shucked today. Now only 60 percent are. The other 40 percent are shipped locally under their own label: Harrison Brand. "It's smart to keep two labels," said Buddy. "When anybody complains about one brand, we ship them the other and they're always pleased with the change. Funny thing is, it's the exact same oysters."

Of course, Buddy makes a better margin on his own brand than by packing for someone else. But it is the boom in the pint trade that has really increased the market share of Harrison Brand. Harrison pints (seven dollars for standards; eight dollars for selects) are sold regionally in grocery stores, mostly for holiday cooking. There's a middleman here, too. Harrison sells first to a distributor, E. Goodwin & Sons, in Jessup, Maryland, who then sells to grocery stores such as Giant Supermarket. People all over the Mid-Atlantic buy and eat Harrison Brand oysters. When shopping, I buy Harrison selects, knowing they're more likely to be dredge oysters. If oysters ever come back strong, Buddy says he might create a label just for dredge oysters, with a skipjack on it. It couldn't come too soon.

Beyond pint sales, the saving grace for the oyster business of late has been the box trade—selling oysters whole to restaurants for serving on the half shell. This represents 30 percent of Harrison's business. (Nationally, 45 percent of the country's harvest is sold through the raw bar trade.) There are only minor labor costs, no shucking or skimming, and a nice margin—eight to ten dollars per box. Packing is simple: about four-fifths of a bushel is cleaned and arranged in a cardboard box and sold for thirty to thirty-five dollars (twenty-eight dollars wholesale). And appetites have been insatiable at the raw bar. Harrison's half shells appear on appetizer menus at Kinkead's on Pennsylvannia Avenue, Washington, D.C., at Hogate's on the Potomac Waterfront, at Mr. Bill's Quarterdeck in York, Pennsylvania, at McGarvey's in Annapolis, and at Harrison's Pier 5 in Baltimore, typically for a dollar a piece. Across the Baltimore Inner Harbor at Phillips Restaurant, oysters on the half shell sell for $9.99 a half dozen. They are hand-tong oysters mostly—long and thin and flat. Only at Faidly's Raw Bar in Lexington Market (Baltimore) are you certain to get a dredge oyster. They reach Faidly's from Harrison via Bellevue Seafood in Oxford, Maryland. They sell "primes," a fat cupped oyster for one dollar a piece, shucked cleanly by an ancient gentleman who looks a lot like Hobo, and served with lemon and cocktail sauce laced with horseradish. None better. With an average bushel containing more than two hundred oysters, the profit on a raw bar is a healthy one.

Formerly, Chesapeake oysters provided over 50 percent of the national oyster harvest. Their succulent meat was in high demand for its unsurpassed flavor, and stocks were abundant. In 2005, however, due to that tangled mix of overharvesting and disease, the Maryland share dropped below 750,000 pounds of oyster meat, or 2.1 percent of the 35-million-pound national catch. As of 2006, the entire Atlantic tallied only a 3 percent share, dead last among the four regional harvests, which include the Gulf States (58 percent), Pacific (35 percent), and Northeast (4 percent). Louisiana is the leading oyster-producing state now, with 12 million pounds last year—34 percent of the national harvest. In Louisiana, seafood packers pay ten dollars for a bushel dockside, and shucking is cheaper (sixty cents per pound). The Chesapeake can't compete. Even with a superior product, it is fast slipping toward last place in the national oyster industry, valued last year at $120 million. These days, Maryland produces less than $5 million dockside, and that's from an expensive oyster. "What we need," said Buddy, "is a cheaper oyster, a more reliable oyster, and more of them."

Historically, the Chesapeake oyster was more than secure. It was solid as a rock. In the 1880s when oyster harvests topped 15 million bushels and through the 1930s, shucked oysters were shipped in barrels by train to Philadelphia, New York, and Chicago for distribution to every major town in the East and Midwest. Baltimore had over fifty oyster shanties along its wharves and hundreds of dredge boats in its harbor. But it has been downhill ever since: Fewer oysters have been caught each decade. Now the catch is only one to two percent of the boom years in the 1880s. And markets have dried up along the way. Boxcars no longer carry oysters to New York and Boston. National seafood packers have cut oysters from their product lines. At the peak of recent oyster supplies in the 1970s, Harrison sold whole oysters to Campbell Soup Company, which produced an oyster stew. But as the market became less stable (and prices climbed), Campbell's dropped oysters from their product line as well.

The seasonal nature of oyster sales and consumption hasn't changed, however. Oysters are traditionally eaten during the R months—September through April. This convention stems from two things: biology and health. The oyster is watery and less meaty during the summer when the oyster's gonads enlarge and spawning begins. But they are perfectly edible. (Recently, the Pacific oyster farms have created a year-round market on the West Coast.) And hygiene is no longer a problem. But before the days of refrigeration, it was difficult to keep oysters fresh during the warmer months, and the demand for oysters dropped off as winter gave way to spring. Today, the East Coast market has remained a seasonal one by tradition more than anything else. "It has one great advantage," said Buddy. "It gives the oyster beds a rest."

The onslaught from oyster disease presents the most vexing problem keeping the dependability and supply of oysters low. MSX can waste the tissues of an oyster, turning a count into a standard or worse. While these oysters are still edible, they are watery, flat in taste, and shuck out poorly. It takes many more of these tainted oysters to fill a pail. The combination of poor oyster quality and low abundance is forcing shucking houses to close down all over the Eastern Shore. Bud was realistic about his chances that day. "We can't hold on much longer," he said. "MSX is killing the industry. And if we're forced to close down, even for a few months, our labor will disappear."

Oystermen have their complaints, too, mostly about prices. As demand slows down after Christmas, the dockside price might be cut by a third, yet retail prices remain high. The watermen scream price-fixing. If the buyers reduce the bushel price paid to the watermen, so the thinking goes, then the price should come down for the consumer. But if the retail price stays robust, then so, too, should the dockside value. Since it doesn't, watermen figure buyers are pocketing the difference. Buyers respond by claiming they're caught in the middle and barely make a profit as it is. The consumer market, so their own logic runs, can't bear higher retail prices. And so buyers and watermen must keep their prices low. That's the argument, but dredgers don't buy it. Such is the distrust among keepers and thieves.

CLOSE TO 2:00 P.M. the last song of the day ignited the voices of the shucking bench. And the oyster house filled again with holiday spirit—though embellishing a bit on the lyrics.

> *Joy to the world! The Lord has come:*
> *Let earth receive her king.*
> *. . . And heav'n and nature sing,*
> *'Til the quitting bells ring . . .*

Everyone joined in. Woody, Hobo, Luggi, Donna, Kenny, and the Lakes. Even Pete was swept away by the tide. Luggi seemed to be right: It was one big family. And nothing brought them together like singing. And ad-libbing.

Joy to the world! Payday has come . . .
. . . Let earth receive her king . . .

Pete turned off the conveyor—the closing bell—and everyone weighed in. Woody had three full pails. So did Hobo. Most of the others had selects and extra selects from the afternoon's dredge oysters and a couple of pints of standards. Sheryl Lake weighed in at fifteen pounds, 50 percent too heavy. She was taken aback until she poured out three large stones. Donna and Luggi smiled in innocence.

In his chicken scratch Pete marked the weights on the chalkboard and tallied the totals for the day. There was quite a spread, ranging from Sheryl's 50.25 pounds (and dollars) to Woody's 92.30 pounds, beyond his expectations. Hobo had 78.5 pounds, coming in second. Luggi, at 72.8 pounds, nearly her own weight, was a close third—besting Kenny. Fifteen shuckers had produced 1,035 pounds from 150 bushels, just over half a ton of oyster meat in eight hours.

Pete was pleased; his quota had been surpassed. Out of the skimmers, he had packed 148 gallons, approximately 130 gallons of meat plus a pint of water to top off the 148 buckets. He had sixty-four standards, thirty-eight selects, and forty-six extra selects for a retail value of $6,522. More likely, Harrison would gross closer to the wholesale value of $5,016. After paying for the 150 bushels ($3,600) and the shuckers ($1,035), the net proceeds, if all sales were wholesale, would only be $380 and change. Even on the occasional days when all sales were retail, the profit would be only $1,887 (before subtracting minimal overhead). Little wonder shucking houses were in trouble. Labor costs stood as their nemesis. While at the same time, skilled shuckers and dredgers were their salvation. Buyers had to balance the two.

After cleaning up, the shuckers headed for the office where Bud would divvy up the thousand dollars in cash among the workers before they walked out into the snow. Woody was the first to be paid—over $140. He took the wad of bills and stuffed them into his back pocket and donned his cap and coat. The other shuckers shuffled forward in line. Just then, Edith rushed forward and threw her arms around the old man and kissed him on the cheek. This was just to distract him. She reached around and stuck her fingers into his hip pocket. Woody grabbed both her hands, looked into her eyes, and said, "Baby, don't leave a nickel." All the shuckers laughed, Edith the loudest. Woody smiled and whispered, "Lordy, yes."

Friday meant payday for dredging crews and shuckers, but it also signaled the weekly oyster buffet at Harrison's Chesapeake House, the family's popular inn. The thought of it made me hungry. I cleaned up on Gibsontown Road and walked over to the hotel. Flurries were still falling and the skipjacks in Dogwood Harbor were cloaked in white. Everything was quiet: no sound of waves breaking on the shore since the edge of the harbor was a shelf of ice. Only my boots made a noise, crunching on the snow. Thirty cars and a couple of trucks filled the hotel parking lot, which was circled with Christmas lights like a skating rink.

The foyer of the restaurant was too hot. I peeled off layers, found a table, and ordered the buffet. I was in a hurry. Woody stood at the shucking table and I began with him.

"I'll shuck 'em for ya good," he said. "Just keep the lights on. I'm a li'l better when I can see." He flashed that gold tooth at me.

"Keep 'em coming," I said, and piled my plate high with raw oysters, scalloped oysters, fritters, and oysters Chesapeake. I really can't say which was the best. They were all freshly shucked just down the road. By a rather large family. Gifted, too. You could almost hear them singing.

7

January, Six Foot Knoll

The predawn palette barely hinted at the theater to come: a pale amber wash, then the eastern sky erupted in gold. Above it, a sharp blue. Two banks of clouds—to the northeast and southeast—burned with orange so that the sun, when it arose like a peach, appeared center stage, flanked left and right by two scorched curtains. The play of colors would tally five minutes at best. Sensing this, Stanley Larrimore glanced over his shoulder at the brief spectacle and smiled. He had seen a sunrise or two in his life. "Sunrises get perty in wintertime," he said, "when the air is clear and crisp."

And cold. We huddled aboard *Lady Katie* in the Upper Bay, sailing southwest toward Baltimore. Close-hauled, she was making good time with a double-reef sail. The fresh breeze—a headwind blowing twenty miles per hour—stung our faces. Twenty degrees at dawn. After a small shiver, Stanley zipped his extra-large jacket and pulled the cords on his sweatshirt hood tight. Placing one hand on the wheel, another on the cabintop, he buttressed himself against the wind. We held a starboard tack. Our destination was Six Foot Knoll, ten miles away.

Nearly half the skipjack fleet had ventured above the Bay Bridge to work the reefs of the Upper Bay. They had abandoned the Choptank, by now picked clean and likely riddled with MSX. The dredgers' first northern targets were Seven Foot Knoll, Six Foot Knoll, and Snake Rip, where the dredgers had been planting seed for years—above the reach of the disease. Traditionally, the skipjack fleet had always traveled north to work these rocks after New Year's. So, over the weekend, eight Tilghman boats had sailed the thirty-five miles from Tilghman's to Tolchester, a small sheltered harbor west of Chestertown on the upper Eastern Shore. From there, on Monday and Tuesday they had worked Snake Rip without much success. It was now Wednesday, a sail day, and all hands were expected on Six Foot Knoll.

"We planted them knolls three springs ago," said Stanley, turning his back to the wind, "so we should have a perty good skim. Unless'n, of course, them patent tongers got thar first." The season for tongers began in October, a month earlier than skipjacks, when patent boats often headed to the knolls to poach dredgers' seed. Stanley turned the wheel to starboard. As *Lady Katie* edged west, the boom swung across the deck, and we ducked out of the way. "Of course," he said, "the ice nearly kept us from getting here."

Earlier that morning, glass ice had coated Tolchester harbor. It had been the coldest night of the year, in single digits. The water temperature of the open Bay, slower to chill, was thirty-seven degrees, but in freshwater harbors like Tolchester, it had fallen below freezing. Luckily, *Lady Katie* and the other skipjacks had copper sheathing at their waterlines to combat the ice panes. Now, as we sailed southwest toward the knolls, the spectacle of dawn diminished and clouds formed, suppressing the promise of warmth. Our southerly headwind grew more moderate.

On a port tack, we crossed Brewerton Channel, one of two main shipping arteries into Baltimore Harbor. A huge red derrick dredged there, deepening the channel for large commercial vessels. Just then an enormous green container ship steamed north along the channel, toward the harbor, dwarfing us and passing us by. Evergreen Lines out of Taiwan. Our wood, their steel: two centuries crossing paths. The modern world dominated our horizon. Even in dawn's first light, Baltimore was lit up like an airport runway. The red-and-white twin smokestacks of an electric power plant flashed steadily—a lighthouse for jets. And the amber lights of Sparrows Point glowed like a furnace. Just south of Baltimore a single sharp reflection bounced off some metal crane or steel building and chased us across the water. One-eyed, it blinked like a Cyclops.

Behind us, the sun climbed steadily. We were an hour late getting to the rock. While six other skipjacks had begun working up ahead, our dredges sat idle on deck. The harbor ice was to blame, but Stanley took it in stride. "We'll get in a day's work," he said, smiling calmly. "I've got a plan." Stanley knew a spot he thought the patent tongers might have missed. "I've got the marks for Six Foot Knoll in my head," he said, "but to get to the little hill where I want to work, I'll need my loran." He punched a code into the navigational gear. This gave him a compass bearing, and Stanley altered his course slightly. "Now my fathometer will tell us when we're exactly on that hill. Sure is easier than a sounding pole."

Stanley knew the marks and depths of hundreds of bars around the Bay, but navigating by sight and feel was an all but lost art. Every captain except Art Daniels now had electronic navigational gear aboard. Still it was a comfort to know Stanley could get by without it, should the need arise.

While the other men slept below, one culler—Solomon, at sixty-six the oldest of Stanley's crew—stood out on deck. He wore a bright yellow slicker with oilskin overalls to match, in sharp contrast to his blue-black skin. Solomon, I came to see on my days aboard *Lady Katie*, continually prepped and cleaned the middle deck, getting things shipshape. He was never idle. Today, in the growing dawn, he tended to the winders. Solomon greased the gears of the windlass with old engine oil from a coffee can. He did this

every day, keeping the winders well lubed. He paid special attention to the starboard pulley block where his hand had been caught
and nearly mangled two weeks ago. Miraculously, he escaped with
only half a finger lost.

"It was his fault," said Stanley, watching him grease the winders. "He put his hand on the cable while he was winding in the
drudge. His hand went with it, right up into that block. Makes me
wince just to think of it. When he done it, he knew he was wrong.
He snatched his hand away, right out of his glove, and left that half
of his finger in the mitt. That glove was all chewed up by the wheel
of the block. He cut part of his finger off, not the tip, but the side of
it. I took that piece of the finger and him up to the hospital. We
should've put it on ice, but we didn't think of it. Anyway, them
doctors sewed it back on. They say it may fall off again, though."
Stanley took a moment to tighten the main sheet, then continued.
"I gave Solomon some money the other day, but I can't keep doing
it. He's got to work to get a share. We have no worker's compensa-
tion in the water business." Watermen learn to adapt to their injuries. Years ago John Lowery, captain of the bugeye *Coronet*, lost
his entire arm as it was pulled into the winders. No need to ampu-
tate; it was hacked off right above the elbow. Captain John kept
right on dredging for many years.

Solomon eyed the captain, oblivious to our conversation. "We're
gonna catch our limit today," he shouted. "I can feel it." At sunrise
anything seems possible.

Stanley's fathometer registered ten feet, then eight, now seven.
We were on Six Foot Knoll, actually on a hill, or lump, on top of the
plateau—about the size of a basketball court. He woke the crew,
and they quickly donned green oilskins and boots. The sails were
set with a double-double reef—two reefs each in the main and jib—
just where the captain wanted them. He came about and sailed on
a starboard tack toward the lump. The fathometer readout climbed
again: 8, 7, 6.

"Heave," Stanley shouted. "Let 'em go." Solomon and Randolph (half asleep) tossed the two dredges overboard. I saw now that Stanley had six crewmembers: five black men and Tommy Briggs, the man I had replaced on my first spatting job aboard *Rebecca*. We had become friends. It was more or less the same crew that Stanley had had all season.

Just when the dredges touched the bottom, the fathometer read six feet again. Stanley smiled at his good luck and dropped a buoy overboard to mark the hill. Almost immediately, he revved the winder engines and Solomon, more carefully than usual, engaged the cable spools to bring the dredges up. They overflowed with "clear oysters," the term for an exclusively live and legal catch. We came about and headed for another lick.

Stanley explained the technique for working a lump right. "My father was a lumper and he raised me to work these hills a certain way—to make them last." The Larrimore method requires perfect timing and dead reckoning of where you are during the course of each lick. "You approach a lump and hold the drudges until ye're just on top of the hill, then you drop them. That way, you don't drag mud up the hill and cover the orsters. On the other end you pull in yer drudges before they drag down the hill. You have to know the shape of the hill so when ya come about ya can hit it right again. Of course, with the Bay so murky, we're all flying blind." Stanley revved the winders, and the second load was pulled up and dumped on deck. "These younger drudgers don't know how to do it. They cover the lumps with mud and kill the orsters. I guess it don't matter anymore. Patent tongers have dug up most of the lumps anyway. We're being tonged into a corner. I guess we're on the way out. Yes, sir."

The second lick tallied as good as the first—about a hundred market oysters in each dredge. Even more small oysters were discarded, shoveled overboard. Culling was a challenge, however. Most of the smalls measured just under legal size, and the keepers registered only barely legal. So they were hard to tell apart. The crew waved an occasional four-inch jumbo at the captain and tossed it into a special bushel basket. "Those are for later," said Tommy, catching his hat as the wind knocked it off his head. "You'll see. We have our ways to fool the law."

Quickly, I saw that hauling the Stone Rock seed oysters up here had been a success. Just about all the oysters coming aboard were living. There were few boxes, so the effect of the disease this far north, this far into freshwater, was minimal. On the other hand, the freshwater was responsible for "dwarfing" the oysters. They grew more slowly here. It had taken four years, rather than three, for the spat to grow to three inches—one year on Stone Rock and three up here. Oyster after oyster came aboard just at the edge between legal and illegal. The marine police could bring trouble today: The law was on the lookout for small oysters.

As each dredgeful crashed on deck, water and mud and bits of shell flew through the air. In between culls, the crew flashed fingers at the captain to tell him the count of market oysters in each lick. In this way the captain could make minor adjustments to stay on the money. Stanley sailed *Lady Katie* single-handed in the lessening breeze, coming about and fine-tuning the main sheet without any assistance. If I pitched in, my motivation was to keep busy, not because he needed it. With the tide ebbing and the wind against him and the water obscuring the bottom, it seemed miraculous that he could hit that little hill each time with such accuracy. Only a skipjack. Only a great captain.

Mussels often draped over the oysters, and the crew employed culling hammers to knock the bivalves away. A couple of bricks came up in one haul. A pair of antique scissors—marked "Baltimore"—in another. But the most interesting artifact to surface was an old whiskey bottle: blown glass, no seam, and a year embossed "1927." The height of Prohibition.

In those days, Stanley told me, you could be thrown in jail for drinking a little or a load. For oyster-dredging crews it was usually, as the sailors dubbed it, "from tying on some freight." Over two hundred oyster-dredge boats—not just skipjacks but schooners and bugeyes—would line the wharves of Baltimore Harbor in wintertime. And captains had a shrewd way of obtaining their crews. At the beginning of each season a captain would walk into the city jail, pick out a few men from the drunk tank, pay off their fines (and maybe offer a small bribe to the police), and carry the drunks one by one to the waiting hold of his dredge boat. By the time the sobering men realized they'd been shanghaied, it was too late. By then, they stood stranded in the middle of the Bay. The captain would keep them aboard all winter, manning the windlass, promising them a share for culling oysters.

But in the spring, more often than not, the men were dropped off in shallow water without pay and told to swim to shore. Others, legend has it, were "paid off with the boom." To avoid a payout, the captain would come swiftly about and the boom, swinging across the deck, would clip the unfortunates in the head and overboard they would go. The captain would then pick up a fresh crew in Baltimore for the next season. Despite criminal penalties imposed by the federal Shanghaiing Act of 1908, the abduction of crews remained commonplace until well after Prohibition ended. And Stanley, for one, had hinted he would prefer to "harr" and "farr" some of his men the old way. Convicts, he said, are accustomed to routine.

THE WIND BEGAN to die down a little, and visibility to the south—down the Bay—dropped off considerably. Over the next thirty minutes a thin haze turned into what looked like a low cloud bank ten miles away. "That's no cloud," Stanley corrected me. "That's fog, and it's coming our way. Maybe an hour or two till it hits. We better make some money before it gets here."

Lady Katie was sluggish in the light wind, so the captain ordered the crew to shake a reef out. Solomon and Tommy lowered the main a few feet so the others could untie the reef points. This allowed the two of them to raise the sail about three feet higher, giving us an additional two hundred square feet of sail to harness the more moderate wind. They let the jib out one reef, too. We picked up speed—just enough to pull the light mud dredges across the top of the lump. Our hill was small, forty by sixty yards at best. But the oysters piled up with every lick.

Around 9:00 A.M. Daryl Larrimore sailed over in our direction. Like the others, he had been broadcasting over the breadth of the knoll, to the north of us, looking for a strike of oysters. He suspected his uncle was on to something since Stanley had sailed to one spot and stayed put. Daryl sailed seventy yards away, nearly on our lump. He was bound to discover it. Daryl got Stanley's attention and flashed ten fingers. The hand signal avoided announcing news of his catch to the whole world over the radio. Stanley responded only by shaking his head, not wanting to give away his success. Daryl persisted, flashing ten again, and Stanley finally responded with fifteen. We may have had closer to twenty bushels. It was enough for Daryl, who sailed over our way to work off Stanley's buoy. Resigned, Stanley let it go. It was family after all.

For the moment the five other dredge boats kept to the north of us, on the main plateau of the knoll—like a wolf pack watching from a distance. Their sails reflected a pale yellow in the morning light. They were still broadcasting, trying to find a spot not cleaned out by the patent tongers. And from their movements it was clear they were being frustrated. Stanley paced back and forth in front of the wheel. He knew it was only a matter of time before another dredge boat found his lump and told the whole pack about it. He wasn't anxious for company. At the lower postholiday prices, down one-third, Stanley had to catch a boatload to make a day's work.

Right then, Daryl came over the radio, complaining about buyers paying higher prices to some dredgers and not to others.

DARYL: Did ya hear Wadey got twenty-two dollars in the river the other day? Everybody else got twenty dollars a booshel.

STANLEY: Everybody gets a different price, though the buyers deny it. I'm always the last in line. Yes, sir.

DARYL: He's on Old Rock today. Let's see if he gets the same as we do.

STANLEY: We'll see.

Daryl was fully aware that Wadey was listening to this down the Bay, but he didn't care. Stanley turned down the volume on the radio and said to me, "Daryl would just as soon ram Wadey as Wadey'd run over him." It seemed there was still no love lost between the Larrimores and the Murphys. The rumor was—perhaps started by Wadey—that he landed a higher price for his oysters because he made sure his crew culled them right—no junk, no smalls. He called his extra pay a second "tip." Whatever it was, the other dredgers were mad as hell about it.

On *Lady Katie*, the crew stationed themselves according to experience. Solomon, as senior man, handled the winder position up forward on starboard, right where he had lost his finger. Across the dredge roller from him, in the starboard aft position stood Tommy. Opposite them on the port side, two brothers—Randolph and Gene—worked in the fore and aft spots with Randolph handling the port winder. Two extra men helped dump the dredges up forward. Leroy, a familiar name to me, had a crazy, wild look about him and bloodshot eyes; he assisted Gene. And Ethelbert "Bird Eye" Browne manned the starboard log, dumping the dredge with Tommy. A yellow ring circled the brown iris in each of his eyes. This gave Bird Eye a raptorlike look.

"I've farred only two men in my life," said Stanley, "and I think Bird Eye's one of 'em. Not sure. I've had a lotta crews over the years and I can't be certain who those two were, but I bet Bird Eye's caught my boot." Stanley spun the wheel and the boom swung across the deck, bringing us to a starboard tack for another run at the lump. "I'd like to farr Leroy—he only shows up half the time— but I'm afraid the rest of the crew would quit if I do. They're all related in one way or another. If I farr one, I lose 'em all." The day Leroy came after Wadey with a shovel was his last day crewing for the Murphys; the Larrimores inherited the whole family after that. Leroy was nearly an orphan—down to his last dredge boat.

Above the din of the winder engine, Stanley shouted to Solomon and Randolph to let the dredge line out two turns, to the next becket. The dredges were not digging as deep now that the wind had weakened, and the extra line would remedy that. The next lick brought up a fuller load, which kept the men busier, culling. Subsequent licks generated seventy to eighty legal oysters in each dredge. Though yielding a few less than at the beginning of the day, the lump still held out.

Captains can predict the day's catch from the look of each haul, even early in the day. The rule of thumb reads that the average number of oysters per dredge per lick, over time, will approximate the number of bushels at the end of the day. We stood on track for a seventy-five-bushel day, half our limit and a good take for the second half of the season.

With the cable lines long, the dredges surfaced with their bags full. Much of this was shell, but many live oysters surfaced as well. When Gene and Randolph dumped the port dredge, a roll of live oysters swelled over the crest of empty shells and crashed toward the winders at middeck. A good culler like Gene saw this quickly and reached for the big oysters on the inside of the pile. Meanwhile, Randolph knelt to cull through the center of the pile. Gene, though, with his long reach swiftly grabbed the biggest oysters right out of Randolph's hand and snapped them like a football center between his legs to his crescent pile. That pile grew faster than Bird Eye's and Randolph's, the two-man effort up near the mast.

"Any legal oysters thar, Gene?" the captain called out.

"A few. Not like before."

"Well, there's a helpful answer," Stanley said under his breath. "How many?" he said a little louder.

"Seventy-two," Gene said, not looking up.

"Gene's my best culler, aren't you?" Stanley whispered so low I could barely hear.

"Yes, Captain! Fastest man on deck."

Up forward, Randolph and Bird Eye took a break to shuck oysters from a pile of small culls. They were fast: Randolph was already filling his second pint jar. "I can sell a pint for eight dollars on the black market," he said, smiling, "but the captain won't let us, so I'm shucking for my mother." Bird Eye shouted, "Me, too." A host of hungry mothers around.

"Every boat up here sells smalls or shucks 'em," Stanley said. "If I can stay on this lump, these men will make enough money, though; they won't need to sell any pints. Yes, sir, the Indians took only what they needed, but the white man ruined everything."

The shellfish that Randolph shucked were not plump and white like Choptank River oysters. His emerged smaller and more grayish with a fringe of green. The green color came from copper that accumulated in the body of the oyster from the effluent coming out of Baltimore Harbor. According to the State Health Department, the concentration of heavy metals in Upper Bay oysters was not sufficient to pose a health risk. But I wasn't taking any chances. When Randolph offered me an oyster, I declined. Choptank oysters were worth the wait.

"I'm looking for a pearl," Bird Eye announced, prying another oyster open. "That's why I shuck so many for my mother." While pearls from the American oyster are uncommon, lackluster, and of little worth, the nacre or iridescent inner shell is beautiful—typically ivory and purple, like a winter sunset—and has traditional value.

Native Americans once used pieces of oyster and clam shells, called wampum, for trading and currency.

Stanley surveyed all the shucking up by the mast and became agitated—by the growl in his stomach. He bobbed under the boom and shuffled to the starboard side of the wheel to get Solomon's attention. He made a signal, turning his hat upside down like a bowl. It was 10:00 A.M.—dinnertime. The fog now hovered about five miles away, resembling puffs of cotton, below some brooding clouds.

"I'm hungry," Stanley said. "I could eat an elephant." This echoed a joke between us, and he chuckled heartily. Stanley had been asked by the Cookbook Committee of the Tilghman United Methodist Church to submit a recipe for *What's Cookin' at Tilghman's Island?* He gave them two. Both registered on the scale of his appetite. One called for crab cakes, serving ten dozen; the other featured elephant stew. The latter recipe had been designed to feed a boatload of people. Stanley recited the recipe: "Cut one elephant into bite-size pieces. This should take about two months. Cover with brown gravy and cook over a high fire for about four weeks. Add salt and pepper to taste. This will serve about 3,800 people. If more are expected, two rabbits may be added. But do this only if necessary, as most people do not like hare in their stew." Stanley chuckled to himself in the deep way common to big men. He got a kick out of the recipe no matter how many times he recited it.

While Solomon cooked our dinner, I took his place on the middle deck. First, I rushed down into the cabin to squeeze on some oilskins and a pair of wet gloves. I also borrowed Solomon's kneepads. Up forward, I took the position next to the log so I could dump the starboard dredge with Tommy. Bird Eye dissented. He shook his head no. He didn't want to work the winder position, and Tommy said he hated to wind, so the task fell to me. The captain revved the engine and I pushed the lever into gear. On the port side, Randolph did the same. The dredges came up full of mud, so we rinsed the dredges by dropping them four feet back into the water and then raising them and drenching them, washing them three or four times. This rinsed the mud off the oysters. Finally, the dredges landed on deck. Bird Eye and Tommy dumped our dredge and stood aside while I grabbed three feet of slack in the cable and tossed the dredge overboard, bouncing it up and over the roll bar in a smooth arc. I watched to see that the dredge bag flew out clearly without catching the teeth. It looked fine to me, but I avoided the captain's eyes. Then, the three of us knelt down to cull the oysters.

I picked a few oysters off the top of the pile but then remembered that the right way to cull was from underneath. "Dig right through them from the side," Tommy said, "so you won't miss any." After two and a half months of culling, I was still learning a trick or two.

Most of the oysters, in that first lick, seemed to be just barely market size. It was hard to tell. I used the culling hammer to measure every other one, which slowed me down. The other men rarely used their culling hammers. "Until you can eyeball them, use your fingers," said Tommy. "Lay the oyster across your palm like this," he said demonstrating with a small one. "If it covers up three fingers of your glove, then it's legal." He threw the little suspect back overboard.

I stood up and straightened my back. December's aches and pains came back to me. I was glad that today I was only briefly substituting for the cook. The winder engines revved again and we engaged the windlasses. The dredges broke the water without mud this time. A gorgeous seafood buffet poured onto the deck: two flounders, six blue crabs, and fifty oysters. Bird Eye picked up a flounder by the tail and waved it at the captain. Stanley nodded his head enthusiastically. You could almost hear his stomach groan. I tossed the dredge over the side and, lifting a shovel, turned to Solomon's pile of oysters—eight, maybe ten bushels (one of four such piles on the boat)—and shoveled Bird Eye's and my keepers onto the top.

"Stop it," Tommy shouted in my direction. "Don't shovel that pile so high. It'll attract attention from the other drudgers. They've all got binoculars. We don't want neither one of 'em coming here this morning." On the Chesapeake, it pays not to advertise. I put down the shovel and stooped to help with more culling. The cable whirred quickly by my ear, reminding me too late about the need for the winder man to slow the dredge's descent.

I had forgotten my job. The dredge hit the bottom unchecked, at full speed.

Immediately, the boat vibrated with a shudder and the cable became more taut. Bird Eye and Tommy jumped out of the way. I backed up and fell onto Solomon's pile. A loud "snap" ricocheted off the deck, as the becket broke on the cable spool and six more feet of cable paid out. The boat lurched forward but the next becket held and *Lady Katie* was sailing smoothly again. After a close call, the dredge was dragging free.

There may have been a small hang on the bottom or just the teeth dug too quickly into the reef. Regardless, the dredge had caught and broken the becket because I had not slowed the cable before the dredge hit bottom. The descending cage gathers momentum like a brick dropped at the end of a string. If the brick (or dredge) falls unchecked, the string (or becket) can break. Checking the dredge was the most important job of the winder man. I had been asleep at the lever. Stanley was nice enough about it, though, and gave me another chance. I was glad to be aboard *Lady Katie*. On *Rebecca*, Wadey would've handed me my hat. When we wound up the dredges next, Bird Eye replaced the becket and we were back in business.

Beyond *Nellie Byrd*, two other skipjacks—*Martha Lewis* and *Minnie V.*—approached us from the north. Six Foot Knoll was half a mile wide, and they had cut the distance to us in half. I could see Johnnie M., the captain of *Minnie V.*, checking us out with binoculars. He was suspicious we had struck gold. "He doesn't know for certain we're on a lump or he'd be on top of us by now," Tommy said. "Bring his friends, too."

Kathyrn and *Wilma Lee* had already shaken out their last reefs: They dredged with full sail, barreling along. That was Russell's and Robbie's style—to dredge at a faster speed with their dredge lines long, digging deep and quick, and bringing up a full dredge of oysters and shell that kept the crew busy culling. What they missed in accuracy they made up in quantity. As Russell explained later at the dock, "We go fast with a lot of line to cover a lot of bottom, so we catch more orsters. I can double the take of guys with short lines going slow." Short-line dredging—either along edges or lumps—was all finesse, easier on the reef, and required less crew. With a smaller payroll, old-timers claimed to clear more money. The rest of the fleet, moving closer to us now, still worked with a one-reef main and jib. But the wind diminished, down to a fifteen-mile breeze. The tide still ebbed but would begin to flood in less than an hour.

"It's fresh now," said the captain as we stood near the helm. "But that's all—it's no longer a strong breeze because of the ebb tide." Stanley was declaring his suspicion, some say superstition, that the tide controls the wind. In this instance, he meant the fair tide—fair because it was running south with us—kept the headwind, the wind coming at us, at bay. "When the tide changes later this morning," he continued, "that flood tide will bring that wind on strong, right up the Bay. Until then, the ebb tide will hold up the wind." There's not a meteorologist on earth that will agree with him that the tides and the wind work together, but the watermen swear by it.

Stanley began to pace again; he did not like the fleet crowding him and began to mutter about finding another spot. The wind fell out, too. Overhead, the clouds were bruised with purple. And the fog gathered just to the southwest, low along the water, like gauze on a wound. Up front, awaiting dinner, the crew was also anxious about the weather. They tried to read the wind and predict what the captain would do.

"Look at that fog," said Tommy. "Gonna be clam chowder."

"Cap'n'll find us another spot," said Gene.

"You can count on that," Tommy said.

"He knows these lumps," said Bird Eye.

"No better cap'n, pushing or sailing," Tommy added.

"It'll be a sad day if'n he sells this boat," said Gene.

I was eyeballing the oysters by now. I employed my hammer only to knock off mussels, and my three-finger technique had given way to a quick recognition of what was legal and what was not. At least I thought so. But many of the marginal, just legal, oysters in the dredge pile became illegal when we shoveled them back. Their bills broke off.

As an oyster grows, a thin crusty brim forms at the edge of the shell, especially in the front. This bill, or "lip," can add an extra half inch to the size of an oyster, but it's fragile. Upon culling and shoveling, many of the bills break off. What was legal on the reef falls short of legal dockside. Since the marine police allow no more than 5 percent of a given pile to be smalls—that is, one out of every twenty oysters—a boatload of marginal oysters is likely to yield a ticket from a lawman.

While we broke for dinner, Stanley pulled his buoys and began a search for new ground. He headed northwest with the wind broad on our port quarter. Daryl followed behind us, but the rest of the fleet converged on Stanley's lump like hungry wolves.

The black men descended into the cabin while Stanley remained at the helm with Tommy nearby. Leroy glanced at the brass plaque on the bulkhead: THE CAPTAIN'S WORD IS LAW. He did not smile. Below, the men removed their oilskins and warmed their hands above the propane stove. Through the companionway Solomon passed three steaming bowls of lima bean soup and a plate of ham sandwiches, carved off the bone.

Tommy said, "I overheard two lawmen yesterday say, 'All drudgers are crooks.' Well, we're not saints, but that's going too far. They're boarding us every day, *ev-er-y day*, looking for an excuse to arrest us."

"No, we don't have no angel wings," Stanley said.

"No," Tommy said, "we don't have no halos."

"No halos," echoed the captain. "Conservation laws are necessary, but just the same they don't have to come aboard like they do. No, sir. They never ask permission. They just pick out somebody and hound 'em to death. They're just waiting for Daryl to make a mistake. After three tickets, the next one, they'll take his license away. A waterman can't feed his family without a fisheries license."

"Yesterday," said Tommy, "I had trouble with the lawman. He come right after me, culled my pile without even looking at the others, same as he done the day before. It was the closest I've ever come to going after one of them lawmen. God help me when I do."

We began working the second hill, slightly to the northeast of a red buoy. Stanley continued to sail each lick single-handed. However, the second hill did not amount to the gold mine that the first one had. Only twenty or so oysters rolled onto the deck on each lick. And some of those were dead. But not from MSX. Half a dozen boxes had tooth marks in them—crushed when the hydraulic jaws of a patent tonger closed on the shells. The patent tongers had discovered this hill and wiped it out, leaving dead oysters behind like buffalo carcasses. Not surprisingly, very few smalls came aboard *Lady Katie*. The patent-tong boats had purged them, too.

Solomon pointed to the meager catch of one dredge and said, "Those patent boats sell the bottom, sell our future right down the road." It was the most he had said all day.

Back at the helm the captain shook his head. "I should've stayed put, but them others was starting to crowd me." He gestured to the southeast where five skipjacks now sailed over Larrimore's lump. "Look at them. I could never get back on it now. No, sir." He sighed. "Well, I got one other spot the patent tongers may not have found yet." He wound the dredges in and we sailed north away from the breeze—fair wind, fair tide.

On the short sail to the far side of Six Foot Knoll, followed by Daryl, the crew cleaned the deck and, since we were out of view of the others, shoveled the oysters higher. Tommy then showed me his trick for fooling the law. He carried the bushel basket containing the oversize oysters (four-inch-plus "monsters") from pile to pile and placed the jumbos on top of the piles. Also scattering a few on the sides of the piles, Tommy further demonstrated the technique of "facing off." The deception assured that the marine police would see only the more-than-legal catch and not bother to sample the piles. Alert to this charade, some lawmen would dig into a pile with a shovel to get their samples from underneath rather than take them from the top. Tommy's countermeasure was to place a layer of jumbos just underneath the surface as he was doing now.

"If they peek under my skirt, they'll see I'm a big girl now," said Tommy. "Mister Law has a date with disappointment. Of course, they have their tricks, too. They take that hammer and, if the catch is only barely legal, they tap 'em and ding 'em and knock the bill right off it. Then if it's still big enough, they hit it on the hinge. You take an orster and you start beating on it, you're going to get him small enough. And that orster's been caught in the drudge, been picked up and thrown back, shoveled up, shoveled again into a tub, dumped into a conveyor, and dropped into a truck. By the time the buyer gets it, that orster is small all right."

Tommy and I returned to the aft deck just as the rest of the crew emerged from the cabin. "Let's shake out that last reef," the captain said. The wind had dissipated to ten miles or less and it lacked any punch. The first fingers of fog wrapped around the fleet, just south of us now, and small wisps reached out toward us. Solomon and Randolph lowered the main a few feet to slacken the sail while the others untied the reefs, then Gene joined them in raising the sail to its full height and breadth.

But we never made it to Stanley's third spot. Within fifteen minutes, the fog enveloped us as well. It engulfed us quickly. Visibility dropped to a hundred yards and the wind all but disappeared. We were cut off from the fleet. The water, rolling waves earlier in the day, was now slick calm. To hold us in position, Stanley ordered Randolph to throw the port dredge overboard to serve as a makeshift anchor. Suddenly, Daryl appeared out of the thick fog and anchored *Nellie Byrd* beside us. He had been following us to the new spot when the fog descended. It was pure luck that he had been able to find us. Pure dumb luck, we discovered: He was sailing without any navigation gear.

At the captain's orders, the crew spread out around the boat to keep a lookout for any approaching vessels. We hovered near the shipping channel, and this proximity made Stanley nervous. Huge freighters, container ships, and tankers would be steaming into Baltimore today. Fog would not stop them; they'd rely on radar—as if it were night.

Two things worried the captain in this fog. The sum of these fears could arrive swiftly, without warning, and be deadly. The first concern was a ship or a barge coming up the channel toward us. The second was a sudden wind. In the fog the captain wouldn't see any of the telltales of a gale-force wind steaming up the Bay. No green water. No wind clouds. No scattering geese. Without these warning signs, a boat like *Lady Katie* under full sail could be hit broadside in an instant and lose a mast or capsize or sink. It had happened before.

There was only one warning system the dredgers could use when the fleet was spread out as it was now: the radio. Daryl raised Bart Murphy on the VHF, and Stanley listened in. Bart was dredging

Esther F. on Coopers Hollow ("Cupper Holler"), an oyster bar just north of Tilghman's. That was thirty miles south of us, just out of the fog. The Chesapeake is big enough that several weather patterns can be active on it at once, and from Bart's report he could have been on a different estuary.

DARYL: Hello, Bart. We're in the thick of it here on Six Foot. Fog and neither breath of wind.

BART: Blowing a gale on the Holler, Daryl. I've dropped my jib and got three reefs in the main. Blowing thirty mile. Can't drudge in this. I'm going home.

DARYL: What's your tide?

BART: Flooding strong, bringing on the wind. You better watch it.

DICKIE: This is the *Caleb W. Jones*. It's breezing up here on Belvedere Shoal. I had fog but it's clearing out now.

STANLEY: How much you got, Dickie?

DICKIE: Stanley, I got fifteen mile and it's strengthening.

Stanley sat down on his wheelbox and thought for a minute. "If Bart's got that much wind on Cupper Holler," he said, "I don't want it to hit us with all our sail up. We'd be in deep trouble." He stood up and gathered the crew around him. "Let's put two reefs in the main and jib—the wind might hit us strong. I don't like fog one bit. Not one bit. No, sir."

Faced with that bank of fog, Stanley recalled previous whiteouts. When fog is whisked away, he said, it can often be carried on the prow of a stiff breeze, or gust, even a sudden gale that can take the boat's rigging with it. And Stanley had lost enough masts for one lifetime. Wind or accident, being dismasted was a frightening experience. Working the middle deck of his father's skipjack *Laura J. Barkley*, Stanley had watched in disbelief as another boat—Gordon Pope on *E. C. Collier*—rammed them, causing the mast to break and topple from about thirty feet up. The top of the spar came down like a sharp spear and harpooned into the deck. It happened on a Saturday, first day of the season. Father and son splinted the mast and were working again on Monday. "We couldn't afford to stop," said Stanley. "Them days was orsters. We caught a boatload each day, *every day*. Yes, sir."

We were sailing in a small circle to stay put, in an area, Stanley hoped, that was safely outside the two shipping channels. Every fifty yards we came about. Our mast cut through the fog like a knife through white icing. But we could only see the length of the boat. Stanley navigated with his compass and his watch, keeping the same direction and time on each leg of his circuit. In this way, theoretically, we stayed in one place. The only unknown was the flood tide, which was now running strong. So we possibly drifted slightly north. There was just enough wind to keep us moving, but the sail luffed and flapped in the light air. The slapping sails produced the only noise. All hands listened for the sound of foghorns that might betray an advancing ship.

Stanley looked around through the fog—visibility was fifty yards—but could only see *Nellie Byrd* tracing his circle. "In this fog with these shipping channels so close," he said, "I wouldn't know which way to head home safely. We'll wait her out." Stanley gripped the wheelbox with both hands, braced for a siege.

The crew was impatient. They wanted either to dredge or head back to port. "Maybe we should drop this yawl boat and power-dredge a little," Tommy said. "In this fog, who can tell it's a Wednesday?" This made Stanley chuckle. Our predicament did not keep him from telling a story about power dredging in the fog.

"Years ago on Stone Rock—it was a Wednesday, like to-day—we 'sneak-pushed' on a sail day. Ca'm day, fog so thick you couldn't see. Half a dozen of us—all pushing with our yawl boats. We thought we were hidden in the fog. But what we didn't know was that our mast tips were above the fog—looking like chopsticks in a bowl of rice. So the law comes by, over top of us, in a plane. They knew what we were doing: Thar's no wind in fog that thick, and they saw our poles going around. We couldn't be sailing, had to be pushing. But they couldn't tell who we were. Those lawmen just knew some of us drudgers was breaking the law. Back at the dock, later that day, they arrested Old Man Wade Murphy. Funny thing, he wasn't even thar. He was drudging in the river that day. They never did catch the rest of us, but they hounded us for a month. No, sir, an outlaw never rests."

Daryl stayed close on our heels, about thirty yards behind us as if we were towing him. As we approached the edge of the shipping channel, he came alongside of us, and uncle and nephew exchanged words. Daryl came to the rail and shouted across the water, "I just got a call on the radio. A tugboat and barge picked up the two of us on radar. We're too close. I didn't call you, so to keep the radio free."

Somewhere in the nearby channel a tug hauled a two-hundred-foot barge full of coal, steaming for Sparrows Point. We lay in their path. And we were sailing blind. Stanley stooped into the cabin to summon the tug on the radio and then came back to the rail to report the latest to Daryl.

"That tugboat captain is confused," said Stanley. "First he said we passed his port bow, then next minute he doesn't think we passed him at all. He's got me worried. I don't know where he is, but he doesn't seem to know where we are and he's the one with the radar. If he comes out of this fog, it'd like to scare me to death." Stanley shook his head, whistled, and then let out his breath. "By the time you *see* a barge in this fog, it's too late."

All around us the dense haze revealed nothing. On the bow Tommy threw up his hands. The barge could have been anywhere. Every couple of minutes the tug sounded its horn, but the sound melted into the mist. We couldn't tell its direction, only that it was generally in front of us, maybe to starboard.

Stanley yelled over to Daryl, "I'm heading northeast to Gail's Lumps. He'll never get to me in that shallow water." Daryl acknowledged with a thumbs-up. Punching the letters "G-A-I-L" into his programmed loran, Stanley received a setting of eighty degrees and a distance of 0.4 miles—the other side of the channel. Barge traffic was no time for a watch and compass. He had to use whatever electronics he possessed. With his yawl boat engaged, we crossed the channel slowly. Daryl followed closely behind. As each minute ticked by, all eyes peered into the white distance. Five minutes turned into ten. Ten into twenty. Finally, we reached Gail's Lumps, and Stanley was relieved. "That barge won't find me here," he said. A half hour later the fog lifted to the west and we saw a huge barge steaming toward Baltimore, a wide, white wake following. We'll never know how close we came to disaster.

Lady Katie nosed through the evaporating mist. We could just see the far shoreline, last night's port of call. Luckily, we crossed the last shipping channel without mishap. The wind kicked up, gusting from the south. The fog lifted steadily and blue sky appeared to the east, over Tolchester. This was a mixed blessing. The law, if they were waiting, would see more than our mast tips coming out of the fog. Stanley hoped we would miss them by coming in early, but, just in case, he ordered the crew to "string together" the four oyster piles, combining them into a single mound. At that point, I did not fathom the utility of the move; my curiosity would have to wait.

Tolchester Harbor had a narrow entrance, and the dredge boats entered single file, only then to diverge within the basin toward their respective buyers. The Oyster Peddler was there, as was Hansen Seafood. So was Buddy Harrison Sr., standing on the wharf. He had ridden with the buy truck from Tilghman's that afternoon as he often did to monitor how the six dredge boats he bought from were getting along. Buddy was Harrison Oyster Company's soothsayer. He could look at a deckload of oysters and tell how well they would shuck.

But not only buyers waited for dredgers at the Tolchester wharf. Two marine policemen stood on the dock next to Buddy. Two other pairs lingered at the next pier, with the next buyers. The police had been tipped off. Tongers had alerted them that the dredgers would arrive early. Unlike at Tilghman's, where lawmen and laymen get along, these police officers did not converse with Buddy. This was Kent County—tonger's country. They stared straight ahead at *Lady Katie* like two armed guards eyeing an intruder. And we were sailing right into their net.

Buddy was the first to speak, yelling across the water as we maneuvered toward the wharf. "How'd you make out in that fog, Stanley?"

"A barge nearly ran us over, Buddy," Stanley said. "I got away from him on Gail's Lumps, in that shoal water."

"Fog's dangerous up in these shipping lanes."

"Yes, sir."

The policemen continued their stares without acknowledging Stanley. For his part, the captain acted like they were not even there. Stanley brought *Lady Katie* parallel to the wharf and Tommy jumped ashore with the bow line.

"What's the price today?" Stanley asked Buddy.

"We had to drop it some," Buddy said. "Not much demand for oysters right now."

"How much?"

"Twenty-three dollars for bay oysters. I'll pay that for these today but yesterday's catch didn't shuck as well as Wadey's. He's on Old Rock—that's a better oyster than up here." Buddy must have heard Daryl's complaint about Murphy over the radio. Just the same, Buddy was threatening another cut if the fleet stayed north catching green oysters.

"I may just return home at the end of this week," Stanley said with a glance at the officers. "It's friendlier thar."

The price for a bushel of oysters had dropped 30 percent from the record start of thirty-two dollars in November. After the holidays, the price of oysters always drops, then rebounds a little in March, as people know the season's ending. "We've never made such a good price as this season," said Stanley to no one in particular, "but neither man likes to make less today than he did yesterday. I guess we missed the chance to strike."

"We'll probably get an increase next month, come Lent," Buddy said.

"I may not be drudging by then if my crew quits," Stanley said. "I may not be drudging anyway. May just sell my boat."

"I hear you, Stanley."

But it's anyone's guess whether the lawmen heard them, or if they cared. Now as we came alongside the wharf and tied up, the pair opened their eyes wide at the sight on deck. The crew had shoveled all the oysters into one heap around the mast, like rocks surrounding a flagpole. Stanley figured if one of the crewman's piles had small oysters, either broken bills or dwarfs, then combining the four, the good and the bad, would give him a better chance. Twelve percent (over the limit) in an original pile became three percent (that is, legal) in the single mound. Any mischief would average out.

Stanley had found a loophole in the law, and the officers knew it. Nevertheless, when we rolled up to the wharf, they boarded *Lady Katie* without a word, not even a nod, to the captain. They huddled in the middle of the boat and turned around and around, trying to figure out what to do. Both of the men were young, looking almost like twins in their polished uniforms. One had sunglasses, the other an oversized gun on his hip. Sunglasses studied the top of the pile and Rambo scrutinized the edges, searching for small oysters. The evidence was there, only hidden. Nervous about it, Tommy threw his culling hammer at a dredge, and Rambo gave him an unhealthy look. Tommy apologized. Each officer then took a shovel to scrape off the large "face" oysters placed by the crew and, afterward, stooped to look over the middle layers. Signaling each other with an index finger, the pair met again in the center of the boat in quiet conference. They must have run into Tommy's hidden layer of jumbos because they shrugged and stepped off the boat. Culling off the big, lone "single pile" on *Lady Katie* just wasn't worth it to them. Stanley and crew had fooled the law once more.

Buddy now helped unload the oysters: forty-two bushels, not bad for a half day's dredging. Lumping was worth it when a dredger beat a patent tonger to the hill; worth it, too, when he beat the rest of the skipjacks to it as well. Stanley Larrimore had reaped the seed. And he would return for more.

Before our drive home in the coming darkness, I looked west across the Bay. There was no hint left of today's fog. The magician had snatched away his white cloak. In its place was the spectacle of a winter sunset, the sun dropping toward the horizon like a ball of molten gold. When it hit the horizon, the orb flattened as if hitting an anvil—like a hot ingot. The yellow light burned a path across the Bay toward us—an amber stream blazing over the water. Then it vanished. And *Lady Katie* was made fast. And the buy trucks drove off down the highway. And we headed home. Ten hours, a short day: the crew could rest. They would need it. The weatherman was calling for a gale tomorrow.

8

—•··•—

The Oyster Wars

No matter how early I stumbled into Gary's Store that winter, Stanley Larrimore had always arrived before me. He was a fixture on the liar's bench—the makeshift pew brought inside for the season. If it were not for his wife Loretta's cooking and the call of the water, he would probably spend all his days there spinning yarns with the boys. And that's how I found him one morning in late January, sipping coffee and jawing two hours before dawn. The day before he had sailed *Lady Katie* home from Tolchester in a screaming blizzard. Harbor ice had driven the entire fleet south, forcing them to brave the storm, which was blessedly short-lived. The skies had now cleared, and the full moon lit up the snow-lined island as if it were the land of the midnight sun. It was homecoming. Skipjacks lined Knapps Narrows and Dogwood Harbor again, their bare masts rising above the snow and ice like a winter forest.

Gary's appeared half empty, though not because of the hour. The hand tongers had already come and gone, getting an early start before the sail dredgers arrived. That reflected their strategy—to beat the dredgers to Black Walnut Sands, just southeast of the island, within the mouth of the Choptank River. A battle over this oyster rock was under way, I learned later. But when I first arrived, I was simply surprised by the absent tongers and by the full roster of sail dredgers milling about. Eleven men: a "drudger's dozen," which Stanley described as twelve men less one captain running from the law.

"That would be Wadey," Freddie Williams said in jest. He had just stepped in from the cold, stomping his feet and rubbing his hands. "Wadey left arly for Old Rock across the Bay. He hit some orsters thar on the outside edge. But he'll never get straight thar today with the wind to the nor'west."

"Patent tongers're the problem on Old Rock, not the wind," Bart Murphy said. "Looting at night, on Sundays, whenever the law's not around. They just about invented overfishing—it's the worst threat to the Bay."

"Patent tongers've been working illegally on Black Walnut Sands, too," Freddie said in his deep drawl, pouring a cup of coffee. "They work right alongside the hand tongers. Tha're not even allowed in the river."

"Maybe that's what loosened them orsters," Bart said. "Before them patent tongers broke the law on Sands, them river orsters were packed tight. We couldn't budge 'em. But they could do it. Hydraulic tongs could dig up asphalt."

Pete Sweitzer of *Hilda Willing* agreed. "Sands—hell, all the big rocks—are always packed hard until we work 'em a bit—either us or the patent tongers. That's why we've always had the river to ourselves. That bottom's like cement to a hand tonger. Tongers wouldn't be thar atall if orsters weren't dying in the creeks."

Bart Murphy blew the steam off his coffee and said, "Hand tongers got nowheres to go. Half of 'em are giving up on the creeks, putting patent-tong rigs on thar boats, and working out in the Bay. The other half are staking out Sands—legal or not. But why should we share it? That's our best place close to home."

The door swung open, letting in a cold bolt of air. Bobby Marshall, thirty-nine, captain of *Virginia W.*, walked in, dropping the hood from his head, kicking the snow from his boots.

"Did someone die?" he asked, looking around. "Where's everybody?" He scanned the captains' faces. "Did you kill all the tongers?"

"Not yet," Pete said.

Bart stepped forward and refilled his Styrofoam cup. "Didn't you hear, Bobby?"

"I guess not."

So Bart told him. It had all happened yesterday, he explained. With the freeze, a bunch of hand tongers had tried Sands over the weekend to see if the skim had loosened up. Tommy Hathaway, a Tilghman tonger, hit them first, bringing home his fifteen-bushel limit in two hours. Come Monday, yesterday, two dozen hand tongers followed him back to the same spot—a shallow, underwater hill about half a mile, maybe eight hundred yards, off Lower Bar Neck Point. They worked there until 3:00 P.M., quitting time for tongers, catching their limit and then some. "Then they got a radio call from some drudger," Bart said. " 'We'll get 'em now,' somebody said. 'So long, you tongers, we're on our way. We've got till sunset on push days.' " Bart looked at Freddie, the second youngest dredger in the room.

"It was a dirty trick," said Stanley, avoiding Freddie's eyes. He stared at his nephew Daryl instead. "Tongers already want to hate us. And one of us just rubbed it in."

"We watched 'em all day, Stanley," said Freddie. "We gave 'em till three o'clock before we left Cook Point. So what if we took over their orsters on Sands? If thar're enough orsters to hand tong, thar're plenty enough to drudge."

"You could've waited till they were back in the harbor," Stanley said impatiently. "Salt water on the wound. We don't do it that way. Didn't use to, anyway. We'd give a man one day to work his strike."

"They shouldn't have tonged on drudgers' bottom," Freddie deadpanned.

Even Stanley chuckled. "That's one way to look at it," he said. "Might be another way, too." Sands was originally tonging ground. Now it was equally shared by dredgers and hand tongers, but each would have liked to muscle the other out of the way. Only patent tongers were excluded by law. The big man stared out the window at the eastern sky, which had lightened, no longer the pitch of night. "Well," he said, "it's an hour till sunrise—we might as well finish it."

"Put the tongers out of their misery," Bart said.

"All's fair in love and war," said Daryl.

Tommy Briggs, still the first mate on *Lady Katie*, winced at Stanley as if in pain. "Half them tongers are kin," he said.

"Chesapeake's open range," Stanley said, stepping out the door into the cold. "Anybody can work that orster rock today that gets to it first." Or steals it from a cousin. On the Chesapeake, sometimes water is thicker than blood.

STANLEY HAD TROUBLE that day right from the beginning. When he arrived at the long pier off Harrison's Chesapeake House where *Lady Katie* was docked, the night held an eerie silence. No voices in the cabin. No twang in the rigging. No waves caressing the hull. To begin with, the crew was late. Tommy had arrived with Stanley, but the rest of the men were nowhere in sight. As it happened, Solomon's mangled finger had become infected and he had to go to the clinic that day. He usually gave a lift to Gene and Randolph, so they were missing, too. Just then, an old car rolled across the oystershell, bringing Leroy and Bird Eye. "Just my luck," said Stanley, "a couple of convicts is all I get today." He would have to settle for a crew of three. Well, four, I suddenly realized. I'd been shanghaied again.

Tommy was the first to discover the reason for *Lady Katie*'s silence. "Ice," he called out. "She's locked in tight."

Harrison's pier occupied a cove at the edge of Dogwood Harbor, and while the main channel out of the harbor was more-or-less clear, the cove had frozen. More than simply covered with glass ice, the surface was choked with blocks of ice a couple of inches thick. The good news: The ice was not a single sheet but rather a scramble of small chunks, each a foot or two wide. Near the channel these broke off from the pack like tiny bergs. Even so, an ice harness gripped *Lady Katie*, held perfectly plumb from keel to waist to mast tip.

"Here I am back from Tolchester," Stanley said, "and thar's ice here, too. It likes to follow me. Yes, sir." Stanley lowered his tailgate, which creaked and landed with a thud. In the back he had secured half a dozen five-gallon cans, full of gasoline for the winder engine. Stanley let us carry these to the boat. Leroy and Bird Eye each carried a can. I grabbed two, one in each hand. Tommy shook his head. First rule for a green hand: Don't work harder than the regular crew. I passed Stanley on the pier twice. He shuttled only his brown-bag lunch but was moving slowly that January morning. The cold had caused his gout to act up. He winced in pain as he settled to his knees in order to climb backward onto the boat. Lowering himself, he said, "When you get to be a hundred, you back onto one of these drudge boats." Stanley's self-deprecation did not disguise the pain in his swollen feet. He moved like a man suffering from frostbite.

"I better warm up the winder engines," Stanley said. "Solomon usually does it. I never thought I'd miss that old son of a bitch. He's never missed a day in thirty years. Hell, he's older than I am. And that's old."

The yawl-boat engine sputtered to life, and Tommy rode it as we lowered it into the water. The propeller dropped onto the ice like an eggbeater. Almost immediately, the ice around *Lady Katie*'s stern started to break up. The ice floe became pliable; each chunk floated away. It would be fairly easy, Stanley said, to plow our way toward the open channel.

Stanley backed her up, then shifted into forward gear and slammed the throttle full. *Lady Katie* lurched ahead. Ice ground loudly against the copper sheathing at her waterline, not unlike fingernails scraping on slate. You could hear it in your spine. *Lady Katie* bucked free. Then, with momentum, she sliced through the ice as if sweeping aside a drift of autumn leaves.

As we pushed through the next section of ice, a procession of skipjacks exited in front of us—from the main channel of Dogwood Harbor. In the faint light the silhouettes were indistinguishable. I counted six dredge boats making for open water. Like us, their sails were still furled against each boom; there was hardly a breath of wind. Stanley pointed to two more boats pushing out of Knapps Narrows. From here we could only see the running lights on their shrouds. But Stanley knew they were brethren. The only Chesapeake sailboats likely to be challenging dawn and ice and bitter cold on a January morning were skipjacks. No one would do it for pleasure.

"That'll be Russell and Robbie," Stanley said. "Looks like nine of us are going to pay them tongers a visit."

THE NINE SKIPJACKS descended on Sands as if they were an armed squadron. Without losing speed they rounded Bar Neck beacon, turned southwest, and set their sights on a dozen workboats hovering at the mouth of Black Walnut Cove. The dredgers did not have exclusive rights to Sands, but today they would claim a portion of it nonetheless. It was seven o'clock, still eight minutes before sunrise, but the tongers were already sounding the bottom with their bamboo poles, trying to get a fix on a "rank patch," or a sizable cache of oysters. The dredgers held their course, drawing a bead on the tongers. At 150 yards it appeared a collision was certain.

At this point Glendi Larrimore, Stanley's father, would have turned his back, absolving himself of the coming impact. But Stanley looked straight ahead. The skipjacks bore down. Closer. One hundred yards. Fifty. Then, at the last possible moment, the tongers scattered. Like a flock of spooked birds, they skimmed across the water and settled down about a quarter mile away. All but one.

Sam Crockett ("Stoney") stood on top of the culling board of his workboat *Striptease*, hands on hips, and stared the dredgers down. Stoney was known as the meanest, most contrary waterman on the Choptank River, a man with a poker face to match. He stood there, calling the dredgers' bluff. With less than forty yards to go, the lead boat, *Esther F.*, turned off the wind. She cut a ring, a wide arc, around Stoney. The rest of us followed, forming a circle like a school of sharks surrounding a wounded man. Stoney just stood fast, as the sun climbed above the horizon and bathed all of us in a reddish yellow light. More weather coming, a waterman would claim. And he was usually right.

"Defiant son of a bitch, ain't he?" Tommy said.

"He's guarding a small patch," said Stanley. "A hill really. That's where them drudgers worked yesterday. After them tongers were kind enough to show Freddie where they were." He smiled at Tommy and me. "If Stoney don't move, we'll never get on them orsters again."

Just then, Pete left the pack, raised his jib, and sailed *Hilda Willing* east into the sunrise to work on Bunker Hill. He had left the table and folded his hand.

Stoney may have taken this as encouragement because he picked up his long tongs and dropped the rakes into the water. He was well anchored, and the sounding pole must have shown something because, when he pulled up the tongs, he had—it looked like—a good catch, which he dumped onto his culling board. Problem was it was only empty shell. Stoney skipped the flat shells back into the water as if they were casino chips. Was he bluffing? Or had the hill been stripped bare? Stoney's face was blank. He set his tongs down, weighed anchor, and motored through our circle. He joined up with the other tongers and was greeted by a rattling of tongs.

The lump was too small for seven dredge boats to work efficiently. Recognizing this, Russell and Robbie peeled off, taking *Kathryn* and *Wilma Lee* across the river to Todds Point, an oyster reef off the southern shore. The rest of us stayed behind to try and break into the hard-packed bottom around Stoney's hill—to see if there were some live oysters still lying about. The wind picked up, but it was a Tuesday, so we would be pushing. Stanley ordered new dredges—flat plates with teeth (toothed gummers)—to be attached. Leroy and Bird Eye hefted these out of the hold, bitching about the weight, and we put them on. It would not take long to see if this hill still held any bounty. And, in fact, it took only a few licks to confirm the problem wasn't that the reef was too hard. The reef was picked clean. The toothed gummers broke into the foundation, but only blank shell surfaced. "The orsters are gone," Stanley said. "What was here, the tongers and us caught yesterday. I'm telling ya—orsters are scarce. You can thank overharvesting. And pollution—it's turning the Bay brown. On top of that, most places the disease is getting worse. Nothing is lasting very long." The captain glanced at the raft of tongers. "Damn that Stoney. Here we stand: fighting over an empty hill."

THAT DAY, ON Black Walnut Sands, wasn't the first standoff. The argument over territory between tongers and dredgers stretched back 130 years to the most colorful time in the history of the Chesapeake—the Oyster Wars.

Throughout the late 1800s, the rivers of Maryland's Eastern Shore set the stage for numerous conflicts among watermen, hostilities that regularly ended in bloodshed. Shortly after the Civil War, when sail dredging was legalized, pirate oyster schooners invaded the Choptank, usually under the cover of darkness, to raid oyster beds reserved for tongers. One famous incident happened in 1873, the first recorded skirmish among the counties where Tilghman's Island, Cambridge, and Deal reside. Then as now, Somerset County dredgers (Deal Islanders), having exhausted the reefs of Tangier Sound, sailed north in their dredge boats to rake up oysters in the northern counties. On one moonless night that year, a small fleet of Deal Islanders entered the Choptank to dredge on tongers' ground, not far from Black Walnut Sands. They had picked a bad night for a raid. Captain James Langrall of the newly formed Oyster Navy, established to stem the conflict, had been hired to patrol the mouth of the Choptank with specific orders to run off oyster pirates from Somerset County. And his schooner *Regulator* was outfitted with large guns. During the gunplay that ensued, Langrall's men killed two Deal Island watermen, setting off a blood feud. In the weeks that followed, animosities among the counties escalated to the point—with more shootings back and forth—that the *Baltimore American* reported a civil war was brewing in the middle Chesapeake.

The Oyster Wars had officially begun only eight years before, the day that the 1865 sail-dredge law passed in Annapolis. Hand tongers, who made up the bulk of Maryland watermen, had always been against dredging. Now that it was allowed, they viewed the dividing of waters—rivers for tongers, the Bay for sail dredgers—as a poor solution to the inevitable conflict. They were right. Almost immediately, dredgers coveted tongers' ground. In the decades after the Civil War the dockside value of a bushel of oysters climbed from five cents to forty-five cents, and a captain could net over $2,000 in a season, four times the average postwar yearly income. The temptation was too great.

Outlaw dredgers preferred fog or nights of the new moon for storming oyster grounds. Many wore black; others coated their sails with mud for camouflage. Trail boards were covered to obscure the name of each boat. Each raiding party selected a lookout boat that had the job of sailing the periphery to watch for police boats. The sentinel had a code. A flag (in the fog) or a lantern (at night) would be quickly raised and lowered from the mast as a signal that a patrol vessel had been sighted. As always with watermen, the tools and techniques of the trade were passed from father to son. Young tongers were taught to defend their boats and their catch with their lives. For dredgers it was a time of desperation: Captains and crews often fired first, tempted by oysters that fetched a price worthy of breaking the law. It was Wild West on the Chesapeake, and nearly every waterman wore a gun.

During the heyday of the wars in the 1880s, some outlaws gained notoriety, even celebrity status. Their skill at outsmarting the tongers and the police regularly made the newspapers in Baltimore. Among the most notorious was Gus Rice. He has been described as a red-faced rogue with a scraggly beard that "made him look every inch the killer he was." In the years since the Civil War he had been an orchard hand, a drifter, a barroom brawler, and an outlaw waterman. When he was hired on as captain of the schooner *J. C. Mahoney*, he rounded up crew from the jails of Baltimore and vowed that no man would keep him from dredging oysters. Anywhere he wished. Rice already had a solid reputation among watermen for plotting the (unsuccessful) murder of Hunter Davidson, commander of the Maryland Oyster Navy. Quickly, he became the acknowledged leader of the pirate dredgers of the Upper Bay.

The Oyster Navy was overwhelmed by the sheer number of marauding fleets on the Eastern Shore. Nearly every river had its band of outlaws. Outnumbered, the police were no match for the dredgers, and Gus Rice began raiding the reefs of the Chester River with impunity. The tongers were left to fend for themselves. In the early spring of 1888 the Chester River tongers positioned a pair of cannon at the river's mouth in a desperate attempt to drive the dredgers away. They fired on *J. C. Mahoney* and the other desperados for a couple of days without hitting anything. Gus Rice tried to ignore the splash of cannonballs around him but at length grew weary. On an April night after a good catch, Rice broke out several jugs of whiskey for his men, and soon the fleet was emboldened to send a raiding party ashore. They discovered a solitary watchman guarding the cannon. Gus ordered the man stripped bare and sent him running naked down the shore to warn his fellow tongers that Gus Rice was here to stay.

The police and tongers fought the dredgers for over fifty years, into the 1920s, but neither defeated nor controlled them. Only the poor prices (as low as fifteen cents a bushel) during the Depression, coupled with a scarcity of oysters, subdued the outlaw fleets. After a time though, perhaps inevitably, a commingling of events reignited the Oyster Wars. In 1942 watermen from Maryland and Virginia hit a big oyster strike on Swan Point in the Potomac River. The oysters were fat and brought a high price, so watermen from both states wanted access to them. Naturally, they fought over the prize. But there was little policing. (During the Second World War, Maryland had difficulty enforcing oyster laws since her boats were on loan to the Coast Guard.) After the war and removal of price controls, oysters climbed to two dollars a bushel, invigorating the conflict even more. Through the 1950s, there was gunfire on the Potomac, and both watermen and policemen were wounded, all this within an hour of the nation's capital. Meanwhile, the Maryland and Virginia legislatures spent ten years arguing over who had fishing rights to the river. The matter was not settled until President Kennedy signed the Potomac River Fisheries Commission into law, which now administers fishing in the river. At that point, Maryland sail dredgers were excluded from the Potomac, and they are not allowed in those waters to this day.

But don't tell a tonger or dredger that the Oyster Wars are over.

Come each winter along the Choptank the feud seems alive and well. Frequently, the watermen argue over the lines that demarcate tonging and dredging grounds. Still, casualties are rare—watermen have been nearly disarmed. (Today, skipjacks, by law, can carry no more than two shotguns of ten gauge or smaller bore—though some would call that a cannon, a sufficient size to put a hole in a boat and sink her.) Rarely is there shooting anymore, but boats do get rammed, and other mischief abounds. Sometimes the tong-dredge boundaries mysteriously move about. Under cover of darkness, a skipjack captain will drag the state oyster buoys up to a quarter of a mile inshore and then set them down on tongers' ground. Of course, the next night the tongers drag them back. Well, back a quarter of a mile and a little more. In memory of Gus Rice, no doubt.

STANLEY HAD FORSAKEN Black Walnut Sands and, raising his sails in a fresh breeze, sailed *Lady Katie* the four miles across the river to Todds Point, where it promptly snowed. Huge flakes fell and clung to the rigging, blanketing the bowsprit and deck, white on white: There is nothing prettier than a skipjack in the snow. Visibility dropped to less than a quarter mile. We couldn't see Art Daniels up the river or Wadey Murphy across the Bay. Stanley hit a nice spot: The oysters were plump, our dredges were full, and we were alone, just our sister skipjacks pushing nearby. No tongers in sight. When a respectable thirty bushels were aboard, we stored the heavy dredges—with much cursing—and set a course for home.

On the way in, the crew's thoughts turned to money. They were earning so little at these prices—twenty dollars per bushel, a drop of 37 percent since the launch of the season—that they decided not to sail anymore. They told the captain they'd only work on power days—Mondays and Tuesdays—for the rest of the season. Stanley seemed to take this in stride. He'd been expecting it. On a sail day, even when the wind ran right, they could only catch half as many oysters as on a power day. Still, Stanley wondered what these men would do for the balance of the week. He, for one, would rather be sailing for half the pay than sitting around earning nothing. These younger men were wired differently than he had been at their age. The old-time waterman's work ethic—and the six-day workweek—was a thing of the past.

Stanley remained on deck, glued to the wheel. His bare right hand gripped a single spoke. Snow gathered on the bill of his cap. His lone boot prints stenciled the snow. Stanley seemed content to stay at the helm of his skipjack, if need be, all day and all night. Perhaps he was holding on to every sail as if it were his last, memorizing the feel of the wheel, the pull of the sheet, the trim of the main. The thrilling look of a dozen skipjacks combing a bar, full sails aloft and surging, their crews bent to culling. But he spoke of other things.

"I traded some orsters for a goose," he said. "I think I got the better part of the deal. Those were common orsters the day I traded them. Green ones from Six Foot Knoll. I think I'll take some of these selects from today and have Loretta make some stuffing for that goose. That'd be fine dining. Yes, sir." Stanley was a man of unfailing appetite.

Lady Katie broke out of the snow and into the sunlight. Her jib and main ballooned with the trailing southerly breeze—a fair wind. She sailed herself. Ahead, the harbor rim had become encrusted with ice again, the floes and leads now covered with snow. Children ice-skated at the edges. We kept to the main channel and tied up in Dogwood Cove. The crew stowed the sails. Stanley lumbered onto the wharf and shuffled over to his truck, which he turned on to get the battery charging. It roared to life, and I inadvertently inhaled diesel exhaust, which had been so pleasantly absent on our sail home. We off-loaded the oysters in bushel baskets, setting them for the moment on the rickety pier. Leroy and Bird Eye drove off down the road with two days' pay in their pockets.

Out of the blue, a grating noise—the screeching sound of rusty metal hinges—came from behind Stanley's truck. There stood a big green Dumpster. Behind it, Mister Boats, the island salvager, was pulling something from among the garbage and refuse discarded from the county dock. He stooped over, shrouded in black— ebony coat and pants—resembling an outsized crow picking at promising trash.

The Dumpster lid shook with Mister Boats's effort, and debris scattered onto the ground, to each side of the sliding door. All of a sudden he pulled out his prize: an upright purple vacuum cleaner. Mister Boats looked pleased. Smiling with a half set of teeth, he placed the vacuum in his metal-mesh grocery cart and wheeled it over to me. Stanley and Tommy had loaded half the oyster baskets into the truck and drove slowly toward the shucking house. As they passed us, Stanley lifted three fingers off the steering wheel in farewell. "Mister Boats," he said, tipping his hat. Oyster shells crumbled under the weight of his tires.

"We rate three fingers from a captain," Mister Boats said. "You must've put in some work today."

Stanley had been a man short, I said, adding that I had tried to lend a hand.

Boats said, "I hear Stanley is selling *Lady Katie*, soon as the season's over."

I allowed as I had heard the rumor, too. But something had kept me from asking the captain about it. I could not imagine a Chesapeake without Stanley Larrimore sailing on it. The Bay would be diminished somehow.

"I'd like to get my hands on them mast hoops," Mister Boats said, looking at the tethered skipjack. "Them wooden blocks and ironwork would fetch a small fortune, too. Whole fleet'll be up for sale soon, I expect."

I hated Boats for saying that.

Perhaps sensing my mood, he lifted his eyes from *Lady Katie* to the horizon and said, "Nothing survives." He glanced at me and looked up the river again. "Nothing except the memory of the thing."

Mister Boats, scavenger, repairman, and drunk, was a philosopher, too. Water will do that to you.

We circled the harbor and made for Gibsontown Road. Mister Boats pushed the vacuum in the cart, which rattled incessantly. The conversation condensed to the peculiarities of "small engines and what-not," as he called his specialty.

Miss Pauline hollered at us from her front porch. "Boys, you're just in time for supper." Mister Boats and I looked at each other. He was twice my age, and Miss Pauline calling me a boy was even a stretch. "She probably thinks we've been playing," said Boats. I nodded. Of course, we had been.

Naturally, there was no refusing food from Miss Pauline. So we stepped inside and washed up, leaving our boots by the door. Max, her dog, and Cat were lounging on the cool linoleum floor. Something was already sizzling in the pan, and the aroma of fried food wandered through the house. "Cakes," said Miss Pauline in answer to my question. "Cakes'll be ready in ten minutes." She must have seen us coming from the harbor since the midafternoon meal was nearly ready: crab cakes cooking in butter and fresh cornbread emerging from the oven. "Now boys," Miss Pauline said, "don't touch this johnnycake till it cools off a little." She set it on a trivet on the kitchen table. "If you must snack, have a deviled egg." Clearly, the implication was that if we did snitch a bit of cornbread, we'd be punished, kept after school cleaning erasers or some such. Just as a precaution she slapped my hand.

Miss Pauline served the crab cakes—two apiece, golden brown and steaming. At last we were permitted cornbread, too. She sat down, said grace, and made an announcement.

"Today, sixty-five years ago, I got engaged," she said, passing the tartar sauce. "Wes loved crab cakes. He was the finest, the funniest man I ever knew." Mister Boats swallowed a deviled egg whole and then lifted his head to listen.

"I remember that day. We were on his skipjack, the *Ruth*, at the dock, and he dropped to one knee, looked up at me, and said, 'I have two questions.' Well, I asked what, and he said, 'First, will you marry me?' Well, 'Wesley Jenkins,' I said, 'of course, I'll marry you. What's the second question?' He struggled on his knee and said, 'Will you help me up?'" Miss Pauline threw her head back and giggled at the memory. "He always made me laugh," she said. "That was our secret."

Mister Boats asked her where they went on their honeymoon. He had been married once and divorced and never spoke of it. The pain of the memory ran too deep.

"That was another trick he pulled on me," Miss Pauline said. "We got married but had to wait until the end of oyster season to go on our honeymoon. He promised me a tropical vacation. 'We'll go south to the islands,' he said. Well, come spring he took my suitcase and stowed it on the *Ruth*. I said, 'What are you doing? Where's the cruise ship? I thought we were going south to the islands.' He laughed and said, 'We are. We're going to the islands in Tangier Sound, starting with Deal. Load up the skipjack.'" She smiled at the thought of her husband. Nineteen thirty-two: a simpler time, when the skipjack fleet and island life seemed like they would go on forever.

Mister Boats helped himself to another crab cake and three more eggs. It was obvious he hadn't eaten in a while. Miss Pauline finished her small plate and looked across the table at us. Her eyes glanced down at the second helpings we had on our plates and then up at us. Her eyebrows arched. "Well?" she said. Now she was fishing.

Mister Boats flashed his toothless smile. He had tasted this recipe before. Being a novice, I tried to be more demonstrative.

"These are fine cakes," I said, wiping the corners of my mouth with a napkin. "Best I've ever eaten." This was no exaggeration. They were backfin crab, delicately seasoned, and golden fried. I suspected a hidden ingredient had made them sweet and tangy at the same time.

Miss Pauline looked bashful all of a sudden. Seeing this vulnerability, Mister Boats took another bite and livened up. "Now, Pauline, I'll ask you again," he said. "What's your trick?"

"No, I don't have a special recipe. A little bit of this. And a little bit of something else. That's all there is to it."

"Something else," said Mister Boats. "See, you do have a secret."

"No, I really don't. I will tell you something, though: If you pick your own crab, you get a little shell in it like today." This was by way of an apology.

Mister Boats had her on the hook and he wasn't letting go. "Pauline," he said, "these simply don't taste like other crab cakes. Now, what do you do?"

"I don't do anything unusual but two things." We leaned forward in our chairs. "I scoop out a little bit of the fat from the corners of the shell and mix that in." Bingo. And the second thing, I asked. "Well, today, I used winter crabs—they're illegal. Maybe that helps."

The "fat" is the yellowish substance, sometimes called "mustard," that is clumped inside the pointed tips of the top shell of a blue crab. Some people eat it when feasting on steamed crabs. Most do not. The flavor is nutty, not unlike almond paste. Adding it to the crabmeat was Miss Pauline's secret ingredient. It gave the recipe a decisive nudge ahead of others. She had revealed the mystery. Boats looked pleased.

Miss Pauline had a suggestion for harvesting the mustard, which, like most things of the water, was lunar. "Catch your crabs a week after the new moon," she said. "Most crabs shed at the full moon and it takes 'em three weeks or so to get the fat back on them." The best crab cakes are hard won.

MISS PAULINE'S CRAB CAKES

Steam 2 doz. jimmy blue crabs (with Old Bay Seasoning).
Pick clean. Save yellow fat.

¼ cup mayonnaise
1 tsp. dry mustard
1 tsp. Worcestershire Sauce
¼ tsp. black pepper
1 pinch salt or a shake of Old Bay
1 slice toasted bread (crumbled)
1 large egg, beaten
Measure: 1 lb. crabmeat (backfin only)

Mix all ingredients except crab in bowl. Add crab fat
and egg. Mix well. Add crabmeat. Slowly and gently mix
ingredients into crab without breaking crab apart. Fry in
butter.

Makes 6-8 patties

A knock echoed off the windowpane of the back kitchen door.
Wadey Murphy burst in. He peered around, and Miss Pauline
waved him over to the table. Wadey had a mischievous sparkle in
his eye, like a boy playing hookey. "Why're ya eating crabs, Miss
Pauline?" he asked. "Tha're not in season."

"You gave them to me, Wadey," Miss Pauline said. "Don't you
remember?"

"Not me. That'd be illegal." Wadey smiled. They had been
through this routine before. "It's the season for oysters, not crabs,
Miss Pauline. You taught me that."

"We didn't have any orsters to fix."

"Now you do," Wadey said. He stepped outside and returned

quickly with his hands full. He set a bushel basket on the kitchen floor. It was half full of oysters, most of them small. "Miss Pauline, these ran a little short. I couldn't sell 'em so I saved 'em for you." He gestured toward Mister Boats and me. "One of these two'll shuck 'em for you. You'll get a couple of quarts from these."

"Oh, Wadey, you're trying to get in my good graces again," Miss Pauline said, shaking her finger. "Will you have some crab cakes then?"

"No, I just came by to get Chris. We have a meeting to go to. It's urgent." I wondered what he was talking about.

Miss Pauline, never fast on goodbyes, pretended not to hear him. "Wadey," she said, "I wanted to thank you for those crabs, so I wrote you a letter. But, I thought, no, I better not mail it. Jackie might open your mail. If she saw another woman writing her husband, she might get jealous." We all laughed, Miss Pauline the loudest.

I stood up, thanked the cook and the company, and followed Wadey through the back door, the same way we had entered of course. On the back wall I noticed a needlepoint sampler that read:

AND ON THE EIGHTH DAY, GOD MADE TILGHMAN'S

And on the ninth, Miss Pauline. She waved from the door. "Be careful, boys," she called. "Supposed to be a chill in the air toward night."

Wadey's truck was idling in the driveway. We jumped in and unzipped our jackets; the heater was on full blast. Knowing of his aversion to meetings, I asked if there really was one. "Yes," he said, "all the drudge-boat captains are meeting at the firehouse to talk about Hooper Strait. It seems the patent tongers want to take it away from us." This was the latest news of the day; Black Walnut Sands was already history. Like Howell Point in the Choptank, Hooper Strait in Tangier Sound was reserved for dredgers. Typically in the domain of the Deal skipjacks, Hooper Strait had not been worked in a couple of years because of the disease, but the state's fall oyster survey results were promising. Here, MSX— now acknowledged by most watermen—was on the retreat. Market-size oysters along the strait were surviving, which fueled the hopes of local oystermen. And not just dredgers. Patent tongers wanted to get ahold of it for next year. How they could change the law and turn a dredge rock into tongers' bottom was a mystery to me. I was about to ask about it when Wadey said, "Let's drink a beer."

I reminded him we were in a hurry to get to the firehouse. "Honey, not that big a hurry," he said with a wink. "I didn't want Miss Pauline to get too sweet on you."

The bar at Harrison's Chesapeake House was crowded. Half of the patrons were guests of the hotel, clad in corduroys and bright crew-neck sweaters. The other half consisted of watermen in plaid flannel. Half a dozen were regulars. Though the oyster prices had dropped steadily after New Year's, the price of a bottle of beer (Budweiser) had stayed the same: two dollars. It was something you could count on.

The only other skipjack captain in the room was Bobby Marshall. Two stools sat empty to his left at the bar. We joined him. Without asking, Buddy Harrison set two Budweisers in front of us. Wadey called for a third for Bobby and began placing six dollars on the bartop. Buddy picked them up, but Wadey was still pinching the other ends. He did not let go.

"You cut me two dollars yesterday, Buddy," he said. "I was getting twenty-two dollars a booshel last week at your dock."

"That's the market—it's twenty dollars now—all you can expect for January," Buddy said. He grabbed the dollars out of Wadey's fingers and put them in his cash register.

Wadey nodded and lit a cigarette; he only smoked Marlboros when he drank. "The market looking bad, Buddy?" he asked, conceding his hand.

"It's a seasonal market for fresh oysters, you know," Buddy said. "Before Christmas we load oysters by the trailerload for the big cities and the Midwest. That market's all but dried up now. It never lasts. At these prices—seven dollars a pint—oysters are a luxury item. People don't have the disposable income for 'em right now."

"When do you plan to cut 'em again?" Bobby asked.

"February or March. You can't lose money and stay in business." Buddy walked to the other end of the bar to greet some hotel guests. Watermen, like Wadey and Bobby, had no choice but to go along with the cut. Or strike. But they weren't temperamentally suited to collective bargaining. Try to place three watermen at a table and they can't agree who should sit where.

"Well," said Bobby, turning to Wadey, "we only got a couple of places left—Todds Point, Sands, maybe you on Old Rock. When those rocks are caught up, you might as well tie these skipjacks to the dock, cause you ain't gonna get neither crew to go out thar for fifteen, twenty, twenty-five booshel. You can't make a living on that. Not at these prices."

"I'll tell you one thing," said Wadey, draining his beer. "It's gonna get a lot worse before it gets better."

Buddy pulled three cold Budweisers from the cooler and set them in front of us. I'd have to catch up apparently. Bobby reached for some money, as did I, but Wadey was quicker. He handed the bills to Buddy and this time let him have them.

Bobby shook his head. "See, Wadey, damn it," he said, "every time I'm about to ridicule you, you do something nice. How come you have such a bad reputation for being a son of a bitch?" Wadey only smiled.

"I'll tell you what," Bobby said, addressing Buddy across the countertop, "Wadey is the best of all to work around. Bart and Wadey, both. It don't matter if they ain't never hit neither orster all day long. If you hit a place, they won't come over your buoy and steal from you. They respect your spot. Not like the rest of 'em. All except Stanley. Maybe Pete Sweitzer, Art Daniels, the older men. Now I don't catch that many orsters. Not like Wadey. I've got a small boat. But when I do get on 'em, I'd like to have a fair chance to catch 'em. I wouldn't sail north with those younger sons of bitches. They can have the Upper Bay to themselves. I'd rather work alone in the river with fewer orsters than have them around."

"They'll all be thar tonight," Wadey said.

"Where?"

"Firehouse. In half an hour."

"Yeah, I heard something," Bobby said. "What's it about— Hooper Strait?"

"Dorchester County patent tongers are trying to steal Hooper Strait from us. They say thar're no more skipjacks in their county, so they should be able to tear up that oyster rock, too, like they've done everywhere else. They've made a petition to Annapolis."

"Patent tongers have no right to that ground. It's drudgers' bottom. Tha'll kill our orsters. We gotta speak up."

"But I can't say anything at the meeting," Wadey said. "If I do, Bart will just take the opposite position to spite me. That's what he did when we tried to make Black Walnut Sands a sail-drudge-only rock like Howell Point. He went against it, and we didn't get a sail bar close to home. Better if I keep quiet."

CHRISTMAS LIGHTS NO longer framed Main Street, nor the firehouse, but the bright interior flooded out of the windows onto the snow. Inside, behind the fire engine bay, the skipjack captains filled the small recreation room. They sat upon or leaned against every available fixture—the furnace, the water pump, the video-game machine, the walk-in freezer. Three skippers—Stanley, Johnnie, and Ed—sat on the edge of the pool table in the center of the space. Wadey occupied a chair in a corner. The recreation area was not actually a room but simply an extension of the truck bay, so the rear of the red fire truck abutted the pool table, and the ladder hung overhead like a canopy. The firehouse was overheated as winter buildings often are.

Most of the Talbot County dredgers had shown up; only three were missing—Gene Tyler (sick), Bunky Chance (boat just sank), and Bobby Marshall, who had left the bar but never stopped off at the firehouse. Daryl came in late and stood next to the engine with one foot on a coiled fire hose. Bart stood at the water pump diagonally across the room from Wadey, at geometrical extremes. Russell Dize, captain of *Kathryn*, stood next to the low freezer along one wall and was the first to speak.

"Well, I guess everybody's heard—the patent tongers want to take Hooper Strait away from us. To get ahold of it, they'd have to change the law, right?" he said, looking at Stanley, next to Pete Sweitzer the most senior man.

"I would think so, sure," said Stanley. "These orster rocks are divided up by law."

Russell said, "If they go to the state legislature, they'd have more power than us. Tha're a thousand boats; we're only eighteen."

"They could do it," said Bart. "Patent tongers took lower Tangier Sound away from us years ago. Now they want the head of the sound, too. Great Rock down thar was the biggest bar in the whole Chesapeake Bay and, when they got ahold of it, they dug it up. Sold all the little orsters and tore up the reef like a strip mine. It's gone now."

"The whole Bay belonged to us at one time," said Stanley. "Hand tongers had the rivers, but we had all the bay bottom. That was before patent tongers came along. Now nothing belongs to just us."

"Nothing except Hooper Strait and this river," Frank Lowery said.

"Patent tongers get all the seed, all the shell," said Bart. "They get all the ground—and still overharvest. Tha're a greedy bunch of people—pigs, that's all."

"A lot of that going around," said Pete.

Missing a beat, Frank said, "Them boys have been working Hooper Strait all winter, catching small orsters. They just want to make it legal."

"Catching smalls ain't legal," said Daryl. "I ought to know." A ripple of laughter circled the room.

"Some days all they catch is smalls," Russell added. "No law to stop them. We're the ones are regulated. We have a history of regulations over a hundred years or more. Maybe it's time we had fewer restrictions, too."

"That's right," said Robbie. "If we have to let them tongers get Hooper Strait, now's the time to get something in return." The younger captains all nodded their heads.

Daryl Larrimore was the first to his feet. "I'd like to see if we can't start arlier," he said. "Start in October like the tongers. Even the skin divers get to start October first, while we sit ashore for four weeks."

"I agree with you," Robbie said. "We're being discriminated against."

"Hell," Daryl continued, "that first month you could make what you do the whole rest of the season. You got good weather, good wind, and you got orsters—"

"You got orsters and price," said another.

"Yeah, the price is best then," said Johnnie, joining the young dredgers in their chorus. "Let's catch 'em when it pays best."

"I'd also like to see a longer season until the end of March," said Frank, upping the ante. "We have no work that time of year." The younger captains smiled in unison but then turned toward Stanley and Bart and Pete. Wadey still sat off to himself.

"Well," said Stanley, "I'm against any concessions like extending the season till April. Why catch 'em when tha're cheap when we can wait and catch 'em the next fall for top dollar. It doesn't do anything for us. No, sir." Stanley then dropped his head. He stared at the floor around his feet, shifting his eyes as if the junior captains were dropping dredges left and right.

Russell turned toward Wadey and asked him if he agreed. Wadey nodded underneath his downturned hat, bit his lip, and fought to keep silent. It took him only a moment to lose his resolve. The room instantly turned quiet. "If we ask to start when they start, then tha're going to want to work the way we work," he said. "Tha'll want two days of power drudging, too. Ya open up a whole can of worms. Leave it alone." Tongers had sought the right to dredge off their motorized workboats for years—contrary to the sail-only law—but at that point the state still restricted them to working their scissorlike tongs.

After a polite moment, Frank said, "I say we ask for the early start and a later finish." It was as if he hadn't heard a word from Stanley or Wadey. Now everybody spoke at once—the young ones calling for a longer season and the old ones lamenting their greed.

Pete's face turned red and he held up his hand to break into the colliding voices. Slowly the voices trailed off and he began to speak. "When ye're young," he said, "ya have the ambition and physical power to do anything, but ya don't know how. Then, when ye're old, ya know how but can't do it anymore. Boys don't listen to old men. That's the way it's always been, I guess. But let me say this: Drudgers and tongers have done it this way for over a hundred years. Thar's a reason for that. It's a tradition. Things are in balance. If ya fiddle with one gear, the whole machine will stop running right. For once, trust the older captains on this. Stanley, Wade, and Bart trusted their fathers and their grandfathers before them. We all make a good living. Leave it at that."

The room was silent for a few seconds. Bart, nodding at Pete, was the first to break the lull. "Before we talk about getting something in return for Hooper Strait, let's ask whether we should give it up in the first place." Bart had been sitting on the water pump, and now he stood up. "If we let the patent tongers have Hooper Strait, what's next?"

"Choptank River's next," said Stanley. "You can bet on it."

"That's the next step all right," said Robbie. "The patent tongers want all Dorchester County waters back in their territory."

"It's a river by river thing," said Russell, "but they'll have one victory behind them."

Just when it looked like everyone was on the same page, Daryl said, "I still don't see why we can't go where everyone else goes, and at the same time." His uncle rubbed his eyes.

Stanley said, "It's important we have a different season than the tongers. That means we're a different fishery with different regulations. Otherwise, like Wadey says, tongers will try to get power drudging, too. How would you like a thousand boats drudging in the Bay?"

Frank shook his head. "I have a compromise: Let's change both our starts to October fifteenth," he said. "That'd give us two weeks arlier and take two weeks off of them."

Wadey Murphy, red-faced, exhaled his breath in a long, low whistle.

"Frank, I'd like an early start," said Daryl, "but make it four weeks."

"I agree," said Bart Murphy. There it was: Despite his senior age, he was going to take the opposite stance of his brother Wade.

Almost immediately, another offer came over the transom. Ed Farley, captain of *H. M. Krentz*, said, "Wouldn't it be wiser to not ask for a new season but, instead, ask for a third push day?"

"We could use three days of power," Daryl said. "Not every sail day has had any wind."

"I'd like to have Monday, Wednesday, and Friday," said Russell.

"Why not let us pick which three we want on any given week," said Daryl. "Without more power days, I might as well quit."

Ed jumped off the pool table, where he had been sitting, and walked over to the ladder hanging off the tail end of the fire truck. He turned around and grabbed the last rung overhead with both hands and addressed the gathering. "The only problem is, if we ask for a third push day, once again we'd see pressure by the tongers for power drudging on their own."

"That's not the only problem you'd have," said Stanley. "If three out of five days was power, who would bother with sailing? We might as well chop off our masts and put an engine aboard."

"You'd wear out the beds, too," said Pete. "The whole reason sailing has lasted this long is that it protects the orsters."

Stanley said, "That's why they made the sail-only law 130 years ago—to give the bars a rest. After all, we only work when the wind is right—"

"It was just about the first conservation law on the Bay," Pete broke in, "and it's kept the skipjack in business all these years, the skipjack and orster both. Why mess with success?"

A minute passed without a word crossing the room.

"One thing's for sure," Bart said, closing ranks, "we gotta fight and fight for Hooper Strait. We gotta keep it a skipjack-only bar if we can."

"But if they do take it away from us," Daryl said, "we need to tell the state what we want in return."

"I agree with Daryl," said Frank. "We ought to fight fire with fire. We should get our heads together and come up with a package of what we want. For starters we want the Choptank River left alone. Some of us want an early start, some want power. We won't get it all, so let's ask for more than we can get." Frank looked around the room at his allies—Russell, Robbie, Johnnie, Daryl, Freddie, and Ed—and locked eyes with each. They viewed the tongers' attack as an opportunity to loosen the restraints on the skipjack fleet, even if it made overfishing more likely. The rest of the room saw the assault as just that, a siege on their way of life.

Ed returned the stare. "Are the Deal Islanders gonna fight alongside us?" he asked Frank.

"Stan Daniels told us he's gonna make sure they do. Tha're having a breakfast meeting. I'll talk to 'em after that. But I'll tell ya, I already told them if we have to give up something, I want to get something in return. That's what I'll tell Annapolis, too."

Pete stood up and made one step toward Frank. "You don't listen," he shouted. "The only thing you'll be getting in return is an end to your profession! Neither orster will be left." Pete then turned and walked slowly out of the station. Stanley and Wadey stole a glance at each other, then returned to their vacant stares.

Frank watched Pete go and then said, almost to himself, "I'm going home." Everybody marched out of the firehouse into the frigid night. The snow crunched underfoot. In the parking lot the men gathered in twos and threes to critique the meeting. They finally relaxed. Watermen are more comfortable under the cold winter stars than in a heated room.

Daryl buttonholed Frank and said facetiously, "Wadey sure was talkative. I can tell he's for it."

"Well," said Frank, "not everybody's gonna be for it."

Freddie was standing with them. "You can bet the Deal Islanders will be for more power days," he said.

"Except Art Daniels," Bart said.

"Yeah, except Art," Daryl agreed.

The other dredgers milled around the lot. Pete and Bart talked briefly about how to save Hooper Strait. Pete said he knew a state delegate and he'd make their case.

Wadey walked up to Stanley and spoke under his breath. "If these boys get what they want, it will open the door for them tongers. As soon as you want more, the other guy will want more. Ye're better off not asking. Anyway, if thar's ever three days of power, that'll be the end of sail drudging. You'll never see it again."

Stanley listened, then nodded and said, "A skipjack will no

longer be a skipjack. All she'll do is power drudge. Her sails will rot."

"It won't happen in my lifetime, if I can help it."

"No, sir."

The two men asserted their allegiance, and Wadey agreed to call Pete Jensen, the head of Tidewater Fisheries. The old Larrimore-Murphy rivalry was briefly set aside. As it happened, Stanley and Wadey drove in tandem out Main Street toward their homes south of town. And the remaining trucks headed out in as many directions as there were men.

9

February, The Deep

The smoky aroma of cut bacon arose from the galley and mingled with the brackish night air. Cookie stooped below in the cabin of *City of Crisfield*, preparing a sumptuous breakfast, his culinary magic illuminated by a single naked bulb that flickered a few times, casting broad shadows before it extinguished. The galley fell into the thick darkness of the last hours before dawn. No moon. Overhead, the constellation Boötes—the Herdsman, where winter watermen find their early-morning compass—dominated the center of the sky.

Cookie poked his head through the hatch and saw Captain Art Daniels standing on the Cambridge dock. Art was talking to three other Deal skippers: his son Stan, Walton Benton of *Somerset*, and Jack Parkinson of *Helen Virginia*. A lone Tilghman boat—*Rebecca*—nestled against *City*; Wadey was just now unlocking his cabin. All five captains were waiting on their crews.

Cookie raised his voice. "Cap'n, we lost the juice. Should I put a hold on breakfast?"

"I'll check on it," Captain Art said. "Keep cooking."

"Keep cooking," Cookie repeated. "Okay, Cap'n." He struck a match. There was a sudden glow from the four propane burners—now the only light on the boat—that silhouetted his head. The cook grabbed a flashlight from the cabintop and returned to the galley. Ice had coated his pots and pans, and he began thawing them out on the stove. It was twenty-four degrees and snowing lightly. Cookie rubbed his hands and held them to the stove flame. The bacon started to sizzle.

Art and Stan climbed onto the boat and each jiggled one of the battery cables that served the yawl boat, the winders, and the cabin. Cookie's lightbulb did not even blink. Stan stood up and looked at his father. "Daddy Art," he said, "I'll get my spare battery and some jumper cables. We'll try to recharge her." Stan stepped past Jack and Walton and marched over to *Howard*, the skipjack with the blue cabin. (She had sunk at the dock in January but had been refloated and was back in operation. Cambridge Harbor had been a better place to founder than in rough seas, and the brief submergence had done little damage to the skipjack— wood fares well in brackish water. But the navigation gear was destroyed; only a clock survived.) Shortly, Stan returned with the spare. He connected it to his father's battery and gave it a try. John-Boy, the latest arrival, started the yawl engine, which roared to life, and Cookie set his flashlight aside. The cabin was bright once again.

Wadey took advantage of the light streaming from the port-holes and climbed over his railing to join the Danielses aboard the *City*. Stan peered over toward *Howard* and dropped his head. "She's leaking all right," he said to Wadey. "Not as bad as she was, but thar's a steady stream. Pumps are keeping up with it, that's all I can hope for. I've pumped the Chesapeake Bay through that boat twice."

"She may be waterlogged, Stan," Wadey said. "She was under-water for, what, two days."

"Three. Yes, she's sluggish sailing all right. That wood at the base of the centerboard is rotten; it just splinters and falls off. I've chiseled cotton into her, but it's only window dressing. She keeps leaking just the same. What I need to do is put a new centerboard well and a new keelson into her. But with arsters scarce, I can't afford it. She's had some bad luck."

Wadey turned to me and whispered two words under his breath: "Blue paint."

Walton Benton joined the trio and stamped his feet against the cold. "I'll tell you what you could do," he said. "You could take these five drudge boats right here, take the best parts off each of them and stitch 'em together, and you still wouldn't have one good boat between them. It's too expensive to keep these boats up. It'd take $100,000 to rebuild one. Tha're all dying."

Wadey changed the subject. "What did you Deal drudgers decide about Hooper Strait? At Tilghman's, we couldn't get our heads together."

The men stood in the near pitch black—the light from the cabin merely scattered across their faces—but their voices were distinctive. In a thick brogue, Stan said, "We had a split decision, like Tilghman's. But neither island matters now. After your firehouse meeting, everybody called Annapolis—Pete, Bart, Russell—and every one of you told Pete Jensen a different story. Everybody had a wish list. That ought to confuse the regulators some. I imagine Hooper Strait is safe for now."

"Better be," Jack Parkinson said, mixing with the other captains. "I'd hate to lose more territory to the tongers."

Wadey said, "This is the Alamo. We've gotta stand our ground."

"In the 1960s," Art said, "the government took the Potomac River away from us. That was the beginning of the end of the arster business. Then they took the western shore—all those grounds between Annapolis and Solomons. Then they dug up Tea Table for oyster shells to make roads. What they should've done, in other words, is kept the whole Bay a drudging ground. We cultivate the bottom. Arsters would have a chance then."

"Hell, even if Hooper is reserved for skipjacks, patent tongers will cross the line anyway, legal or not," Walton said.

"I guess we'd do the same thing," Jack said.

"Not Daddy Art," said Stan. "He wouldn't cross the line. Would you, Daddy?"

"Probably not."

Jack said, "Remember, Art, in the seventies, we was all drudging on France bar in the Lower Choptank? And all twelve of us busted through the ice to cross onto tongers' ground, everyone except you. We caught a hundred booshel each and you only caught twelve. Why'd you hold back?"

"I live by the laws of God and the laws of man."

"I knowed it," Wadey said, in defense of his mentor. "That's what I figured."

Glancing at some shadows along the wharf, Jack and Walton stepped off the *City* and turned toward their boats. Their crews had arrived. Bob and Kevin Thompson, two of Walton's men, headed for *Somerset*. The brothers were the sons of Wallace Thompson, the last black captain, owner of the skipjack *Claud W. Somers* (1911), which sank in Tangier Sound in rough seas, a March squall, in 1977. All men drowned, including the captain, another son, a nephew, and an uncle. Like many watermen who had suffered drownings in their families, the Thompson brothers returned to the water all the same. Water was the only calling they knew.

First light had appeared to the east, extinguishing Arcturus (the brightest star in Boötes), and the faces of the captains and crews emerged from the shadows. A paper plate from the galley skittered across the deck and caught Stan's eye. A telltale. He pointed to the eastern sky, where a thin layer of black stratus perched on the horizon, like the rim of a volcano. This is known as a "lee set," a thin line of dark clouds in the sky opposite, leeward of, a building wind.

The signs of inclement weather stalled the Daniels's departure. They waited at the dock for breakfast and courage. Robert Daniels looked over his shoulder for his father, but the old man was pacing the middle deck. "He's getting a little age on him," brother Stan said, "so whenever he sees bad weather coming, he gets a little nervous."

"Daddy Art's my hero," his grandson Bobby said.

"I know he is," his father responded. "He's got ten or fifteen years more on this boat. You can bank on that. Daddy'll make eighty-five on the water."

"That's Daddy Art," said Stan. "Never surrender."

At that point, an old man in his nineties labored up to the wharf, straining under the weight of a bushel basket clasped tightly in his delicate hands. It was Walter Scott, a former waterman and a friend of Art Daniels. He had purchased a bushel of oysters off the *City* the evening before, had shucked them, and returned now with a basket of empty shells.

"Cap'n," he said to Art, "these orsters were plump. I could use another booshel this evening."

"Okay," Daddy Art said. "We should catch a few."

"I'd be in your debt if you'd take these shells and dump 'em back on the rock. Plant 'em somewhere that'll bring another booshel or two next year."

"Happy to do it. Why don't you stay and dine with us this morning?" Art extended his hand and helped the older man onto the boat. They counted 166 years between them.

Cookie Jones had prepared a full breakfast. Flavors of oatmeal, fried eggs and bacon, beaten biscuits, blackstrap molasses, and coffee brewed in the cabin. He had been whipping up such meals all season. Though he kept threatening it, he never had gone to Seattle to salmon-fish. Like all his brothers, Cookie was loyal to Daddy Art, regardless of his griping, showing up even when oysters were scarce. He had two siblings aboard this morning, Clarence and John-Boy, who hovered near the galley impatiently. Larry, the heavy eater and brother number four, was absent. He had asked Daddy Art for a day off to tend his chickens. The three Danielses—Jimmy, Robert, and Bobby—comprised the other half of the crew. Crewing *City of Crisfield* and *Howard* today were nine members of the Daniels clan. This was some sort of record, though every captain in the harbor had some kin on every boat.

And Daddy Art had a foolproof method of rounding them up: Cookie. The crew always arrived in time for his breakfasts. Waiting on Cookie now were five men crowded in the cabin and three on deck—Daddy Art and his two sons, Robert and Stan. With a "Ready for you, Cap'n," Cookie passed the first plate up to the afterdeck. Stan took the plate and lifted the plastic fork, but his father stopped him fast.

"Thar's only room on this boat for one captain, Stan," he said. Then, turning toward Robert, he said, "And that goes for you, too." Looking at these two huge men (and their much smaller father), it was easy to imagine that they had eaten their way out of house and home as young men. Daddy Art drew a chalk line on the deck and held his ground. Stan passed the plate back to his father, saying, "All this drudgery makes me hungry." Stan and Walter got the next two plates, and without a word to Cookie, Stan finished his eggs fast and jumped off the boat. He climbed aboard *Howard,* where his second breakfast awaited him. His wife, Ruth, deckhand and cook, only permitted him one helping, but she couldn't control Cookie. Or a wayward Stan.

Back on the *City,* the crew was laughing in the cabin while Cookie tried to flip the eggs without breaking them. "This cabin's so small there's not enough room to change your *mind*," John-Boy said. "Now let me have my eggs before I kick your *behind*." John-Boy, always the prankster, measured out his day in limericks and rhymes.

"Don't give me no hard eggs," Bobby said.

"Hard eggs. I don't cook no hard eggs," Cookie said. "I keep them yolks running wet."

"Hard yolk's bad for you," said John-Boy.

"Kill you," said Jimmy, in his husky voice. "Some sort of fancy name."

"Cholesterol," Robert said. "It's in the hard yellow but not in the white."

"That's it," said Jimmy. "It'll kill you."

Art leaned down through the companionway. He had been listening. "Don't believe it," he said. "Cholesterol is one of those fancy doctor's words. Ain't nothing to it at all 'cept it makes a lot of money for them doctors. Fat in your blood is all it is. In other words, that's your energy."

"I'd like to eat some of that ham," John-Boy taunted Cookie, while he gulped down another biscuit. A ham shoulder sat in a pot on the stove.

"You keep away from that ham. I've got it soaking in salt and brown sugar. That's our dinner." It was easy to imagine that the same routine was repeated each day. Cookie trying to feed everyone. John-Boy stealing more than his share. The captain taking it all in stride. Robert and Jimmy finished breakfast and climbed the stairs to see what help Daddy Art might need in order to get under way. The younger men stayed below, eating whatever was not nailed down. They would burn it off. Nothing burns calories like culling oysters and shoveling shells. Quickly, the mood in the cabin changed. Without the captain's brother and son as witnesses, talk loosened up. Once again, the state of ill repair of the *City* fell under scrutiny.

Setting his plate aside, John-Boy said, "Cap'n won't take her to the mouth of the river. It may be too rough down thar most days, but that's where the arsters is. Cook Point. Tilghman boats are catching a boatload thar."

"The *City*'s in no shape for open water," Clarence said. "Can't you hear them pumps."

"Yes, sir," John-Boy agreed. "She leaks like a sponge. Still, on a ca'm day, we should go to Cook Point. Somebody ought to ask the captain about it." He looked at Bobby.

"Not me. Daddy Art decides where we go. It's up to the captain." Bobby lit up a cigarette.

John-Boy said, "Hell, I'll ask about Cook Point when the captain's ready."

On deck, captain and crew prepared to cast off. Wadey had departed the harbor, so the *City* was no longer wedged in a raft, and the Jones boys only had to release the spring and stern lines. Afterward, only one line tethered the *City* to land.

"Throw off my bow line, would you," Art called to Walter Scott.

The old man pushed us away from the wharf, tossed the line like a seasoned cowboy, and waved farewell. The sun was rising, and the snow had stopped. To the east the bank of clouds turned scarlet. I pulled my collar up to shield myself against a sudden rush of wind.

We rounded Cambridge Light and set our sights downriver. Daddy Art seemed more relaxed now. "That light has been here for more than a hundred years," he said. "If she could talk, she'd tell you some stories. Seen some storms. And some boats that didn't make it home."

John-Boy and I raised the mainsail; Robert and Jimmy handled the jib. It was blustery—blowing about twenty miles per hour. We left a reef in the mainsail. Taking the halyard in hand, John-Boy hesitated before cleating it to the crooked mast. "The Indians could have really done something with this crooked bow and arrow— won a *fight*," he said. "She's bent just *right*." He stomped his feet rhythmically, pleased with his joke.

"Second dawn," said Robert, pointing. The sun had disappeared behind the line of red clouds and was now rising above them. The sphere was a dark yellow, not white as it was on its first appearance above the horizon. Watermen believe a double dawn foretells falling weather. Even now, there were rings around the sun—ice crystals, called "sundogs," that also announce bad weather is on its way. But we sailed on, each captain assuming he had a window in which to work. The *City*'s crew was upbeat, joking around, as if preparing for a barbecue.

Stan Daniels pulled alongside us, gaining slightly with full sail, no reefs. As he came even, he spilled some of the air from *Howard*'s sails, to align with us, for his weekly performance—a serenade, from a voice I had only heard previously in his Deal Island church. Throughout the Chesapeake, Art's oldest son was known as "the singing captain." Stan was a classic baritone and just now, simultaneously switching on the radio mic and broadcasting over the water, he sang his favorite tune in rich cadences that echoed across the river:

Drudgin' she's my drudgery
Sailing she's my pride
That's been my joy
Since I's a boy!
Come Monday she's a pushing day
Tuesday's pushing, too
Wednesday she's a sailing day
I stop missing you
Thursday I get happy
As I lick across the rock
Friday she's a payday
Put her to the dock
Drudgin' she's my drudgery
Sailing she's my pride
Bend my back to labor
Ride out on the tide
That's been my joy
Since I's a boy!

The wind was gusting from the southwest off our port bow. We were sailing west, beating directly for the green buoy (number 19) marking the outer edge of Howell Point bar, known for its large single oysters. The edge, the steep slope running from the reef to the channel, required more cunning than the top of the bar, and a special dredge. "It's a perfect wind for that edge," Daddy Art said. "I knew it would come sooner or later—in its own time." The river was rolling that morning, and spray showered the bow as we plowed through the waves. Halfway to the buoy, the *City* passed over hand tongers' bottom, a bar called Sandy Hill. Bobby, recognizing the oyster ground, lifted Walter Scott's basket of shell to dump it. Daddy Art shouted in anger, "Stop that, Bobby." Bobby set the basket down and glanced at his grandfather sheepishly. "Ye're only hurting yourself," the captain continued, "throwing those shells on tongers' ground. That's yer foundation. If you don't have a foundation, you got nothing."

"Sorry, Daddy Art. Where do you want 'em?"

"Howell Point. We'll be thar in a few minutes. It ain't many shells, but it's the principle."

Once we were on Howell Point, the captain signaled his grandson, who then scattered the shucked shells over the bed. Daddy Art waved Bobby over to the afterdeck and put his arm around him. "That booshel will produce ten once it catches spat and they grow," he said. "Fresh shell like this, just opened with the knife, attracts baby arsters the best."

When we reached the southwest edge, the wind shifted, toying with us in our quest for a perfect lick. The gusts turned clockwise, each puff now originating from the west. And far off between Horn Point and Castle Haven, two fingers of land to the west, the water suddenly turned a pale green. "Here comes yer flaw," Jimmy said to his brother. Daddy Art let out the sheet on the mainsail and changed his course slightly, rotating the point of sail as the wind direction changed, like two hands on a clock. But there would be no sailing the edge—that breeze was lost. The clouds closed in, dropping like a blanket. Still, there were few whitecaps, just the odd one here and there that caught your eye like a leaping fish. The new wind was a mile off. We savored the brief calm, all two minutes of it.

The arriving gusts slapped us like a screen door slamming shut. Our sails flapped wildly, making a *thwop-thwop* sound. Quickly, *Howard* sailed again in our direction, with a double-double reef—to work in tandem. The breeze topped twenty-five. Behind Stan, *Helen Virginia* and *Somerset* lowered their yawl boats, abandoning Howell Point, forsaking the river. They had had enough wind for one morning.

"The wind giveth and the wind taketh away," said Jimmy, watching them.

The geese also headed home. As the wind hit, great numbers of them lifted off the river and flocked toward the northern shore. They passed over the *City* causing a racket, as if trying to get our attention.

"We'll have to move away from here," the captain said.

"We need the money, Daddy. Prices have been low," Robert said. "Let's keep drudging. We can always scud home if need be." With that, the two skipjacks, father and son, and uncles and brothers and grandsons, sailed a couple of miles west into the eye of the breeze.

Approaching the next bar, the Diamonds, the wind—forever moody—dropped out, down to fifteen miles per hour. Part of the abeyance was thanks to the sheltering effect of Castle Haven Point, but the wind was fickle, like it hadn't yet made a stand. "Plenty of wind," John-Boy said, "just not much motion to it." The tide was slack now. It would be an hour before it ebbed, an hour before whitecaps colored the sea.

Two skipjacks were already catching oysters. *Rebecca* looked majestic, bright white with her enormous sails unfurled, harnessing all the available breeze. *Maggie Lee*, in contrast, seemed broken down, unpainted and her stern "hogging"—hanging low in the water, her waterline submerged. As young men, Jimmy and Robert had crewed on *Maggie Lee* when she was owned by Art's father-in-law, Clifton Webster. They both looked over at her now and shook their heads. "She's seen better days," Robert said. "I expect she's dying. It's just a matter of time." As if on cue, *Maggie Lee* dropped her yawl boat, pulled up her dredges, and motored toward Oxford.

Farther downriver two other skipjacks—*Lady Katie* and *Hilda Willing*—were sail dredging on Todds Point, the next bar past Castle Haven. The pair looked like two gulls bobbing amid the waves. Daddy Art and Stan chose to steer clear of Wadey on the Diamonds and Stanley on Todds Point. With the wind moderating, they decided to risk the Deep, the spot between the two. It was exposed—a ready target for the wind. Nevertheless, the two Daniels's skipjacks, on watch for each other, the reasoning went, would have a margin of safety.

The Deep is not an independent oyster bar but rather the long edge of the deepwater channel that runs between Chlora Point and Castle Haven on the north and south sides of the river. It is cinder bottom—broken shells—and mud; that is, soft bottom up to sixty feet deep. Mud dredges are required. And since the channel is narrow, forming a tight funnel in the lee of the wider expanse of the Lower Choptank, it is the roughest place in the river. On a flood tide with a northwest wind the water rushes fast through this strait, churning waters into a maelstrom. But Daddy Art counted on the tide ebbing soon, that it would hold back the wind. His marks were easy: The edge of the channel ran between two red buoys to the northwest of the Diamonds. The only trick was that the main drag was in forty to fifty feet of water, more than twice the usual depth for dredging.

Bobby and John-Boy each held a knife and set about cutting all the beckets from the dredge cables. It would take all the line—two hundred feet on each spool, running at an angle—to handle that depth. This channel was at about the limit of where oysters could grow. Any deeper, the water is nearly anoxic, devoid of oxygen. The Deep held a cache of oysters because it was rarely worked, and the cinder bottom caught spat there. The crew was excited. They had caught seventy bushels here earlier in the season.

Arriving at the eastern end of the trough, the captain ordered, "Ho." The dredges slipped over the rollers into the cold, green water. The cable played out for a long time. Robert grabbed hold of the port cable to feel when it hit the rock. "Ye're on 'em, Daddy," he said. "Feels like the mother lode."

After ten minutes, running toward the next red buoy, Daddy Art reeled in the dredges. Amid the thin broken shells were only a couple of live oysters. But the dredges had scooped up nearly a bushel of large blue crabs, mostly number-one jimmies. The crabs had been hibernating in the channel when we stumbled upon them. Winter crab dredging was illegal in Maryland, so the bushel of crabs was put in the hold, out of view. Jimmy and Robert, the senior men on the starboard and port sides, stepped aft for a conference with the captain. The problem was that they needed the dredges to dig deeper, but all the line was already out. There was only one answer.

"Divers," Jimmy said. "We got to put the divers on them drudges." The captain agreed, and so Bob and Jimmy descended into the hold to extract another illegal measure. The divers they were talking about had nothing to do with scuba gear. A dredge diver is a thin metal plate about six by twelve inches long, the shape of a license plate, which is tied to the dredge frame. It acts like an airplane wing flap and forces the dredge to dive faster and more steeply through the water. On the bottom it causes the teeth to dig more sharply into the bottom. (They are especially useful when it's gusty, which can cause dredges to bounce.) Under Maryland law, divers were not permitted, and simply having them aboard brought a heavy fine. Daddy Art considered them a minor infraction and above, or rather beneath, his own code of ethics. He thought they should be legal. So he kept them aboard. The captain whistled to the crew and yelled, "If the law comes, cut 'em quick."

The second lick came up with a few oysters, say fifteen to twenty in each dredge, and it got better with each catch. By the fifth lick, Daddy Art had settled down on the contour of the channel, the divers were digging, and the men were busy culling. Nearly fifty keepers emerged from each dredge. In between culls the Jones brothers (and Robert Daniels) used up their spare time by shucking oysters for the black market. Over the course of a day, they produced a gallon each, clearing forty dollars tax-free. Daddy Art had tolerated the shucking all season; with oysters sparse, the men needed the cash. But it cost him three or four bushels a day, three or four bushels that never made it to the legal market. That set him back personally up to sixty dollars. "Sooner or later I'm gonna have to farr them Jones boys," he said. He'd been saying that for fifteen years. And there was no firing kin.

Reverend Robert shucked slowest, accompanied by a little cussing and a little preaching. "Damn, I nearly cut myself with this knife—it's too dull," he said, and then, catching himself swearing, he healed it with a "Praise Jesus." He popped an oyster in his mouth and said, "Eat arsters and you'll have a mess of boys like me."

Robert selected another large oyster, a palm-size specimen, from his bucket and shucked it with a single wiggle and twist. The inner shell, or mantle, typically white with a mother-of-pearl center, was yellow, like tobacco-stained teeth. Robert pointed out the discoloration to the captain and me. "What is this, Daddy?" he said.

"Something else is hurting the arsters in this river," Art said. "Something new is killing 'em. It's not MSX. Thar's no such thing as MSX. That's just a fancy word that scientists use when they don't know what's going on. You can't see MSX. But this new parasite is another thing. Just look at it. I've seen that blemish everywhere this season. In other words, thar's a second disease, this one for real." Faced with the evidence, Art Daniels had accepted half the crisis and rumor circulating around the Bay. He seemed unaware that both protozoans, now on scientists' radar, caused similar bruising of the shell.

The captain pulled the cord to draw the dredges back aboard. Robert and I remained with his father at the helm, leaving four men on deck to do the culling—Jimmy, Bobby, John-Boy, and Clarence.

"Arsters are scarce, Daddy," Robert said. "If we don't find a few more today, all these boats will be sailing home to tie up to the dock for the rest of the season."

"Tha're still a few to catch," Daddy Art said. "A few on this Deep. Shoal water and deep water are the last places to get caught up. The Deep's hard on yer winders. All that winding, all that line out. Nobody comes here until the skim is caught everywheres else."

"But, Daddy, it ain't like it was. Only five years ago we were catching our limit everywheres before ten thirty in the morning—one hundred fifty booshel—either day, either year." Art did not answer. He didn't agree oysters were lost, but he didn't deny it, either.

Robert had captained the skipjack *Stanley Norman* but sold it right about the time the catches plummeted. "Good timing," he said, "but I miss it from time to time. Sail all day. Pick yer men. No one to tell ya what to do. Being a captain is like ruling the world."

The tide began to ebb, flowing downriver to the west. Whitecaps took shape and slapped against the hull. And, as for Daddy Art's prediction, he was half right: The wind did shift, but it doubled rather than halved in force. Light green water churned to the west of us, and it began to gust, high off the water near the top of the mast. Everyone looked downriver. Row after row of whitecaps combed the river, and cold gusts swept down every few seconds, darkening the water as they came. The charcoal-colored cumulus that had hugged the horizon in the early morning had tripled in size and was now advancing to the center of the sky. Lined with black, the clouds looked ominous. It began to drizzle. Within minutes it was blowing twenty-five again.

Jimmy was happy for the rain. "As long as it's raining, we're okay," he said. "It won't blow hard. But if more wind does come, it'll blow the rain away."

Daddy Art had difficulty handling the *City*. She bucked wildly and the rudder was even less responsive than usual. To subdue her, he headed up into the wind to shorten the sail. The mainsail, flapping violently, with reports like cannon fire, was lowered down the mast. The crew tied the third reef and raised the sail again. With the shortened sail, now just half the size of full canvas, the captain had more control. He pointed the *City* into the wind to spill some of the air from the straining sails. Luckily, this port tack was the same course as the contour of the channel we were dredging, so he was able to get back on track. Naturally, that was his plan: A gale wasn't going to stop Daddy Art. We were close-hauled, no longer on the preferred beam reach, but with this breeze the captain felt he could keep on dredging.

The wind brought lower temperatures, and the crewmen ducked below to don more layers of clothing, placed underneath their oilskins. Or perhaps it was just to smell dinner cooking. Either way, Cookie swiftly kicked them out of the galley. Dinner would be late today. The crew slowly emerged from the cabin and shuffled toward the middle deck. Their eyes lifted, their enthusiasm gone. To them, the sky looked threatening even if the wind had settled some, to about twenty-two miles per hour. But everyone knew a squall could brew at any moment.

Off the stern, more waterfowl—this time rafts of bay ducks (scaup, canvasbacks, redheads)—took flight as we came about to take another lick. They flew low over the water toward the leeward shore, likely to a sheltered oyster bar where they would feed.

"We going in, too, Cap'n?" Clarence said, the last to bob out of the cabin. "Them birds are smart."

"We have some more drudging to do yet," Daddy Art said, with an edge to his voice.

Clarence backed off and returned to his station, but Bobby tried his luck with his grandfather.

"How long we staying out, Daddy Art?" he said.

"Until we catch twenty booshel. That all right with you?"

"I'm for drudging, Daddy Art. I want to be a waterman."

"Okay, then, you gotta take the good with the bad. Sometimes the wind is right and we make some money. Other days it may be flat ca'm or blowing like this. But you gotta show up every day and hope for the best. Take it as it comes. Thar's no waiting on the wind." He looked across the horizon and saw something that was clear only to him. Bobby and I looked that way and could only shrug our shoulders.

"Take the helm," Daddy Art shouted to Bobby above the wind. "You'll be a captain someday." His grandson smiled with delight as he grabbed the spokes of the wheel.

Art stepped forward to assess the starboard team. "Jimmy, how many we got?"

"I'd say sixteen booshel, Art. Four in each pile."

"Right. We'll stay a little longer."

"We've drudged in rougher waters than this," Jimmy said, just as he caught the top spray of a wave right in his face. "I've come up on twice this wind and kept on drudging. In waves eight feet high. Blowing about forty miles."

Art turned to me. "He exaggerates. Forty is a lot of wind. The most you can drudge in is thirty—a little more than now—or thirty-five."

Jimmy heard this and smiled. "Art," he said, "you can always put four reefs in the main and take down the jib."

"If we have to do that, I'll be heading home. I'm not losing my boom or the mast or a man just for a pile of arsters."

The captain now walked aft but didn't interfere with his grandson at the helm. Bobby pulled the winder engine cord, signaling the crew to bring in the dredges. When they came aboard, the catch was meager. The number of legal oysters was down to twenty in a dredge. In the rougher seas, with the wind bucking the tide, the oysters were harder to catch. The dredges were bouncing off the bottom, dragging poorly and spilling the take. But the captain's remedies had been exhausted. The lines had been lengthened to the maximum; divers had been attached. Three reefs had been placed in the main and the jib to slow the boat down. With all measures taken, there was little else to do. They had to dredge the best they could. That or quit, which wasn't an option aboard the *City*.

The poor catch did, as always, prompt complaints from the crew. "Days like this cut into yer whole week," Cookie said. "I should've stayed home house painting. You gotta pay yer bills. I must be crazy to keep coming out here."

"Arsters are scarce," John-Boy said. "But I won't give up on the water. I'm looking for the big *catch*. We should go to Cook Point and make some *scratch!*"

Bobby came about and completed his turn. Daddy Art called, "Ho," and the dredges rolled into the water. The men bent over to cull.

A cry rose from the starboard side. Jimmy had made a discovery. He held up a fist-sized black stone. "Look at this," he called in his coarse voice. "I've got an ax head." On inspection it was clearly a chopping tool made by a Native American. The sharp edge of the tool had been pressure-flaked.

"You've got yourself a relic," Daddy Art said.

"I'll add it to my arrowhead collection at home," Jimmy said. As a boy on Deal Island he had collected many artifacts from the Nanticokes of the Algonquian Nation, who fished and hunted the

Chesapeake and its shores long before the Europeans arrived by sail.

"Nanticokes were the last of their breed," Jimmy said. "Modern times done them in."

The rain stopped. From far off, another piece of wind raced across the water. The waves suddenly changed direction, and the sea turned dark green, now to the northwest. The tips of the white-caps fell like dominoes, frothing the water a few hundred yards away. Like a descending hood, the sky cast a shadow and there was, for a moment, an eerie silence.

The hush did not last for long. Five minutes. Then, chaos. The wind hit Stan's boat first. She heeled over sharply. Daddy Art saw this and took the helm from Bobby, quickly turning the bow into the wind, the safest point of sail. The sails fluttered, then flapped and cracked as the flaw hit, like whips snapping in the wind.

"Blowing thirty-five mile now, maybe forty," the captain screamed above the loud reports of the sails. The dredges happened to be aboard when the latest wind hit, so the captain had time to assess the situation. He trained his binoculars on *Howard*. Stan had now turned his boat into the wind and was getting his dredges aboard. Father and son waited out the northwest blow for ten minutes or so, as spray crashed over their bows. Our boom swung wildly back and forth above the deck. Everyone kept their heads down. The crew secured the loose items on deck: bushel baskets, water buckets, plastic buoys, shovels. Jimmy's hat flew off and bounced across the waves. Bobby stumbled as the boat listed to one side, and his father told him to be careful. "Untie your boots," Robert shouted. "If you fall in, you'll want to kick those boots off fast." Most winter drownings happen because a waterman's boots drag him down to the bottom. Bobby did as he was told. The rest of the crew squatted on their knees and looked expectantly at the captain.

"Twenty booshel or three o'clock," he said to them, "whichever comes first."

The crew respected the captain's call and bent to the culling with their usual good humor, as if the storm was a million miles away. Even with the wind howling in the rigging, John-Boy just laughed a little louder. He had to accept the mandate of the captain as final. From time immemorial the commander of a vessel has been master and mentor, judge and jury, and that's how it was on *City of Crisfield*. The captain's word was law.

Still, John-Boy saw his chance to raise a question, if not an objection, to the captain's future plans. "Cap'n," he said, stopping by the helm. "Are you thinking about going to Cook Point anytime soon?"

"Maybe, John."

"I was just thinking them Tilghman boats are catching ninety booshel thar. We could catch a few, too. We've caught up everything thar is to catch on Howell Point—till next year."

"We might go thar next Monday if it's ca'm."

"Yes, sir, Cap'n, I want to go to *Cook*. And take a li'l *look*." John-Boy stomped his feet and did a little dance. The captain couldn't help but smile. He came about, circling his buoy.

By now we had nineteen bushels on deck according to the captain's eye. "Ho," he called into the din, and the dredges splashed overboard for another run between the red buoys. "One more good lick," said the captain, "and we'll be done."

When the dredges came up, they were loaded with oysters, easily half a bushel in each dredge. The captain had called it correctly. He had his twenty. He waved frantically to Stan and flashed twenty fingers and pointed east toward Cambridge. Stan flashed back fifteen fingers and pointed to port as well. They would run home together. No one realized at this point that *Howard* was taking on water. She had loosened her centerboard well, turning broadside, when the last wind hit. Her hold was filling slowly but at a steady clip.

Just as we jibed to run up the river, the wind picked up—gusts on top of the burgeoning storm. Loose gear—quarts of oil, tin cans—flew around the deck. Cookie was blown against the mast. I was smacked on the head by the boom. Gusts flirted with forty, the threshold of a true gale.

To the captain's eye, the gale was just a warning, the trumpet announcing the main charge. We had no sooner turned around to scud home than everything, overhead and afar, mutated. The sky, already somber gray, turned pitch, and visibility dropped to half a mile. To the northwest, behind us, it looked like rain was slashing the water—actually gusts of wind slicing the tops off the whitecaps like a scythe. Foam blew across the river. My yellow oilskin jacket caught a flaw and pinned me like a kite against the boom. I crouched for cover. Waves crashed on deck and washed over the winders, the dredges, and us. Anything not pinned down floated out to sea. The crew checked the hatches, made sure they were tight, and then ducked behind the cabin to escape the next blast of wind.

The nor'wester was now roaring, screeching through the rigging. A piercing, shrill cry. The captain shouted some orders but nobody heard him. Each crewman held his hat with one hand, and grabbing the cabintop, anchored himself with the other. After each gust, the men staggered backward as if there was an undertow between each assault.

There are no wind gauges on a skipjack, so clocking the speed of a sudden blow is guesswork. But, the captain told me later, the brute force of that blow was over fifty miles per hour, maybe with gusts of sixty. The wind came in waves and felt like it was spanking the boat with an enormous hand.

The captain wished he had put a fourth reef in the main or taken down the jib. But it was too late for that. To reef now he would have to bring the boat around again into the wind, briefly passing broadside—exposing the boat to the possibility of capsizing. As it was now, with half his main unfurled, he was in danger of breaking the mast. A rogue gust could snap it like a matchstick.

Having no choice, he rode out the storm, tearing through the water on his flight upriver. Cambridge Harbor and safety were four miles away.

We raced by the easternmost buoy marking the end of the Deep and the edge of Castle Haven Point. Lecompte Bay was due south. *Rebecca* roamed about that cove and, sheltered from the northwest blow, looked secure. Daddy Art deviated from his Cambridge course and turned south toward her. Ten minutes passed. The detour brought the wind broad on our starboard quarter. Each time a gust hit, the boat heeled over and surged ahead. But something had shifted: The wind was no longer wailing in the rigging. It was down to a roar. Castle Haven Point had blanketed us again. Just about then, in the relative peace, some noise came over the radio. It was Stan. "I'm leaking like a crab pot, Daddy," he said. "You better follow me to shore. I've got to pump her out and I need to do it yesterday."

By now, *Howard* had sprung a full leak in her centerboard well, and water was racing into the hold. The rough seas had loosened the makeshift repair after her sinking last month. Stan had discovered the gusher by accident today when his son Teddy, his first mate, was checking the hatch covers at the height of the storm. Water had nearly filled the hold; it looked like a bathtub. Stan was making for the shallow, leeward corner of the cove in case his crew had to walk or swim ashore.

Now passing over Diamonds, Stan found some relief from the storm, but he was still hemorrhaging. If water topped off the hold, the boat would drop to the river bottom. Luckily, Stan was prepared for a major leak. He carried a gasoline-powered, high-capacity pump on board, and he fired it up. The nervous crew looked on, expectantly. After fifteen minutes the pump began to make headway. Stan was relieved. The pump was outpacing the inward flow of water. When Stan radioed his father that he would be able to sail home on his own, we could hear the cheers.

Nonetheless, Art Daniels waited until the pump had nearly emptied his son's hold. The black clouds had passed overhead without any rain being dropped. The wind moderated, lessening by ten or fifteen miles per hour. Down to thirty-five. It had been a "gray" squall if not a black one. After a hairy half hour, the skipjacks seemed to be out of danger. In the protected waters of Lecompte Bay, the Danielses waited another twenty minutes or so before dropping their yawl boats for the voyage to Cambridge— with a fair wind. Stanley Larrimore and Pete Sweitzer, it turned out, had rushed home ahead of the storm. Immediately to windward, *Rebecca* was making another lick. Throughout the gale, Wadey Murphy had simply kept on dredging.

Daddy Art glanced over at Wadey and said, "Young men and sailboats don't mix. That's what my father used to say when Jimmy or I would set sail in a storm."

"Young men and sailboats," Jimmy said, hovering by the cabin door. "Old men, too."

"We risked a swim today," Art responded. "Had to—to catch enough to satisfy the crew, to make up for a poor season."

At the helm, Bobby turned to his grandfather and volunteered that the gale had been the worst he had seen yet. Daddy Art tilted his cap down over his left eye and stared over Bobby's shoulder. "The drudge-boat fleet has seen worse, a lot worse, right here in this river," he said. "The worst tragedy in skipjack history ended here, just a little farther along on Howell Point thar, but it began across the Bay, off the western shore. I was drudging for my father."

"We both was," Jimmy added, coming close to the helm. "Art and I were crewing on *Robert L. Tawes*. It was a Friday. February 3, 1939. We were working on a bar called Under the Cliffs between Annapolis and Solomons. It had been raining all morning, drizzling and blowing northeast like."

"Northeast, that's right," Daddy Art took over the story. "A nice breeze. We had about fifty booshel on deck."

"And another one hundred fifty booshel in the hold," said Jimmy. "Arsters we had caught the day before and not sold yet. That's what saved us, them arsters."

"It was just like today," Daddy Art said. "Quitting time and most drudgers were headed for home. We were still drudging with single reefs, a light breeze. All of a sudden the sky above the cliffs to the northwest turned dark—black as tar."

"Father yelled, 'Take yer jib in, get yer sail off,'" Jimmy said.

"Well, we got the jib down, but the wind hit before we could get the mainsail half down. Wind was blowing maybe sixty-five miles, maybe more. All five of us pulled downward on that sail but we couldn't budge it. Bringing that boat up into the wind was like hitting a wall. We threw two big anchors in the water to steady her."

"That squall hit us hard," Jimmy said, "and heeled us right over worse than I've ever seen. We were having a pretty time of it. Water on deck, up to the winder boxes. Waves coming right over us. We had to close the cabin door to keep the hold from flooding."

"We nearly capsized," said Daddy Art. "The only thing that saved the boat was that hundred fifty booshel we had in the hold. The weight was in the bottom, in other words, and acted like a heavy keel. Ballast. Kept the boat upright."

"Thar were half a dozen drudge boats under the cliffs that day— five that I remember: us, *Maggie Lee*, *Ruth Thomas*, *Esther W.*, and a little schooner we called the *Glen*," Jimmy said. "The *Maggie Lee* took the worst of it because she had full sail. When she heeled over, the hatches filled with water. We only had hand pumps in them days and it took them hours to get the water out."

"That violent storm lasted just eight or ten minutes, ten minutes at the most—that squall of wind," Daddy Art said.

"That was the hardest blow I've ever seen come across this water," Jimmy said. "Worse than today. And we got the easy bit of it. She kept spinning right across the Bay."

"We were spared," Daddy Art continued, "but the Cambridge

drudge boats, working in the river, had no idea what was coming. They were caught in fog. We didn't have radios back then, so we couldn't warn them. We only heard about the disaster later."

From his memory and from newspaper accounts, I pieced together the second half of the calamity.

The black squall and its waterspout—essentially a tornado—traveled across the Bay, spinning like a top. Within minutes the twister, with winds in excess of seventy miles per hour, entered the Choptank. It bypassed Tilghman's Island and carved a course right up the river, lifting water into its funnel. It literally dug a trench through the water.

In the Upper Choptank nearly a dozen dredge boats, all out of Cambridge, were finishing their day in the fog. The one-masted bugeye *Agnes* had been working on Benoni bar. The gaff-rigged topsail sloop *J. T. Leonard* had been dredging on Castle Haven. Most of the other boats—including the skipjacks *Geneva May, Annie Lee,* and *Ethel Lewis,* captained by Emerson Todd's father—were on Chloras, just below Howell Point, sheltered from the northeast wind.

Actually, the wind had been light all day, barely puffing through a drizzling fog. At 2:00 P.M. some of the boats—*Agnes* and *J. T. Leonard* among them—were still dredging, but most, frustrated by the light winds, had stowed their dredges and were either pushing or sailing home upriver to Cambridge. Behind them, the sky became dark, so dark, one witness said, that "it seemed like a curtain had dropped over the sun." Clearly a major storm was descending, but in the fog, no one had seen it coming. Too late now. Everyone tried to get their sails down. A sudden blow hitting full sails could dismast a boat, snapping the mast like a twig. The leading wind—from the northwest now—grew fierce, topping sixty miles per hour. And the main twister had not even hit yet.

Orville Parks, dredging *Joy Parks* that day, was one of the first to react. He saw that his barometer on board had dropped precipitously, and the needle was jumping around. The black sky clinched it for him, and he dropped his push boat to dash for the harbor. "We better get out of here," he called to Lloyd Kerwin, captain of *Reliance*. Captain Orville made one mistake. He left his sails up, thinking he could harness the storm to scud into port.

The wind kept coming. When it was a hundred yards away, it looked like black smoke over the water. No whitecaps. The wind was faster than the waves. Then it rolled right over the fleet. By the time it reached Howell Point, the wind was near hurricane force. No one measured it, but it was the worst any old-timer had seen in the century. "The storm bore down on us like a rushing freight train," said Willie Parks, crewman on *Joy Parks*. The lazy jacks, an integral part of the rigging, broke. Their long lines dropped from the mast like circus ropes, and the mainsail crashed to the deck. That spared the mast and kept the skipjack from upsetting. "Those lazy jacks saved my life," Captain Orville said, lucky to be speaking after the storm.

Will Jones, captain of *J. T. Leonard*, was also there with full sails aloft when the skunk hit. "Skunk. That's what we call 'em," he said later. "A squall that sneaks up on you. Blew the topsail off. Then we couldn't get the mains'l down. The boat fell off the wind and scooted up the river. We couldn't do a thing but hang on and hope. Couldn't get the dredges in. They were jumping up and down behind us like porpoises."

Parks and Jones were lucky all right. But three other dredge boats—*Annie Lee*, *Agnes*, and *Nora Lawson*—were hit hardest. They were right in the path of the twister, two with their sails up. The wind had turned into a terrifying, high-pitched squeal.

The bugeye *Nora Lawson* was forced into shoal water on Howell Point, where the crew safely furled the sails. Bevel North, captain of the *Lawson*, must have thought he was in the clear with just two bare poles exposed, when a gust of wind capsized the bugeye anyway. In the shallow water the boat hit bottom and the crew clung to the side of the boat. Within moments of the squall's arrival, the seas became violent. But the men held on until rescue came. Only crewman Forney Ruark was hurt; he suffered a gash to the head but recovered.

With full canvas up when the skunk hit, *Agnes*, however, didn't have much of a chance. Captain Bill Bradford, seventy-three, and four crewmen perished when the boat capsized and sank in the deep water off the Howell Point edge.

"It was an old boat and an old skipper," said Will Jones. "Too old, I guess. He kept sail on her too long and sailed her right under."

Meanwhile, Captain Theodore Woodland of *Annie Lee* tried to respond when the squall appeared out of the fog—he ordered the crew to drop the sails—but it was too late. The full force of the storm smacked into the skipjack. It spun her around into the wind, but as soon as she was broadside, the boat capsized—knocked right over. The captain and his four men, including crewman George Wheatley, jumped into a small skiff that had been trailing the skipjack. (Wheatley cut loose the towline so the skiff was free of the foundering boat.) Almost immediately the skipjack sank to the bottom of Howell Point bar. The men looked on from the skiff in disbelief.

By chance, one of the crewmen saw the anchor line that was tied to the sunken skipjack float by, and he grabbed it. Holding on, he was able to steady the skiff in the rough seas. But it was a brief safety. The line suddenly pulled out of his hands and the skiff rolled over. In an instant the five men were in the water.

Their heavy hip waders dragged them right down to the bottom of the river—twenty feet below—like stones. Remarkably, all five were able to climb out of their boots and swim to the surface. Once the dead weight was off their feet, with air in their lungs, they shot up like corks. The skiff was a few yards away, overturned in the water. They swam to it and reached for the keel, actually a narrow skeg that formed the spine of the boat.

In the five minutes they had been in the frigid water, the men had become scared and tired. This was February. Hypothermia was setting in. In desperation they grabbed at the skeg and tried to pull themselves onto the bottom of the skiff. This was a mistake. Each time the men dragged themselves on top of it, the boat rolled over like a log, knocking some of them in the head.

This may be why Captain Woodland was the next to go down. He seemed to be hurt or unconscious when he dropped again like a rock to the bottom of the river. This time he didn't resurface.

Most of the men kept crawling onto the boat, only to be flung off by a wave or by the rolling boat. The first mate, Emerson Wingate, was cast off the skiff and sank toward the captain. Jim Scruggs and Herb Robinson were hit by waves and never resurfaced. Only George Wheatley seemed to keep his cool. He treaded water at the stern of the skiff. Each time the boat rolled, he let go of the skeg and waited for it to surface before grasping it again. Ten minutes after *Annie Lee* sank, all of George Wheatley's companions were dead.

The wind had cut the fog into shreds, into streamers. Visibility was better, and the carnage was clear. The masts of *Agnes* and *Annie Lee* poked above the waves and *Nora Lawson* foundered on shore. All three were in a straight line, the path of the twister. Holding on to the skiff, Wheatley looked past them, upwind and downwind, for some sign of rescue. He saw a mast, then a bowsprit, then two men standing on a bow.

It was *Geneva May*. Her captain and crew had spotted Wheatley between two waves. Skipper Bill Hubbard aimed the boat at the bobbing skiff and crewman. The skipjack was bearing down on Wheatley at full speed with the wind behind her. She was flying. Hubbard had only one chance to throw a lifeline since she couldn't possibly turn around in that wind.

As *Geneva May* came alongside Wheatley, Hubbard threw the hawser line to him. The spare anchor line was heavy so he got some distance. Still, it barely reached him. Wheatley grabbed the knotted end in his teeth and made a quick loop around his arms. As the line became taut he held the line with both fists on either side of his mouth. This man was not letting go. The boat rushed by. The abrupt yank on the line, as it took hold, nearly broke his neck.

On board the skipjack the crew had spliced the hawser line onto the dredge cable, a makeshift winch. They began winding him aboard as the boat continued its flight in the prow of the wind. Wheatley planed atop the river like a body surfer. With a smack, his body slammed into the side of the boat, and the crew reeled him up the side of the boat and across the dredge roller like a load of oysters.

Once on deck, Wheatley passed out. Only then did his jaw and grip relax. His skin had turned purple and he was shivering uncontrollably, nearly frozen. The crew covered him with blankets. But Hubbard left him on deck and sailed for Cambridge to get medical help. Wheatley did not come to until they reached the long wharf in Cambridge Harbor. His first question was about his boat mates. Had they survived?

Out of ten men in two boats—*Annie Lee* and *Agnes*—all were lost except Wheatley. The crew of *Nora Lawson* was rescued. Within fifteen minutes the center of the storm had passed, but it left behind the worst dredge-boat disaster of the century. If it had hit an hour later, most of the boats would have been safely tied up in Cambridge.

Over the next few days, Amos Creighton, commander of the Oyster Navy and captain of *Governor McLane*, recovered seven of the nine bodies. One body was extracted from the rigging of *Agnes*. Six others were dragged from the river bottom. Two were never found.

Maybe the most remarkable piece of the story is what happened to George Wheatley, the sole survivor. "I was only nineteen then," he said one spring. "I thought I was invincible. Nothing bad could happen to me. Then I nearly died. By all accounts I should've died. But I didn't give up the fight. I was a waterman all my life. It's what I am. I figured if I capsized again, I'd fight all the harder. This life is worth fighting for." George Wheatley was back dredging again on the Choptank River the following season.

Sailing into port, Art and Jimmy Daniels told me bits and pieces of the Choptank disaster, that which they remembered. Jimmy promised me a newspaper clipping. But they were mostly thankful the February squall of 1939 had only dealt a glancing blow to the Deal fleet an hour before it hit the Choptank. "We were lucky," Jimmy said. "We saw it coming and got our sails down. Those Cambridge boats never knew what hit 'em. We had a close call today, too."

Bobby looked at his great-uncle and grandfather and shook his head. "Why would you get back on a skipjack after that?" he said.

"You'll know the answer to that by the time you become a captain," said Daddy Art.

THE *CITY* AND *HOWARD* passed by Howell Point beam to beam. The tailwind was helpful, no longer a threat. The two captains exchanged thumbs-ups to assure each other that Stan's leak was under control. Now *Howard* would have to be repaired. Still, Stan would try to make it through the last four weeks of the season before tackling the inevitable. Like many captains, he kept his boat in just good enough shape to make it through another month.

At Jimmy's lead, the crew began cleaning up the chaos left in the wake of the storm. All the tackle and tools, buoys and debris, that had blown across the boat were retrieved by the Jones boys and stowed safely away. Robert and Jimmy tied down the sails. The youngest, Bobby and I, washed and mopped the deck. Afterward, it was impossible to tell a gale had ravaged the skipjack only an hour before. After Cookie served dinner, the faces of the crew brightened. Like George Wheatley, they already had their minds on tomorrow.

"Can't we just catch some good weather, Uncle Jimmy?" said

Bobby, as we rounded Cambridge Light and took aim on the harbor. He speared a piece of ham with his fork.

"That's the Choptank for you—either slick ca'm or blowing a gale. Either way you can't catch neither one on those days. That's sailing."

"We'll have a perty day on Monday," Daddy Art said. "These nor'westers tend to blow themselves out."

"Then we can go to Cook Point," John-Boy said. "That right, Cap'n?"

"If it's perty, John, not too rough."

"I know it'll be perty. Got to be. Our luck's gotta change."

"You make your own luck," Cookie said.

"Then I'll be ready. Cook Point—oh, yes, indeedy. Catch me some arsters. Make a boatful of *money*. And none for my *honey*." John-Boy did a little jig and stomped his feet.

10

The Second Death

March opened with ambivalence: A freezing night gave way to a balmy afternoon. Not a complete surprise, however, for the signs had been rearing up for days. Like a slow ebb tide, winter had backed off, in steady retreat. The harbor ice had first thinned, then broken into shards, melted, and finally disappeared altogether. A thin sheet of glass ice would "make up" each evening, coating the harbors, but this never lasted past noon. Snow, on the island had faded, too, withdrawing into small patches and tiny circles underneath the more expansive trees. At the wharf, only a few icicles still clung to pilings and posts. Days were longer, and the skipjacks now returned each day before dusk. They set sail before dawn each morning and reached the oyster rocks in full sunlight. The crews dressed in sweatshirts and sweaters, foregoing their heavy coats. Oilskins were discarded in the cabin. The skies had transformed as well. On that first day of March the daily platinum cast overhead had turned light blue, the color of a robin's egg. Spring was begging and the sail-dredging season was coming to a close.

On that first day, a Friday, the skipjacks were stranded in port. A week of heavy winds had given way to dead calm. The river and

Bay were both flat as a millpond, so the sail dredgers huddled at Gary's Store or ran errands. Even if there had been wind, crew would have been scarce. With spring looming, deckhands were off scrambling for the next line of employment. Stanley's and Wadey's dredging crews had not had any luck.

But there was some hope. With only two weeks left in the season—till March fifteenth—watermen were thinking about spatting again, that spring ritual of transplanting oyster seed. While the state administered the effort, the oystermen's license fees and surcharges covered a large portion of the budget. They would have to build frame boxes to hold the seed, which meant hunting down lumber. Captains also had spatting on their minds because of the meeting that night. Tidewater Fisheries would convene the county watermen committees in Annapolis to "discuss" that spring's oyster replenishment program, the government title for the twin task of spatting and planting old oyster shells, on which larval oysters might adhere. With more than one million dollars at stake for distribution to different harvesters, the annual discussion was always volatile, more a shouting match than a dialectic. Dredgers and tongers from Talbot and Somerset counties would be there, fighting for their respective quotas. Other county clans as well. And there was big news: The governor had just cut the budget for planting shell on the oyster beds. Watermen would try to get the money restored, so the debate promised to be all the more contentious.

Yet the haggling was hours away. And fireworks are best observed at night. Still, on Tilghman's Island, watermen tested their arguments in favor of Talbot County—in huddled groups around the island. This I knew from rumor, but when I arrived at Gary's that morning, only tongers were on hand. Wadey's and Stanley's trucks were nowhere in sight. As usual, the tongers were not as friendly toward me, less likely to confide. But they were especially dismissive that day: My allegiance to the skipjacks would make me an adversary that night. As I stepped through the door, I was pushed aside, back against the glass. Several beefy watermen filed past me without a word. Then a few more exited the store and gathered next to the gas pumps. Something had caught their attention. They searched the skies to the east.

Set against the rising sun, black smoke billowed up from behind the maple trees that lined Chicken Point Road, just off Main Street. Without a breath of wind the ebony column rose to form a mushroom hanging over the northeast of the island. "A boat's on fire," someone said with the waterman's instinct for distinguishing between domestic and marine. I would have guessed a house, not knowing that diesel fuel burns a certain shade of smoke. A few of the men piled into their trucks to follow the fire. I was on foot and hustled down the lane toward Severn Marine.

The marina was home to Bobby Marshall's *Virginia W.* (1904), so I immediately feared for the life of one of the last active skipjacks. As it turned out, it was one of the retired boats that was in trouble. Two old skipjacks in ill repair—*Ruby G. Ford* (1891) and *Claud W. Somers* (1911)—had been sitting on blocks at the marina, awaiting money and a carpenter and the chance to sail again. One of them—*Ruby Ford*—was ablaze.

Copper-red flames sprouted from her bow and stern, fueling two separate fires. Ahead of the mast, the paint of the weathered foredeck ignited—peeling and searing and releasing an oily, black smoke. Behind the helm, a fiery wave, four feet high, crested above the rudder. The twin conflagration gathered speed, racing toward the middle, but it stopped short.

Perhaps it was not too late to save the skipjack, but nobody was volunteering. It was up to the captain. But apparently he had torched her. That was the word from three firemen of the Tilghman VFC who lingered nearby, next to an idle fire engine. Four spectators huddled in front of the boat, all Murphys: Lawrence,

Jimmy, Karen Sue Tyler, the daughter of the boat's skipper, and Bart, the owner himself. Bart stood farthest back. He looked uncomfortable, kicking at the oyster shell underfoot.

Fire now circled the clipper bow, its paint feeding the flame as if Bart's "bowsplit" was a welder's torch. The helm also ignited. The marine latex blistered and bubbled like boiling-hot tar.

Ruby Ford was not Bart's most recent charge but she was his fondest. He had dredged her for nearly fifteen years from the early 1970s to the mid-1980s, before he put her aside to sail *Esther F.* He found her in December 1972 after a ninety-mile-per-hour storm had dragged her out of Knapps Narrows, nearly sinking her. At that time she was owned by Edward and Daniel Harrison, two brothers from Smith Island. They were so distressed at her near destruction that they agreed to sell her, as is, to Bart. He restored her and began dredging her the following year. The oysters culled aboard *Ruby* paid for his growing family. When he looked at her he saw his kids.

But the greatest significance of *Ruby* was her age. Built in 1891 in Fairmount (not far from Deal), she was one of the earliest skipjacks and the first recorded V-bottom dredge boat from Somerset County. She was the oldest skipjack still living, at least before her torching. Long ago she had been registered with the National Trust for Historic Preservation. But that status (which many skipjacks share) did not bring funds for her restoration. For years she had needed rebuilding. Her sides were rotten, porous as a sponge. Her centerboard well leaked. Even her keel was warped. As the watermen say, she hogged—her stern had dropped below the waterline. It had been cheaper for Bart to buy *Esther F.* than to fix *Ruby*.

So he had put her up on blocks at Severn Marine, hoping to get the funds someday to bring her back to life. But the oysters never came. Eventually, he could not pay the yard bill any longer. So he applied for a permit to Billy Lednum, captain of the firehouse, for an open burn. Nobody was warned. Not the press. Not the National Trust, not even the Chesapeake Bay Maritime Museum. Somebody might have claimed her, but Bart no longer cared.

"Last chance," Billy Lednum said to Bart, as he looked at the middle deck, still untouched by flames.

"She died long ago," Bart said. "Let's get this over with." He nodded at the box of matches Billy held in his hand.

The very middle of the boat was already soaked in diesel fuel. Billy lit a rag and threw it onto the deck. An audible "swoosh" rippled over the frame as curls of fire raced across the deck, around her waist, and beneath the hull. The herringbone planking of her bottom was the next to flare up. Quickly, the planks pried loose as the nails popped like buttons. A rush of air flew through every crevice, feeding the flames. By now her galley was consumed, the cabin where a dozen captains and countless crews had awoken, dressed, eaten, boasted, laughed, lied, and slept for a hundred years.

Bart stepped forward once the inferno was raging, after there was no turning back. He caught Lawrence's attention. "Forty-four years I've been drudging," he said to his cousin. "Ever since then I've heard we're a dying breed. Well, now I believe it." For Bart, for everyone, she was the last of her kind—a classic skipjack from the nineteenth century.

I returned to Gary's to find the same tongers in residence, speaking in hushed tones. On Tilghman's it was impolite to speak of the dead. No dredgers had arrived, for unlike most island news, the word had not yet spread. I asked the tongers if they knew where Wadey Murphy and Stanley Larrimore were. They shrugged. I couldn't call; nobody on the island uses the phone. If you need to talk to someone, you drive to their house. But my car had broken down. That was the problem: I was on foot. So I grabbed a bicycle to peddle to the Larrimores to ask for a lift to the meeting in Annapolis.

In Fairbank, at the south end of the island, I was surprised to see the Larrimore house finished. The façade and trimmings were painted yellow. Loretta must have won—Stanley had to spring for something more expensive than marine white, though perhaps as thin. The entire renovation, inside and out, had taken five months, a slow pace while Stanley dredged.

Loretta opened the door. "Stanley is down at the harbor showing Scott Todd the *Lady Katie*," she said. "That boy wants to buy her." This was news to me, but I knew Scott. He was a Cambridge waterman, the grandson of Emerson Todd, former skipper of *Rebecca Ruark*. Since Cambridge sat across the river in Dorchester County, moving *Katie* there would cancel the patent tongers' argument that, without skipjacks in their county waters, Hooper Strait should be in their domain.

"He wants to try his hand at drudging," she continued. " 'Runs in his blood,' he says. I guess that makes my blood seawater. Just talking to him will probably make Stanley give up on selling her." This was a common affliction among older captains. One old-timer retired and sold his dredge boat—a sloop—only to buy it back again before the next season. Captain Will Jones, who had survived the February Storm of 1939, missed sail dredging too much. He was ninety years old.

I wondered out loud why the Larrimores were considering selling.

"It's time," Loretta said. "The orsters are dying, the boat's getting old, and so are we. It's been one gale too many. Steve, our son, has a good land job, and Daryl's got his own boat. He may sell, too. The crew is a headache at best, and it's more dangerous with a poor crew. Half of 'em are jailbirds. I worry about Stanley with that bunch. Yes, winters without the worry of crews and weather and the boat breaking down—I'm ready." She smiled, convinced for a moment. "Stanley will miss it terribly, though, watching those sails from the window, seeing the others leave from the dock. Winters will be hard on him. I just hope not harder than they are now."

Loretta searched past me, through the door, out over Black Walnut Cove.

"The whole island is changing," she continued. "Not just the older captains retiring or skipjacks being sold. Property is being bought up. The rumor is that a developer has snatched up the old farm fields around Dogwood Cove. Won't be long before town homes pop up instead of corn." She shook her head and seemed bewildered, like a nurse who can't get the pulse on a patient. Her eyes wandered, following a great blue heron at the edge of her yard.

Suddenly, her gaze returned to mine and she asked if I would stay for dinner. Loretta offered a sandwich and iced tea. Eleven o'clock in the morning. Even on land, watermen families are on a sea clock. I begged off but first asked about the seed-and-shell meeting that night. She said Stanley was planning to go but would likely drive there from Cambridge, where he had some hardware to pick up. I would need another ride.

Cycling back to town, I turned onto Bayshore Drive. Wadey's truck was not in front of the Murphy house but a car sat idling next to the old tires and rusty refrigerators in the yard. The car was Jackie's old Buick, so I walked around back and rapped on the door. Billy, ever the man of the house, opened it. His mother in a new blouse hovered behind the twelve-year-old. Her head was turned. Suddenly, Li'l Wade stepped from behind the door with a long face, fresh from some dispute, and made for his truck. Jackie frowned and whistled gently, now glancing at me for support. Unfazed, Billy was still smiling. "Hello, Mister Chris," he said, and with a flick of his finger ushered me in.

"He's not here," Jackie said, anticipating my question. "Here it is a day off and Wadey can't keep still but for the want of wind blowing in his hair. I imagine he's down at Gary's talking to anyone who'll listen. Either that or messing around on that boat. I think he mentioned something was broken."

"Can I go help?" Billy said.

"Better wait another year," his mother said. "You'll make a better crew than the one he's got." Billy smiled and returned to his bedroom and toys.

"Li'l Wade should be helping his father right now—that's what I told him. But he's off to Easton to work on a carpentry job. Moonlighting. Well, I guess I can't blame him. It's been slack all week, since Tuesday. No crew. No orsters sold. And he's trying to save up for a truck." She blew out a long breath and placed her hands on her hips. "A little wind, a little snow, and the crew won't show up. They look for an excuse not to work. It's unreal. As soon as those Crisfield boys get a little money in their pockets, tha're off to Ocean City. Tha'll never raise a family with that attitude. It's a shame. I guess all Wadey can get these days is them young boys. Tha're not dependable like the old crews on *Sigsbee* were. But that bunch are old men now."

Jackie reached for a rag and began cleaning the pile of dishes in the sink. "Check his boat," she said. "He had some trouble with his winders, I think." She set the rag down. "If you see him, tell him this house needs fixing more than that skipjack does. Lord knows, I'd have to raise a mast on this house to get him home."

REBECCA AND *LADY KATIE* were rafted side by side. They looked in remarkably good shape for a pair of dredge boats that had endured the extremes of winter. Their decks were chewed up from oyster shells and dredges and shovels, but the white sides looked new, and the pine mast, boom, hoops, and other brightwork held varnish of a golden hue. Surviving this winter was only half the battle, of course. There were other winters to come.

No sign of Wadey or Stanley. For a few minutes I walked across the decks, refreshing my memories. In retrospect, the season had been short, flying by like all serendipitous moments. I had been ambushed by the nineteenth century and grown accustomed to its comforts, to having skipjacks around. It would be difficult to see

Lady Katie or any boat sold from the Tilghman fleet. The trouble with holding on to something too tight, though, is that it vanishes all the faster. I touched *Katie*'s wheel for a second and promptly stepped off the boat.

Just beyond Gary's Store at the edge of the narrows was the small inlet known as Tongers Basin. A dozen workboats were harbored here, winter and summer. Hand tongers and crab boats. *Mistress, Double Trouble, Hard Times.* And one lone patent tonger, *Lady Brooke.* Nearby, two abandoned skipjacks, *Lorraine Rose* and *Ralph T. Webster,* rotted in a marsh. That was where I found Wadey and Stanley, talking, with two young watermen at their sides. Tommy, first mate on *Lady Katie,* and Moe, a sometime crewman on *Rebecca,* seemed relaxed, as relieved as two seconds would be after a duel had been called off. The four watermen were talking about the governor's planned cut of the shell program, when I walked over.

"—he's just another politician," Wadey was saying. "He doesn't give a damn about the watermen."

"And to think I voted for him," Moe said.

"Cutting our shell just when we need it," Stanley said. "A good spat count this summer might bring the orster back."

"Yeah," said Tommy, "if this year's spawn is as good as last year, we'll need it. Them little orsters need shell to attach to."

"But can't you see it, the governor wants to drive us out of business," Wadey said. "This is all part of his plan. He wants to force the watermen out and then lease the bottom of the Bay to seafood companies. Like they've done in Delaware Bay. That's his slogan: 'Farm the Bay.' He's got to get rid of the cowboys first."

"Orster farming will never be prosperous," Tommy said. "All us watermen will stampede them beds and rob 'em blind."

"At night," Wadey added. "That's when some of us do our best work."

"Okay, men, but how do we fight the governor?" Moe said. "The

Watermen's Association doesn't represent much of Talbot County, certainly not drudgers. They lobby mostly for the Upper Bay—for tongers. We have no say in Annapolis."

"Now listen," said Wadey rocking on the balls of his feet, "those tongers—I don't dislike them any more than I dislike anyone else—but they've been catching small orsters all winter, and I'd just as soon see them in jail. I'm planning to give both them tongers and the government a piece of my mind tonight. They complain about the disease killing the young ones and then let everybody catch what's left. Sure we need shell, but we need the law, too."

WADEY AND I ARRIVED in Annapolis after an hour and a half drive. It was ten minutes before the meeting. The room was beginning to fill with watermen and bureaucrats and reporters. Now on the Western Shore, Wadey and the other watermen looked out of place with their billed hats, checkered shirts, and sunburns. The state officials wore coats and ties. The two camps sat on opposite sides of the room, around a conference table. The newspapermen huddled by the door. So far nobody was speaking. The mood was tense, like a gathering of farmers and bankers before the foreclosure on a family farm.

The state officials were far outnumbered. Roy Scott, John Hess, and Steve Koontz—all members of the crew from the annual oyster survey, which had measured fifty-three bars for spat, disease, and survivorship—sat along the head of the conference table. Next to them was their boss, Pete Jensen, Director of the Fisheries Division of the Department of Natural Resources's Tidewater Administration. Surrounding the other three sides of the huge table, two deep, were twenty-two watermen, all with distrust of the dais. Most were county chairmen of seed committees, like Wadey Murphy and Bobby Hathaway, the chairs of the Talbot dredgers' and tongers' committees, respectively. But others had come, as well. Jerry Phillips, a

Tilghman patent tonger, was there. And a few Tilghman dredgers—Stanley, Russell, and Robbie. A little late, the Somerset watermen arrived. Art and Stan Daniels walked around the table and sat next to Stanley. Art broke ranks: He wore a coat and tie. Maybe he had just been to church.

Wadey viewed his chairmanship of the Talbot dredgers with some irony. He often disagreed with three-quarters of the captains whom he had been voted to represent. But they didn't elect him because he would always follow their wishes. They chose him because he would stand up to government personnel and give them hell. Last year he got so angry at Roy Scott, the senior shellfish biologist, for moving seed contrary to his instructions, that he threatened to quit. Russell and the others talked him out if it. "Tha're afraid of Wadey," said Russell. "That's why we need him." Murphy had his own version: "I tell them state boys the way it is. I don't give a damn what they think. They'd love to see me quit and gone; that's why I stay around."

For the first time the annual meeting was being held in the Department of Agriculture building rather than at the Department of Natural Resources, which regulates the public oyster fishery and commercial watermen. Agriculture would, in the governor's new plan, oversee seafood farming, a private fishery, a distinction not lost upon the watermen and adding to their discomfort. The seed committees would address not only the allotment of seed among counties but also the distribution of shell on open bars—that is, if the governor did not succeed in blocking the budget. By law, the state had to consult the committees before allotting seed and shell to specific counties, although the final decision resided in the hands of the regulators. In theory, the state was supposed to distribute seed based on a scientific model of where it would best survive. But in practice the officials typically deferred to the oystermen, thus absolving themselves of responsibility if something went bad—something awry, such as a load of seed dying on a diseased oyster bar, an error that had been happening more and more. Watermen have the ear of the legislature and often get their way, right or wrong. Politics prevails over biology.

Besides the official agenda of allocating quotas of seed and shell, the meeting has an unofficial purpose. It is a soapbox for complaints from watermen about real and perceived mismanagement of the oyster program. Watermen arrive primed with their own agendas and sometimes primed with beer.

Roy Scott cleared his throat, and the throng turned its attention toward the front of the room. A slight man, he glanced at the spreadsheets on the table in front of him, results from the fall survey aboard the state vessel *Miss Kay.* Roy would run the meeting: He drafted the county quotas each year. But first he would deliver his report on the health of the oyster grounds—spawning and "spat fall" and survivorship. He spoke in a low voice.

"We have a lot to cover tonight," he said, "so I'll be brief. You have a summary of the fall survey in front of you. We have good news and bad. Probably thanks to last summer's drought we had a record spat set, larval oysters settling on the bars, in Tangier Sound. We have plenty of good seed to move. And it's free of MSX, which, despite the drought, has been on the retreat." The watermen looked across the table at each other, pleased. "But the bad news is that a second parasitic disease, called Dermo, caused by the single-celled protozoan *Perkinsus marinus* (and formerly mistakenly attributed to the fungus *Dermocystidium marinum,* from which it gets its common name), has now infected nearly every bar in the Bay. We are up to our gills with Dermo; we've been blindsided. And it has infected the fresher areas that were always out of range of MSX." Roy paused, with a guilty look on his face, the countenance of a man who did not want to deliver bad news. "Dermo has infected our creeks, our brackish rivers, most of the open Bay. It's worse in the fresher tributaries where hand tongers work, but it's also gotten hold of our seed areas. Just about everywhere oysters are dead or dying. It takes a couple of years to kill a bar, however; so you'll be able to work next year, but it's gonna get tougher each season after that."

At first, the audience was stunned. Then they began thinking of ways to sail out of the storm.

"I guess I'll put that patent-tong rig on my boat," said one hand tonger, "and head for deeper water."

"I might go diving," said another.

"Where did this Dermo come from?" asked a third.

"Nobody knows," Roy answered. "It may have been here all along, but something made it more active. Maybe pollution makes the oyster weak and more susceptible to the disease—sort of the way drought makes trees more prone to Dutch elm disease."

"If MSX backed off after years of killing," Russell asked from the sidelines, "why can't Dermo do the same thing?"

"It could," Roy said, "but unlike MSX it never disappears from an oyster. Fresh water, from a lot of rain, might make it dormant, but sooner or later it raises its head again."

"Roy, I heard all bars with Dermo will die," Robbie said. A buzz circled the room.

Roy held up his hands, and the crowd settled down. "Most will, but they're not all gonna die. When disease prevalence gets above 40 percent, then mortality reaches 50 percent a year. Half your oysters of a given age class are gonna die each year. It thins out the bar and makes it unworkable. When it gets to the third year, you have 12 percent still living. That's if Dermo is on a roll. On a drought year, when salinities elevate, both diseases come on strong; on the other hand, wet seasons and cold weather hold them back. The death comes in waves."

The Choptank River, he offered, was typical of the pattern throughout the Bay. The three creeks on the northern side of the river—those that enter from Talbot County—were riddled with Dermo. They had fallen like dominoes, one after the other, east-ward up the river. Harris Creek—what Roy called "Tilghman

Wharf" and the locals called Middle Ground—had 100 percent Dermo, a graveyard. Broad Creek, a former seed area, had 60 percent. The third creek, the Tred Avon, was also dying. Double Mills, one of its biggest bars, was hit with 40 percent prevalence. Half the bar was now boxes—coffins—empty shells.

"I see it different," Bobby Hathaway, the tonger, said. "Places in Broad Creek that were stone dead are coming back—little orsters the size of a dime, fifty to a lick. It's coming back."

Roy stared at him in disbelief, his jaw slack. "Dermo doesn't stop the spawning," he said. "Don't you see, it kills the little ones after a year or two."

"Well, if that's right," said Bobby, "I'll work the main part of the river—Lighthouse Middles."

"Lighthouse Middles has 56 percent prevalence, and mortality is around 60 percent."

"That's one of our best bars in the Choptank," Bobby said.

"Especially the tongers' part," said Wadey. "That's why I like to drudge thar." Everybody laughed, taking a little of the edge off the discussion.

Art whispered something in his son's ear. "How about the drudgers' ground in the Choptank River?" Stan said out loud.

Roy looked down at his spreadsheets and flipped through several pages, coming to the data he was looking for. "At midriver, well you heard about Lighthouse Middles. Downriver, Black Walnut Sands has 60 percent Dermo. I wouldn't plant any seed there. Where you want 'em is Howell Point, upstream. It's relatively safe, with only 4 percent mortality. Funny thing, just across the river channel on Sandy Hill we found 100 percent disease. Just shows how patchy it can be. We don't know what'll happen next." He scanned his figures again. "Well," Roy said, "that more or less shows the picture in the Choptank."

He smiled anxiously and looked around the room for other questions.

A Kent County waterman said, "Why are MSX and Dermo up here when they started in Virginia?"

"Cause we moved it up here," said another. "We hauled infected seed up the Bay. Now she's all ruined."

"Chances are," said Roy, "the disease would have spread everywhere on its own whether we moved the seed or not."

"But the orsters are dying a lot faster cause you did, Roy Scott," said another waterman. "If you knew spatting would spread the disease, why did you let us do it?"

"That's hindsight," said John Hess, one of the heavy-set state employees. "Y'all probably would have been out of business without us hauling seed. Thar'd be no tonging oysters in the Chester River without it."

"Yeah, if we can catch 'em and sell 'em before they die, we'll be all right," said the Kent County man, "but, if we can't, then I'll have to drive my boat up into a marsh and let *her* die."

Russell now spoke up. "I don't hear anyone talking about all the orsters we have in the main Bay. Everybody's talking about the creeks and rivers. Hand tongers are switching to patent tonging because it looks good out in the Bay. Doesn't it, Stanley? You've worked the Bay all your life?"

Stanley Larrimore turned his head toward Russell. "Looks better to me than it has in a long while," he said. "Kent Shores. Gum Thickets. Snake Rip. The northern Bay."

"Moving those seed orsters a couple of years ago off Stone Rock up to Six Foot Knoll and Snake Rip was a huge success," said Russell. "We have orsters above the Bay Bridge we never had before. That's our future: moving seed on long hauls to the Upper Bay."

"Which brings us to the seed program," said Roy, looking around the room. "Let's talk about the plans for moving and planting seed oysters this spring. We want to transplant baby oysters from our seed areas to commercial bars, as free of disease as we can. We don't have many options, but the o-options we do have, look perty goo-od." Roy sometimes spoke with a thicker Eastern Shore accent in front of the watermen, rounding his vowels and clipping his gerunds. Despite the affectation it was doubtful that the audience would accept him as one of their own.

The good news was that Roy's two new seed areas—the mouth of the Little Choptank and Kedges Strait in Tangier Sound—had both produced counts of over 1,300 spats per bushel—more than ten times the spatfall Stone Rock had last year. These two new strikes had low Dermo infections (16 percent on Kedges; 8 percent in the Little Choptank), enabling Roy's gambit to get away from the creeks and into open water. That's why he planted over one hundred acres of bottom in Kedges Strait with old shell last summer—to catch oyster larvae. Same with the Little Choptank. These offshore locations were traditionally high in spawning success. MSX had abated. And the strategy worked.

Roy boasted, "Now we have plenty of seed—"

"—but not enough money," Robbie interrupted. "The whole problem is that a year when we have good seed thar's not enough state dollars to move it. Two years ago, we had a 1,500 count on Stone Rock. We moved some but not all of it. You said thar wasn't enough money. Well, all the seed left behind is dying. The seed we actually moved north is living."

"That's true, Robbie," said Pete Jensen, Roy's boss, smoothing over his tie like a banker, "but the last two or three years we've only had $400,000 to move seed. That doesn't go far when we're talking about two thousand oystermen on contract to haul it."

"I'm one waterman—and I know a lot of others—that would pay double their license fees to keep this program going and moving more seed. Shell, too."

"That's right," Stanley said.

"Count me in, too," said Wadey.

"All the drudgers would pay more," Art said. "We might as well vote on it."

Pete Jensen nodded. "We'll consider that option. Of course, it won't help for this year—not enough time—but maybe next year. Roy, you have $400,000 *this* year—what're we gonna do with it?"

"Most of it will pay watermen to haul seed in their boats," Roy said. "Same as last year. We will try to move 300,000 bushels of seed again. That's more than a billion spat. Our strategy is to plant that seed strategically in the Upper Bay above the Bay Bridge and in the main stem of the Choptank and Chester and other rivers, avoiding the creeks. That's where the seed will have the best chance for survival, where the water is fresher and thus the disease is milder. Even then it'll be a bit like playing roulette: We'll place our chips on a number and see how lucky we are."

Roy had developed a quota allocation system over the years whereby the total seed budget was divided into counties based on the number of watermen licensed in each county, and within those counties the allotment was further divided pro rata among dredgers, tongers (hand and patent), and divers. This calculation produced, for example, the number of bushels allotted to sail dredgers on Deal Island (Somerset County). The oystermen of each county and harvest group were given free rein on where to plant their seed quota. The state only made suggestions. Usually this resulted in wise placement, but sometimes one group would choose to plant seed in a certain spot just to keep it out of reach of another group, even if that spat was in a high-disease zone.

Just then, Roy announced the seed quota for Talbot County, which included Tilghman's Island. For dredgers and tongers, a combined total of 23,500 bushels would be allotted, a little less than 8 percent of the state budget. Of this, 9,000 would go to dredgers and the balance evenly divided among hand tongers and patent tongers. The dredgers' quota was one-third what it had been in previous years. The conventional wisdom had been that a minimum of 10,000 bushels of spat were needed to seed one bar adequately. Now the dredgers had less than that perhaps to spread over more than one bar.

And the choice of those bars had no consensus. Last year most of the dredgers' seed had been planted on Howell Point. This had been a traditional site—low in disease and accessible to both dredging fleets. However, over this winter a rift had widened between the dredgers. The Deal fleet had stayed in Cambridge all season and worked Howell Point nearly every sail day. Meanwhile, the Tilghman fleet, farther downriver, had only worked Howell Point at the beginning of the season, preferring to reserve the balance of its oysters for the next autumn. The Tilghman captains had come to regret planting last spring's seed on Howell Point, since it was easy pickings for the Deal boats. They swore not to do it again.

Roy asked the Deal Islanders where they wanted their seed planted—4,500 bushels.

"Howell Point," Art said, loosening his tie.

"And Tilghman?" said Roy.

"Black Walnut Sands," said Wadey. "We want 'em close to home."

Stan Daniels straightened up in his chair and said, "Tilghman Islanders find out what you want first and then they go different."

Art said, "We didn't come to Annapolis to argue with Tilghman Islanders about where to put 9,000 booshels of Talbot seed. It's not enough to fight over. We'll take our Somerset County allotment."

"I'd like to have enough so it *was* worth fighting over. Yes, sir," said Stanley. Laughter eased the tension in the room.

Roy said, "If we plant any of this seed on Sands, it's probably gonna die. It's heavily infected. Howell Point is safer."

"We'll take our chances," Wadey said. "If I thought they'd die, I wouldn't plant 'em thar. I've drudged Sands all winter. Tongers had their biggest strike on it. Orsters are living."

"The tests show the disease is multiplying on Sands. The dying comes a year or two later."

"Not always, right?"

"No, not always."

"So, we'll take our chances. It ain't many. And we want to take a chance. Just remember: Tilghman has twelve drudgers and Deal has six, so we get most of it."

"If you want to plant it on Sands, be my guest. Just remember I advised against it. So we'll place 4,500 bushels on Howell Point and 9,000 bushels on Sands. Maybe your gamble will pay off." And that's how it played out: The Tilghman captains risked next year's crop just to keep it away from the competition. And the authorities rubber-stamped it. A discretionary allotment was reserved for Six Foot Knoll.

For the next hour both sets of tongers from the other counties debated where to place their seed. None of the haggling was as acrimonious as the dredgers' had been, and the allotments were made in favor of disease-free grounds rather than where rival watermen were scarce. Hand tongers and patent tongers were no longer in competition; they were all of the same tribe.

After the tongers spoke, Pete Jensen made an announcement. "Some of you patent tongers," he said, "and some dredgers have called my office in the past few weeks about Hooper Strait, about access to it. Enough dickering: That bar will remain dredgers' ground. And no season limits or power-dredging regulations will change this year. Only skipjacks can power-dredge and them only two days a week. The oyster wars are over—we're keeping the status quo." It seemed skipjacks would live to sail another season.

The dredgers smiled, and the tongers, stone-faced, pulled back into their seats.

We had come to the last item on the agenda: the shell program, the forty-year tradition of depositing old oyster shell onto seed areas and other bars so that larval oysters would have access to a hard substrate in order to begin a reef. Roy began by explaining the original budget plan and the threatened cut by the governor. Apparently, the governor had read newspaper accounts on this year's oyster season that had reported harvest levels far above what was really being caught. This led him to question spending money on improving oyster grounds when they were already in good shape. However, DNR's in-house projection for the season was 175,000 bushels, 10 percent below last year. For now, Roy kept the figure to himself but suggested that the governor might reverse his decision and reinstate the $750,000 shell budget in time for this spring's program.

Wadey offered to call the governor's office and give them the skinny. Roy blanched at the thought but said nothing. He was noticeably relieved, however, when Russell said he would call his congressman. Russell was more of a diplomat than Wadey.

"We'll see if any politician wants the weight of putting two thousand watermen out of business," Russell said to the crowd.

"Seafood is the biggest industry in the state," Robbie said. "Even if the governor has forgotten the skipjack fleet, he can't turn his back on *all* the watermen."

"Nobody loves a drudger," Wadey said under his breath.

Art, the senior captain, took over the discussion with a nod all around; the other drudgers stopped to listen—they gave way to the older man. "We all pay for this shell program—seed, too—out of our licenses and booshels," he said. "The rest comes from our taxes, from every Maryland citizen. There's a reason for that: A law was passed that channels our contribution and our taxes to restoring the arster grounds. In other words, it's our right to have our money spent as promised. If not, this governor won't be governor much longer."

At this, Wadey leaned forward, his eyes opening wide. "A-men," he whispered, his breath barely passing his lips, but he stole an approving glance at his mentor and risked a wink.

Roy cleared his throat again. "If things do turn around and we do get some money, we better put shells on the seed areas we've set aside—Kedges and Little Choptank. If we only get a little money, that's where it *all* should go. If we get more money, then we can plant shell on some wild bars—bars you can harvest."

Bobby Hathaway, the hand tonger, raised his hand. "How much shell is budgeted for Talbot County?" he said.

"About 200,000 bushels—75,000 for the dredgers and the rest for you," said Roy.

"We had 600,000 last year," said Bobby.

"And 300,000 booshels went to private planters," said Joe Hudson, another tonger. "Those oyster farmers must be the governor's friends."

"Roy, you wanted to put that private shell on Stone Rock," said Wadey. "It ain't right to put shell for private leaseholders on a public oyster rock."

Roy responded by saying a new law says Maryland can plant shells for oyster farmers anywhere in the Bay—to catch seed for them. "That makes Stone Rock fair game," he said. "We're already placing four private nurseries down around Smith Island."

"It's just not right," Wadey shouted. He was flushed with anger. "The governor would like to see us all work for private planters all right. I'm a third-generation waterman and I'll work wherever I damn please. But I'll be damned if a private planter will. They have no business on our ground. And no business on Stone Rock. That's one of our best orster beds."

Then John Hess made an unforgivable mistake. He contradicted the word of a waterman, Wadey Murphy no less. "Why do you care about Stone Rock?" he said. "It's nothing but a sandbar."

Wadey and Stanley nearly came out of their seats. "Turn out the lights," Stanley said.

Wadey clenched his fists. "That's no sandbar," he said, the blood rising to his face. "It's loaded with orsters. Always has been. How'd ya get yer job, John? I've caught my limit thar many mornings by ten o'clock."

"I've caught mine, too," Russell said. "It's a living rock. John, you better come out on my drudge boat sometime and I'll show you a few things."

Robbie simply said, "Good Gawd Almighty." The moment passed but the department's credibility had suffered another setback.

Roy, sensing anarchy, took back control of the meeting. "If we get the budget back in full and we have shell left over after planting the seed areas, where do you want them dumped?" Roy looked at Wadey first.

"In the river on Black Walnut," Wadey said. "Same as the seed. Different areas on the same bar."

"Okay," Roy said in an act of appeasement. This time he withheld his criticism. Then, he turned to Art Daniels and nodded.

"Todds Point," he said. "We want to catch some spat in the river, too."

Once Roy had recorded the locations for the various county quotas, he had some good news for the watermen.

"We're gonna begin planting shells earlier this year," he said, gathering up his charts. "In early May." This would be a few weeks *ahead* of spawning. Only token applause filled the room—how do you forgive decades of error?—but the department's reputation had climbed back up a notch. For one of the few times in forty years the shell would be planted at the right time of year. When oysters first spawned in June, the larvae would now have a ready surface to adhere to and grow on.

"What does the harvest look like for this season?" someone asked, when the bureaucrats signaled the meeting was coming to a close.

"Well," Roy said, "the season has two weeks left and we don't have the figures for February yet, but, based on the first half of the season, landings are low. It may be one of our worst harvests on record—less than 175,000 bushels."

"If ye're talking legal orsters, it's even lower," Wadey said, leaning forward in his chair. He had been looking for a chance to make his voice known. This was it. "All year long, tongers—some of 'em in this room—have been catching and keeping and selling small orsters. Thousands of booshels, I expect. It's a shame. These watermen are damn outlaws. The buyers are to blame, too. They could refuse 'em, but they don't." Wadey's voice had jumped an octave, and nobody was interrupting. "MSX and Dermo get blamed for something else that's actually killing these bars—it's greed. I'll tell you what: The orsters just aren't gonna be around next year. Every little one's been sold.

"Now, I'm no angel"—this brought laughter around the room—"but I've never boosheled off small orsters in my entire life. That's the lowest you can go. That's our future. We would have had a load next year. But tha're all gone now. No, I'm no angel, but catching li'l orsters is my heartache. I wouldn't think a moment about going on tongers' ground. I'd catch 'em on a state seed area. Hell, I hope to Gawd the orsters on Stone Rock Sanctuary don't get big enough cause I'll cross the line and catch some of them, too. But they'll be legal size."

All the watermen chuckled at his admission. So did the four state officials charged with protecting the oyster grounds. Wadey was simply too outrageous to resist. Left unsaid was the tongers' motive: Catch the oysters before they die. Why wait, tongers figured, until the oysters were legal but dead. (Scientists argue against this mistaken "logic": The three-inch cull size actually saves the broodstock, they say.) For the bureaucrats' part, no promise was made to crack down on the poachers. Enforcement was not Maryland's long suit. But Wadey already had something else on his mind. He had softened up the audience and was preparing for the kill. "And another thing," he raised his voice to say, "you can tell the governor for me and all the Tilghman drudgers: We want the shell budget back or we're going after somebody's job."

"Well, that about wraps it up," Roy said with a smile.

Outside, the watermen gathered around John Hess's truck—to pick up red flags for spatting—while the other three officials stood off to the side, watching. Steve Koontz, a state scientist, turned to Roy and quietly said, "You want to double our bet?" The two had a running wager on the date of the demise of the oystermen. "Dinosaurs," they called them. Roy declined, adding, "Next fall we'll be doing a death survey. Then we'll know for sure." He looked on as John handed the flags down from his truck. "Of course," Roy said to the moonless night, "if they're put out of a job, I guess we're out of one, too."

THE CRISIS WITH the shell budget had a swift resolution. The next day, an investigative reporter grilled the governor's staff about the missing funds for the shell program. He asked for a reaction, on the record, to a waterman's quote, which was terse and barely civil. At least that was the rumor. But before the article was printed, there was a reversal. On day two, the budget was reinstated, in return for higher license fees and surcharges next year. The waterman quoted in the political backroom was reportedly Captain Wade Murphy, local legend and voice of reason.

11

March, Black Walnut Sands

By mid-March the night canopy was altogether different. No longer a winter sky, not yet spring. The stars had shifted; bearings had changed. With the shorter nights the morning sky brightened earlier—by more than a minute each day—and thus fewer stars were visible. The evening stars and planets that appeared around sunset—like Venus—had mostly set by 5:00 A.M., and those still aloft in the hour before dawn flickered softly before their light was swallowed by the sun. The last lights to shine were the brightest. Arcturus in Boötes. Vega in Lyra. Spica in Virgo. These midnight risers were still aloft at sunrise, perched between one world and the next. Their moment would be brief.

At 5:30 A.M., on March fifteenth, I arrived at Gary's under a clear, star-studded sky for the last day of the sail-dredging season. Outside the store I kicked the mud off my boots and opened the door. The lilt of the Tilghman dialect reached my ear. Someone said, "Over thar, yesterday, I caught a farr breeze on Cupper's Holler." Inside, Wadey and Moe, *Rebecca*'s newest deckhand (and a friend of the captain's), shuffled about. He had crewed for Daryl for most of the season, but since Wadey was shorthanded, he would be lending a hand, as would I. A dozen other crewmen huddled with their captains in the four corners of the store. From his stance behind the counter, Gary Fairbank gathered the quarters tossed on the countertop for white Styrofoam cups of coffee. With a fast smile, Moe offered to flip a coin for the next cup, but Gary picked up the last quarter and shook his head. He wasn't about to lose a certain sale to a coin toss.

Only the four senior men had shown up to close out the season: Wadey, Stanley, Pete, and Bart—the eldest men standing among the brothers. Combined, the four captains had more than 120 years of sail-dredging experience, which if the years were stretched end to end, would reach back before the skipjack was born. As I approached, they sipped their coffee in silence. Sometimes these men bent my ear, but that day they had nothing to prove. The young crowd had challenged them, but the old skippers had prevailed—to them, the natural order of things. For the time being, skipjacks would continue to sail. Now, the junior men stayed home, contemplating their future—whether to sell their boats. Just before leaving for the dock, the senior captains briefly spoke of the weather, and the conversation turned quickly to dredging.

"Well, I might as well get this last day in," Stanley said, setting down his cup on the counter. "Last day for *Lady Katie*. Last day for me, too. Yes, sir. The best thing about retarring is you don't have to worry about yer crew showing up."

"My crew is giving me a heart attack," said Wadey. "I may not even get in this last day if they don't show. Hell, they haven't showed all week. Only got two men—a skeleton crew. I'm looking for anybody—"

Li'l Wade then walked through the door. "Thar's my boy," his father said. Then turning to Stanley, he called, "Ya got yer crew?"

"Same bunch." Stanley's crew had agreed to one more sail day, in honor of his last voyage.

"So, ya really sold *Lady Katie*?"

"Sold her just up the river. I'll make it a short goodbye."

Wadey nodded but had nothing to say. He was superstitious about a skipjack retiring. More so, the man. At 6:00 A.M., still a hand short, he downed his coffee and said we might as well get going. It was nearly blowing a gale northwest, very gusty and cold. "Well, boys"—he winked toward us—"last day for Black Walnut Sands. I want to be on the rock when the sun comes up."

We emerged from the store. Wadey looked up at the North Star, Polaris, and glanced northwest, perhaps looking for wind clouds or some other private sign of the day's weather. "It's going to blow all morning," he said, turning away, his voice muffled by a flaw. We walked down to the wharf to untie *Rebecca*. She was facing west, away from the drawbridge and into the near gale. A good day, I thought, to lay low, but the captain had already read the wind and made up his mind. "Let's spin this boat around and head for the bridge," he called out, a notch louder than the roaring wind.

"Cap'n, I'll bet you we cross under that bridge without a scratch in just under ten minutes," Moe said. It was his second wager of the day. Wadey smiled and shook his head like he had heard it all before. Moe was the island bookie; he'd place odds or money on anything: football, boxing, crab races, the weather. He barely broke even, yet the captain was not about to challenge him, not about to bet against *Rebecca*.

The wind rattled the old corrugated roof of Buck's Seafood with a clamor like the crackle of soda cans being crushed. Bushel baskets skidded across the icy wharf. Upwind, in the private yacht marina across the narrows, halyards strummed against aluminum masts. *Rebecca* was silent, despite the wind. Her nylon lines gently tugged at the wooden mast and spars. Gathering around, we cast off the lines, setting her free in the current.

The crew and I quickly lowered the yawl boat off the stern. Moe, who was forty, looked at the captain's young son and said, "Ye're first mate today. Don't worry about me—I'll stay out of yer way."

"I've been that all season. Not that Dad always remembers."

"I heard you earned it." At that, Li'l Wade did a double take and stole a glance at his father. Wadey was busily coiling the spring lines and hadn't noticed. Li'l Wade said, "Doesn't matter. This is my last day. I start a carpentry job next week."

Rebecca lurched forward. Just in time, the jaws of the drawbridge opened up and we shot through—propelled by the wind more than the yawl boat. Nine minutes flat. Moe cracked his knuckles and blew a breath onto his hands; winning for practice rather than money, without a bet from Wadey, held some sting. It was cold enough in the wind that our fingers and ears were numb. March held on to winter with a clenched fist for one last blow.

Behind us in the growing light, Polaris shut her eye and old Regulus, the bright blue star in Leo, winked to the west and was gone. Arcturus, Wadey's favorite star, which had been an eastern beacon for him each winter morning, was high overhead—not east, not west, and no longer a useful compass. But *Rebecca* knew her way around the island. When we passed Avalon Island, the small oystershell isle adjacent to Tilghman's on our right, the captain turned the helm over to me so he could repair a dredge up forward.

He gave me a few directions, softened by the wind. I steered due south for two and a half miles, then as Avalon disappeared behind Upper Bar Neck, I watched the depth sounder climb from 12.4 feet to 7.9, just as Wadey had told me. I pushed *Rebecca* to the edge of Black Walnut Sands, alone at the wheel. The captain came aft. "I'll take her now, honey." That's all he said.

Abruptly, at 6:30 A.M., under a bright orange dawn, Wadey called all hands on deck to unfurl the sails. It was a Tuesday, but we'd sail anyway—as in the old days. He turned *Rebecca*'s nose into the wind, a gusty, thirty-two-mile breeze, and cuffed Moe and me, as we ascended from the cabin. "Heist the main," he shouted. "Two reefs." The three of us climbed atop the cabin and winder box to untie the sail stops. But she was already set at two reefs, from yesterday, so we quickly raised the sail. The jib was even easier. Moe stayed on the bow; Li'l Wade and I stepped back to the afterdeck.

"I'll handle the port drudge again," Li'l Wade said to his father, "but it's not catching as well as the starboard, so don't hold it against me. No reason to yell."

Wadey nodded. "We'll try to even 'em up; the bag on that drudge ain't right. It's not yer fault." He braced himself on the railing; the chop rocked the boat from side to side and made the footing precarious.

"Right," said Li'l Wade, as he lit up his first cigarette of the day, with a windproof lighter, and shuffled toward the winders. "Damn drudges," he spit into the water.

At 6:45 A.M., we arrived on the captain's spot. Wadey had found his marks—a beacon falling like a bead in the gunsight of Harris Creek—so he was fast on his favorite station on the south side of Sands. "Let 'em go," he said, and Li'l Wade and Moe cast off the dredges, which slid in without a splash. They ran free for five minutes, then came up full. Wadey quickly threw overboard his lucky red-and-white buoy—three plastic jugs tied to iron slag. The jugs bounced in the whitecaps like party balloons. His marks were right on the money. With my hand on the main sheet, the captain turned *Rebecca* northwest into the wind and came about. The boom crossed the deck, and I eased it to the other side. By instinct, Wadey adopted a northeast-southwest course, wind abeam.

Moe culled eighty-two big oysters, I landed seventy, and Li'l Wade selected sixty-four out of the first lick. Beautiful oysters: large and round. "That's half a bushel combined," the captain smiled. The oysters arrived as single shells, not clumped or clustered, a result of the winter's cultivation. Buddy Harrison would be pleased.

Wadey made diagonal runs across the bar, winding the dredges every hundred yards or so, then coming about and doing it again.

On each change of tack the captain now handled the main sheet himself, guiding the boom across the deck. The tide was slack, so it was easy to stay on course. The wind was steady, if violent. The cream-colored sails snapped and swelled on each tack, like a tarp. Tiny wind clouds raced across the sky, dissolving against the horizon upriver. A perfect dredging day. "Life is sweet," Wadey said.

Moe jumped to his feet and ran aft with a black stone in his hands. The rock was dappled with little white crowns—dozens of them. "How many barnacles on this cobble, Wadey?" he asked. The captain took a long look, resigned to the inevitable contest. "Forty," he said, pulling a dollar from his wallet. Moe guessed thirty-eight. I counted them. Thirty-six. And thus began Moe's winning streak, which was tough to cut into all day long.

By 9:00 A.M., even as a skeleton crew, we had settled into our roles. As each dredge came up, Wadey and I stepped forward to dump with the other men; then I culled from both piles while Wadey brought the boat around. In the morning light the crew and the boat appeared to move in unison, almost in slow motion. The wide, hesitant swing of the boat, reluctantly coming about. The bow dipping into the trough between each wave, then rebounding like a bubble of air. The rhythm of the men hauling and dumping dredges in synchrony, each man kneeling to cull, then rising, as if from a prayer. The elliptical flight of the dredges, cast over the rusty rollers, slipping into the Bay, while the glistening chain bag caught the sharp light as muddy water flew off its back. Sometimes everything on a skipjack appeared in monochrome, like a series of sepia photographs.

Upriver, another dance. *Lady Katie* and *Hilda Willing* dredged with triple reefs on Dawsons in a tight circle. Broadside now, the sails were backlit by the soft March light, giving them an amber glow. The stretch of water between us shimmered with silver, like the scales of a fish. Here, on Sands, Bart worked *Esther F.* outside of us, away from the shore. Bobby Marshall arrived on *Virginia W.*, wearing his trademark sunglasses and waving a bottle at Bart. "What the hell," said Moe, "it's the last day of the season."

Farther east, Daddy Art's crooked tree was visible on Benoni bar. The *City* had both sails up, each reefed twice, as did *Howard* sailing right alongside. Art and Stan, I learned later, caught more oysters than anyone on the river that last day, more bushels than on the few power days in March. Only the best sailors can do this—making a living with the wind, keeping the fleet elite and small—a good argument for sail dredging.

"I guess we're the last holdouts," Wadey said, "the end of an era."

By midmorning, we had exhausted Wadey's spot and were searching for another. After canvassing about, he settled on a small promontory and began prancing at the helm, peering over the cabin as each dredge came up. We were on our third hill. Ten minutes later, our fourth, and luck finally surfaced. *Rebecca* made a good lick. Li'l Wade yelled, "Ninety-eight," back to his father, who visibly relaxed, choosing not to notice the twenty-odd coffins that had surfaced, too.

"Blowing now," said the captain, just after the strike. "Thirty miles." Green water and whitecaps raced over the bar, less so in the main river. Stanley sailed toward us, to the relative safety of Sands. Farther upriver, Pete, Art, and Stan reefed their sails down to patches of cloth. The Danielses pushed upriver, seeking a sheltered bar. The Choptank had only a few places to work in a northwest blow: Trappe, Chloras, Sands. Skipjacks headed for each.

Eleven A.M.: dinnertime. Without enough men aboard to rotate through the galley, *Rebecca* came to a halt. The captain nosed her into the wind to give the sails and crew a rest. Wadey attacked a bologna-and-cheese sandwich, on white bread. Li'l Wade grabbed his brown paper bag marked with a 3 by his mother, to signify Wade Hampton Murphy III. And I ate from another bag that Jackie Murphy had sent along—a cold venison burger. Moe was more enterprising. He pulled out a Tupperware box of homemade spaghetti, which he proceeded to heat up on the stove. Li'l Wade was unusually talkative, like a teenager after school.

"This orster season couldn't end quicker," he said. "I've gotta get my workboat ready for crabbing. Then thar's carpentry next week, every afternoon."

"The geese have left, flown north," Moe said. "I'll be shedding crabs soon."

Wadey looked us over. "We have spatting for two weeks, if you want to make some money, boys. Crabs are still a ways off yet."

Li'l Wade set down his sandwich and took a long pull from his Coke. "I'll come along, I guess," he said.

"Fine, that's fine," his father answered, barely containing his excitement. The boy had come full circle.

Moe looked at Li'l Wade. "You gonna drudge next season?"

"Guess I'll have to. Somebody my age can't make better money than this. I made $570 the best week this winter and only $350 as a carpenter's assistant last summer. The water business is still top dollar as I can see it, as long as the orsters and crabs last. But I'll do some carpentry this summer, on weekends and afternoons. Crabbing the rest o' the time."

"You might be a winter carpenter soon enough," Moe said. "Nobody's betting the orsters are holding out."

"I am," said Wadey. His crew responded with an awkward silence.

Then Li'l Wade broke in: "Lot of gapers and boxes today." His father emptied his lungs with a whistle.

"Where ya going after spatting, Cap'n?" Moe asked, breaking the impasse.

"Florida."

Moe smiled at this. Wadey had been threatening to go on a vacation for years. He never did. Trouble was he couldn't get the Chesapeake out of his veins.

After a fifteen-minute break, captain and crew returned to dredging. The wind had kicked up more seas; waves splashed readily over the sides of the boat. Telltales were everywhere. Sail stops blew horizontally off the boom; oilskins flapped on the cabintop; plastic buckets blew across the deck with the wind. And the whitecaps kept breaking steadily from the northwest.

But at noon, after five hours' dredging, the wind suddenly dropped to twenty miles. Sailing became smoother; the boat ceased rocking back and forth. We culled in safety. Working next to him, I noticed that Moe could sort faster, better than young Wade, who carelessly tossed some markets overboard, angering his father. Moe used a culling hammer, but Li'l Wade simply eyeballed them and sometimes he was wrong.

"Watch yer culling," the captain yelled. His son glared at him and lit a cigarette. I strolled back to the helm, and the captain buttonholed me. "Li'l Wade's the best man I had all winter; those other boys weren't worth a damn. He just needs to listen more— he'll make a good waterman." Wadey glanced toward his son. "I may lose him. If he goes with carpentry full-time, I'll have to accept it. Thar's not much real money on the water anymore."

I stayed with Wadey while the dredges raked across the reef. He was reflective that day; his thoughts often returning to the exploits of old-time dredgers, men of his father's generation. "You didn't know Funny Parks," he said, coming about on a starboard tack. "He had the *Dorothy*—a skipjack the size of the *Hilda Willing*, with the same low cabin. Old-time dredger from Holland's Island. That's his house over thar next to Stanley's." Wadey pointed to Fairbank at the edge of Black Walnut Cove. "Funny's gone and the *Dorothy*'s gone and that island he come from is gone, too. Washed away. But he was a good drudger." Wadey straightened out the boat and continued. "Old Captain Funny would do anything to keep his crew busy, culling nonstop. He sailed that boat single-handed. He would climb over the cabin, over the winders, to release his jib rather than bother his men with it. 'Keep 'em culling,' he used to say. It was money to him. Orsters were money in them days."

Wadey didn't interrupt his crew, either. He only asked us to cull that day. There were no beckets to change; no sails to reef—the second reef held just fine. We had no free time to cause trouble. Three men doing the work of six. Everything was coordinated, like a baseball team going for the pennant, trying for one last great day. On one catch, a couple of dozen markets fell on deck with a mess of open, large coffins and healthy smalls. Only the youngest oysters showed good survival; the older bivalves were dead. Wadey picked up a couple of smalls and tossed them in the river, then he held up a box and looked at it, shaking his head.

"Yes, Roy Scott says Dermo has invaded the creeks—Harris Creek, Broad Creek, Tred Avon—and now the river. He says Black Walnut Sands has it bad. I guess he's right. We've been catching dead orsters all morning. Not many, but it's getting worse. This river will never be the same." Wadey looked out over the oyster grounds, past the mouth of the Choptank to the rough, green water beyond. "I'm still hopeful but I'm not gonna wait for the Bay to die. I'm gonna buy a new suit of sails for *Rebecca*, and get her Coast Guard certified. Maybe get a sponsor—like Old Bay. Then I can take charter parties—make some money between seasons, when it's slack." Without a glance, he flipped the coffin back overboard. The captain then selected a few medium oysters to take back to the helm. From the cabintop he took a shucking knife and opened one of the smalls to gauge its health. It was white and plump, and he held it out for me to eat, on the half shell. I didn't resist. Salty and cold, the oyster was one of the best I'd ever had on the Choptank.

Wadey said, "That orster has fed my family for three generations. I'm having my doubts she'll serve a fourth. Too many being caught or killed." The captain's optimism after the Annapolis seed meeting was fleeting, like the wind on a flawy day.

"It's not just the death or patent tongers," said Moe, approaching us at the helm. "Some of the young drudge-boat captains—you got it, 'the grinders'—they sold smalls all winter, too." His voice trailed off. "I'm not naming names," he whispered, "but I've seen it." Moe worked for Daryl aboard *Nellie Byrd* for two months this season. "I quit New Year's Day; we weren't making enough money," he continued, a little louder. "Daryl's not the sailor or drudger Wadey is. One day I'd make thirty-five dollars, another day fifty-five, then a hundred, then back to thirty-five. The young drudgers are inconsistent. They keep their lines too long, bringing drudges aboard full of empty shells. If Wadey sees the drudges coming up with shells, he takes the lines in a few turns, so they won't dig as deep. Not the other drudgers. Daryl just grinds 'em and winds 'em—as soon as you've got the shells off the deck, he's bringing 'em up again. You don't catch as many legal orsters, but the captain thinks he's making a killing. With Wadey, I know I'm gonna make one hundred dollars every day. And you don't miss many days. He's out here like today in a living gale—worse than this—when no one else will work. You betcha I'd rather work for Wadey. Some won't. He's got the biggest mouth on the Bay, everybody knows that. But I'll say this much: You get a day's work each day, *every day*, and he doesn't have to catch smalls to do it."

By midafternoon the catch slowed down. The port dredge bag tore, and Wadey had to stop the boat for twenty minutes to fix it. The repair partially corrected the disparity that had been Li'l Wade's complaint. Afterward, Moe walked aft to munch on a candy bar and made his forecast: "We'll catch forty—make it a day's work. We need, maybe, ten more booshel. Three more hours till sundown—we'll do it if the pace picks up." The skipjack fleet used to land ten bushels a boat in as many minutes; today the scale had changed, expectations had diminished.

"Okay," said Moe, "how many in the next lick?" The captain bet a dollar it would be a bucket or better—half a bushel, around one hundred oysters. Moe clapped his hands, rubbed them together, and went forward to cull what he hoped was fewer than that—self-defeating for a culler. But the game was on: Moe betting low, Wadey betting high for the rest of the afternoon.

Shortly, the dredges rose out of the river. Moe was quick to cull and count them. "Only twenty single orsters that lick," said Moe, stepping aft again. "That'll be a dollar, Wadey."

The captain smiled. "We better find another spot to finish up the day."

ON A WHIM, Wadey moved to the Swash, a channel that cuts through the southwest corner of Sands. It was softer and deeper than the top of the bar, and although the captain didn't like mud, moving there got us away from Bart, Bobby, and Stanley. Blue crabs now came aboard, dislodged from the mud, a thick gunk that forced the lever man to wash the dredges on each lick. So many farmers had lost their topsoil on the bottom of the Bay, an unlikely culprit in the demise of the oyster. Nobody profited from the erosion: The farmers forfeited their greatest asset and the watermen watched bed upon bed choked with silt. Here, on the Swash, despite the sediment, we had some success, though not quite keeping up with the earlier pace of four bushels per hour. Wadey was relaxed though, enjoying the day. The wind dropped out, moderating to fifteen miles, northwest. As a consequence, *Rebecca* slowed down even more. At the captain's order, we pulled the sails down fast, untied a row of reef points, and hoisted the main and jib again. We regained our speed under a "dredger's breeze." I thought of Daddy Art upriver.

Signs of spring surrounded us like flags signaling a boat race. A great blue heron flew by across the mouth of the river, from Cook Point, over us, toward Tilghman's. Canvasbacks took flight and would soon return to Canada. To the north of us, a beautiful male oldsquaw, adorned in black and white, swam with his drabber mate nearby, ideas of mating no doubt in his head. Like troubadours, birds and boats announce the change of seasons on the Chesapeake Bay.

Up forward, father and son debated the merits of switching dredges, to keep Li'l Wade on par with Moe, but the only substitute available that day would be a pair of hard dredges that Henry Reecer had repaired in November. They were too heavy for the Swash. The captain decided to stick with the edge dredges, even if an imperfect match. "The twine bags are fair now," he said to his son. "Good culling can make up the difference." After dumping the port dredge, Wadey turned to me as he came aft. He said, "Honey, I've got to shuck a few for Miss Pauline. Take the wheel. Keep her"—he pointed with four fingers of his right hand northeast toward Change Point—"straight until she comes up to ten feet. When we wind the drudges, turn her hard to starboard and go back down the hill. Drop the drudges again only after yer straight and clear. Wind'ard first." His instructions sounded like directions for landing a plane on an aircraft carrier—only blindfolded, with the deck underwater.

Wadey walked around to the starboard side of the cabin and, selecting a mess of oysters, began shucking them with a little wiggle of his knife, as I kept the wheel steady. Inside the first oyster, Wadey found a black pearl—rare for the American oyster. "Now that's valuable," he said. "My luck's bound to change."

We were a mile offshore, about five hundred yards due southwest of *Nellie Bly*, a shipwrecked schooner. I looked through the cabin hatchway at the video sounder: 15.9 feet. Suddenly it jumped to 13.4. The captain peeked up from shucking, cast his eyes around, saw the buoy up ahead, and then trained his eyes on me.

"Twelve point one," I said. "She's coming up fast."

"When she comes up to ten, as soon as we wind 'em, turn her

hard to the right, take her sou'west. Go down to sixteen feet and come on back."

"Ten point four."

Wadey grabbed the throttle cord and revved the winders. Moe and his son kicked the levers down. The drums engaged and labored under the strain, under the weight of the cable and the dredges and the catch.

When the dredges were just breaking out of the water, I turned the wheel hard to starboard, pushing it away from me. I ran forward to dump the port dredge with Li'l Wade. *Crash.* Oysters and stones and mud hit the deck. A good haul. I ran aft to grab the wheel again and continued to bring her about—a wide circle to the right. Then I straightened her out. The compass said we were headed southwest. The buoy was dead ahead. I was drudging. Like the Daniels boys, I felt like I was "ruling the world."

We released the windward dredge and she dug in, scooping up oysters in her path. Once *Rebecca* came southwest, I turned her back south for a few seconds to allow the second dredge to bite into the bottom. Then, with the dredges both behind us, I gently turned her southwest again, bringing her straight, aiming for Sharps Island, the sunken isle washed away by the currents, just south of the tilting lighthouse.

Wadey looked up briefly, cast his eyes at the dredge cable as it came along the boat, and returned to shucking. Not a word. We must be working the edge all right, I thought to myself.

After a minute, he added, "Now turn her all the way south—toward James Island. I want to try farther east of the Swash, away from shore. We may do even better over thar."

I brought *Rebecca* around south in the direction of James Island, down the Bay at the mouth of the Little Choptank. I watched the depth sounder closely and called out the digits:

"Twelve point four . . . Thirteen point five . . . Fifteen point nine . . . Fifteen point nine . . . Fifteen . . . Fifteen . . . Fourteen . . . Twelve. She's coming back up."

Wadey looked around, dropped his shucking knife on the cabin-top, and came around to examine the depth sounder.

"Come about," he ordered. I tacked and ran into the trough. He looked over the side as the dredges descended. Again the depth sounder climbed up from its low.

"Thar's a hole out here. I knowed it. The edge comes up on both sides of it. Try turning her north-south and we'll try this outer edge. It's got three sides—it's shaped like a horseshoe. My good fortune." He winked.

We climbed up the hill. The dredges bit weakly into the edge, their teeth worn down from a season of combing the bottom of the Bay. The dredges surfaced as we reached "the hard"—the ten-foot plateau above the horseshoe on the south side of Black Walnut Sands.

Clear oysters. The bags were brimming full. Moe and Li'l Wade filled two white buckets apiece. A bushel or more to a dredge, double what we were doing this morning. "In all my years drudging I've never found this spot before," said Wadey, his faith restored, as he took over the helm. "It won't last long, but we'll be leaving a good skim for next year—if it lives."

Li'l Wade looked up from his impressive catch and shouted, "Where'd this place come from?"

"Looked for a strike all season long and here it is with an hour to go. Good Gawd Almighty! You can't win but for losing."

"It's the mother lode," said Moe.

"We could catch our limit—a hundred fifty booshel—if we had the time," said L'il Wade.

"Let's stay out," said Moe, waving his arms like a traffic cop. "After sunset, nobody'll know."

"I'd know," said the captain.

"Buddy'll know," said Li'l Wade, coming aft. He looked at Moe intently. "Other drudgers will know, even if we don't get arrested." L'il Wade was turning into a Murphy after all.

"I won't get caught," said the captain, "because we're going in at sunset, not a minute later. I'll catch these orsters next year. That's *my* wager. They better live—'cause I'll be here next November with the best of 'em. Eight months, that's all, then we'll reap the harvest. You gotta be patient to be a waterman." Wadey sounded like a man with his last bet on red.

The northwest breeze subsided to less than ten miles per hour, hardly enough to fill the sails on each tack. Each dredge began surfacing with too few oysters in the bag, too few for what was there to be caught. Clearly, *Rebecca* was crossing the bar too slowly. And the wind was to blame. I expected the captain to shake out another reef but he surprised me with another piece of folklore from generations past.

"Go on, Moe," he said, "throw some money overboard so we can catch a little breeze."

"I'd rather buy some wind with yer money," Moe answered and turned his coat pockets inside out, in the universal expression of poverty. I reached in my pocket and handed him a dime. Without missing a beat, he flipped the coin to Wadey, who tossed it north over the stern, where it hung in the air briefly before dropping into the cold waters of the Choptank River.

"I hope a dime wasn't too much," said Moe.

Wadey smiled. "Yeah, once a Somerset County waterman was becalmed in Tangier Sound, so he threw a quarter over the side and hollered, 'Let me have a quarter's worth!' Ten minutes later a gale came and nearly capsized his boat. The captain said, 'Lordy, if I'd known the wind was that cheap, I'd only've thrown a nickel.'"

"Maybe a dime is just right then," Moe said.

It better be enough, I thought. I was out of change.

Wadey made half a dozen more licks running north-south on the Horseshoe, which had been christened properly by the captain with a cold cup of coffee, while the sun descended into a bank of clouds. Between culls, Moe came aft to bet on the size of the last two licks of the day. Wadey already owed him four dollars. "Let's make it an even five," Moe said, spreading his hands and cracking his knuckles.

"What's your bet?" Wadey said.

"A buck. Half a booshel or less—each drudge. Ye're high, I'm low." Moe smiled, then in a low conspiratorial voice, said, "It's not how you play the game; it's how much you win."

"Fine." Wadey slammed a dollar bill on the cabintop. He did not have the constitution to bet against *Rebecca* and had called for the higher count, the rosier forecast, all day. As we came up the hill one last time, Wadey looked over and saw Stanley and Bobby still had their dredge lines out. Ten minutes remained till sunset. So he said: "Let's head for my last buoy." On cue, I tossed the windward dredge in with Moe. After a pause, Li'l Wade did the same on the leeward side. "We'll make one last lick on the way to my mark," the captain said.

To arrive at the buyers first, some dredge boats had already quit. Pete had pulled his dredges two hours earlier and was now at the dock. Art and Stan had returned to Cambridge. Even Bart had sailed to Knapps Narrows an hour before sunset. This left three skipjacks on the river to vie for the title of the last boat at work. The contest was an old one, as old as racing to port.

Wadey stretched out his last lick, even as the sun nearly touched the horizon. The breeze kicked up a bit, maybe to twelve miles. Wadey responded with a grin. The wind purchased, the captain could hold on to the rest of the pennies in his shoe. His attention turned to the last two skipjacks in the fleet, framed in his binoculars.

Moe said under his breath, "He'd never hear the end of it if he quit before Stanley or Bobby. Wadey's a hard roller—hell, he busted two masts out of the *Sigsbee* in just one week. Yes, they say he dredged in a living gale rather than be the first one in." Moe turned toward Li'l Wade and raised his voice, "Broke the mold with yer father, son."

"If it was up to me, we'd be headed home right now," said young Wade. "Let's give this drudging a rest. Next November will come soon enough."

Wadey, out of earshot, said, "Okay, boys, let's wind 'em and get a booshel this time." He winked at Moe and tipped his hat farther back on his head.

The sun, a spectacular crimson, descended through a bank of reddish gray, almost pink, clouds and seemed to hover briefly before setting over Tilghman's Island. Balanced there over the trees, it resembled Henry Reecer's forge: a brilliant hot coal surrounded by smoldering embers. In two minutes the furnace was gone. At that moment the last dredge came over the roller and was dumped aboard *Rebecca*. The catch was gloriously chockful of oysters. Each landed with a *plink* in the pile. Wadey waved the prize money at Moe and put the greenbacks in his wallet. *Rebecca* had won. It was just after sunset: We were minor outlaws and—since reputations mattered most—the last ones on the rock.

Wadey spun the boat around to the north, and Li'l Wade picked up the last buoy with the boat hook. We were headed home with a fair breeze behind us. To our right, ahead, and to leeward, sails were being unreefed on *Lady Katie* and *Virginia W.* In the long evening light the sailcloth was bright white, almost translucent— like a bedsheet pinned to dry—in the fresh northwest breeze. The tall plumb mast of *Lady Katie*, well varnished, was yellowish red, almost cedar, and tall—like the neck of a crane. A big man stood at the wheel.

"Shake out all those reefs and heist the sail again," Wadey shouted. "We have a challenge race on our hands." In a few minutes the three of us had untied the reefs, relaunched the main and jib, and secured the halyards. We paraded full sail.

A racing skipjack puts a crew on its toes, and the three of us ran around the deck preparing for an offensive. Wind filled the canvas, and we quickly gathered speed. Wadey adjusted the mainsail by letting out the sheet about six feet. Li'l Wade freed the jib. With the sails now set right, the crew was free to clean up the deck. Moe shoveled each oyster pile into a tighter mound, almost cone-shaped—out of the way and stacked high for inspection. He pointed to his own cache next to the starboard chain plates. "That's probably twenty-two," he claimed. Then he looked over at Li'l Wade's pile. "Wade, you'll go eighteen thar. That's forty total, I believe."

"Not a bad day's work," said Li'l Wade. "We'll make a hundred thirty dollars each."

"I'll bet I have four more booshel than you," Moe said. "One buck."

"No, I'm not betting," said Li'l Wade.

"Cap'n, forty on deck."

"Okay," Wadey said. "I say forty-four. One dollar. Even money." Moe looked pleased. "Ye're on."

With the resurrected breeze now pushing sixteen miles per hour, *Rebecca* was in sailing trim. She gathered speed on a port tack, with the boat close-hauled, heading north toward home. We came alongside *Virginia W.*, then promptly raced ahead of the little skipjack. Wadey said, "She can't match us—a bigger boat's always faster; the hull speed is greater. Bobby should know that."

We braced into a headwind for the sail north toward the narrows. Directly ahead was *Lady Katie*. She had a head start on us; this was not a handicapped race but a free-for-all. Stanley had started off at sunset, too, but he had been slightly to the northeast, a better position.

Rebecca and *Lady Katie* spread their broad sails and heeled over slightly. *Rebecca* may have been gaining. But as they exited Sands and crossed onto tongers' ground, *Lady Katie* jogged left, turning into the wind. Stanley was one tack ahead of us. He rounded Middle Ground beacon, dropped his sails, lowered his yawl boat, and motored in. By the time we sailed by the beacon, Stanley had already threaded the channel between Avalon and Devil's Island, the harbor just ahead. Wadey said, "It's good to see Stanley win." The big man didn't glance back. His season, his sailing career was over. The Larrimore dynasty had come to an end.

Rebecca sailed north, dropping her sails at the last possible moment. Nearing the narrows we left green beacons number 3 and 5 to port. Both markers held the first twigs and branches of new osprey nests, harbingers of spring. Two of the fish hawks stood guard, picking at rockfish in their talons. Passing red beacon number 6 to starboard, we crossed into the mouth of the narrows. As *Rebecca* glided home, we passed the older skipjacks—the resurrected *Claud W. Somers*, the derelict *Ralph T. Webster* and *Lorraine Rose*, the sunken *Oregon*, and the charred embers of the *Ruby G. Ford*. Wadey recalled that just about every oyster boat on the Bay had passed through Knapps Narrows at one time or another. A thousand dredge boats, perhaps half of them skipjacks, he said. The Cambridge boats: *Rosie Parks* and *Sallie Bramble*. The Smith Islanders: *Geneva May* and *Annie Lee*. And the Deal boats: *Thomas Clyde, Susan May, Mamie Mister, Robert L. Webster*. And others. Few were living, their legacies nearly lost, no longer secure in the memories of captains and crews.

The Tilghman fleet had survived the best, if a hundred boats cut to twelve was surviving. And even Tilghman's last stand had been a struggle. Most of the old Tilghman fleet was lost—Glendi's *Laura J. Barkley*, Stanley's *Reliance*, Wild Bill Berridge's *Anna May Rich*, Bart's *Lena Rose*, the Old Man's *George W. Collier*. Even now, with *Lady Katie, Martha Lewis*, and *Nellie Byrd* retiring, the local fleet would number less than ten.

Farther ahead, at the Harrison Oyster Company wharf, Billy Murphy was waving to his father. He had waited patiently for *Rebecca* for two hours; his mother had driven him to the wharf after school. Jackie now sat in her car nearby with the heater on, preparing checks for the crew. *Rebecca* pulled into the "falls," the oyster landing section of the wharf.

"Hey, Billy!" the captain called, tossing a stern line to the wharf. "How's my best boy!" When the skipjack came alongside, Billy jumped aboard, stepping past his older brother to wrap his arms around his father's waist. Lee Daniels, Art's grandson and new employee of the Tidewater Administration, had been standing on the wharf with Billy; he stepped aboard now as well. "Are ya gonna be a drudge-boat captain?" Lee asked the boy.

"Someday."

"Which skipjack you gonna drudge?"

"This one. *Rebecca.* I'm only going to sail her; power drudging's too noisy. I'll grab a drudger's breeze any day." This seemed to satisfy Lee. He gave a thumbs-up and walked past Wadey to the oyster piles—to assess the quality, the health, of the day's catches. They exchanged winks. The captain then glanced at Billy with a wistful look in his eyes.

Little Buddy was on hand to buy our oysters—twenty dollars a bushel. He caught a bow line thrown by Moe and put the loop on the piling at the corner of the bridge. Sonny Murphy was in the counting booth, ticking off the bushels. With each bushel, the conveyor belt groaned like an elevator engaging. Wadey shoveled the port side, which was closest to the wharf, and Moe shoveled starboard. Li'l Wade handled the buckets swinging back and forth to the conveyor. The entire catch was being loaded into a Daiger Brothers truck destined for Virginia. Wadey and his oldest son worked in tandem, silently, no words needed after a season together. His youngest kept count. After thirty minutes of off-loading, Sonny called out his eighth tally, making forty, and then counted four more bushels. The captain asked, "How many?" Sonny came out of the tally shack. "Forty-four, Wadey," he said.

Wadey looked at his young son. "Forty-four, Dad," Billy confirmed.

Moe threw up his hands and shook his head. "Wadey," he said, "I'll be damned—ye're right on the money. How'dya manage that? You should try predicting the future." Wadey blanched. Who can see past a turn in the road?

At that instant, Lee Daniels stepped back onto the dock, and Wadey cuffed him. "Where's yer grandfather today?" he asked.

"Daddy Art's out sailing—last day, his sixtieth season in all his glory—loving every minute. Ya know, he'll die at the wheel of a skipjack." Wadey nodded and looked off into the distance with a knowing smile. "Perty arsters," Lee said, but by then the captain wasn't listening.

We cast off and floated into the narrows. Wadey picked up the microphone on the VHS radio: "Knapps Narrows Bridge, I'm coming through—"

"I've got you, Wadey," answered the faceless voice, hovering above in the bridgehouse. And she swung open. *Rebecca* held the course, like an old horse that knows her way home.

Underneath the bridge, Moe and I discovered a green street sign, tacked to the pilings, that announced SKIPJACK RD. Moe said some kids had stolen it from North Tilghman, as a prank, and nailed it here. The law had spotted it but left it in place. Seemed like some justice had been served. It may be the only epitaph for the countless men and ships that have run these waters, sails aloft, to strike out for another season or to scud home with gale astern.

Rebecca's mast cleared the span and her bow swung toward the next wharf. Like a towering sundial, the mast tip was bathed in the warm evening light. Then the drawbridge descended and closed the narrows for the night. Billy Murphy caught his father's stern line again, and L'il Wade tended to the bow. The crew roped in *Rebecca* and pulled her in to the berth. She was secured one more time.

Wadey walked over to his truck and climbed in. No goodbyes. He started to drive off to have a beer with his friend Hunky, only to suddenly hit the brakes. The truck jolted to a stop. Reaching across his seat, Wadey grabbed something. He held out a quart glass jar of shucked oysters. "Honey, take these to Miss Pauline for me," he said. "I'm her favorite, even if Hunky thinks he is." I nodded that I would and he drove off, oyster shell flying from his tires.

I walked along Main Street toward Gibsontown Road. Soon I would be leaving the island, and it was time to begin packing up. The last light was fading, and the island had settled down for the first springlike night. Lights were shining from the windows; dogs barked in the yards. From Gibsontown I could see that the other skipjacks were tied fast in Dogwood Harbor, all battened down. At the end of the road, on the dock next to John B. Harrison's house, I saw two silhouettes outlined against the river. It was Miss Pauline walking Cat on a leash.

"There you are," she said. "I was worried about my boys. That wind was fierce today. Blowing nor'west."

"We're all safe."

"I thought Stanley was out still. He always played late, after dark. Maybe I should call Loretta. Were you working for him today?"

"Wadey. I was with Wadey. He sent you these oysters. He shucked them himself."

"Teacher's pet. My, I might just keep him after school for that." She tugged and yanked at the leash, making Cat snarl. "I love all my boys, drudgers every one. Is Stanley in yet?"

I convinced her he was, that all her captains were safely home, and then we walked back to our shared lawn. Miss Pauline wished me good night, and then she returned to her piano. "Summertime" trickled out of her bungalow and down the street, a wish for another season.

THE NEXT DAY the wind picked up, and from my window, I saw two skipjacks under sail on a starboard tack, slowly making for the mouth of the river against a broadside northerly breeze. The sickle-shaped jibs and unreefed mains were full of wind. Figuring it was a couple of Deal dredge boats sailing home after five months at their northern port, I grabbed my field glasses and drove to the south end of the island—to see who was returning to Tangier Sound.

Past the cornfields in the middle of the island I turned left, east toward Bar Neck. I passed by the old schoolhouse, where Miss Pauline had taught, and the old Larrimore houses lining the cove. I was too late. The skipjacks were already out of sight, behind the broad peninsula of Bar Neck Point. Revving the car, I backtracked toward the southern tip of the island. Suddenly, I realized I was driving fast, too fast, and slowed down as I rounded Black Walnut Cove. At the memorial cross to drowned sailors· on Black Walnut Point, I hit the brakes and skidded to a stop.

Ahead, one mile across the mouth of the Choptank the two skipjacks made way. Through the binoculars, the mast of the lead boat was clearly bent. Crooked tree. *City of Crisfield* and *Howard*. Art and Stan. Father and son. Grandsons were certainly aboard. As they cleared Cook Point, the Danielses jibed, allowing their booms and mainsails to cross to starboard. They turned their wheels and began a new heading south toward Deal Island. Their jibs stretched to port, across from their mains. Wing and wing: The two sails opposite each other looked like the spans of two giant birds. Two white swans flying south. And Daddy Art in all his glory. The clouds were low in the sky—almost like fog—and against this backdrop the two skipjacks floated dreamily. I begged them not to disappear, but by then they had set their course on the far horizon. I stood for an hour, watching patiently as the two sailboats slowly vanished, twin white dots fading into the blue. I thought I could still see them long after they were gone.

OUT OF THE THOUSANDS of lights that had brightened the Bay, fewer than fifteen now glittered in the twilight of the century.

Eighteen had ventured that season, and nearly all—80 percent—had returned to sail another day. But for how long? As I watched the last two sail home to their families, I had no illusions: Their prospects were poor. For the moment these captains clung tenaciously to the past. Yet their grip was failing. Their world would inevitably change. Inexplicably, though, a feeling of calm washed over me: We lived in a world where skipjacks were still possible. That brought on a smile. And, in an instant, I saw beyond that: a world lucky to have them. They give us so much—beauty, history, balance, grace—and we give them nothing in return. They are a gift. Even as they disappear one by one, it almost seems enough to know hundreds had once sailed and sailed well, in all their glory. They had their moment in time. It will have to be enough.

Fair wind, captains. Fair tide.

Epilogue

Every Chesapeake story not only begins but ends with the wind. Late in the day a strong breeze can precipitate a sea change, and such a turnabout is how this story concludes. Attitude and attention toward skipjacks from both bureaucrats and politicians shifted a few years ago, like born-again conservationists. Unfortunately, it took more than a breeze—it required a full living gale and a near tragedy—to bring this about. Even then, the conversion came too late.

It was the second day of the 1999–2000 season, a few years after my farewell to the island. *Rebecca* was dredging at the mouth of Trappe Creek, near Howell Point, in the upper Choptank with three crewmen, a man short. I was the missing deckhand, delayed on my flight from the Rocky Mountains, where I had moved. Since leaving the Chesapeake, I had returned each November to open the season—a few days of sailing on those crisp autumn mornings and afternoons for which the Bay is renowned. But on this day, Wadey and his crew battled driving rain alone to land seventy bushels of prime oysters before heading home at three o'clock. The captain made this unusual concession in the face of a green crew—two brothers, Ward and Walker, and their friend, Mike, from Crisfield.

They were cold, soaked, and tired, and when Wadey quit early, relieved. The wind was spiking to twenty miles. Visibility was poor. Rainsqualls danced around the boat.

Rather than retreat to Cambridge, as the Deal boats had done two hours earlier, Wadey turned *Rebecca* downriver, casting caution to the wind. The two-hour voyage to Tilghman's began as a routine, if wet, trip. The yawl boat did all the pushing, and *Rebecca* cut through the whitecaps with ease. The rain continued to plummet, stinging the faces of the crew. Later, Mike said sheets of water slapped him as if he had stepped through a waterfall. Each gust brought another bucket of rain. The wind—picking up to twenty-five now—streamed from the south, creating a following sea. Swells approached six feet. With the wind behind him, Wadey feared for his yawl boat. If she sank, he'd be dead in the water, or worse, she'd pull *Rebecca* down, too. When the wind hit thirty, Murphy ordered the men to haul aboard the auxiliary. *Rebecca* turned into the wind, and the crew tied three reefs in the main and raised her tight. From the shore a mile away, where I was standing, the shortened sail resembled a scarf, a bandana between the boom and the mast. The wind howled. *Rebecca* came about and, with fair wind, she scudded toward home. This was barely an hour into the trip, and she was only halfway there.

With the rain, Wadey couldn't see the squall line, wind clouds, or a darkening sky. He hoped the wind would cap at thirty; he counted on less than a gale. But the wind and seas almost immediately began to build. The wide mouth of the Choptank gave the waves a broad fetch to grow. Whitecaps topped eight, maybe nine, feet. The wind, now double the strength of his morning at Trappe Creek, worried Wadey. It wasn't a steady blow; it punched like a boxer and seemed to multiply in strength all the time. The wind screamed through the rigging, climbing an octave with each notch in velocity. And, in turn, the waves rose up, peaking at ten feet. The captain winced each time a swell washed over the deck; the boat had several rotten boards nailed to the foredeck, and he worried about water seeping below. But as long as they were sailing northwest toward the island (away from the wind), the waves did little damage—no water came over the stern—and the three electric pumps held their own in the hold. Still, Murphy, clutching the wheel, knew to prepare himself for the worst.

When the wind topped fifty, the mainsail shattered. The sail literally blew up, torn into a dozen pieces, like little rags. Wadey had been smart to shorten the sail; fewer reefs could have brought down the mast. In any case, his propulsion was gone; he was dead in the water.

Thinking quickly, Wadey ordered the anchor dropped over the bow, to stabilize the boat and bring her head into the wind. The greatest danger would be for *Rebecca* to lie sideways to ("beam-to") the gale; waves would likely swamp her with her profile exposed. Now with the bow and anchor chain nosing the wind, Wadey felt better, but he still feared he might lose her. Waves were spilling over the front rail, penetrating the bad place in the deck. Water always discovers a weakness. So the second thing Wadey did was call his wife, Jackie, over the radio. He told her he was taking on water, to send a couple of boats out to tow him in. She ran next door to Robbie Wilson's house, and within minutes, Robbie and his son Jason were driving their workboats, *Miss Brenda II* and *Island Girl*, out of the harbor, bearing south toward *Rebecca*.

Halfway out, a rogue wave smashed Robbie's windshield, but he kept on coming, barreling through each crest, diving into each trough. By now a strong ebb tide was retreating against the wind, producing monster waves, perhaps twelve feet tall. Meanwhile, Wadey was taking on water. The pumps were no longer keeping pace. He began to bail with a bucket, by hand. The crew didn't join him; they were too scared to descend into the hold, where the water was up to the captain's knees. Nobody thought to put on life vests; they sat in factory wrapping in the cabin. It took the Wilsons half an hour to reach the wounded vessel. When they did, they attached a towline to *Rebecca*. Wadey cut loose the anchor, and the tow home commenced. As dusk descended, everyone thought they'd be okay. But it was a race against time.

Time and water. Each wave that broke over *Rebecca* added to the surplus in the hold. And the skipjack "broached," nose-diving into each trough, which caused more water to penetrate the leaking foredeck. Wadey bailed until his arms ached and then returned to the helm, where Mike stood, hanging onto the davits. The two brothers, Ward and Walker, clung to the shrouds near the mast. Another twenty minutes to safety, but that was to be outside everyone's grasp. As *Rebecca* passed over Bar Neck onto tongers' ground, the Bay landed a one-two punch. First, a huge wave swamped the boat, listing her to port. Then, as she came back even, another, larger assault plunged into her, and she went down. She sank fast, right underneath the feet of captain and crew in twenty feet of water, spilling her cargo of oysters on the bottom. The stern went down first, submerging Wadey and Mike. Both were certain they would drown (Mike couldn't swim; Wadey had cracked three ribs), but Robbie threw them a life ring, which landed nearby. They struggled over it while something pinned down their legs—perhaps the boom or the topping lift. But they drifted free. Up forward, Ward and Walker still hugged the shrouds, the most stable element of the rigging. As the boat sank, water rushed past the hatches into the hold, and the brothers feared they would be sucked into the bowels of the skipjack. They were spared one death to face another. *Rebecca* rolled over on her starboard side and the brothers spilled into the turbulent, near-freezing water.

During the ensuing rescue, any number of lethal incidents might have claimed them. A hundred-pound hatch cover might have knocked out a crewman; a dredge might have pinned him under water; the mast might have rolled out. As it happened, the only treachery in the water was the array of lines and rope and cable from the rigging. If a foot or a leg or an arm became entangled in one of those snares, drowning was likely. The lines threaded the water like spaghetti. Just as Ward entered the water, a line or halyard pressed against his throat and pushed him under. He pushed away from it and popped up just in time to grab a second life ring. His brother, Walker, gripped the port log rail, frozen in fear, even as the boat went down. When Jason handed him the end of a boat hook and yelled, "Hold on," Walker shouted into the wind, "Are you kidding? I'm never letting go!"

The four men bobbed like corks in the swells. Miraculously, Robbie and Jason plucked the men from the water without mishap. *Miss Brenda II* and *Island Girl* motored back to Dogwood Harbor with the men, leaving *Rebecca* on the bottom with only three feet of her mast exposed above the waves. When I met Wadey at the wharf, he was already paying off the crew—$300 each for their trouble. Looking them over, he said, "I'm just glad you boys are all right. I can get another boat, but you can't replace a life." For the crew's part, they acknowledged they were lucky to get out alive. Walker summed up their feelings: "No, I ain't never going out on neither dredge boat again. No way. I quit." I had never heard that many double negatives before in one sentence, but the day deserved it. The rest of the crew agreed. "Not on your life. Neither skipjack for me."

The wind had been clocked ashore at sixty-eight miles per hour. Several old oak trees toppled on the island—one of them upended, flinging clay and oyster shell into the air. Wadey had never seen it blow that long, that hard. His brother, Jimmy, passed judgment. "Wadey," he whispered, "plenty of times you stayed out thar when it weren't fit for man or beast. The beast finally got you is all."

Rebecca preyed on Wadey like a bad dream for three days; he retied knots in his sleep. He was anxious to raise her before the rough seas ground the starboard side into pulp on the oystershell bottom. So he hired divers to refloat her, but they failed in their efforts. Finally, at week's end, the governor's office, breaking with their hands-off policy with regard to skipjacks, sent a barge and crane at a cost of at least $10,000 to lift her from the water. The crane succeeded. Then *Rebecca* was taken to St. Michaels for eventual repairs, and Wadey spent the rest of the season gathering funds in order to save her, to put her back on her feet.

But I'm jumping ahead of myself. Wadey had something to settle first: the fate of his seventy bushels. They lay out of any dredger's reach—on tongers' bottom. Trading on his notoriety with the press during the salvage of *Rebecca,* Wadey solicited and received permission from the state to dredge up his lost oysters from forbidden ground. "That should really piss off them tongers," he smiled. The recovered shellfish fetched over $2,000, not a bad take for the second day of the season.

The rest of the Tilghman fleet that day worked the Upper Bay, in moderate winds on the knolls outside Baltimore. While the weather and old age conspired to nearly ruin *Rebecca,* the northern fleet dredged in apparent safety, landing the light skim off bars just above the reach of the disease. Yet these boats were simply spared one storm for another. Over the past few years, MSX and Dermo have elevated their attack, like an underwater maelstrom, laying siege to the Bay and its rivers. The oysters in the Choptank have died; the plague has spread northward; the diseases have played ruin with the fleet. Today, most of the remaining boats—five or six skipjacks—work the far Upper Bay with modest returns. Harvests are at a record low. Most captains have simply given up.

Skippers and boats tend to succumb in step. When a skipjack retires from the fleet, the captain often walks away from the water. He fishes no more. And the name of his skipjack is only whispered, in female company, with longing and regret. Like a death in the family, the loss of a dredge boat is irreversible; a once-living thing cannot be conjured up.

Some boats have seen worse fates than *Rebecca*. The skipjack *Howard* sank again in Cambridge Harbor and was towed to Baltimore for repairs. Captain Stan Daniels could not raise the cash to rebuild her, so she was chainsawed to pieces and thrown into a Dumpster. He has not commanded a skipjack since. Even after the destruction of *Howard* (1909) and the burning of *Ruby Ford* (1891), both registered with the National Trust as historic landmarks, no one stepped forward to save *Maggie Lee* (1903), one of the two extant round-bottom skipjacks. She was also considered of national rank but was broken up into kindling, nonetheless. Of more recent vintage, *Esther F.* (1954), Bart Murphy's boat, sank in Harris Creek and was left there to die. Bart passed away shortly thereafter. His ashes were scattered off Bar Neck, where, says Wadey with no little irony, neither crab has been caught since.

With so few oysters, the younger captains have sold their boats into private hands. Three, including *Wilma Lee*, have become pleasure yachts, and four have been adopted by nonprofits as educational envoys on the Bay. (Another four skipjacks had already been engaged as "living classrooms," taking children out on the Chesapeake.) With nearly half the fleet slipping into private hands, few boats remain that could still be employed for dredging, even if the oysters should bounce back. Few captains stand in reserve. And young watermen are losing their chance to apprentice on a dredge boat. There is no line of succession by either blood or bravado. The lineage is dying out.

The rituals of retirement are starkly absent for watermen of advancing years. There are no ceremonies, no gold watches, no handshakes or speeches. While the younger skippers have turned to other trades—Robbie Wilson to pound netting, Bobby Marshall to charter fishing, Ed Farley to tourism—the older men do a little crabbing or count their memories. In summer, Stanley Larrimore trotlines a bit, but in winter he steers clear of oysters. How do you follow an act like *Lady Katie*? He can be found at Gary's Store on any given winter morning, recounting tales of the water trades. From the shore he reads the wind, notes its character, and watches the watermen go into the predawn light. Then he sits on the old bench and spins a few. Every breeze has its story. And each story has a breeze.

"I miss sail drudging," he says. "The competition is what I loved. We competed in drudging, culling, sailing, whatever. Everyone wanted to win. The last night of October, you could hardly sleep, just waiting to go."

Stanley sees the old crew from time to time. He told me that one of the crew had been arrested for murder. Gene, at seventy, begged Stanley to buy another skipjack. "I believe I could still handle them drudges," he said. Solomon, he reported, is in a nursing home, and failing. Oftentimes, he sits up in bed, scooping his hands back and forth, as if culling oysters. It's all he ever knew.

Daryl Larrimore died last winter, from a childhood form of cancer that recurred, leaving the Larrimore family with no heir apparent. Without his wit, the docks are quieter now. And as for *Lady Katie*: Scott Todd, the new owner, dredged her for the first year but has made neither lick in the seasons since.

Wadey Murphy has retired from dredging, too. After refloating *Rebecca*, he spent $60,000 repairing her and bringing her up to Coast Guard certification so he could run summer charters with up to forty-nine passengers aboard. A third of his restoration budget came from donations. He also outfitted *Rebecca* for dredging, and worked her for a couple of winter seasons. The oysters were poor while the charter business boomed, and Wadey made the logical switch to full-time tourism. A dredger at heart, he never thought he'd see the day when he'd take his winders off the deck. But he is adaptable, unlike most. Today, from March through November, Wadey takes out up to four parties a day, for a two-hour sail, essentially sailing *Rebecca* single-handedly. The guests get a taste of the Bay. They get a lecture, too—the history of Wade Hampton Murphy—worth every dime.

Like the Larrimores, the next generation of Murphys has walked away from the water. Li'l Wade and Billy are both carpenters, remodeling homes along the Eastern Shore corridor. "My boys can't afford to live on the island," says Wadey. "I'm upset they can't drudge, can't crab to make a living. The decline in seafood is to blame, and that's thanks to mismanagement by Maryland. That and the oyster disease." The terrible irony is that these problems have overshadowed youthful avarice and old age as threats to the fleet.

Rebecca's old crew has also turned its back on the water. The Langfords and Welches work on land at odd jobs. Two didn't survive the turn of the century: Aaron died of a drug overdose; Moe drowned while eel-potting in Harris Creek. Only the racing crew has stayed the same. At Deal Island each Labor Day, nearly ten skipjacks compete, some sailing out of retirement in a regatta as lively as before. Wadey has now tied Art Daniels's record with nine wins. It's hell or high water every time.

For now, Deal Island is pretty much the same: churches and cottages and peeler shacks. It hasn't caught up to the new century. It is still down-at-the-heels, almost seedy, unlike the tectonic shift on Tilghman's Island, where land speculation has brought more than fifty new houses and condominiums. Too often the new residents—retirees and weekenders—move to the island for its charm and open spaces then immediately try to shut it in. Exclusive yacht clubs. Swimming pools. The new homes are rimmed with fences, on an island where there were none. Miss Pauline would lead the charge to tear them down, if she was living, but Alzheimer's claimed her a few years back.

Conflicts are inevitable. One vacation renter rode her bike past Dogwood Harbor and was overwhelmed by the stench of bait. She asked the guilty crabber if he would "do that" somewhere else. Another weekend sailor had trouble launching his Boston Whaler at the county boat ramp because a stack of crab pots was in the way. Rather than talk to the waterman involved, he reported the incident to the marine police. The narrows has been divided: fiberglass to the north, wooden boats to the south, a swift tide running in between.

Next to the narrows at Gary's Store, men still sit on the benches telling lies, some of them true. Amid the fishing tackle and dry goods, however, there are subtle changes. California wines and imported beer crowd out Budweiser in the coolers. Outside, by the gas pumps, the old men look bewildered when a rush of Volvos and BMWs stream by, outnumbering the pickups.

Across the street at Harrison Oyster Company, the shucking-house room is quiet for most of the year. Bud Harrison still buys oysters from one skipjack—*Thomas Clyde*, operated by Lawrence Murphy—and from tongers, but 70 percent of the catch is shipped to Virginia for shucking. From November through Christmas (and beyond), however, the old gang assembles to shuck a few thousand gallons for holiday customers. On Friday evenings all winter, Woody King, now ninety-four, also works the raw bar at the Chesapeake House to a grateful crowd. But his tasty morsels are in short supply. Just as the future of the skipjack is uncertain, the prospects for Woody and the shucking house are bleak. The oysters just aren't there.

During the 2007–08 oyster season, Maryland watermen landed just over 80,000 bushels—bringing in less than 2.5 million dollars dockside. This harvest represents half of what was caught eight or ten years ago, just short of a total collapse of the fishery. Disease is the number-one culprit, having bitten a large chunk out of the annual crop each year since 1987—twenty-two seasons now under siege. Most of these years have seen periods of drought, elevating salinities and promoting the spread of MSX and Dermo. Nearly every oyster bar in the Bay has been infected with one of these pathogens. There is no refuge; disease is here to stay. The number of active oystermen also fluctuates with the drought, or more accurately, with the cycle of disease prompted by the weather. During the 2003–04 season, after a four-year drought, only 273 watermen reported an oyster harvest, and the catch was less than 30,000 bushels, an all-time low. More recently, over the wetter 2006–07 season, 800 oystermen were active, though only 325 reported selling over 100 bushels for the season. Eight bushels per man were landed for each day of effort, on average, which is half the showing for the same effort thirty years ago. When a fishery shows a decline in catch per unit effort, most scientists see it as a confirmation of overfishing. In the case of Maryland oysters, state regulators disagree. Shellfish managers claim the diseases act like a "second predator," thinning the population so that oysters are harder to catch and thus require more effort to land the same harvest. They see disease as preempting any harvest pressure, making a moratorium inappropriate—though others are calling for it. In the managers' view, a temporary ban on oystering (or any intermediate restrictions on harvest) would not restore the population. Many experts beg to differ. They suggest both disease and overfishing may be at work simultaneously on various natural bars. To add just one more perspective, some scientists hold the view that harvesting adults that have survived to market size on an infected bar may cripple the development of disease resistance in the population. Those hardy adults may be the best hope for building sustainable reefs. The practice of catching them, they offer, is another brand of overfishing and reason enough for a harvest ban.

In sharp contrast, all parties agree the blue crab fishery is under pressure, and recent plummeting harvests are the result. For many watermen, crabbing is still the only summer harvest and offers the best chance to recover losses from winter oystering. The combined Maryland and Virginia harvest recently (2007) was approximately

43 million pounds, exceeding the overfishing threshold by 2 percent—a formula comparing the catch to the estimated adult population. (The adult stocks are considered overharvested when the
ratio exceeds 53 percent; the exploitation rate is now 55 percent.)
Even so, the catch was the lowest on record. At the same time, the
ratio itself was high because reproduction and recruitment into the
adult population was also low. Besides overfishing, pollution and
loss of habitat inhibit a comeback. Presented with the news of a
rock-bottom harvest, Maryland has imposed new restrictions: cutting the season for female crabs by six weeks—to achieve the goal
of reducing the number of females caught by 34 percent. Environmentalists at the Chesapeake Bay Foundation (CBF) doubt that
curtailing the season alone will provide enough relief for a full recovery. The shortened season, CBF contends, might boost the population short-term but to rebuild the stocks to a healthy, sustainable
level over the long haul will require nothing less than a fundamen-
tal restructuring of the fishery. In a market-based approach, gear
allotments or catch quotas could be transferred from one waterman to another, while scaling back the overall ceiling on each.
Thus, the effort (e.g., the number of crab pots in the water) or catch
(i.e., bushels) statewide could be monitored and fine-tuned to
achieve an optimal harvest. In the absence of such a new system,
crabbers may be fishing themselves right out of business.

Without the crabs and oysters to sell, watermen are turning to
the land for income. There has been approximately a 40 percent
drop in the number of active watermen on the islands. Baywide (in
Maryland), of more than 2,000 active harvesters ten years ago,
only a third still work. On Tilghman's, the men who have stepped
ashore often take care of the new housing developments: mowing
lawns, painting, all-purpose repair. Others learn the plumbing,
electrical, or carpentry trades. Today the island sits somewhere
between a working watermen's community and a tourist haven.
It's inevitable which way it will move. If the watermen do disap-

pear, so will Tilghman's Island. What remains will just be waterfront real estate.

Farther south, on Deal Island, a lone skipjack ties up at the edge of Tangier Sound: *City of Crisfield*, lassoed to a rickety pier like a forgotten stallion, the last one standing after the stampede. In Art Daniels's youth, over one hundred dredge boats filled Deal's two harbors, so thickly tied abreast that he could walk across their decks from shore to shore without getting wet. Today, at eighty-eight, Daddy Art is the last skipper working out of Deal. He has no intention of quitting. With over thirty great-grandchildren, he has some help keeping the *City* in shape. Most of his progeny have moved off the island, however. Similar to Tilghman's turnover, "foreigners" have been buying up property on Deal. Wenona, the harbor at the southern end of the island near Daddy Art's house, will soon be surrounded by condominiums. His old skipjack and his crab shanty could not be more out of place.

Come each November, Daddy Art suits up for dredging and sails into Tangier Sound. Aboard are two or three Jones brothers, always loyal to the captain, sometimes a green deckhand, and a few kin, most often son Bob and grandson Jonathan, who is Bobby's younger brother. Bobby, now married and a father, gave up the water and now works as a prison guard alongside his older brother, Jason. The crew culls thirty to fifty bushels of oysters on average and lands over thirty-five dollars for each bushel. Mostly, the *City* goes power dredging two days a week, but Daddy Art got in fifteen or twenty sailing days last season, in November and December, the only skipjack to raise its sails. Even when he's pushing, he often sails in and out of port, the pleasures of sailing never far from his mind.

"Yes, sail dredging is so quiet and peaceful," he told me recently, "that I miss it when we skip a week—in other words, when either of the crew is too inexperienced. When a skipjack gets wind in her sails, she becomes alive. You ask her something—like when you let out the sheet—and she responds. When she has too little wind, she luffs—she talks back to you, tells you what to do. We communicate. She knows me as well as I know her. She's my pride. I bought her in 1951 when I was thirty; she was two. We grew up together. I'd hate to lose her."

Losing her almost happened in 2001 when the *City* sank at the dock in Cambridge Harbor, a fate shared by the boat of Art's son, Stan. After years of neglect, she was riddled with holes; it was clear she'd sit out the season. Daddy Art raised her and towed her to the Chesapeake Bay Maritime Museum in St. Michaels where a skipjack restoration project was just getting underway. The sinking of *Rebecca T. Ruark* had prompted the Maryland legislature the year before to appropriate $150,000 toward the repair of the fleet. Recognizing that meager oyster catches had kept the captains from tending to annual upkeep, thus leaving boats like *Rebecca* prone to accident, the legislature intended to stimulate private donations to round out the restoration budget for the fleet. A maximum of $50,000 would be allocated to service each skipjack, though most could use more. The National Endowment for the Arts and others took up the slack, so that three skipjacks—*City of Crisfield*, *H. M. Krentz*, and *Lady Katie*—could be restored in the first year. The philosophy of the museum was to not only preserve the boats as historic vessels but to restore them as working sailboats. This mission is unique in maritime preservation: the first large-scale effort to save historic craft still in active use. That first year, master boat carpenters attended to the ailing *City of Crisfield*, replacing her bowsprit and transom and most of the planking in between. She returned to sail dredging the following season. Subsequently, the museum teams rebuilt or maintained another six skipjacks, including *Rebecca Ruark*. However, in the third year they ran out of money. Today, the Chesapeake Bay Maritime Museum is exploring other ways to maintain the boats, with a new emphasis: preserving traditional boatbuilding skills as a means to saving the skipjacks.

But you can't save the skipjack without saving the oyster. A working oyster boat is tied to the health of the fishery, for a dredge boat without its quarry is simply a museum piece. So we turn to the public sector. Traditionally, oyster renewal has been the mission of the state government. Curiously and quite suddenly, however, the Maryland Department of Natural Resources abandoned its annual oyster replenishment program.

The seed-and-shell program, as it is informally known, has operated in Maryland waters for nearly fifty years. Over that time, the combination of planting shell and moving seed to commercial bars for harvest has been a winning formula: millions of bushels of spat have been transplanted outside the primary sphere of the two diseases—though spreading the pathogens somewhat. Of late, with poor landings in the Lower Bay, this program has sustained a northern oyster fishery. To a limited extent, the shell component has helped create sanctuaries that nurture a breeding population (broodstock). The weak link in the chain has always been the acquisition of fossil shell, mined from deposits in the Upper Bay, which required an Army Corps of Engineers permit. Last year, two sportfishing groups opposed the permit on the basis the mining was disruptive to finfish. DNR, in light of this public opposition, abandoned the mining program. The state could have forced the issue—hundreds of watermen jobs were on the line and there is evidence that fish habitat recovers from the mining—but they backed off. Without the shell, there will be little seed produced, no spat to haul. And, consequently, watermen in the northern Bay will have few oysters to harvest. Skipjacks will be forced to sail in southern waters, where the disease is worse and dredging prospects are poor. Still, DNR is unapologetic. "Because of political pressure, we could no longer get the permits to dig the shells," says Chris Judy, former director of DNR's Shellfish Program. "It was just too hot of an issue." He does acknowledge the fallout, however. "A crisis is coming. The loss of the seed program spells a dramatic decline in the fishery in the very near future." A crisis of their own making. Once the existing oysters mature and are harvested—two years from now—the northern reefs will likely fall dormant, too sparsely populated for harvest. As many as three hundred oystermen will be put out of work.

"Incompetence. That's all it is," says Russell Dize, owner of the skipjack *Kathryn* and vice president of the Maryland Watermen's Association. "DNR didn't have the backbone to stand up to the sportfishing lobby. Oystermen pay for much of the program and the state still throws it away. Well, you can forget the skipjack: She's finished." Lacking resources, the Maryland Watermen's Association is unlikely to bring suit against the state.

"DNR simply caved in," agrees Bill Goldsborough, senior scientist at the Chesapeake Bay Foundation. "Fossil shell is essential to hatchery and restoration efforts, as well as the seed program. Without digging more shell, we are left with no alternatives for restoration activities—central to our mission—to rebuild bars and sanctuaries. Critics of dredge shell need to look at the net benefits of restoring reefs in the Bay." Goldsborough believes the seed program should be reinstated, given the availability of shell, only if a way can be found to prevent the spread of disease, for example, by transplanting seed locally within one given salinity zone. CBF and the Maryland Watermen's Association are lobbying DNR to reapply for the fossil shell permit.

The Oyster Recovery Partnership, a nonprofit agency created by the state of Maryland, is an alternative program that may provide some relief, though its benefits on a large scale are still unproven. Its mission is to promote the ecological and economic restoration of oysters in the Chesapeake Bay, a goal that, in both the short- and long-term, benefits watermen. At least two-thirds of its efforts have been to provide oysters for harvest; the rest of the initiative has focused on building oyster sanctuaries. The ratio may even out in future years. Since 2002, the partnership has received 9.9 million dollars in federal funds—through a congressional earmark—to help the oyster recover as a self-sustaining species, one that will filter the water of the Bay, create habitat for fish, and provide other ecological and economic benefits. Primarily, the agency contracts the University of Maryland's Horn Point oyster hatchery to plant very young, disease-resistant spat on oyster bars, most of which are then closed for four years, only to be reopened for harvest. The hatchery employs fresh shell from shucking houses (as opposed to fossil shell) to grow the seed. While DNR typically planted up to one billion spat at a time, the hatchery usually deposits spat in the 300-million range—spiking to 525 million in 2008. It's a smaller operation, but with additional funding and efficiencies, it will expand in the next few years, more than tripling its output of seed. At that level, the partnership can plant over a thousand acres annually, an improvement, but less than half a percent of Maryland's historic oyster ground. Critics doubt hatcheries will ever have the capacity to repopulate the Bay, especially if a majority of adult oysters are made available to watermen.

A third initiative is even more controversial: the proposed importation and release of the Asian oyster, *Crassostrea ariakensis*, to restore shellfish stocks in the Chesapeake. Maryland and Virginia have just published a draft environmental impact statement that evaluates the risks and benefits of introducing this alien species. On the upside, the Asian oyster, a native of China, is highly resistant to MSX and Dermo; also, it grows to full size in one year, rather than three. It ranges over a similar environment and salinity range in China, and is edible—though its culinary ranking has yet to be measured in a Chesapeake challenge. A similar species from Japan (*C. gigas*) has been cultured in the Pacific Northwest and in France successfully, with only modest problems. Nonetheless, the risks of introducing exotic species are real. The Asian oyster would most likely compete with the native bivalve, possibly overtaking productive reefs, and thus potentially upsetting a fragile ecological balance. Another fear is that a nonnative oyster may bring an unexpected disease with it that could further decimate the local species or other shellfish. This concern finds support among scientists who theorize that MSX arrived in the late 1950s in the same way; it now infects the whole Atlantic seaboard. For this reason and others, coastal states from Maine to Florida oppose the plan. The Asian oyster would likely spread beyond the Chesapeake, colonizing the entire Atlantic coast. These impacts, if they were to come to pass, are irreversible: Once the Asian oyster is here, it will be here to stay. A sign of how desperate the watermen are for recovery is that most embraced the introduction before the risk-benefit analysis was complete. Because of protest from other quarters, the plan is unlikely to move forward anytime soon. More likely is a temporary (or area-specific) harvest moratorium on native oysters, while restoration efforts and aquaculture are expanded. Meanwhile, the $17 million spent on the environmental impact statement could have paid for eight years of a tailored seed-and-shell program, with enough money left over to restore the entire skipjack fleet.

All options are on the table for Maryland's Oyster Advisory Commission, established in 2007, to give guidance on managing and rebuilding the oyster population. In addition to reef rehabilitation (with shell, slag, concrete, or stone) and hatchery expansion (to 2 billion spat annually), the commission is looking into the creation of oyster sanctuaries beyond the current 1,475 acres now in Maryland. These large-scale refuges, potentially entire rivers or creeks, would establish a secure broodstock population, essential to any restoration plan. (CBF sees sanctuaries as potentially providing a large share of spawning needs, which, with broodstock protected, could then make efficient harvest gear suitable elsewhere.) The broad sanctuaries, essentially harvest closure zones, would also foster the buildup of disease resistance and allow greater ease of enforcement. More revolutionary than these initiatives, the commission is already pushing to close down a large percentage of the remaining public oyster bars to make them available for private leasing, possibly all of them—the worst of all watermen's fears. One of the justifications for the move is that private ownership would prevent overharvesting. Baywide leasing may be inevitable: Nearly every oyster fishery around the world, except Maryland's, is based to some degree on shellfish farming. In the words of Bill Eichbaum, the commission's chairman, "The greatest opportunity for expanding the economic production of oysters in Maryland is through privatization and aquaculture." Those oystermen who believe the greatest opportunity is proper management of the public fishery—that is, a wild harvest—will fight their plan every step of the way.

Another management issue that hangs in limbo is the old controversy over Hooper Strait. Although the sail dredgers won the day following the firehouse meeting, patent tongers have been snapping at their heels ever since. They may win this time, securing the strait for themselves. With only Art Daniels working in Tangier Sound (and no active skipjacks in Dorchester County), the dredgers have little leverage to prevent it. Meanwhile, in the Upper Bay, the skipjacks won a decisive victory on another matter by forcing DNR to change the regulation on when patent tongers have access to Six Foot Knoll and other northern bars. The tongers must now wait until November to work the knolls, coincident with the dredgers. A third debate has also been resolved: the issue over the number of power days allowed. Ceding to the wishes of the older captains, the state still limits power days for skipjacks to twice a week, but— because there is the perception that Wadey pushed *Rebecca*'s luck on an inclement Tuesday—skipjack captains can now pick which two days they want to use power, on any given week. Presumably, that flexibility will keep them out of the roughest weather.

In the waterman's mind, the largest controversy on the table, besides abolishing the seed program and promoting aquaculture, is DNR's leniency toward a new method of harvesting oysters. Breaking with the wisdom of the sail-only law again, the state recently allowed powerboats to dredge for oysters with scoops similar to those of skipjacks. Power dredging had been banned since the Civil War (with the exception of skipjacks twice a week), and yet the state regulators allowed the more efficient technology in 1999 at a time when oyster stocks were at an all-time low. Even in the face of the collapse of the industry, they considered harvest gear to be a minor issue, so why not allow more? At first, only eighteen motor vessels participated but, as they recognized the advantage, the number climbed—to 429 in 2007. By then, DNR had opened up 25 percent of the oyster bottom to them, including parts of the Choptank River and all bars south of Tilghman's Island. Now up to 50 percent of the statewide harvest is caught by power dredgers; skipjacks account for less than 3 percent.

Stanley Larrimore is suspicious of DNR's motivations. "The only way I can figure it," he says, "is that they want to wipe out the native orster so they can bring in the Asian one." Like the watermen who believe DNR wants to close down the public fishery (in favor of aquaculture), Stanley's apprehensions point to a general distrust of the government after years of mismanagement.

When, in 2003, DNR proposed the expansion of powerboat dredging outside Tangier Sound (where it began), scientists and environmentalists also objected. "It's almost unprecedented that in the face of declining abundance of oysters, you increase the efficiency with which you can catch the remaining ones," said Roger Newell, a professor of marine biology at the University of Maryland, at the time in the *Bay Journal.* "The best chance to build up these [oyster] populations is to stop fishing them out." Yet DNR went ahead with their plans anyway.

DNR's Chris Judy says, "We felt as long as the dredging gear was used in an area where oysters are repopulating—that is, the lower and mid Bay—then it's doing no harm. Disease is the problem there, not gear or overfishing. Too few watermen are working to have an impact." Judy claims DNR is conservative in doling out territory to power dredgers. "We haven't allowed them in the far upper Bay, where oyster reproduction is low." A small consolation. That's where skipjacks roam—free of powerboat dredgers for now. But for how long?

Without extensive sanctuaries, hundreds of powerboats will likely overdredge the Bay, especially if DNR gives them even more bottom, as the motor dredgers now demand. The Upper Bay is in their sights. Even now, they're cleaning out most small oysters in their path, trespassing on sail-dredging ground, and poaching on reserves. State enforcement is wanting. Motors were the fear of the Maryland legislature in 1865, and now they're here. First with hydraulic patent tonging, then yawl-boat dredging, now with outright power dredging, DNR opened the door and welcomed them in—once again accommodating the fishermen rather than protecting the resource. Of course, the watermen only suffer in the end.

The mechanization of the Chesapeake mirrors the progress of most global fisheries, besieged by industrial trawlers, factory ships, and other innovations. Yet, with seafood harvests crashing at home and abroad, lessons can still be learned from the Chesapeake's 145-year "experiment" with wind power. Thanks to its inefficiency, the skipjack and oyster stayed in balance—from 1925 to 1960—until modern technology (and disease) tipped the scales. As we slice our way through every other fishery, trample each resource, every other wild tribe and tree, we might realize that better technology doesn't always benefit mankind. Limiting efficiency again could help preserve fisheries in the Bay and around the world. If Maryland adopted a low-tech, low-impact strategy, it would perhaps be unnecessary to close down any public oyster grounds. Many watermen contend such a well-managed wild fishery would be sustainable—fished within the limits of the resource.

THE REMAINING, ACTIVE skipjacks—either five or six boats, depending on how you're counting—are sequestered in the far northern reaches of the Bay, where the diseases are less prevalent. All of them, that is, except for *City of Crisfield*, which stubbornly clings to Tangier Sound, the home waters of the Daniels clan. Pickings are better in the northern Bay, with the fleet typically landing twice or three times the catch of Art Daniels. At the start of last season, the northern boats caught their limit on some days, thanks to the last load of seed planted two years before. For now, this vestige seed is off-limits to powerboat dredgers but free pickings to patent tongers. In any case, it won't last: The seed is almost gone. Two of the sailing skippers are old hands, pushing sixty-five: Walt and Delmas Benton, brothers who captain *Somerset* (1949) and *Fannie Daugherty* (1904), respectively. Barry Sweitzer, fifty-four, commands *Hilda Willing* (1905), which he inherited from his father, Pete. And Lawrence Murphy, fifty-five, cousin and sometime crew to Wadey, dredges *Thomas Clyde* (1911). *Martha Lewis* (1955), owned by the Chesapeake Heritage Conservancy, occasionally works the Upper Bay as part of her charter, bringing the overall count to six. Between these sailboats, the oyster harvest last year was less than 5,000 bushels.

With the exception of Art Daniels, who sail-dredges from time to time, the fleet restricts its efforts to push dredging, on those two random days of the week when more oysters, more money, can cross their decks. The captains would like to sail, but they are nearly powerless to do so. Crew is the limiting factor: The young deckhands today are inexperienced with tending sails. Even if they were skilled, modern crews would quickly grow frustrated with both the calm and blustery days that inevitably keep sailboats in port from time to time. They are accustomed to making $150 a day and can only be guaranteed that by a captain who is pushing with his yawl boat. Despite the odds, if you listen to the northern captains, some may harness the wind again: They can't let go of the halyard. Daddy Art manages to keep the sail trade alive through the rare fidelity of his Deal Island crew. He would sail every day if he could, taking up permanent residence in the nineteenth century, denying the passage of time. For, in the end, sail dredging is an act of defiance. And there's poetry in this rebellion. Daddy Art wanders across the water each day a free man.

Unfortunately, indifferent forces crowd that freedom. And thus Daddy Art's glory may be brief. Powerboats, overfishing, mismanagement, pollution, the twin diseases, aquaculture, a proposed moratorium, the curtailment of seed—all threaten to close the oyster fleet down. Reacting to DNR's recent actions (or inactions), the remaining captains are incredulous.

"Here we are symbols of the state of Maryland and they cut the keel out beneath us every time," says Lawrence Murphy, the lone oystering survivor of his clan. "The government comes to the aid of farmers when they've had a bad crop, but neither dollar floats on the Bay."

Whenever I close my eyes, I can hear the captain's voices: bewildered, ironic, hopeful, resolute, sad. They try to make sense of their lives, of their time at the helm, of the end of the only life they ever imagined. Nonetheless, the last skippers have painted up their boats and suited up for another season, making their best of a world already lost. They don't ask for much, only hoping to preserve their place in the world for a few more years, without any wish to improve upon it. These men would be content to follow the water for the rest of their lives.

For now, the rhythms of the waterman's life continue. He rises early, even on a slack day, and wanders over to Gary's Store for the news. The first edition rolls off the lips of the men at 5:00 A.M.

Editorials are offered on the intent of the wind. The phase of the moon and reach of the tide are discussed. After much commentary or none, the timing of the launch of a boat or the laying of a line is set. Seasons bring oysters or fish or crabs, but the daily cycle is pretty much the same. More than anything, the weather and tide set the schedule for the day.

There is a symmetry, a logic to this life that cannot be escaped when you stand in its presence. The course of a waterman's years is printed on the curve of the water. The shape of his life is a rolling wave, made of arcs that return to their origin. Where else do three generations of a family work together on the same boat? The children of watermen grow up with the Bay perched on the horizon, their eyes trained on the coming and going of boats. If landscape is destiny, then so, too, is the water. A boy like Wadey knew his calling before he could spell. So did his father. And his grandfather before them. Modern lives don't trade in such certainties.

In local lore, there has been much romanticizing the waterman. He has entered the pantheon of the noble savage. Clearly, he has his shortcomings: stubborn, xenophobic, often greedy, competitive to a fault. Nobody is being nominated for sainthood here. Yet, after the myths have been peeled away, we see that rare self-confidence of knowing one's place in the world. For what they have is community, tradition, and a sense of belonging. That's why the men step back in time to follow the water. And if they struggle with the balance between self-interest and altruism, with the tragedy of the commoner and the commons, then don't we all?

The longevity of the skipjack fleet—over 125 years—gives weight to the belief in nurturing the common good. Once the dredge-boat fleet fell off to a manageable and sustainable two hundred vessels after the First World War, captains looked after the oyster grounds, and conserved them through proper sail dredging—cultivating the bottom with a modest fleet. For the first few decades, the skipjacks dredged alongside older boats—schooners, sloops, and bugeyes—that sailed the great waters. It's the ships and boats, the captains, I now realize, that make the waters great. The majestic skipjacks and their skippers have outlasted them all. And now it's down to a handful of boats to carry the last canvas of the Age of Sail. Their brethren are gone. Progress has never stepped aside for beauty.

So, it's fair to ask the question: Is the oyster fleet an anachronism, irrelevant today? Certainly, wind power has its advocates. Who can afford gasoline or diesel fuel? Obviously not the planet. And the inefficiency of sail dredging for decades protected the reefs. But let's put a human face on the question. When we look at the whole life of one of these boats—from her origins on the heels of the Civil War, to her captain, his family, to the lineage of skippers and crew that have sailed her, to the boom and bust and its revival, at the way of life and its values—it describes the arc of the American experience, a reminder of what we are, where we've been: a symbol of how sustainable a society could be, at its best. That's their final relevance. If water has a memory, then skipjacks are etched indelibly on the sea.

And what will we feel in their passing? Sorrow? Yearning? Loneliness? A sense of wonder? Lives go on as if nothing happened. Well, some will. Others will know the fullness of having seen a great work of art, an original tribe. It must suffice, in the end, to know they once sailed across the wide water, their pine masts glowing red with the light of dawn, their sails billowing and whispering in the breeze.

The tide recedes. The wind drops out. The horizon flattens. What is left is the broad smile of water. The dredge boats have come and gone, but what matters is that the world witnessed their beauty, their defiance, their authenticity. For a moment in time the skipjacks held forth.

I hold that memory tight and revisit each autumn to take the pulse of it one more time. Come the first of November, I cross the

Bay Bridge and turn north to Tolchester or south to Deal. The signs of autumn are colorful, the trail well-worn. Perch yourself with me at the edge of a quiet harbor, where each thoroughfare enters the Bay. Beyond the thinning mist, look for the raked masts—half a dozen as tall as trees. Cloth and timber: The last fleet is under way. Men in oilskins scurry on deck. If we're lucky, they've been sailing all morning, and it's late afternoon. The orange sun is low on the horizon, and the long white hulls and alabaster sails are reflected in the water. If the breeze is right, the jibs are aloft, and no reefs in the mains. It's full sail, a dredger's breeze, and the crews are bent to culling.

"Only a light skim," a first mate warns, but today the crewmen aren't complaining. Neither one.

Suddenly, a racket: Geese lift off the water and make for shore. The captains smile and train their eyes on the horizon. They read an ancient language in the sky and between the waves. "Thar's green water to west'ard—storm's a coming." No matter, it's almost quitting time.

Feel the wind as it freshens, as the ca'm water whips into a brew. And lift your eyes. The boats come about and tighten their sheets. The sails fill, bellied out to bursting. Now slack the boom: a beam reach for the final run. And heave. The dredges fly outward, sparkling bright in the sun. The promise of a bushel well caught. "It's one more lick across the rock," the captains say.

One more lick across the rock and we're done.

Author's Note

For clarity, the sequence of a few events has been shifted. Also, some names have been changed. These alterations are minor in scope.

Acknowledgments

This story comprises what was experienced, overheard, and directly asked on the decks, piers, and shores of two islands in the Chesapeake Bay. I can't overestimate the importance of a good yarn, and the participants in this book all took time and patience in talking about the finer arts of sail dredging, blacksmithing, boat carpentry, racing, shucking, and shooting the breeze. I thank them all, though only a few names are repeated here. First, I am grateful to the three captains around whom the story revolves. Art Daniels, Stanley Larrimore, and Wade Murphy were generous with their sailing experience and family traditions that reach far back into American maritime history. Without their help, my voyage with the skipjack fleet would not have been possible. Their wives and families opened up their homes to me, often tolerating an unlikely guest at four o'clock in the morning and at evening meals. LaDelle Daniels, Loretta Larrimore, Jackie Murphy, and my neighbor Pauline Jenkins epitomize the island women who hold the fabric of their communities together.

I am also indebted to the captains of the rest of the fleet. All were enormously helpful as I collected information for the book. I am especially thankful to Stan Daniels, Russell Dize, Bobby Marshall,

Lawrence Murphy, Robbie Wilson, as well as the late Daryl Larrimore, the late Bart Murphy, and the late Pete Sweitzer. Additionally, three retired captains from their fathers' generation, all now deceased, sat down to talk with me on several occasions: Ellis Berridge, Jesse Thomas, and Stanford White. They opened a window into days long gone.

Other island friends generously gave of their time. I would like to thank a few: Donny and Joanne Cummings, Mary Dyer, Gary Fairbank, Rose Garvin, Buddy and Bobbi Harrison, Bud and Leslie Harrison, David McQuay, Jimmy Murphy, Evelyn Reecer, Grace Sweitzer, and Donna Wilson of Tilghman Island; Lee Daniels, Ruth Daniels, Teddy Daniels, Arby Holland, Phil Thomas, and Jack Willing of Deal Island.

My first forays as a Chesapeake writer grew under the guidance of my first editor, Will Lockwood, who continues to be a mentor and fine friend. He is an editor and gentleman of the old school. Will joined me on several skipjack voyages, shucked and slurped a few prized oysters along the way, and otherwise encouraged me through the years of this project. His wife, Eleanor, offered hearth and home during my travels, a port in many a storm. I thank them both.

Various experts on wooden boats and the Chesapeake estuary kindly offered their advice: Earl Brannock, Mary Ellen Hayward, Fred Hecklinger, Pete Lesher, and Andy Mutch on skipjacks; Stephan Abel, Torrey Brown, Chris Dungan, Bill Eichbaum, Bill Goldsborough, Philippe Goulletquer, Pete Jensen, Chris Judy, George Krantz, Tom O'Connell, Roy Scott, Harley Speir, and Mitch Tarnowski on oysters; and Lynn Fegley on blue crabs.

Very little has been written about skipjacks and oyster dredging over the years, so most of my research relied on firsthand accounts. Still, there were four books that were very helpful to me: Larry Chowning's *Harvesting the Chesapeake*, Robert Hedeen's *The Oyster*, Pat Vojtech's *Chesapeake Skipjacks*, and John Wennersten's *The Oyster Wars of Chesapeake Bay*, all from Tidewater

Publishers. Various pamphlets from the Chesapeake Bay Maritime Museum, including Howard Chapelle's *Notes on Chesapeake Bay Skipjacks*, were also beneficial. A more complete list of references is given at skipjackthebook.com.

The job of transcribing three hundred hours of audiotape and five thousand pages of notes was a prodigious undertaking. I'd like to thank Susanna Hesch, Sandy Grodin, and Marilyn Colborn for taking on this job. Marilyn also supported the project in other ways, with her big heart and by clipping news articles about the fleet. News clippings were also provided by Jim Lynn, Tom Hardie, Roger Hart, and Rodger McHugh. Additional help came from Clinton Daly and Tom Lewis, who supported the wrap-up, often with a place to stay. Ted and Jennifer Stanley assisted with another project that overlapped in time with this effort somewhat, and I thank them for it. Over the course of a long illness, which stalled the book for a few years, Alan Brody, Jeff Davis, Bill Hug, and Ellen Lefkowitz helped restore my health so that I could return to the story again.

My first professional readers were Elizabeth Lyon and Polly Bowman, who edited early drafts. Elizabeth was instrumental, a midwife to the book. Other readers who helped with finding a home for the manuscript include: Will Baker, Rick Carey, Trevor Corson, Leslie Leyland Fields, Gil Grosvenor, Patrick Noonan, and George Reiger. Others assisted the project in a variety of encouraging ways: Susan Armenti, John Barber, Dan Beigel, Johannes Brahms, Debra Boldt, Melanie Hornstein, George Moose, Bill Paca, Jack Parsons, Alex Parsons, Ray Saunders, Rob Wilder, Tom Wisner, and my parents, Dorothy and Don Sherwood.

I have been blessed with a fine editor and staff at St. Martin's Press. Many thanks to Michael Flamini for his critical eye, for his enthusiasm, and for championing this book in the marketplace. Vicki Lame, his assistant editor, was always gracious and helpful.

My gratitude also extends to my agents at Strothman Literary

Agency: Wendy Strothman and Lauren MacLeod who shepherded the book with patience and care. Their early editing was critical to its success. All along, they transformed a daunting enterprise into a joy.

In closing, I want to express my unending appreciation for the support of my family, who rallied around the various trials, false starts, and successes that gave birth to this story. Donna was always passionate about the journey even when I occasionally ran aground; she kept the lighthouse burning all these years, making it all possible. Thanks also to the next generation—to Lexi, David, Hovey, and Kristina.

With all these helpful hands, I had the wind at my back for the finish.